The

HUMANITIES
and the
LIBRARY

SECOND EDITION

Edited by
Nena Couch and Nancy Allen

American Library Association
Chicago and London
1993

Project Editor Joan Grygel

Cover and text designed by Interface Studio

Composed by Interface Studio in Avant Garde and Caslon

Printed on 50-pound Glatfelter, a pH-neutral stock, and bound in Roxite B-grade cloth by Braun-Brumfield, Inc.

The paper used in this publication meets the minimum requirements of American National Standard for Information Sciences—Permanence of Paper for Printed Library Materials. ANSI Z39.48–1984. ∞

3-25-94- 1713061

Library of Congress Cataloging-in-Publication Data

The Humanities and the library / edited by Nena Couch and Nancy Allen.
   —2nd ed.
    p.   cm.
   ISBN 0–8389–0608–7 (alk. paper)
   1. Humanities libraries—United States. I. Couch, Nena.
II. Allen, Nancy, 1950–
Z675.H86H85 1993
   016.3'00973—dc20   92–32610
                                                     CIP

Printed in the United States of America.

97 96 95 94 93   5 4 3 2 1

CONTENTS

In 1957 the American Library Association published *The Humanities and the Library* by Lester Asheim et al. This present edition updates that source, that, for most of the intervening 35 years, served faculty and students in librarianship as well as librarians in the field. The original work helped librarians and students understand the vital connections between librarianship and the fields of scholarship served by libraries in practical as well as theoretical ways. This new edition not only updates but greatly expands the coverage by including chapters on two additional disciplines—history and the performing arts—with newly written chapters on the original disciplines: religion, philosophy, fine arts, music, and literature.

The Humanities and the Library revised edition is intended for experienced professionals who need a convenient overview of the issues and resources for librarianship in these disciplines, as background reading for beginning librarians, and for students at graduate library schools who have completed basic library science course work. While college and university library service is the primary focus, the work will also be useful for librarians of larger public libraries that support serious study and consideration of subjects within the humanities.

The main purpose of this work is to enrich the understanding of library school students or practicing librarians so that they may link their knowledge of the techniques of librarianship with an understanding of the subject fields. In the context of and as appropriate to the particular discipline, the chapters address the mission of librarianship and the way in which that mission affects collection, organization, and service; special facilities and equipment requirements; the training of the librarian and related professional organizations; users' needs and interests; cataloging and classification issues; and the literature of the discipline, including primary and secondary sources as well as any special forms of materials.

Systematically providing guides to the literature is not within the scope of this work; however, many individual titles are cited to aid conceptualization of the points under discussion. Bibliographies cited within the chapters provide access to more titles in the disciplines than would be possible to include here. Following Asheim's practice, complete bibliographic information is not given for titles that serve as examples only. Titles to which the reader is referred as particular sources are followed in the text by full bibliographic citations. Each chapter includes a selected bibliography of professional literature for librarianship in that particular humanities discipline to lead the reader even deeper into the field of librarianship under discussion.

Given the diverse circumstances in which library collections in the humanities exist, this book cannot be the definitive work on librarianship in these subjects; rather, it should serve as a guide to the major topics in the area.

A great many faculty, students, and library and university administrators, as well as librarian colleagues, have shaped the professional experiences that the contributors have brought to their chapters. In addition to these who are too numerous to name, the editors would like to express their appreciation to Dee Baily and her "Resources in the Performing and Visual Arts" class at San Jose State University and to Martha Friedman, head of the History and Philosophy Library at the University of Illinois. The editors would like to acknowledge the support, advice, and encouragement of Peter Coccia and of James F. Williams II. The collections and administrative and institutional support of The Ohio State University, Colorado State University, and University of Denver are gratefully acknowledged. The work of the chapter contributors was indispensable, of course. Charles Bunge and Susan Wyngaard were instrumental in developing this work by serving as editors at earlier stages. The project was initiated by Valmai Fenster, whose untimely death interrupted its completion. She appreciated the difference that some books make in the way people think. In her final months, she ensured continuance of the tradition represented by the first edition. The editors of this edition reshaped the work by using both the tradition of the original edition and the contributions and visions of all those who aided in its completion.

Nancy Allen

The nature of the humanities is better understood through observation of their characteristics than by reading definitions. Similarly, the nature of humanities librarianship is shaped by the understanding that librarians charged with providing information, collections, and services to humanists hold for each field of the humanities.

If the fields of interest—together called humanities—are analyzed in search of commonality, or generalizations, a number of themes are found. There is a concern for the individual and for the thoughts, imagination, achievement, creativity, performance, and impact of individuals. There is a concern for culture and for all kinds of human behaviors that produce cultural artifacts. And perhaps all these concerns are framed by the larger concern for values, for quality, and for expression.

One way to seek understanding of the humanities is to compare them to the sciences. John M. Budd has looked at past and present studies of humanistic and scientific scholarship in his article "Research in the Two Cultures." He found that a number of cogent points of difference continue to exist over many years and that heated debate over the defense of scholarly behavior in each "camp" continues. (Those who work in general research libraries are not surprised by the heat of these debates, since the information demands of historians and chemists are so divergent that most attempts to serve both with the same current periodicals room results in hostility approaching the name-calling level.) These differences in the fields translate into differences in research methods, which directly affect library collections and services. Budd notes that Aldous Huxley looked into differences in humanistic and scientific uses of language, that J. Robert Oppenheimer looked for peace between the separate professions through respect for mastery and expertise, and that critical differences have been the basis for emotional critique by many writers over the years. Generalities spur the search for exceptions; nevertheless, as Budd says:

> There are inherent differences between the scientist and the humanist primarily because the two conduct their business in different realms. The purposes of inquiry are seldom identical; the humanist usually focuses on the less tangible, the less concrete. In terms of what is generally included among references to previous work, humanities scholars rely less on the empiricism of the laboratory study and more

on informed opinion. The humanist seldom deals with that which can be measured as a quantifiable entity.[1]

There is also the argument that scientific research is cumulative while humanistic research is not.[2] However, most librarians contributing chapters herein provide evidence that many scholars in music, religion, history, performing arts, and the fine arts work to understand the achievements of the past—at least in part by studying previous analyses and by looking at the effects of one performance or piece of art or music on another—and that there is definitely an element of cumulative research in the humanities.

Some other generalities comparing humanists to scientists are found in *The Humanities.* Among them are the observations that

> ... the humanist finds research to be such an intimately personal matter that it is more difficult than in other disciplines to function as a member of a team. ... Humanistic research is differentiated most sharply from research in the natural sciences by the constant intrusion of questions of value. To the scientist *qua* scientist, such considerations are, indeed, intrusions ... [whereas] humanistic scholarship has traditionally been intimately intertwined with considerations of value.[3]

On the face of it, these types of judgments seem to be value judgments themselves, and it is interesting to see that some of the generalizations pronounced over time have been proven to some extent by quantitative studies that focus on how humanists and scientists refer to previous sources and findings. A discussion based on comparisons between citation indexes in the arts and humanities and in science show that scientific writers cite source writings vastly more than humanists, that science authors make use of journal literature greatly more than do humanists, and that book literature is the predominant kind of reference for humanists.[4] Further, numerous studies show that humanists cite much older material than do scientists. And indeed, the publication rate of scientific books is far below that of books in the humanities.[5]

So, how do humanists use libraries? What information do they need when undertaking research and writing projects? What is the relationship of the nature of the humanist's pursuits to his or her pursuit of

1. John M. Budd, "Research in the Two Cultures: The Nature of Scholarship in Science and the Humanities," *Collection Management* 11, no. 3/4 (1989): 4.

2. D. J. Urquhart, "The Needs of the Humanities: An Outside View," *Journal of Documentation* 16 (Sept. 1960): 22.

3. Ron Blazek and Elizabeth Aversa, *The Humanities: A Selective Guide to Information Sources,* 3d ed. (Littleton, Colo.: Libraries Unlimited, 1988), 2–3.

4. Budd, "Research in the Two Cultures," 11–12.

5. Budd, "Research in the Two Cultures," 14–15.

information held by a research library? What does a humanities librarian need to know about the humanities in order to succeed in serving information requirements?

Each chapter in this book is designed to answer these questions, and again, some commonality is found among the observations of the various humanities fields.

There are many interrelationships among the humanities fields. Religious studies and philosophy ponder reasons for being, the nature of humankind in the world, and the significance of a deity. Art and architecture both feature works based on religious and philosophical questions—church architecture and religious art are fundamental elements of any study of art and architecture history. Religion and music are similarly linked, and the history of music ranges into secular links with theatre and performance. Narrative expression is central to the study of literature as well as to music and theatre and painting; and literary works are often springboards to artistic expression in the media of theatre, dance, and film. It is increasingly impossible to look at any field of the humanities in isolation from others, and, in fact, the humanities and the social sciences are increasingly connected. History has always straddled the line between humanities and social sciences, but social elements and societal impacts of performing arts, visual arts, music, and film are studied by scholars in every college and university in the world. These interrelationships are far more apparent now than they were to readers of Lester Asheim's *The Humanities and the Library.*

If the humanities are increasingly intertwined, so are aspects of the literatures of the humanities. There are many commonalities of the literatures described in these chapters. The value of humanities publications is retained over time, as felt by librarians and as proven in empirical studies of citations. This literature is found in both academic and public libraries since humanities are of interest to the general public as well as to university professors. Going to a play or to a movie, museum, or gallery is an act that triggers a reaction in the visitor. Curiosity to know more, see more, or feel more drives families to their public libraries to seek information on what they have experienced.

The complex netting of primary and secondary works about the humanities reveals something of the nature of each field, much of which is common to them all. Each field has unique primary resources, including oral history tapes, articles in yellowed newsprint, artists' books, authors' manuscripts, music scores, theatre handbills—each representing the work itself or some kind of byproduct of the work that is laden with information.

One of the generalities already mentioned is that humanists tend to work alone. This is interesting, given that many creative works studied by humanists are collaborative works. Musical writing and performance, theatre, dance, literature, film, and many forms of art are the results of the creativity and thought of pairs, teams, groups, and sometimes even companies. This collaborative nature of humanistic efforts often leads to interesting scholarly challenges.

Stepping back from the characteristics of the specific humanistic disciplines, Stephen Wiberley and William Jones talked to a group of eleven members of the Institute for the Humanities at the University of Illinois at Chicago to look for patterns in their information-seeking practices. This group did indeed publish largely alone, rather than working with coauthors. They used information-seeking procedures based less on efficiency and comprehensive searching and more on a limited set of personal choices of tried-and-true current information sources. They avoided consultation with librarians, although they relied heavily on archivists and special collections staff. All relied to some extent on library collections but preferred a self-reliant, independent use of collections and catalogs. The increase in interdisciplinary work is bringing humanities scholars into contact with unfamiliar areas, and it is in these areas that they needed formal bibliographies. However, four of the eleven reported that they do not use formal bibliographies at all. None of the group was interested in comprehensive literature searching. Much of the research of the members of this group had little to do with libraries; rather, it related to personal records, interviews, genealogical records, etc., with the work of greatest importance being a phone book.[6]

Wiberley and Jones also asked their eleven humanists about computer use. In this group, library online catalog searching was the most common use of a computer, followed by word processing. None had personally conducted an online database search.[7]

Dr. David Hoekema, a philosophy professor serving as executive director of the American Philosophical Association, observed that avid computer users and staffs of computer centers have designed systems with the ideal of the scientist in mind rather than the humanist.[8] He also observed that the computer has assisted scholars who work closely with texts in both sciences and humanities. Perhaps it is the increase in textual databases in recent years that is sparking the interest of humanists who in the past were left unhelped by computer files oriented toward

---

6. Stephen E. Wiberley, Jr., and William G. Jones, "Patterns of Information Seeking in the Humanities," *College and Research Libraries* 50, no. 6 (Nov. 1989): 638–45.

7. For a discussion of issues involved in online services in the humanities see Peter Stern, "Online in the Humanities: Problems and Possibilities," *The Journal of Academic Librarianship* 14, no. 3 (July 1988): 161–64.

8. Phil Schieber, "Faculty, Computerists, and Librarians View New Alliances at RLAC Conference," *OCLC Newsletter,* no. 185 (May/June 1990): 7–8.

manipulation of data. With this increase, humanists have been shifting from the use of computer systems that index printed works, such as online catalogs and journal indexes, to machine-readable files, such as those to be controlled and accessed by the Princeton-Rutgers Humanities Text Center now being developed.

Each author in this edition has commented on computer files available in the specific fields of humanities. Most of the files cited are indexes or catalogs, a few are text files, such as concordances, and a few are data files, such as the Medieval and Early Modern Data Bank. Although computer files are of great interest to a few humanists, they continue to be used by only a small minority of scholars. There are many reasons for this. One is that humanists dislike approaching reference librarians. This, in and of itself, is highly likely to prevent a scholar from being aware of machine-based resources, and if the scholar is only distantly aware of such resources, the appropriate comfort level with machine-based information retrieval methods is not going to develop without assistance. Therefore, it is most likely that the humanist will learn from colleagues, but humanities librarians sensitive to the traditional scholarly research methods used by humanists can step in by supplementing these methods with different research strategies that are needed for computer-based systems. And humanists who become computer users will "spread the word" about alternate (electronic) paths for scholarly communication.

Several large projects underway serve more than one of the humanities disciplines. One is an electronic mail forum for the discussion of humanities issues called HUMANIST. Another is the Electronic Text Service of Columbia University, established in 1988, that exists to:

> focus on research and analysis using machine-readable texts, the creation of bibliographic databases, and computer-based literature searching ... [and] to collect, examine, and evaluate software and text files, consult with students and faculty, and teach courses and workshops on new information technologies.[9]

In addition to such interdisciplinary efforts to support access to machine-readable text files as the two just mentioned, individual subject-oriented projects are making headway in most humanities disciplines: the American and French Research on the Treasury of the French Language (ARTFL), the Dartmouth Dante Project, the Global Jewish Database project, the Perseus Project on classical Greece, or the Thesaurus Linguae Graecae.

---

9. Margaret Johnson, et al., *Computer Files and the Research Library*, ed. Constance C. Gould (Mountain View, Calif.: The Research Libraries Group, 1990), 17.

With many data and text files in use and under development, a third type of computer file is emerging, along with the necessary networking, holding great promise for humanistic research—image files. A number of the authors note that many, and perhaps most, scholars depend heavily on primary collections in archives, manuscript collections, special format collections, museums, etc. When such collections contain images, scholars encounter a set of difficulties, especially when close analysis of an image is critical to research. Access to image collections from a distance is virtually impossible, reproduction is problematic, and retrieval of the right image is difficult in large and often underindexed collections. The Library of Congress American Memory Project demonstrates a possible solution. The images in several Library of Congress special collections have been scanned and indexed and are stored on either CD-ROM or videodisc (depending on the existence of movement) along with user-friendly retrieval software. The Library's experiments with this kind of technology include a mainframe version of the image files available through dial access over national high-speed networks. If these experiments are received well by the library and scholarly community, it will show that images previously available only to the select few who travel to visit rare or special format collections will soon be available for study and analysis in local libraries or through computer connections.

The Research Libraries Group (RLG) conducted three studies of information needs in order to guide the policies determining the inclusion of databases in the PRIMA (Program for Research Information Management) project list. The study on humanities identified information needs, especially online information, in classical studies, history, art history, literature, philosophy, religion, music, and linguistics. More than one hundred scholars were consulted in the study. They pointed to several common concerns: The increase in interdisciplinary research is causing an increased need for general bibliographies. The paucity of funding for humanities research makes scholars wary of databases that, although potentially useful, are expensive to use. The younger scholars who are not part of the traditional "invisible college" or who are working in interdisciplinary areas are suffering from a lack of easy access to recent works. Established scholars use established information retrieval methods and are not interested in investing time to learn complicated new search procedures for machine systems. Finally, in many areas of the humanities, there is new interest in popular culture and the many diverse information sources about daily life throughout the history of religion, literature, music, film, photography, etc. Gould suggests that machine-readable files helping scholars locate visual material, archival (unpublished) material, subject-specific data files, and older printed materials would be of great interest to humanists.[10]

Many of these conclusions are reflected in the chapters of this book. Each author addresses problems of library collections and services, and in addition to those identified by Gould, there are other common concerns. Information retrieval, even in an electronic age, seems to be universally hampered by inadequacies in classification systems and the thesauri used to control search terms in both paper and machine catalogs. Most authors point out that keyword searching and other powerful computer search capabilities have the potential to release far more relevant citations to the literature than any printed bibliography or card catalog ever did. But the state of the art of online library catalogs (designed by librarians) does not take advantage of these powerful assists as much as do the indexes to journal literature (designed by commercial interests). With the humanists' reliance on book literature rather than journal literature, the limits of the standard online catalog are greatly felt. Another online catalog issue that causes acute inconvenience to the humanist is that few large research libraries have yet funded the complete conversion to machine-readable format of all bibliographic records. Older books are often accessible only in the card catalogs. Thus, humanists (who rely heavily on older literature) must look in two places for needed references.

Problems of inadequate language systems to describe, categorize, label, and retrieve literature are connected to problems in the basic way many humanists approach research problems. Donald Case notes that historians and philosophers are especially concerned with categorization of knowledge and of human experience, and that categorization is a fundamental part of the way scholars define and analyze research issues.[11] It is obvious that categorization is also basic to librarianship, and each author has used a set of categories to clarify and analyze the field of humanities with which she or he works.

Despite the longtime influx into librarianship of people with educational backgrounds in the humanities and social sciences, there is a concern about the lack of specialized programs on humanities librarianship in library education. Higher education seems to be reducing emphasis on language skills, and the need for foreign language proficiency is seen as problematic in finding qualified humanities librarians. Possibly because of these concerns, there are strong library associations and developing

---

10. Constance C. Gould, *Information Needs in the Humanities: An Assessment* (Stanford, Calif.: The Research Libraries Group, 1988).

11. Donald Owen Case, "The Collection and Use of Information by Some American Historians; A Study of Motives and Methods," *Library Quarterly* 61, no. 1 (Jan. 1991): 63–64.

discussion groups in many fields of humanities librarianship, so that continuing education through professional associations is emphasized.

The preservation of library material is a widespread concern. This is especially acute in the humanities, where older material is as valuable—and often more valuable—than recently published material. The horrifying disintegration of millions of books published on acidic paper threatens humanities research. And the preservation of nonbook materials used by humanities scholars is also alarmingly underfunded. Included in this category are moving pictures produced on nitrate stock, videotapes, photographic archives, letters and manuscripts, artworks, music scores, etc.

Although the authors write largely from the perspective of the research library, they note that special collections of great importance are located in special libraries, personal libraries, or even corporate libraries. And as has already been pointed out, many resources have nothing to do with libraries at all. Still, those librarians serving the information needs of humanists are likely to be based in university settings or in large public libraries with research collections. This concentration is not surprising given the finding of a National Endowment for the Humanities report that "our society's understanding of the humanities ultimately depends on colleges and universities."[12] It is increasingly problematic for librarians to keep themselves informed about the incredibly diverse and far-flung sources of information and expertise. No more can a librarian consult a few key bibliographies and guides to manuscript collections to find the most relevant sources. The new proliferation of machine-based information sources, combined with variability in the computer use abilities of humanists due to the past paucity of computerized resources, requires new skills and considerable ingenuity on the part of the librarian ready for the twenty-first century.

---

12. Lynne V. Cheney, *Humanities in America: A Report to the President, the Congress, and the American People* (Washington, D.C.: National Endowment for the Humanities), 32.

CHAPTER 1

Fine Arts

Susan Wyngaard

The term *fine arts* appears in general use in the English language in the eighteenth century as a translation of the French term *beaux-arts*. The establishment of separate academies in France for the study of music, dance, and beaux-arts did much to influence current use of the term. As with the French term, we usually refer to fine arts as only the visual arts and do not encompass music, dance, or the literary arts in our definition of the term.

Fine arts libraries differ from other humanities libraries in many ways. While music libraries contain musical works and literature collections contain literary works, art libraries do not collect art objects; they collect information about art, or secondary source materials. Art libraries also differ from art museums. Unlike an art museum, the art library attempts within its walls to document the entire world of art. While an art museum will carefully select or deselect specific artworks to focus its collection, perhaps around a historical or geographical theme, an art library brings together in one location information about the art of all times and places. The art library attempts to unify and present artistic concepts in a way that does not exist in the real world due to geographic, historic, or economic barriers.

Art libraries often contain a large number of rare and expensive items requiring special physical care and security precautions. Art books are generally more expensive than their counterparts in other collections due to an abundance of high quality reproductions and the necessity for special printing processes. In the methods employed to provide special security and physical care for materials, fine arts libraries often more closely resemble rare book collections than other types of libraries.

The field of fine arts is one of the most diverse disciplines for the librarian to master. Because the works of art themselves are the primary subject matter, the art librarian must have a grasp of the technical processes involved in creating the art objects, an understanding of the features that distinguish different types of art, and an appreciation of the history and criticism of different art forms. Beyond this familiarity with the art object, the art librarian must have a thorough knowledge of the literature of art. The literature of fine arts covers such diverse elements as broad histories of art, art criticism, collection catalogs, biographies of artists, handbooks of collections, how-to books, technical analyses of art works, exhibition catalogs, *catalogues raisonnés*, and guides to art appreciation, to name just a few. To know art objects is not necessarily to know art literature, and vice versa, and the art librarian must be facile in both. The fine arts librarian usually is responsible for the areas of sculpture, drawing, painting, the graphic arts, decorative arts, design, crafts, and contemporary art movements, such as performance art and electronic art, and often is responsible for architecture and photography. This requires an understanding of the history, techniques, and literature of a large number of fields.

Profile of Fine Arts Librarianship

The many challenges of art librarianship have fostered the emergence of professional associations, distinct professional identities based on type of art library, specialized educational programs, and an impressive body of literature. Professional societies dedicated to art librarianship have developed to further communication among members and to establish standards for the profession. Within the profession, distinct identities or roles have developed to distinguish the functions of the academic art library, the museum library, the art school library, and the art collection of the public library. Educational programs now exist to prepare new art librarians and to continue to educate those already working in the field. A growing body of literature documents the past and directs the future of art librarianship. All of these indicate the importance art librarianship has attained as a specialty within the profession.

Professional Associations

Several professional societies now cater to the needs of art librarians. As early as 1924, the Art Reference Round Table was established within the American Library Association (ALA). Shortly thereafter, in 1929, the Museums Division was created in the Special Library Association (SLA), which has been known as the Museums, Arts, and Humanities Division since 1979. In 1959 an Art Section formed within the Association of College and Research Libraries. However, the most significant developments occurred between 1969 and 1972 when two independent art library associations were born. In 1969 the Art Libraries Society (ARLIS) was established in the United Kingdom, quickly followed by the Art Libraries Society of North America (ARLIS/NA) in 1972. The emergence of these two organizations heralded "a unified art library profession which embraced traditional printed work librarianship and visual collection management."[1] ARLIS and ARLIS/NA have provided art librarians with a forum for formal exchange and channels for cooperation, as well as documents to assist librarians in achieving desirable standards. The annual conferences of ARLIS/NA, held in the United States or Canada, are valuable avenues for exchange of professional information. *Standards for Art Libraries and Fine Arts Slide Collections* (Tucson, Ariz.: Art Libraries Society of North America, 1983) was published to address standards for staffing and collection development and was followed by a lengthy study of standards for physical facilities for art libraries. Art librarianship was recognized on the international scene in 1976 when the first International Conference of Art Librarians and the International Conference of Art Periodicals were held in England. A year later the precursor of the Section of Art Libraries was formed within the International Federation of Library Associations and Institutions (IFLA). This section aims to promote international understanding and cooperation in visual arts librarianship and attempts to provide a global forum for associations of art libraries and art librarians. Since the organization of the IFLA Section of Art Libraries, professional societies for art librarians have formed in Australia, New Zealand, and Norway.

Training and Continuing Education

The art librarian should be equipped with a subject background in art, knowledge of foreign languages, and professional studies in librarianship. American educational opportunities in art librarianship were outlined by Antje Lemke in 1982.[2] Professional literature as a form of continuing education has flourished in the past ten years with an increase in published information. With the emergence of journals devoted solely to art librarianship, such as *Art Documentation* (Tucson, Ariz.: Art Libraries Society of North America, 1982–) and *Art Libraries Journal* (London,

---

1. Wolfgang Freitag, "The Indivisibility of Art Librarianship," *Art Libraries Journal* 7 (Autumn 1982): 28.
2. Antje B. Lemke, "Education for Art Librarianship: The First Decade and Beyond," *Art Libraries Journal* 7 (Winter 1982): 37–38.

Eng.: Art Libraries Society, 1976–), art librarians have established a forum for discussion of professional concerns. These two journals are concerned with the documentation and bibliography of art and art librarianship. They serve a multipurpose function of newsletters to disseminate timely information, such as job postings or announcements of conferences; vehicles to provide information to support scholarly research, such as union catalogs or specialized bibliographies compiled by art librarians; collection development tools with art book review columns; and forums for discussion of issues of professional concern, such as automation and the art library or changes in the copyright law and its effect on art libraries.

Other, general library journals have recognized the growing specialization of art librarianship, and art librarians as articulate spokespersons for their profession, by dedicating entire issues to problems of the field. The *Drexel Library Quarterly*, *Library Trends*, and *Microform Review* have provided single issues that focus on examinations of art research collections, unique needs of art scholars, and the current state of art librarianship. The *Art Libraries Society News-Sheet* (London, Eng.: Art Libraries Society, 1976–) contains a regular "Professional Literature Update" that is of particular interest to art librarians, and the *Art Libraries Journal* offers a "Bibliographies Update" contributed by the IFLA Section of Art Libraries to provide a current awareness of art bibliographies. Paula A. Baxter's *International Bibliography of Art Librarianship: An Annotated Compilation* (Munich, Ger., and New York: K. G. Saur, 1987) provides a summary listing of professional readings. These publications are indicative of the degree of specialization that art librarians have attained and demonstrate a commitment to continuing education within the profession.

Types of Art Libraries

Art libraries have a longer history than is implied by the relative youth of the specialized professional societies. Early art libraries often formed around museum collections. In the nineteenth century great museums were founded in Europe under government patronage and in America under private sponsorship. These museums built library collections to support the scholarly investigations of the museum staff. Other art library collections evolved in the nineteenth century in the art school environment or through art museums or galleries associated with American colleges and universities. At that time art education for the public, including the education of many artists, was left to the public libraries in the United States and Great Britain. It was deemed part of the public library mission to refine the taste of the public and to aid in the develop-ment of several areas of recreation, among them arts and craft skills.

Today's art library collections are still commonly found in colleges and universities, museums, art schools, and within public libraries. In addition, a growing number of design agencies, architectural firms, art galleries, and industries employ art librarians to organize and manage their libraries and visual resource collections.

These different types of art library collections are relevant to an equally wide variety of patrons: artists, architects, art historians, art collectors, art critics, art dealers, art educators, curators and museum professionals, designers, and dilettantes. The traditional areas of art history studies have expanded to include the social, economic, and ethnic aspects of art that have, in turn, increased the interdisciplinary nature of art history research. Studio arts have broadened to include design, the crafts, performance, photography, and electronic media. The materials collected by art libraries reflect this dynamism. Art libraries contain materials for the study of visual expression from prehistoric time to the present. The geographic focus of these materials has grown from a preoccupation with Western civilization to a global fascination. The art librarian serves people who create art, people who study art, and people who use art. To effectively work with this diverse group of patrons in such a wide variety of subject areas, the art librarian must be well trained, indeed.

Academic Art Libraries

Many universities and colleges maintain several separate subject collec-tions, such as art, in addition to their central library, a tradition that was established in the nineteenth century when seminars became a popu-lar supplement to lecture instruction. Today academic art librarians must keep in mind the interests of the university community as a whole. While the primary clientele is most certainly the faculty and students of the art and art history departments, other disciplines, including history, anthropology, religious studies, and area studies such as women's studies and Black studies, rely on the art library to support their teaching and research activities. A scholar of ancient history or a classicist, for exam-ple, would depend on the Greek and Roman art materials in the art library for the study of these civilizations and cultures. An anthropologist might use art library materials documenting the culture of the Aztecs, Native Americans, or other groups. A Buddhist scholar would come to the art library to use works describing the cave temples of India. In a time of increasingly specialized scholarly investigation, the role of the academic art library as a home of interdisciplinary research is heightened. While the academic art librarian still builds and services the collection to support the teaching and research of the faculty and students of the primary teaching departments, there is now the added responsibility of supporting the numerous interdisciplinary fields of investigation throughout the humanities and social sciences.

In addition, the academic art librarian must be alert to new subjects not yet considered a significant part of the university curriculum. The art librarian must be able to anticipate the demands of future scholars and acquire art materials not well recognized today. In the nineteenth century, for example, the *carte de visite*, a photographic form of the calling card, was considered a throwaway, or ephemeral, item. Few collectors or librarians had the foresight to maintain large files of these items, even though many cartes were produced by the finest photographic artists of the day. Today the carte is a highly sought-after research source in the study of the popularization of nineteenth-century portraiture. Today's academicians might not yet be studying performance art or artists' books, but can the art library afford not to acquire materials on these subjects as resources for future art scholars?

Rare Book Collections

Many academic art libraries have their own rare book collections and provide special areas of the library with added security and temperature and humidity control to house these materials. Other art libraries unable to provide the proper conditions for their especially rare and valuable materials send the items to the rare book room of the general library. Art books might need special protection for a variety of reasons. Some are considered rare because they are very old or were printed in extremely limited editions, such as original editions of art inventories or guidebooks published in the seventeenth or eighteenth century. Others are valuable because of the cost of production. *Das Goldene Evangelienbuch von Echternach*, a recent publication, contains 272 magnificent color facsimile plates with hand-gilding in 23½ carat gold, each leaf singly cut true to those of the manuscript, and a full silk cover with gilded copper clasps reproducing the original tenth-century cover. Some books require protection because they contain original artwork, such as *Le Poete Assassine* by Guillaume Apollinaire, which contains thirty-six original lithographs by Raoul Dufy.

Occasionally the binding of the book has artistic interest, and the librarian must take special care to protect these pieces because rebinding would destroy their value. *The Temple of Flora* by Jim Dine is boxed in a portfolio that contains relief sculpture on the lid. Such a work could not be rebound or repaired without destroying its artistic value and, therefore, must receive special physical care to protect the original state.[3]

The academic art library often has the broadest collection of any type of art library. Information on all fields and ages of artistic activity is required by the diverse faculty and student body of the university environment. Everything from the ephemeral to the rarest material is the responsibility of the academic art librarian.

Museum Libraries

Art museum libraries have a different origin and serve a different purpose than other art libraries. Museum libraries in the modern sense developed in the eighteenth century as reference collections for staff use only. Today, the American museum's identity as a research institution with an educational mission is clearly reflected in the library collection. This might mean the development of a major research collection to provide in-depth coverage of a wide variety of fields, such as painting, textiles, sculpture, ceramics, etc., as in the library of the Metropolitan Museum of Art. Specialized libraries support museums concentrating on single subjects, such as the library of the Corning Museum of Glass. Whatever the nature of the particular museum collection, the art museum library must be able to respond to a variety of specialized information needs. Photographic archives, slide collections, and extensive vertical files are often maintained to document special collections within the museum's areas of interest. Photographic files and slide collections are essential for documenting works in the museum's collection as well as for providing a record of related pieces in the collections of other museums. Special collections of auction and sales catalogs will be maintained to trace the *provenance* of artworks in the collection as well as to inform the curatorial staff of the current market. Catalogs of art exhibits at other museums are considered essential research tools. Often, the art museum library houses the museum's archives or history file, and the museum librarian might serve the dual role of art librarian and archivist. Archival material in the care of the museum library might typically include the correspondence of past museum directors or curators, a complete listing of all exhibitions that have taken place at that museum, as well as installation photographs of museum displays. Art museums often acquire the papers of artists featured in their collections, and these can come under the care of the art librarian. These materials

---

3. For interesting illustrations of artists' bindings, see Roy Harley Lewis, *Fine Bookbinding in the Twentieth Century* (New York: Arco, 1985) and Kerstin Tini Miura, *My World of Bibliophile Binding* (Berkeley, Calif.: University of California Press, 1984).

may become primary research resources for future art scholars and must be carefully indexed and preserved.

The art museum librarian might be called on in the course of research to develop special information packets to be routed to staff members who need to know "everything" on a given topic. This could involve searching the museum archives and the photo files, abstracting periodical articles, or compiling research bibliographies. Some museum librarians regularly route to curatorial staff photocopies of the title pages of recent journals to provide an in-house current-awareness service.

More and more often in the United States the public is invited to use the art museum library, a strong statement of the importance of the educational role of the museum. The art museum library is not necessarily viewed as a means to increase the number of visitors to the museum but to enrich the visitor's experience and to deepen understanding of what is seen. This goal can lead to interesting challenges that can be met with innovative services on the part of the art museum librarian. In communities lacking strong art collections in their public libraries, the art museum libraries may be called on to fulfill a public library role.

Art Collections in the Public Library

In contrast to those of art museum and academic librarians, different resources are provided by the art librarian in the public library. Typically, the more popular aspects of the arts will be the focus of the public library collection, such as how-to books explaining artistic techniques, broad histories of artistic disciplines, and books with an emphasis on well-illustrated surveys of art movements or styles. Certainly, there are contradictions to this generalization in scholarly art research collections located in such premiere institutions as the New York Public Library. The local artists' file is a source of information, often found only in the public library, with particular value to a large number of art scholars. These files may consist of printed announcements or invitations to artists' exhibits, newspaper clippings of local exhibition reviews, or artists' biographies. They may also contain the only information documenting the early, developmental years of certain artists' careers and may prove to be important research material in later years. For example, information contained in the exhibition catalog *Women's Spheres: Celebrating Three Centuries of Women in Middlesex County and New Jersey* was gleaned from the New Jersey's artists' files maintained by the Newark Public Library. A public library may have a commitment to collecting information on artists from that particular community or from the entire state. In either case, this service can be an important asset to serious art research.

Art School Libraries

The library in the art school reflects the curriculum of the institution, which emphasizes visual education rather than history. This might require the art librarian to develop an "image library," a file of visual aids or pictures maintained with the artist/teacher in mind, rather than the traditional art research collection emphasizing text with images, organized around the needs of the historian.[4] Beyond the traditional book collection, important resources in the art school library might include picture files, motion pictures, posters, trade catalogs, clipping files of graphic design materials, and catalogs of fabric swatches or wallpapers, as well as charts of all colors and types of paint chips. Especially important resources in the art school library are the current periodicals and exhibition catalogs of contemporary art that allow artists to stay abreast of new work in their fields.

Cataloging and Classification

The Dewey decimal system and the Library of Congress classification scheme handle the fine arts somewhat differently. In the Dewey system, part of the 600s are devoted to the Useful Arts, such as welding, metalsmithing, woodturning, and leathercrafting, and the 700s include the Fine Arts, that is, architecture, sculpture, painting and drawing, photography, music, and amusements. However, "amusements" can range in scope from dancing and stage design to areas not generally considered fine arts, such as card games and sports. In the Library of Congress system the majority of the visual arts fall into the N classifications, such as architecture (NA), sculpture (NB), drawing (NC), painting (ND), graphic arts (NE), and art applied to industry (NK). However, there are art forms such as weaving, pottery, glassblowing, and photography that fall into the Ts as technology, while aesthetics, an important aspect of the study of fine arts, often falls in the Bs. It is not unusual for primitive art, folk art, and many areas of archaeology to fall outside the N classification and, therefore, be excluded from the art library collection.

In both the Library of Congress system and the Dewey system the major divisions of the fine arts (paintings, sculpture, architecture, etc.) are subdivided in several ways. For example, in the Library of Congress system, painting can be further described by subject (landscape, portrait), by time period (medieval, modern), by technique (watercolor, gouache),

---

4. For a fuller discussion of this issue, see: Stan Lewis, "Experiment with an Image Library," *Special Libraries* 56 (Jan. 1965): 35–38.

style (baroque, abstract), nationality (American, Chinese), or by a combination of these factors. Architecture can be described by historical period (ancient, Renaissance), function or purpose (school buildings, monuments), or by style (rococo, Gothic).

A few very specialized art libraries have found it necessary to devise their own classification systems for entire collections or portions of their collections. The *Library Catalog of the Metropolitan Museum of Art* (2d ed., Boston, Mass.: G. K. Hall and Co., 1980; *First Supplement*, 1982), one of the many art library catalogs published in book form by G. K. Hall and Company, illustrates a specialized classification scheme devised for art that has been constructed from a modification of the Dewey system. Most art libraries, however, find that the great expense of revising schedules, training catalogers, and explaining the system to users does not merit the invention of specialized systems.

In both of the major classification systems, Dewey decimal and Library of Congress, there is much overlap in art, while some areas are sadly overlooked. At best these systems serve as guides, and it is essential that the art librarian have a good understanding of the qualities that distinguish art forms from each other, the technical problems of creating art, the history and development of art, as well as the rich literature that documents and aids its creation.

Problems and peculiarities of cataloging, such as choice of entry or bibliographic description, are important issues to art librarians. The main entry is a topic of continued discussion. The "artist as author" rule is applied when printed reproductions of an artist's work are assembled in a book by a compiler or editor and the critical or explanatory text accompanying the reproductions does not exceed a specific number of pages. This can be very confusing for the researcher who does not consider the artist to be the author of the book. Exhibition catalogs might be found entered in the library catalog under the name of the artist, the name of the person who wrote the critical essay in the catalog, or the name of the institution that organized the exhibition. If the name of the exhibiting institution is chosen, the city in which the institution is located might or might not come before the institution. Would one look under B or M for a catalog from the Boston Museum of Fine Arts? Is it "Boston. Museum of Fine Arts" or "Museum of Fine Arts. Boston"? Is it "New York. Metropolitan Museum of Art" or "Metropolitan Museum of Art (New York, N.Y.)"? Many libraries have these institutions listed both ways. Often, the subtle interpretations and changes in cataloging rules are very difficult to understand. While the Fogg Art Museum of Harvard University is listed as "Fogg Art Museum," the art collection of the University of Rochester is listed as "University of Rochester.

Memorial Art Gallery." Also, the commonly used name for an institution may not be recognized in the library catalog. What is commonly referred to as the Guggenheim Museum in New York is found under "Solomon R. Guggenheim Museum." Further, if an exhibition catalog has been issued by one of the national museums in the United States, such as the National Gallery of Art or the Smithsonian Institution, it might be found in the government publications department, remaining unlisted in the central catalogs.

The collation of the book, i.e., the number of plates, types of illustrations, etc., is of special importance to art library patrons and, therefore, is often provided in more detail than for other types of materials. It would not be unusual for a researcher to request only works on Japanese ceramics that contain color illustrations. With the help of a detailed collation statement, books on this topic without the proper illustrations could be eliminated at the beginning of the search.

Subject access to art information can be problematic. With subject headings as general as "Painting—Exhibitions," it is difficult for the art researcher to narrow the scope. In other cases, valid and recognized art movements are not used as subject headings. It would not be uncommon for an art library patron to request information on contemporary art styles or movements such as funk art, drip painting, or food art. Although the library might own several books on these subjects, because the library catalog does not use these terms as subject headings the patron might not find the information needed. It is the rare library catalog that keeps abreast of new terms applied to contemporary art movements. In other cases the subject headings used are not what the patron would most likely look under in the library catalog. It is a seasoned searcher who knows to look under "American wit and humor, Pictorial—Exhibitions" for an exhibition catalog documenting comic book artists of the United States. Online catalogs with keyword searching capability can help users with these problems but only if the keyword search term appears in the title or elsewhere in the record.

The Literature of Art

The literature of art has a long history and broad profile. It encompasses biographies and autobiographies of artists, guidebooks, historical surveys, technical treatises in many fields of art, and theories of aesthetics and criticism, to name but a few traditions. The earliest forms of art literature—biography, guidebooks and surveys, handbooks of collections, and instructional treatises—date back to antiquity.

Biography and Autobiography

Biographies of artists were known in ancient Greece and Rome. Douris of Samos (second half of the fourth century B.C.) compiled a collection of biographies of artists based on established and fictitious material. Cornelius Nepos (first century B.C.), in his sixteen books of biographies of famous men, included a section on the lives of painters. Later, during the Middle Ages, artists were relegated to the role of artisans, and biographies were more likely to be written about art patrons than about artists. Although diminished during the Middle Ages, artistic biography found a new life during the Renaissance, as evidenced by Giorgio Vasari's *Lives of the Most Eminent Painters*, first published in 1550. Lorenzo Ghiberti's *I Commentari* (reminiscences) contained biographies of trecento artists as well as his own autobiography, the first written in a literary form by an artist.

Since that time biographies of artists have continued to be valuable sources and documents in the study of art. Today, information about an artist's life and work will often be the first step in art research, and art libraries usually contain a large number of biographical works. Many well-known artists, such as Andy Warhol, have been the subject of several biographical studies, and it is important for the art library to make available as many of these studies as possible to provide readers with more than one view of artists and their works. In addition to biographies of individuals, art libraries contain many dictionaries of biography and indexes to biographical information. The two most frequently consulted biographical dictionaries concerning historical artists are Emmanuel Bénézit's *Dictionnaire Critique et Documentaire des Peintres, Sculpteurs, Dessinateurs, et Graveurs* (Rev. ed., Paris, Fr.: Librarie Gründ, 1976) and Ulrich Thieme and Felix Becker's *Allgemeines Lexikon der bildenden Künstler von der Antike bis zur Gegenwart* (Reprint ed., Leipzig, Ger.: F. Allmann, 1964). Bénézit's ten-volume set includes 300,000 entries for painters, sculptors, designers, and graphic artists of Eastern and Western art from 5 B.C. to the mid-twentieth century. In addition to providing short biographies for each artist, entries often include lists of awards won, prices obtained for sale of the artist's work, locations of some art works, brief bibliographies, and facsimiles of artists' signatures. Thieme and Becker's thirty-seven—volume set is considered one of the most scholarly biographical dictionaries in the field. Signed articles are valued for their completeness and the usefulness of the bibliographies.

Hans Vollmer's *Allgemeines Lexikon der Bildenden Künstler des XX Jahrhunderts* (Leipzig, Ger.: E. A. Seemann, 1953–1962) is a six-volume supplement to Thieme and Becker, covering artists born after 1870. *Contemporary Artists* (3d ed., Chicago and London, Eng.:

St. Martin's Press, 1989), a listing of more than 1,000 recently active artists, provides biographical sketches, bibliographies, reproductions of artists' works, chronologies of exhibitions, and statements by artists.

Numerous biographical dictionaries have been compiled to document artists of particular nationalities, artists working in a single medium, or artists concerned with a specific subject. Specialized biographical sources such as Chris Petteys's *Dictionary of Women Artists: An International Dictionary of Women Artists Born before 1900* (Boston, Mass.: G. K. Hall, 1985) and Adolf Placzek's four-volume *Macmillan Encyclopedia of Architects* (New York: Macmillan, 1982) prove indispensable in reference work.

A tour of an art reference collection will reveal a wide variety of avenues from which we can approach biography. Indexes to biography assist the user by citing a large number of biographical sources. Patricia Havlice's *Index to Artistic Biography* (Metuchen, N.J.: Scarecrow Press, 1973; first supplement, 1981) provides the user with a guide to more than 100 different biographical dictionaries. Havlice does not reproduce biographical information, but she tells the user where to locate information for more than 100,000 artists. *Mallett's Index of Artists: International-Biographical; Including Painters, Sculptors, Illustrators, Engravers, and Etchers of the Past and Present* (New York: Peter Smith, 1948) cites more than 1,000 biographical sources for information on more than 40,000 artists. Although biographical indexes require a two-step search process, they are valued tools because of the large numbers of sources indexed in each volume.

Artists' autobiographies and anthologies of writings by artists are essential documents in interpreting works of art. Important commentaries by historic artists have been compiled in Elizabeth Gilmore Holt's *Documentary History of Art* (Garden City, N.Y.: Doubleday and Company, 1957–1966) and Horst Janson's *Sources and Documents in the History of Art* (Englewood Cliffs, N.J.: Prentice-Hall, Inc., 1965–1972). Autobiographical commentary and discussions of artwork by more contemporary artists are found in Barbara Rose's *Readings in American Art Since 1900: A Documentary Survey* (New York: Frederick A. Praeger, 1968), Cindy Nemser's *Art Talk: Conversations with Twelve Women Artists* (New York: Scribner, 1975), and *Art of Performance: A Critical Anthology* (New York: E. P. Dutton, 1984) edited by Gregory Battcock and Robert Nickas.

Guidebooks and Surveys

Guidebooks were written by the ancient Greeks to survey and record great art treasures. The work of Pausanias (second century A.D.) documents important artworks of interest to travelers of his time. In ancient times collectors and connoisseurs increased in number as a fascination with art objects developed, and handbooks for collectors are often considered the most important contribution of the Romans to the literature of art history. Two notable examples are Philostratus the Elder's *Imagines*, which describes sixty-four paintings in a villa in Naples, and Callistratus's *Descriptions* of thirteen pieces of sculpture. In the Middle Ages guide-books were often directed at religious pilgrims and described items of religious interest rather than significant works of art. A renewed interest in the material world during the Renaissance resulted in a revival of art documentation, and guidebooks recording important artworks again appeared. This tradition continues to represent an important resource for art research, and today art libraries collect guidebooks and surveys that record and document art in all areas of the world. Karl Baedeker's many *Handbooks for Travellers*, well known to tourists around the world, are often found on the shelves of the art reference collection. Although these guides are quite dated, the descriptions of artistic works and monuments are often helpful in research. More up-to-date guidebooks continue the tradition by providing overviews of particular regions and presenting detailed descriptions of architectural sites and artistic monuments.

Several ambitious projects that attempt to survey all of the art or architecture in a specific region are quite important. The *Historic American Buildings Survey* (*HABS*) (Teaneck, N.J.: Somerset House, 1980), a state-by-state inventory of measured drawings, photographs, and written descriptions of significant American structures, is available to libraries in book format and on microform. The multivolume *Buildings of England* series (London, Eng.: Penguin Books, 1951–1974) by Nikolaus Pevsner surveys and records great numbers of churches, houses, and other structures from ancient to modern times in all of the regions of England and is useful for its descriptive data and reproductions. Although not always considered "art" books, guidebooks and surveys make important contributions to the documentation of the world's art.

Handbooks of Collections

The eighteenth and nineteenth centuries were very important in the development of art history as a scholarly discipline. Noble families of the eighteenth century became increasingly interested in art, and their heightened awareness resulted in the development of great art collections. In 1764 Johann Joachim Winckelmann published *Geschichte der Kunst des Altertums*, the work often credited with giving birth to art history as a scholarly discipline. The field gained further notice when the

University of Berlin established art history as an academic discipline with a chaired professorship in 1844. Such formal recognition encouraged art history studies, and major inventories of the world's great art collections were undertaken.

Today many museums publish detailed catalogs of objects in their collections. These catalogs are valuable to art researchers for several reasons. Catalog entries usually contain full descriptions of each piece, including size, medium, indications of signature, and inventory number, and are often well illustrated. Furthermore, collection catalogs may provide the only way to trace the ownership of a piece, and catalogs of private collections may offer the only means of access the public has to those collections.

Many major museums have published collection catalogs, and numerous volumes documenting objects in the Musée National du Louvre in Paris, the Tate Gallery in London, or the Metropolitan Museum of Art in New York are commonly found in art libraries today. Recently visual catalogs have been made available on microfiche, and publications such as *Paintings in the Kunsthistorisches Museum, Vienna* (Teaneck, N.J.: Chadwyck-Healey, 1985), which reproduces on color microfiche all the paintings displayed in the gallery, make it possible for art researchers to have visual access to important collections.

Related to collection catalogs are *catalogues raisonnés* and *oeuvres catalogues*. These catalogs are critical or descriptive studies of all of the work of a particular artist. While both of these catalogs present complete listings of the artist's work and usually include an illustration of each piece, the catalogue raisonné additionally provides descriptive entries for each item, citing dimensions, dates, locations, related bibliographies, and other pertinent information. Catalogues raisonnés and oeuvres catalogues have not been compiled for all, or even a majority, of artists, but those that exist are considered essential to the serious study of individual artists and their works.

Technical and Instructional Works

Xenocrates of Athens, a sculptor of the third century B.C., described the development of art by analyzing problems and solutions experienced by artists and, in doing so, recorded artistic techniques from simple line drawings through the use of total color harmony. Medieval university education excluded the fine arts from the *trivium* (arithmetic, geometry, and grammar) and the *quadrivium* (astronomy, dialectics, music, and rhetoric), which resulted in a lack of academic studies of art. However, this did not completely deter the production of technical literature. The strict organization of medieval artisans' guilds and the apprenticeship system encouraged written records, in the form of rule books, to document specific formulas for grinding pigments, preparing panels, etc.

The medieval monastery was also an important source of technical documentation. The monk Theophilus, in his *Diversarum Artium Schedula* of the tenth century, carefully described in detail artistic techniques such as applying gold leaf to icons and manuscripts and painting on glass. Builders' drawings, plans, and sketchbooks were maintained and preserved in monastery libraries. The writings of Abbot Suger concerning the abbey church of St. Denis have survived as a major source of information on medieval architecture and building methods. In his treatise *De Re Aedificatoria*, Leon Battista Alberti explained the mathematical techniques employed during the Renaissance to determine the correct proportions of a building. In addition, well-known artists such as Leonardo da Vinci and Albrecht Dürer wrote treatises on human proportion, perspective, and other artistic issues that have been published in many editions and translations over the years and that will always be considered classics.

Today, instructional works continue to represent an important segment of the art library collection. Josef Albers's *Interaction of Color*, a key work in understanding how the eye experiences color, is used by artists, art educators, and art historians. The numerous volumes explaining techniques and formulas of the old masters, handbooks of artists' materials, and works on the conservation of artworks are often requested by patrons and are considered essential elements of the art library collection.

Art Periodicals

A significant body of literature in any art library is the periodical collection. Art magazines are read by many groups for a variety of reasons. Artists depend on them to communicate with the art world; scholars use them to share their investigations of art through the ages; art collectors and art dealers use them to stay current with the art market; and art lovers of all kinds find pleasure in browsing through their beautifully illustrated pages. In 1976 the periodical shelves of the art library of the Victoria and Albert Museum stretched one and three quarters miles in length. Few art libraries are fortunate enough to have such a sizable collection of journals, although periodicals are a key component in any art library.

Art periodicals have a legacy of more than 200 years. *Der Reisende und Correspondirende Pallas oder Kunst-Zeitung*, the first art periodical in Germany and perhaps the world, appeared in 1755. Shortly thereafter, in 1785, the first English art periodical, *Artist's Repository and Drawing Magazine*, was issued. The first French art journal, *Novelles des Arts*, was published from 1801 to 1805. By the early nineteenth century several journals dealing solely with fine art were established. Some contained lectures on art and articles on art history, some published news items and notes on artistic works in progress, while others issued reviews of art exhibitions or important art sales. In the United States, art periodicals began as museum news and publicity vehicles, such as the *Bulletin of the Metropolitan Museum of Art*. These bulletins soon took on a more serious educational role by introducing the public to important works or collections and by publishing scholarly research. The *Art Bulletin*, begun in 1913 as the organ of the College Art Association of America, continues this role in the United States by publishing seminal articles by outstanding art historians.

In addition to scholarly research-oriented journals, art libraries today subscribe to art appreciation journals. Magazines such as *Artnews* or *Art in America* contain regular feature articles that review and help the reader understand contemporary artwork or work currently on exhibit. Other art periodicals are published for practitioners of specific art forms. While magazines such as *Stained Glass* or *International Sculpture* can be enjoyed by a variety of readers, the notices of artistic competitions, the classified advertisements for employment opportunities, and the product advertisements are clearly compiled with a specific audience in mind. Most art libraries find it necessary to subscribe to a mixed selection of scholarly, art appreciation, and professional journals in proportions determined by their patron user groups.

Art libraries collect current periodical titles and maintain large back files of earlier journals. The periodical collection is one of the many areas of the art library where the value of the material increases with age. Early art journals may have added value because they contain original prints by known artists. *Revue Wagnerienne* (1885–1932) published prints by Odilon Redon and others. *Merz* (1923–1932) was published in a limited edition of numbered copies in the form of a folder containing lithographs by important Dada artists.

Some journals are valued significant documents of specific art movements. *Ver Sacrum* (1898–1903) served as the organ of the Vienna Secession and is considered to be one of the best examples of art nouveau graphic design. *Der Blaue Reiter* (1912), published by Wassily Kandinsky, Franz Marc, and Gabriele Munter, stands as a hallmark of expressionism although only one issue was ever published. *Lacerba*, published in Florence from 1913 to 1915, played a fundamental role in the development of futurism as an important outlet for "written pieces" and manifestos. *La Révolution Surréaliste* (1924–1929), the chief periodical of the early surrealist movement, and *291* (1915–1916), published by Alfred Stieglitz and a major vehicle for introducing modern art to America, are considered rare and valuable documents today.

While several of the older and rarer periodical titles have been reprinted or issued in microform, many others are found only in the original editions in some of the better art libraries of the world. The researcher's access to these collections has been greatly improved by specialized union catalogs of art collections. Two such particularly help-ful catalogs are *Art Serials: Union List of Art Periodicals and Serials in Research Libraries in the Washington D.C. Metropolitan Area* (Washington, D.C.: Washington Art Library Resources Committee, 1981) and Marianne Prause's *Verzeichnis der Zeitschriftenbestände in den kunstwissenschaftlichen Spezialbibliotheken der Bundesrepublik Deutschland und West-Berlins* (Berlin, Ger.: Mann, 1973).

Reference Tools

Art reference work is not limited to the use of a single group of materials or a smaller number of works. Any of the previously mentioned types of art literature, such as biographies, guidebooks, handbooks to collec-tions, catalogues raisonnés, technical works, or even periodicals, can be used in reference search strategies. There are, however, certain types of works that attempt to provide quick, factual answers to questions. These dictionaries, encyclopedias, and indexes are heavily used by art librarians in answering the large number of miscellaneous factual queries received each day.

The numerous encyclopedias and dictionaries available in the art reference collection are useful both for defining specific terms and concepts and for providing summary treatments of different aspects of the field. The *Encyclopedia of World Art* (New York: McGraw-Hill, Inc., 1958; supplement, 1983) is one of the standard tools in an art reference collection. Its lengthy signed articles have been written by experts in the field and are accompanied by numerous illustrations and extensive bib-liographies. Dictionaries of art abound. Numerous general art dictionaries, such as the *Oxford Companion to Art* (Oxford, Eng.: Clarendon Press, 1970), are supplemented by dictionaries covering specific periods of art, for example, John Walker's *Glossary of Art, Architecture and Design Since 1945: Terms and Labels Describing Movements, Styles, and Groups Derived from the Vocabulary of Artists and Critics* (2d ed., London, Eng.: Clive Bingley, 1977), Robert Atkins's *Art Speak: A Guide to Contemporary Ideas, Movements, and Buzzwords* (New York: Abbeville Press Publishers, 1990), or more technical dictionaries, such as Ralph Mayer's *The Artist's Handbook of Materials and Techniques* (4th ed., New York: Viking Press, 1982).

Bibliographies guide the researcher to the most significant works on a topic or in a particular field. A standard review of the history of art bibliography is contained in the essay "Historiography" by Luigi Salerno, in the *Encyclopedia of World Art*.[5] Basic bibliographies, now considered classics in art reference collections, include Edna Louise Lucas's *Art Books: A Basic Bibliography on the Fine Arts* (Greenwich, Conn.: New York Graphic Society, 1968) and Mary W. Chamberlin's *Guide to Art Reference Books* (Chicago: American Library Assn., 1959). These two works have been updated, respectively, by Wolfgang Freitag's *Art Books: A Basic Bibliography of Monographs on Artists* (New York: Garland Pub., 1985) and Etta Arntzen and Robert Rainwater's *Guide to the Literature of Art History* (Chicago: American Library Assn.; London, Eng.: Art Book Company, 1980). Donald L. Ehresmann's *Fine Arts: A Bibliographic Guide to Basic Reference Works, Histories and Handbooks* (2d ed., Littleton, Colo.: Libraries Unlimited, 1979) provides a different approach to art bibliography as he organizes information by world geography.

Several art periodical indexes are typically found in the reference collection. The *Art Index* (New York: H. W. Wilson, 1929–) is organized by the H. W. Wilson Company's usual form for periodical indexes and covers a variety of international art journals and museum bulletins. *RILA: International Repertory of the Literature of Art* (Malibu, Calif.: J. Paul Getty Trust, 1975–1990) provided an abstracting and indexing service for publications in the history of art, including periodical articles, conference proceedings, exhibition catalogs, doctoral dissertations, and *Festschriften*. *Répertoire d'Art et d'Archéologie* (Paris, Fr.: Centre de Documentation Sciences Humaines, 1910–1990) was a French quarterly of international scope that selectively indexed more than 1,500 periodicals on Western art from ancient times to the present. In 1991 *RILA* and *Répertoire* ceased and were superseded by *BHA: Bibliography of the History of Art* (Santa Monica, Calif.: J. Paul Getty Trust, 1991–). *BHA* and the entire RILA database, 1975–1989, are available online through DIALOG's Art Literature International No. 191. Several other indexes related to art are available in online databases. The Arts and Humanities Search, ARTbibliographies Modern Database, ERIC Database, On-line Avery Index to Architectural Periodicals Database, and the RILA Database are only a few with which an art librarian must be familiar in order to assist patrons to quickly and efficiently access the broad variety of periodical literature available.

The printed catalogs of major art libraries are additional important reference sources. Although many libraries report their holdings to major

5. Luigi Salerno, "Historiography," in *Encyclopedia of World Art* (New York: McGraw-Hill Book Co., Inc., 1958), 507–59.

online bibliographical databases, the printed book catalog allows the researcher the convenience of subject access and the pleasure of browsing the collection. Major art libraries, such as the Metropolitan Museum of Art, the Museum of Modern Art, the Harvard University Fine Arts Library, and the Avery Memorial Architectural Library of Columbia University, have published their library catalogs in book format. Specialized collections, such as the library of the International Museum of Photography at the George Eastman House and the Manuscript Collection of the Archives of American Art, have added their printed library catalogs to this growing body of research literature. Catalogs such as these can open a world of research possibilities to the user of any individual art library.

In addition to basic tools, art library collections contain specialized reference works unique to the area of visual studies. Patricia Havlice's *World Painting Index* (Metuchen, N.J.: Scarecrow Press, 1977) or Jane Clapp's *Sculpture Index* (Metuchen, N.J.: Scarecrow Press, 1970), for example, can help the researcher quickly locate a particular illustration and can thereby prevent the frustration that comes with having to scan many volumes to find one specific reproduction. Pamela J. Parry's *Contemporary Art and Artists: An Index to Reproductions* (Westport, Conn.: Greenwood Press, 1978), *Photography Index: A Guide to Reproductions* (Westport, Conn.: Greenwood Press, 1979), and *Print Index: A Guide to Reproductions* (Westport, Conn.: Greenwood Press, 1983) are examples of more recent specialized reproduction indexes that can streamline searches for art reproductions. The iconographical dictionary is another type of reference tool essential to the art library collection. Works such as Gertrud Schiller's *Iconography of Christian Art* (Greenwich, Conn.: New York Graphic Society, Ltd., 1971) and *Emblem Books* (Zug, Switz.: Inter Documentation Center, 1980) that help interpret the subjects and symbols in art are numerous. Dictionaries of signs and symbols, handbooks of mythology and legends, and works on the visual symbolism of the world's major religions are necessary to aid in the understanding and appreciation of artwork.

Art Exhibition Catalogs

Artists' participation in art exhibitions, and the subsequent literature that grew out of art exhibitions, has a long and colorful history.[6] Although the formal and organized display of art objects can be traced back to the earliest times, the publication of catalogs to document this activity is

---

6. For a discussion of the history of art exhibitions, see Kenneth W. Luckhurst, *The Story of Exhibitions* (London, Eng., and New York: Studio Publications, 1951).

a tradition that developed much later. One of the earliest known catalogs was published in 1699 to document an exhibition of three hundred paintings in the Grande Galerie of the Louvre. By 1738 the French Academy had begun to publish catalogs, or *livrets*, to guide spectators and to aid in identifying unlabeled works of art in an exhibition. By 1780 the Royal Academy of Arts in London required that the spectator purchase a catalog in order to be granted admission to an exhibition, evidence of the growing acceptance of such publications. However, the major growth in the literature occurred in the nineteenth century in France with the juried public exhibitions known as *salons*.

The salons were enormously popular events, and the public attended the showings in masses. Art reviews were covered by the popular press as well as by serious art critics of the day. Eventually, accounts of exhibitions were a regular feature of nineteenth-century newspapers, and many were published separately as pamphlets or books.

The first illustrated catalogs of the salons were published in 1808 by Charles Landon, curator at the Louvre and well-known author of many art publications. Works of art were illustrated with engravings, which proved to be costly and complicated and resulted in limited editions. Illustrated catalogs containing photoengravings, first published in 1875 by Henry Blackburn, allowed larger editions to be published. Shortly after, in 1879, F. G. Dumas began to publish his *catalogue illustré* containing facsimiles after drawings. As the official catalog of the salon had no illustrations, these forms of illustrated catalogs became very popular documents. Today salon catalogs, both the illustrated editions and the official nonillustrated editions, contain a great deal of information and are considered essential research documents for the study of nineteenth-century French art.

Since the era of the salon catalog, the exhibition catalog has expanded in scope, and today a typical catalog will include biographies of artists, chronologies, scholarly essays, and bibliographies, as well as detailed descriptions of the works of art shown.

Exhibition catalogs also come in many sizes, shapes, and formats. While most exhibition catalogs are still published in printed-book format, some are issued as sound recordings, packets of slides, and plastic mattresses or other unusual objects in their own right. *A Third World, Painting, Sculpture,* the catalog of an exhibition held at the San Francisco Museum of Art in 1974, came wrapped in a denim bag. *Technics and Creativity II* consists of a plastic box inside of which are a cardboard target and tablets of red, blue, and yellow watercolor paints. The catalog *Miniatures Exhibition* from London in 1977 was published in the form of a miniature card file.

Some catalogs document temporary exhibitions that are assembled and displayed for a brief time, while others document permanent collections owned by museums or individuals. Exhibition catalogs can be simple summaries or lists of items displayed or scholarly research catalogs that make important new contributions to the literature of that field.

Exhibition catalogs are extremely important materials in the art library collection. They may provide the most complete source of information on contemporary artists yet to have monographs written about them. A catalog of a retrospective exhibition of a more well-known artist may be the most authoritative statement on that artist's work. Also, exhibition catalogs may provide the public with the only access to important public collections that do not travel or to significant private collections that are not generally accessible to the public. These catalogs often publish scholarship in progress. A catalog can be a means for a scholar to disseminate research before a major monograph or research article is published. For that reason exhibition catalogs might provide the most current source of information on an artist or movement.

Usually, an exhibition catalog is the only record of a temporary exhibition after the display has been dismantled and the collection dispersed. Anyone needing to refer to the exhibit after dismantling must depend on the catalog for documentation. Catalogs frequently contain important critical essays, extensive bibliographies, and chronologies and biographies of the artist, as well as illustrations not reproduced elsewhere. An exhibition catalog often will also cite the present owner of a work on display, perhaps the only source of that information. Even small catalogs, which if retained at all are often treated as ephemera by libraries and kept uncataloged in pamphlet files, may at a later date prove to be primary source material in the study of an artist or artistic movement.

Artists depend on exhibition catalogs to keep abreast of the latest work in art centers such as New York, Paris, London, or Los Angeles. Art historians use catalogs for the scholarship they provide. Museum curators and private collectors use them to stay in touch with new information that may affect the value of their collections or the direction their collecting might take. Unfortunately, while exhibition catalogs are important documents to the users of art libraries, they are among the most difficult items for the user to locate.

Estimates of the number of exhibition catalogs published each year vary from 6,000 to 8,000 titles.[7] However, even the best indexing sources cover only 2,000 to 3,500 exhibition catalogs per year. Considerably fewer

---

7. Lois Swan Jones, *Art Information: Research Methods and Resources,* 3d ed. (Dubuque, Iowa: Kendall/Hunt, 1990), 25.

than this are added to the typical library catalog each year. Whether the patron is using an indexing source or the library's catalog, the exhibition catalog simply may not be listed. If the patron is working from an exhibition review in a journal, it may not be clear whether or not a catalog was published—not all exhibitions have catalogs. Furthermore, not all catalogs have the same titles as their exhibitions. Reviewers do not always make these facts known to their readers.

Exhibition catalogs are usually published in small editions and are available only at the time of the exhibit. They are not often reprinted when all copies have been sold, so the library must act quickly to acquire a desired title. When the library does acquire a catalog, it may be treated in a variety of ways. Some libraries catalog exhibition catalogs and classify them by the Library of Congress or Dewey decimal system and shelve the catalog in their stacks with related materials. Other libraries, with very large or specialized collections of exhibition catalogs, keep them as a separate collection and devise a special access system for them. The art exhibition catalog collection of the University of California at Santa Barbara Arts Library is a good example of a separate collection with its own cataloging system. Still others do not catalog exhibition catalogs but keep them in pamphlet files with ephemeral materials. Some libraries have large backlogs of uncataloged exhibition catalogs because they do not know what to do with them. Even when the library elects to catalog exhibition catalogs through a well-known system, access can be difficult due to the lack of standardization for selection of the main entry and the problems of assigning subject headings in art. Finally, as a further obstacle in the difficult path to locating an exhibition catalog in an art library, the issue of variant catalogs for a single exhibition must be mentioned. With the advent of the very popular large spectacle exhibitions that travel to several countries, such as the Archaeological Finds of the People's Republic of China in 1975, the Treasures of Tutankhamen in 1976, or the Vatican Art Collections in 1982, it is no longer uncommon for several catalogs to be published for a single exhibition. These catalogs are not simply translations to accompany the exhibit on its journey to different countries, but actually are different catalogs. Different scholars may write the essays, and different pieces may be on display; hence, the documentation changes.

In spite of all these difficulties, exhibition catalogs continue to be heavily used items in the art library. Art librarians and art library patrons are aided by several review sources that can help to make the catalogs known. Reviews of art exhibitions are cited in *Art Index, NewsBank Review of the Arts* (Greenwich, Conn.: NewsBank, Inc., 1975 –), and *Répertoire d'Art et d'Archéologie*. *Répertoire* has the added advantage of listing titles of exhibition catalogs in the *index des matières*.

Of greater assistance are the reference tools that index or abstract catalogs. Some of these tools are quite general and attempt to cover a very large portion of exhibition catalogs published. Others index only the catalogs held in a particular collection or are limited to a specific type of catalog. Good examples of indexes attempting to cover the broad range of published exhibition catalogs include *The Art Book Biannual* (Ithaca, N.Y.: Worldwide Books, 1992–), *BHA: Bibliography of the History of Art*, and *ARTbibliographies Modern* (Santa Barbara, Calif.: American Bibliographical Center–Clio Press, 1969–), which is available on DIALOG from 1974.[8] In addition, each of these reference tools provides abstracts of the exhibition catalogs indexed. The *Catalogs of the Art Exhibition Catalog Collection of the Arts Library, University of California at Santa Barbara* (Teaneck, N.J.: Chadwyck-Healey, 1977–1990), available on microfiche, is an index to the more than 70,000 exhibition catalogs held in that collection. Indexes of major collections such as these can greatly assist the art librarian or library patron in locating a specific exhibition catalog because of the depth of the collections and careful indexing arrangement.

More specialized indexes such as *Boston Athenaeum Art Exhibition Index 1827–1874, Modern Art Exhibitions 1900–1916, Nineteenth Century San Francisco Art Exhibition Catalogues: A Descriptive Checklist and Index*, and *The Archives of American Art Collection of Exhibition Catalogs* are examples of indexes limited to exhibition catalogs of a specific time period, a particular exhibiting institution, or a certain geographic region.

This is a very brief overview of only a few of the indexes to exhibition catalogs, yet the large number of available indexes testifies to their need. Additional help has been offered by publishers who reprint exhibition catalogs. Chadwyck-Healey (formerly Somerset House) has reprinted thousands of exhibition catalogs since the 1970s. Its *Subject Index to Art Exhibition Catalogues on Microfiche* (Teaneck, N.J.: Chadwyck-Healey, 1982) lists titles that have been made available on microfiche. Garland and Chadwyck-Healey have reprinted the *livrets* of the Paris salons: Garland has published the salon catalogs from 1673 to 1881 on paper, while Chadwyck-Healey has reissued the salon catalogs from 1673 to 1925 on microfiche. The extensive collection of more than 6,000 exhibition catalogs held by the Knoedler Library has been made available on microfiche in the *Knoedler Library on Microfiche* (New York:

---

8. *The Art Book Biannual* was preceded by *The Worldwide Art Catalogue Bulletin* (Boston, Mass.: Worldwide Books, 1963–); *BHA: Bibliography of the History of Art* was preceded by *RILA: International Repertory of the Literature of Art*; and *ARTbibliographies Modern* was preceded by *LOMA: Literature on Modern Art*.

Knoedler Gallery, 1973), although due to the price only a few libraries presently own the complete set. These publications serve as examples of a trend in reprinting exhibition materials.

In sum, both historical and current exhibition catalogs are essential to art research. The art librarian must anticipate the needs of users and understand the value of exhibition catalogs in answering those needs. While exhibition catalogs can be difficult to locate in the art library, specific reference tools and the recent increase in reprints have helped to improve the situation. As with other art materials, interlibrary loan of exhibition catalogs is somewhat restricted; however, it is possible to obtain catalogs for patron use through loan. The art librarian must have a good understanding of this entire picture to get the catalog into the library and to then unite the catalog with the end user.

Auction and Sales Catalogs

Auction and sales catalogs document works of art sold in the art market. While many libraries will have sales catalogs from the nineteenth and twentieth centuries, a few will have titles dating from the seventeenth and eighteenth centuries. Early sales catalogs are a rich source of information for the history of art, and new catalogs help us to understand current market trends and even predict the future.

The fact that auction and sales catalogs are used by a broad range of art historians, curators, dealers, collectors, and artists for a variety of different reasons is indicative of the great amount of information they contain. Auction catalogs often include high-quality photographs that show fine details of works for sale. Individual works are often carefully documented with data concerning medium, size, present location, previous owners, and exhibition history. Recent sales catalogs assist collectors, dealers, and curators in keeping abreast of the current art market. Prices from a specific auction must be viewed with caution, however. Several factors can affect prices at an art sale, including the weather, the intensity of "auction fever," and the types of buyers that are predominant at the sale. While such conditions can drive the prices up or down, auction catalogs will not provide this type of inside information. To make a judgment on the market value of an artist's work, one must examine auction prices over a period of time. For these reasons, the art library collection is greatly enriched by a solid collection of auction and sales catalogs.

The expense of auction catalogs often limits the number to which a library can afford to subscribe. Three major auction houses are Christie's and Sotheby's in London and Sotheby Parke Bernet in New York. Christie's catalogs are issued in more than fifty categories, such as furniture, European painting, or ceramics, and it is the rare art library that can afford to subscribe to even half of them. In addition, the library with a commitment to auction catalogs will want to acquire catalogs from Sotheby's and Sotheby Parke Bernet, as well as a few other auction houses of international importance. Art museum libraries often have the largest collection of auction catalogs due to the museums' involvement in the art market and the curators' need to document artworks in their own collections. University art libraries often follow the museums' lead and attempt to provide their faculty and students with art sales resources to support their research and teaching programs.

Beyond the cost of catalog subscription, auction and sales catalogs are considered expensive because of the large amount of space they occupy in the library and the amount of staff time required for their care. Rather than dedicate a large section of book shelving in the main collection, many art libraries elect to house auction and sales catalogs as separate collections. Auction catalogs of major houses such as Sotheby's and Christie's are usually issued well in advance of a sale. They serve to announce the "menu" of a given auction and prepare the purchasers for the minimum opening bid or estimated sale price. The price lists, which quote the actual final sale price at auction, are not issued until several weeks after the auction. Most libraries keep the price list inside the auction catalog so that they are housed together, as this greatly increases the research value of the catalog in future years. Art libraries with a strong focus on auction catalog collections will sometimes annotate auction catalogs after the sale with prices, names of purchasers, and other interesting pieces of information. Whereas publication of the name of the purchaser used to be common practice, reasons of security have made this less common today. Auctioneers will now release this information only with the permission of the purchaser.

Separate collections of auction catalogs are often organized by the name of the auction house and then shelved chronologically by the date of sale or sale number. Because the contents of the sale catalog are rarely analyzed in detail in library catalogs, or even on the cover of the auction catalog, separate indexing tools must accompany the collection and guide the researcher in search of information.

Indexes to auction and sales catalogs are published in book format as well as being available in online databases. Those published in book format can be divided into two types: indexes to past auctions and sales, and indexes to recent sales. Graves's *Art Sales from Early in the Eighteenth Century to Early in the Twentieth Century, Art Prices Current,* and Hippolyte Mireur's *Dictionnaire des Ventes d'Art Faites en France et à l'Étranger Pendant les XVIIIme et XIXme Siècles* are good examples of indexes of past auctions and sales. Recent auctions and sales are indexed in Enrique Mayer's *International Auction Records: Engravings, Drawings, Watercolors, Paintings, Sculpture* (Paris, Fr.: Editions Enrique Mayer, 1967–), *Leonard's Index of Art Auctions* (Newton, Mass.: Auction Index, Inc., 1980–) and the *Annual Art Sales Index* (Richard Hislop, ed., Weybridge, Eng.: Art Sales Index, Ltd., 1969/1970), as well as several other sources. Indexes usually cite the name of the auction house and the date of sale so that, should the library organize its collection of auction catalogs by the auction house and date of sale, the user can easily refer back and forth from the indexes to the collection at hand.

One of the more helpful developments in art library technology in recent years has been the advent of online databases that index records of art auctions and sales. ArtQuest: The Art Sales Index Database (Weybridge, Eng.: Art Sales Index, Ltd., 1970–) contains a file of auction records for paintings, drawings, and sculpture. Initially the database contained records for more than 700,000 works of art, and 100,000 entries are added each year. SCIPIO (Sales Catalog Index Project Input Online) (Stanford, Calif.: The Research Libraries Group, Inc., 1980–) is an online database begun in 1980 and currently available to libraries through RLIN. SCIPIO functions as a union list and provides bibliographic control and access to the sales catalogs in several major research libraries in the United States. Currently the SCIPIO file contains records for more than 95,000 catalogs, and approximately 6,000 records are added each year. Even art libraries that cannot afford to collect huge numbers of sales and auction catalogs will attempt to provide their users with solid collections of printed or online indexes. The indexes often provide enough information to satisfy the researcher's need in place of the actual sale catalog. It is not unusual for these indexes to cite a full description of each work sold and the price at sale.

Other reference tools of service to art libraries without full back files of auction and sales catalogs are the published library catalogs of special collections of auction and sales catalogs. The *Répertoire des Catalogues des Ventes* by Frits Lugt (The Hague, Neth.: Martinus Nijhoff, 1938–1964) cites sales catalogs in 150 libraries, 25 of them in the United States. The *Catalogue des Catalogues de Ventes d'Art* (Boston, Mass.: G. K. Hall, 1972) of the Bibliothèque Forney in Paris cites approximately 14,000 sales catalogs housed in that library and, as such, is considered a major resource. The Fogg Art Library of Harvard University has issued *Catalogue of Auction Sales Catalogues* (Boston, Mass.: G. K. Hall, 1971) and the Metropolitan Museum of Art has issued separate volumes of sales catalogs in its catalog *Library Catalog of the Metropolitan Museum of Art* (Boston, Mass.: G. K. Hall, 1980; first supplement, 1982). These are but a few of the library catalogs of sales catalogs that can be of great assistance in the interlibrary loan process.

Even libraries with a current commitment to collecting auction and sales catalogs might have large gaps in their back files. This situation is being remedied by increasing activity in the reprint industry. The complete run of sales catalogs issued by Sotheby's in London from 1734 to 1970 is now available on microfilm from University Microfilms International in Ann Arbor, Michigan. Approximately 13,000 sales catalogs from the Knoedler Gallery in New York are available on microfiche in the *Knoedler Library on Microfiche* set.

Art auction and sales catalogs provide a wide variety of users with information important for both historical research and analysis of current trends. While auction and sales catalogs can be expensive to collect and costly to house and access properly, many art librarians feel their research value offsets their expense. For those libraries unable to afford large collections of auction and sales catalogs, large numbers of published indexes prove essential. These libraries are further aided by the growth of available reprints of early catalogs as well as published library catalogs of special collections that can facilitate interlibrary loans. Caroline Backlund's article, "The Cutting Edge: New Auction Sources and Computer Projects," provides a thorough overview of research resources available in the field of art auctions and sales.[9]

Artists' Books

When artists make artworks in book form the products are known as artists' books. The terms *book objects* and *bookworks* have also been applied, although *artists' books* is the term most often used.[10]

These are not art books that present the viewer with reproductions of artworks or portfolios of prints, nor are they books on art, such as critical reviews or anthologies of artists' writings. Nor are artists' books in the same tradition as the craft object, the *livre d'artiste*, which is a limited edition of original artwork treated as a precious object.[11] Artists' books are works of art in their own right. They are created using mass-production methods such as photocopiers or offset presses, in large quantities, at low prices. They can be purely visual, purely verbal, or a combination of visual and verbal. The important characteristic is that they are artworks conceived in the book form.

---

9. Caroline Backlund, "The Cutting Edge: New Auction Sources and Computer Projects," *Art Documentation* 9, no. 4 (Winter 1990): 175–78.

10. Clive Phillpot, "Books, Book Objects, Bookworks, Artists' Books," *Artforum* 20 (May 1982): 77–79.

11. For further information on the *livre d'artiste,* see Walter J. Strachan, *The Artist and the Book in France: The 20th Century Livre D'Artiste* (New York: G. Wittenborn, 1969).

Artists' books find their roots in the socially conscious 1960s. In an attempt to rebel against the use of art as a commodity by a capitalist society, the growth of art as a big business, and the elitism of the art world, artists began to make books. These were books as conceptually whole and as visually legitimate as painting or sculpture.

Artists' books are often published by the artists themselves or by a few small presses or galleries. One of the important thrusts behind their creation is the desire to make art more accessible to a larger number of people. There is no single original of an artists' book—each mass-produced, inexpensive copy is a work of art. Artists' books are meant to be a truly democratic art form, and accessibility is enhanced by direct purchasing methods. Art in book form allows the artist to avoid the commercial art gallery system, as these books can be ordered directly from the artists and sent through the mail.

These works present a unique opportunity for art librarians to purchase and disseminate art in its primary state. The low cost of the material (usually between $10 and $30 per book) places it within the realm of possibility for almost all libraries. The art library's role as a promoter of art is heightened with a collection of artists' books. This material can draw to the library those artists, art students, and faculty who may not otherwise use the library extensively, or who avoid the card catalog and prefer to browse the book shelves. Collections of artists' books can also be the source of regular library exhibitions or lectures and can serve as an important element in outreach programs. And the archival qualities and format of the material further enhance the library as a logical home for these art objects.

Acquisitions of artists' books are not accomplished through the normal library channels. Artists' books are not supplied by major library vendors and are rarely handled by commercial book stores, museum book shops, or art galleries. A small number of specialty stores, such as Printed Matter in New York City, have emerged to fill this gap. The most useful selection tools for artists' books are the excellent catalogs published by these specialty stores listing their complete stock of artists' books. Evaluation of the material is also difficult. Artists' books are rarely reviewed either as books or as works of art. However, criteria exist to aid the librarian. Some artists have reached such a position in the art world that the art librarian needs to buy nearly everything published by or about that person. The work may be particularly controversial, and providing access to it could be a valuable service rendered by the librarian. The few catalogs of exhibitions devoted to artists' books serve as basic bibliographies and help the librarian learn of specific works that have been exhibited by galleries or other institutions. *Artists' Books* (London, Eng.: Arts Council of Great Britain, 1976) and *Artists' Book-*

works (London, Eng.: British Council, 1975) provide very helpful listings of artists' books exhibited. The more recent *Artists' Books: A Critical Anthology and Sourcebook* (Joan Lyons, ed., Rochester, N. Y., and Layton, Utah: Visual Studies Workshop in assoc. with G. M. Smith, Peregrine Smith Books, 1985) contains a thorough bibliography on the topic and several essays on the development of the art form. Artists' books also provide an excellent area for the librarian to draw on years of experience and training. Inexpensive gambles on unknowns can result in a rich collection of material that may be unobtainable later.

Unfortunately, bibliographic control of artists' books is quite poor. Whereas the usual single authorship presents few cataloging problems, artists' books can be short on the details of publisher, date, and place of publication. Subject headings can be quite problematic. A well-known tale among art librarians is that of Edward Ruscha's *Twentysix Gasoline Stations*, a collection of photographic images of gasoline stations and one of the early and important artists' books of the 1960s. A well-known and highly respected library had assigned the subject heading Automobiles—Service Stations and shelved the work in the science and technology collection. Similar is the case of another work by the same artist, *A Few Palm Trees*, which had been given the subject heading Palms—California—Los Angeles. Clearly the problems exist because the artist employed photographic images of gasoline stations and palm trees. The classifier assumed that the subject content of the images, and not the book as object, was the main concern to the reader. Had the cataloger been confronted with a book of reproductions of paintings of palm trees, the book most probably would have been assigned a subject heading under a subdivision of Painting or possibly both Painting and Palms. There is a Library of Congress subject heading Artists' Books, but it is not always used by catalogers unfamiliar with the medium. This is a good example of an area that requires oversight by a subject specialist.

Collections of artists' books are treated in a variety of ways in art libraries. Because of the philosophy behind their creation, and because they are often produced in large editions, sound arguments can be made for not restricting their use. Some libraries, therefore, catalog artists' books and shelve them in the open stacks. However, other libraries have pulled together their artists' books as separate collections. Many artists' books will not be reprinted, and in time some titles might become rare items and acquire financial value. The lack of good bibliographic control and poor subject headings may mean that the library catalog will fail to lead the searcher to all artists' books owned by the library. Therefore, separate collections of artists' books, pulled together in one location, can perform a great service for the user. If a separate collection of artists' books is kept out of view of the public eye, periodic displays of the material can bring it to the attention of library patrons.

The physical condition of artists' books also influences some art librarians to create separate collections. Most artists' books are paperback books printed on inexpensive paper stock. Also they are often victims of "perfect" binding, and after a few years the spinal glue can give way and pages will come loose. This action is encouraged by the method of viewing "flip books," a popular format of artists' books. While other paperbound materials subjected to the wear and tear of the open book stacks can usually be rebound, rebinding might seriously violate the significance and value of book art. Also, artists' books come in all sizes. While some are the size of a typical paperback book, many are very small (one or two inches square), and could easily be lost in the book stacks. For all of these reasons, separate pamphlet boxes are often the preferred method of housing collections of artists' books.

Artists' books are an exciting component of the art library collection. They allow the librarian to bring together the reader and individual works of art. In the library the reader can hold an artwork in hand, experience it intimately, and sometimes take it home. Artists' books offer the reader a firsthand experience with new art, an experience that might be particularly valuable outside major art centers. Art libraries with collections of books that are art, not about art, take on a new significance as patrons of the arts, rather than being branded as warehouses of second, third, and fourth generation reproductions of art. Finally, the large number and variety of books produced, and the different methods employed by librarians to select them for purchase, almost ensures that one art library's collection will not duplicate that of another. While the country's largest public archive of artists' books, Franklin Furnace in New York City, requests three copies of all artists' books produced for archival and exhibition purposes, art libraries are not this specialized. Artists' books are an area in which the art librarian can leave an individual stamp on the collection.

Nonbook Materials

Ephemera

The role of ephemera in the art library is still in the early stages of recognition. Art librarians are beginning to call attention to the ephemeral, fugitive items that pass through our society documenting the taste of the time and presenting potential keys to understanding the visual history of our century.

An enormous variety of ephemeral material is of interest to some art library collections: advertisements using typographic work by specific artists or designers; sample books; bookplates; matchboxes; theatre, circus, or rock posters; and record album covers are but a few examples.

Ephemeral items can provide a record of the production of visual artifacts. They note the beat of the artistic rhythm to which a particular culture or society moves. A collection of well-chosen ephemeral items can present future researchers with a representative selection of the art and design environment of a particular period. These collections are important both to art historians, who attempt to reach an accurate appraisal of an era, and to practicing artists and designers who want to better understand and examine recent traditions.

A good ephemeral collection in an art library might provide examples of printing and typographic styles, package design, or examples of product designs by specific artists, designers, or groups. A collection of fashion catalogs will become an important source of study of the costumes of a period. A solid collection of advertisements for a specific product, perfume or cigarettes, for example, can illustrate the powerful relationship between visual imagery and expectation in a particular society. Record album covers have been a popular format for the work of a large group of artists in the past three decades. John Johnson has said, "The waste, the ephemera of today are the evidential data of tomorrow."[12] The library that can provide a good collection of original examples will prevent forcing its researchers to wait to study this genre until books on the topic appear.

Acquisition methods for ephemera are worth noting, as they differ considerably from methods used to collect other types of materials in the art library. Time is of the essence when collecting ephemera, as it is extremely important to acquire the materials when they are current. Timely collection allows the librarian to make a careful selection from the widest range of available materials and circumvents the need to purchase from expensive specialty dealers who cater to private collectors. Although true in many areas of collection development, in selecting ephemera it is especially important for the librarian to remain without personal bias and to aim for broad coverage of whatever item is being collected and preserved. This enables a freer rein in future interpretation and appreciation of the material. The librarian collector of ephemera should try to avoid any single viewpoint and attempt a balanced presentation of that particular phenomenon, including both a comprehensive overview of the topic and a number of good representative pieces.

12. *The John Johnson Collection: A Catalogue of an Exhibition* (Oxford, Eng.: Bodleian Library, 1971), 9.

The clubs and newsletters of private collectors as well as directories of special library collections can lead to important personal contacts helpful for swaps or exchanges of duplicate materials. A very important source of acquisitions is one's own community. An exhibition of the library's collection of ephemera or an article in the local newspaper can alert citizens to the librarian's interest in specific items and encourage donations. Most people would prefer to find a good home for their castoffs rather than throwing them in the trash, and it might only be necessary to bring the library's interest to their attention.

The difficulty of caring for ephemeral materials may be the primary reason many art librarians ignore this rich research resource. Physical treatment of each individual piece can be costly and time-consuming. Depending on the type of material collected, archival storage boxes, portfolio cases, map drawers, or specially compiled albums might provide the best means of caring for the material. It may be preferable to microfilm the collection or to make available a full file of photographs or slides of each piece, together with any other existing documentation, and to keep the collection in storage. Collections in storage can be made available for exhibit or for specific research requests. Such documentation has the added benefit of being able to be sent through the mail to provide other institutions or interested scholars access to the collection.

Traditional library classification schemes do not do justice to ephemeral art collections, and the librarian usually must rely on other methods. Many devise classification schemes specific to their area of specialization. Depending on the items collected, material might be arranged by artist or designer, by form or function, or by chronology. Separate catalogs to these collections are usually necessary.

Other librarians opt for a system based on accession number as call numbers. Such a relatively simple system can work very well if the catalog provides adequate descriptions and subject headings to pull like items together in a meaningful grouping. This solution is made even more feasible today with the growing use of microcomputers.

The rewards of creating, building, and caring for an ephemeral art collection are numerous. The art librarian is presented with an unusual opportunity to collect and service primary research materials. Preserving items that reflect our view of the past and create influences on the future can be an important contribution not only of the book librarian but of the nonbook librarian as well. Also, exhibition of a library's ephemera collection can educate viewers about the art of our everyday lives and heighten appreciation of our visual world. Each collection of art ephemera will be a unique contribution to recording our visual milieu.

Microforms

Several issues relating to microforms deserve special study when examined in the context of the art library. The comparative merits of microfilm versus microfiche, positive versus negative copy, color versus black and white, or silver halide versus diazo have particular importance in the art research collection.

In the art library microfiche has several advantages over microfilm. In many of the large pictorial archives now available in microformat, the researcher is often interested in one specific image. Reproduction on sheet microfiche allows the searcher to locate a single image more rapidly and efficiently than scanning through rolls of film. Also, students and instructors in the visual arts make heavy use of projected images in the classroom. Microfiche readers, which can project images onto a screen or wall, allow microfiche art collections to be used as traditional slide art collections have been used in the past. Art journals and art books often print reproductions sideways, and when these publications are reprinted in microformat, the same pattern is maintained. Several newer microform readers feature optical image rotation, allowing images to be viewed vertically or horizontally. Previously, with older microform readers, viewers often had to bend their necks in the most awkward fashion to study text and reproductions together.

Due to the high proportion of illustrative materials, the issue of positive versus negative film takes on added importance in art libraries. The patron in the art library will prefer positive film since photographs and reproductions can then be viewed in a meaningful way. The positive images appear as conventional prints and are easier to study and reproduce.

The selection of types of film, silver halide or diazo, may also be different in the art library than in other types of libraries. Silver halide film has a longer storage life than diazo film; therefore, it is normally recommended that diazo film be limited to temporary records. In many other types of libraries, periodic supplements to indexes and updating services are produced on diazo film because it is understood that they will be discarded when superseded or out of date. However, most materials produced in microformat for art libraries are produced with permanence in mind, rather than short-term use, and large collections such as the *Historic American Building Survey*, which contains more than 45,000 photographs on microfiche, or *Photographic Views of New York City* (Ann Arbor, Mich.: University Microfilms, 1981), which contains 54,000 images of the history of New York City architecture on microfiche, are purchased with permanence in mind, and storage life is an important consideration in their selection.

In the early years of micropublishing, black-and-white film was accepted as the norm. To the great advantage of art libraries, more and more titles produced in microformat are now available on color film. The quality of color film can be excellent, as evidenced by *The Index of American Design*, which reproduces on color microfiche a visual survey of decorative, folk, and popular arts made in America between the settlement years and 1900. However, color fiche is more costly to reproduce and, therefore, is not as readily available as its black-and-white counterpart. Much has been written on the permanence of both black-and-white and color film, but the fact is that both will fade. When expensive collections of color microfiche reproductions begin to fade, what should the art librarian do? Few art librarians can afford to replace these collections every fifteen or twenty years. Even for those libraries able to bear such an expense, what reassurance is there that the condition of the master copies will be constantly monitored by the publishers? When the value of a reproduction depends on the veracity of color tones, color becomes a very important issue in the art library. Image collections stored on compact disc may answer some of these questions, but the longevity of compact discs is also under study.

The increase of availability of art microforms is quite remarkable. In 1972 the *Subject Guide to Microforms in Print* (Westport, Conn.: Meckler, 1962/1963 –) contained two and one-half pages of citations under the fine arts headings. The 1990 edition of the same work contains sixty-two pages of entries under the same subject headings. The reasons for this growth are not difficult to understand. Unlike titles in libraries in scientific disciplines, titles in art libraries do not become obsolete with age. Most areas of art studies enjoy periodic resurgences of importance, and even works documenting art of questionable merit are important to historic studies of taste and criticism. The recent surge of reprints of art books and journals in microformat makes available important titles lacking in many collections. The economy of microforms allows art librarians to enrich their collections in a cost-effective manner. It is currently possible to purchase ten separate microform editions of illuminated manuscripts for the price of one fine facsimile edition in book form.

Also, publication on microform now allows libraries to house collections that were previously prohibitive in size and expense. One of the more helpful developments in art publishing has been the reproduction of major collections of visual materials in microformat. Even if an art library were able to afford the cost of the photographs, few would have the space to house the 200,000 photographs of Italian works of art contained in *The Alinari Photo Archive* (L. D. Couprie, ed., Zug, Switz.: Inter Documentation Company; Florence, It.: Alinari, 1983) or the approximately 930,000 photographs of German art contained in the

Marburger Index (Munich, Ger.: Verlag Dokumentation, 1976–). Until recently these archives were available only to advanced scholars with the time and means to travel to the original photographic files.

Unfortunately, an art library might go to considerable expense to acquire major research collections in microformat, but fail to catalog them properly and, therefore, impede their use. Although much space in the professional literature of art librarianship has turned attention to the quality of image reproduction, the permanence of color microforms, and the veracity of color reproduction, the most important drawback in the use of microforms is lack of adequate cataloging and poor bibliographic control. The lack of analytics for individual titles contained in large multivolume microform sets leaves hundreds of titles unrecorded in the library catalog. For example, the *Emblem Books* set published by Inter Documentation Company reproduces on microfiche all known emblem books with the exception of identical later editions and reprints. Libraries purchasing this set often list only the set title, *Emblem Books*, in their catalogs, and do not catalog separately the 354 titles included in the set.

In the absence of adequate bibliographic control the "Union List of Microform Collections" was published by Paula Chiarmonte in *Art Documentation* [2 (Dec. 1983): 172–76] to alert users to the great number of resources available and to encourage their use. This project surveyed the microform collections in four major research libraries in the fine arts and annotated their holdings of seventy important microfiche sets in the visual arts.

Art librarians must demand not only high technical quality in the microform publications they purchase but also adequate library access after they have been acquired. The especially large and expensive sets now available in the visual arts are excellent candidates for shared purchasing and cataloging projects.

Visual Resources

"Photographs! Photographs! In our work one can never have enough,"[13] exclaimed Bernard Berenson. Today, picture and slide collections are standard research resources associated with the art library, and more art libraries are collecting videotapes, videodiscs, and optical discs. Such collections can provide users with access to works of art scattered around the world or preserve records of artworks that have been destroyed, lost, altered, or are decaying. Visual substitutes are essential to art research and education, as it would be impossible for an artist or art historian to assemble in one place all the works of art needed for study. Many

---

13. *Berenson and the Connoisseurship of Italian Painting: A Handbook to the Exhibition* (Washington, D.C.: National Gallery of Art, 1979), 45.

scholars consider a good collection of reproductions their most important tool in the study of art history, connoisseurship, or criticism. A well-developed visual library has two advantages over the traditional library collection: the researcher can have access to unpublished images of works of art, and the individual images can be arranged in different combinations for side-by-side comparisons in a way not often possible when working with reproductions in art books.

Many academic art departments, art schools, public libraries, and art museums maintain picture and slide collections as separate visual libraries. The picture collection, often containing photographs, original drawings and graphic prints, and printed reproductions, might fall under the care of a print curator. The slide collection most often is under the care of a slide curator or slide librarian. Although visual libraries are usually maintained as separate entities, they are mentioned here as a resource closely related to the art library and, therefore, part of our discussion of art research materials.[14]

The existence of reproductions of works of art dates to ancient times. However, it wasn't until after the invention of engraving in the late fifteenth century that graphic reproductions of works of art were widely produced for the purposes of study and documentation. Engraved reproductions, however, were unable to show the brush strokes or individual artistic style found in the original works. At best they were interpretive views of the compositional scheme of the original. The introduction of photography in 1839 remedied some of these shortcomings. The application of photography as a study tool for art historians and connoisseurs was recognized as early as 1844 by William Henry Fox Talbot in his *Pencil of Nature* (reprinted, New York: Da Capo Press, 1969), one of the earliest books to include original photographic plates of works of art. Talbot noted that, "Fac-similes can be made from original sketches of the old masters, and . . . multiplied to any extent" and that, "statues, busts and other specimens of sculpture, are generally well represented by the photographic art."[15] Not long after, in 1855, the Louvre began to photograph the art objects in the museum and make copy prints available to scholars on demand. This effort was followed by similar projects in other major museums and art research institutions around the world.

---

14. For a further discussion of the care and arrangement of visual resource collections, see Betty Jo Irvine, *Slide Libraries: A Guide for Academic Institutions, Museums and Special Collections,* 2d ed. (Littleton, Colo.: Libraries Unlimited, 1979), and Karen R. Lewis, *A Manual for the Visual Collections in the Harvard University Archives* (Cambridge, Mass.: Harvard University Library, 1981).

15. William Henry Fox Talbot, *Pencil of Nature,* reprint ed. (New York: Da Capo Press, 1969), text opposite Plate XXIII and text opposite Plate X.

The slide was introduced as an aid in teaching art history in the late nineteenth century at the University of Berlin. Initially the use of slides and photographs for the study of art history was highly controversial because it was felt that students would no longer study the original works of art. "Photography and Art History," a special issue of *Visual Resources: An International Journal of Documentation* [7, no. 2/3 (1990)] traces the use of photography by art historians and connoisseurs. Today slides and photograph collections are considered essential resources in art studies, and it is difficult to conceive of a good research collection without either one. In fact, Wolfgang Freitag has quoted André Malraux, ". . . Art History has been the history of that which can be photographed."[16]

New visual technologies of the twentieth century, such as color microfiche, videodisc, and computer graphics, will permit the creation of even more sophisticated visual libraries. Kodak is now marketing a system to transfer color images from slides and negative film to compact disc. For use with a television, a specialized compact disc player is necessary; however, the discs can be used on computers with CD-ROM drives. Although directed at consumer and business markets, the technology has implications for the library in its ability to store and to retrieve multiple images. Equally promising are the possibilities of advanced cataloging and retrieval methods as well as resource sharing that these technologies can bring. It is feasible that in the future we will have a visual databank of the world's art, fully cataloged and retrievable from a wide variety of access points. The quality of art reproductions, whether engraved, photographic, or electronic, is a subject to which the art librarian must be very sensitive. Even Bernard Berenson, an early believer in the value of photographs as study tools, came to conclude that photography was unable to reproduce the "object as it is."[17] The point of view and lighting techniques used by the photographer can lead to a highly subjective interpretation of a work of art in even the seemingly straightforward black-and-white photo. When one adds the element of color, the tonal variations achieved in the reproduction can differ dramatically from the character of the original. True color, scale, and an appreciation for the handling of materials are very difficult to convey in even the best reproductions. When working with plates in art books, reproductions in picture or slide collections, or electronic images, the researcher can be several generations removed from a firsthand experience with the art object. Recognizing this helps the art librarian remember the necessity

---

16. Wolfgang Freitag, "Early Uses of Photography in the History of Art, *Art Journal* 39 (Winter 1979/80): 117–23.

17. *Berenson and the Connoisseurship of Italian Painting,* 49.

of providing a variety of reproductions, to balance the complexities of reproductive techniques, and the importance of combining textual descriptions with reproductions in the research collection.

Library Facilities for Fine Arts

No discussion of art libraries would be complete without mention of some of the unusual problems and special considerations to keep in mind when working with these collections. Perhaps the most conspicuous is the dilemma of deliberate mutilation. Art libraries are victimized by this activity more often than other types of collections because they house a large number of beautifully illustrated volumes as well as books containing original artwork. Art books are very expensive to purchase, and often the library cannot afford to buy second copies. Many art books are printed in small quantities and go out of print rapidly; it is not always possible to replace damaged volumes. Therefore, the librarian must take special precautions to curtail these malicious acts. It may be necessary to shelve some materials in closed stack areas and, thereby, to deny general access. In this case measures must be taken to balance security of materials with issues of public access in order to avoid developing a pattern of censorship in the visual arts. This solution creates an extra burden for the library staff who must screen users, and it can alienate patrons who feel that their rights are being denied. Another solution to the problem is the establishment of noncirculating collections that require patrons to use the materials on the premises. Libraries opting for this method of control may be arranged so that the reading area is under direct supervision of the staff and all user activity is in clear view. To facilitate this, flat study tables might be provided, rather than enclosed carrels, to deter destruction of materials.[18]

Art libraries face special preservation problems because of the fragile nature of visual materials. Volumes containing loose prints, photographs, and original works of art on paper require special processing and shelving conditions. The impermanence of photographic processes, especially in slides, photographs, and color microfiche, creates many challenges for the librarian in charge of these collections. Issues of conservation and

---

18. For further discussion of art library security issues see the following four articles in *Art Documentation* 10 (Winter 1991): Marcia Reed, "To Catch These Thieves: The Librarian as Protector of the Book," 175–77; William J. Dane, "A Major Challenge to Security: The Theft/Mutilation of Art Materials or the Triumph of Art over Betrayed Trust, Rampant Mendacity, and Vanished Guilt," 179–80; Sgt. J. Steve Huntsberry, "The Legacy Thief: The Hunt for Stephen Blumberg," 181–83; Ann B. Abid, "Loss Liability: Risk, Responsibility, Recovery," 185–87.

preservation are rapidly growing concerns for art librarians, as reflected in the professional literature.

In general the physical arrangement of art libraries is usually different from other library collections. Great numbers of oversized art books require special shelving units. Most art libraries will have at least three shelving sequences for regular, oversized, and portfolio volumes. Art exhibition catalogs are issued in every imaginable size, shape, and format and often require special shelving provisions. Ephemera collections, usually filed in archival storage boxes or cabinets, occupy a special location in the library. In addition, libraries with visual resource collections need special facilities to care for print and slide collections properly. Adequate space is a pressing issue in art libraries. As in most areas of the humanities, the literature of art does not decrease in value with age. To the contrary, older materials often contain the most sought-after information in the collection. This results in few weeding projects and book stacks that are ever-expanding in size. Added to this is the problem of adequate seating. Because art collections contain a higher percentage of noncirculating materials than other collections, it is necessary to provide more seating space for users. The large number of shelving sequences needed, the rapid rate of stack expansion, and the number of open seating units required combine to make crowding a daily dilemma of the art librarian.

Users and Their Needs

The librarian must also make special considerations for the unique needs of the library patrons. Artists and art historians are visually oriented people who rely on their own methods to locate materials in the library. While the numerous art encyclopedias, dictionaries, and indexes in the reference collection are essential to many areas of research, browsing is an irreplaceable method of information retrieval for the majority of art library patrons. It is not unusual for artists not to know what they are looking for until they find it. Often the artist is in the library to seek visual stimulation. An index, no matter how efficient, cannot fill that need. Art students may want to see all the current issues of art journals in the library. Because these students want to look at great quantities of good reproductions of other artists' work as "food for thought," they have little use for periodical indexes that direct them to specific articles. Art historians and curators often seek illustrations to use in comparative studies. A person researching a particular Louis XVI chair will need to see many reproductions of other Louis XVI chairs in order to make a study of the particular piece in question. The best way to achieve this might be to browse through the appropriate area of the book stacks to look at as many illustrations as possible. The art librarian must recognize that browsing is not only a pleasant way to while away hours in the library but also a valid means for the artist and the art historian to retrieve information. The scholarship of art and art history is dependent on fact and personal observation, and the art library should provide the necessary tools for both.

Professional Readings

AICARC Bulletin. Zurich, Switz.: International Assn. of Art Critics, 1974– .

Art Documentation. Tucson, Ariz.: Art Libraries Society of North America, 1982– . (Supersedes *ARLIS/NA Newsletter.* Glendale Calif.: Art Libraries Society of North America, 1972–1981.)

"Art Libraries." In *ALA Yearbook of Library and Information Services.* Chicago: American Library Assn., 1978–1990.

Art Libraries Journal. London, Eng.: Art Libraries Society, 1976– . (Supersedes *ARLIS Newsletter.* London, Eng.: Art Libraries Society, 1969–1976.)

Art Libraries Society News-Sheet. London, Eng.: Art Libraries Society, 1976– .

Art Libraries Society of North America. *Current Issues in Fine Arts Collection Development.* Occasional Papers, no. 3. Tucson, Ariz.: The Society, 1984.

———. *Historical Bibliography of Art Museum Serials from the United States and Canada.* Occasional Papers, no. 5. Tucson, Ariz.: The Society, 1987.

———. *Procedural Guide to Automating an Art Library.* Occasional Papers, no. 7. Tucson, Ariz.: The Society, 1987.

———. *Reference Tools for Fine Arts Visual Resources Collections.* Occasional Papers, no. 4. Tucson, Ariz.: The Society, 1984.

———. *Space Planning for the Art Library.* Occasional Papers, no. 9. Tucson, Ariz.: The Society, 1991.

———. *Standards for Art Libraries and Fine Arts Slide Collections.* Occasional Papers, no. 2. Tucson, Ariz.: The Society, 1983.

The Art Press: Two Centuries of the Art Periodical; An Exhibition Held at the Victoria and Albert Museum, London, 8 April–26 September, 1976. Cambridge, Eng.: Chadwyck-Healey; Teaneck, N. J.: Somerset House, 1977.

Arts Council of Great Britain. *Artists' Books.* London, Eng.: The Council, 1976.

Backlund, Caroline. "Art Sales—Sources of Information." *ARLIS/NA Newsletter* 6 (Summer 1978): 65–72.

———. "The Cutting Edge: New Auction Sources and Computer Projects." *Art Documentation* 9, no. 4 (Winter 1990): 175–78.

Baxter, Paula A. *International Bibliography of Art Librarianship: An Annotated Compilation.* Munich, Ger., and New York: K. G. Saur, 1987.

British Council. *Artists' Bookworks.* London, Eng.: The Council, 1975.

Burton, Anthony. "Exhibition Catalogs." In *Art Library Manual,* edited by Philip Pacey, 71–86. London, Eng., and New York: Bowker in association with the Art Libraries Society, 1977.

Chiarmonte, Paula. "Union List of Microform Collections: Microform Collections Survey in the Fine Arts Research Libraries." *Art Documentation* 2 (Dec. 1983): 172–76.

Dalberto, Janet. "Collecting Artists' Books." *Drexel Library Quarterly* 19 (Summer 1983): 78–87.

Davis, Clarice. "Annuals of Auction Sales." *ARLIS/NA Newsletter* 5 (Dec. 1976): 16–19.

DeLaurier, Nancy. "Visual Resources: The State of the Art." *INSPEL* 17 (1983): 179–92.

Dwyer, Melva J. "Microforms and the Fine Arts." *Art Libraries Journal* 7 (Winter 1982): 23–29.

"Electronic Visual Imaging in the Museum." Special issue of *Visual Resources: An International Journal of Documentation* 7, no. 4 (1991).

Freeman, Carla Conrad. "Visualizing Art: An Overview of the Visual Resources Profession in the United States." *Art Documentation* 7 (Spring 1988): 6–8.

Freitag, Wolfgang. "Art Libraries and Collections." In *Encyclopedia of Library and Information Science*, edited by Allen Kent and Harold Lancour, 571–621. New York: M. Dekker 1968–1982.

———. "Early Uses of Photography in the History of Art." *Art Journal* 39 (Winter 1979/1980): 117–23.

———. "The Indivisibility of Art Librarianship." *Art Libraries Journal* 7 (Autumn 1982): 23–39.

Gibson, Sarah Scott. "The Past as Prologue: The Evolution of Art Librarianship." *Drexel Library Quarterly* 19 (Summer 1983): 3–17.

Haskins, Katherine. "Decennalia: An Editorial Essay." *Art Libraries Journal* 7 (Winter 1982): 6–10.

Hoffberg, Judith. "Ephemera in the Art Collection." *Library Trends* 23 (Jan. 1975): 483–94.

Houghton, Beth. "Acquisition of Exhibition Catalogues." *Art Libraries Journal* 9 (Autumn/Winter 1984): 67–78.

Hughston, Milan. "Preserving the Ephemeral: New Access to Artists' Files, Vertical Files and Scrapbooks." *Art Documentation* 9 (Winter 1990): 179–81.

International Bulletin for Photographic Documentation of the Visual Arts. Ann Arbor, Mich.: Visual Resources Assn., 1974– .

Irvine, Betty Jo. *Slide Libraries: A Guide for Academic Institutions, Museums, and Special Collections*. 2d ed. Littleton, Colo.: Libraries Unlimited, 1979.

———, ed. *Facilities Standards for Art Libraries and Visual Resources Collections*. Englewood, Colo.: Libraries Unlimited, 1991.

Jones, Lois Swan. *Art Libraries and Information Services: Development, Organization, and Management*. Orlando, Fla.: Academic Press, 1986.

Keaveney, Sydney Starr. *Contemporary Art Documentation and Fine Arts Libraries*. Metuchen, N.J.: Scarecrow Press, 1986.

Kirkpatrick, Nancy. "Major Issues of the Past Ten Years in Visual Resources Curatorship." *Art Libraries Journal* 7 (Winter 1982): 30–35.

Leach, Elizabeth. "Sales Catalogues and the Art Market." In *Art Library Manual*, edited by Philip Pacey, 87–99. London, Eng., and New York: Bowker in association with the Art Libraries Society, 1977.

Lemke, Antje B. "Education and Training." In *Picture Librarianship*, 228–39. Phoenix, Ariz.: The Oryx Press, 1981.

_____. "Education for Art Librarianship: The First Decade and Beyond." *Art Libraries Journal* 7 (Winter 1982): 36–42.

Lippard, Lucy. "The Artist's Book Goes Public." *Art in America* 65 (Jan./Feb. 1977): 40–41.

Logan, Anne-Marie. "Optical Media: Their Implications for Archives and Museum." *Visual Resources: An International Journal of Documentation* 5 (Summer 1988): 177–82.

_____. "Videodisc and Optical Disk Technologies and Their Applications in Libraries, 1986 Update." *Visual Resources: An International Journal of Documentation* 5 (Summer 1988): 183–86.

Lyons, Joan, ed. *Artists' Books: A Critical Anthology and Sourcebook*. Rochester, N. Y., and Layton, Utah: Visual Studies Workshop in association with G. M. Smith, Peregrine Smith Books, 1985.

Marco, Guy A., and Wolfgang Freitag, eds. "Music and Fine Arts in the General Library." *Library Trends* 23 (Jan. 1975).

"Microforms and Libraries." *Microform Review* 10 (Summer 1981).

Olin, Ferris, ed. "The State of Art Librarianship." *Drexel Library Quarterly* 19 (Summer 1983).

Pacey, Philip, ed. *Art Library Manual*. London, Eng., and New York: Bowker in association with the Art Libraries Society, 1977.

_____. *A Reader in Art Librarianship*. Munich, Ger., and New York: K. G. Saur, 1985.

Pezzini, Isabella, and Jacques Gubler. "Architecture in Journals of the 'Avant Garde': Part I." *Art Libraries Journal* 9 (Spring 1984): 3–42.

_____. "Architecture in Journals of the 'Avant-Garde': Part II." *Art Libraries Journal* 9 (Summer 1984): 40–64.

Phillpot, Clive. "Artists' Books and Book Art." In *Art Library Manual*, edited by Philip Pacey, 355–63. London, Eng., and New York: Bowker in association with the Art Libraries Society, 1977.

_____. "Books, Book Objects, Bookworks, Artists' Books." *Artforum* 20 (May 1982): 77–79.

_____, and Beth Houghton. "Periodicals and Serials." In *Art Library Manual*, edited by Philip Pacey, 140–67. London, Eng., and New York: Bowker in association with the Art Libraries Society, 1977.

"Photography and Art History." Special issue of *Visual Resources: An International Journal of Documentation* 7, no. 2/3 (1990).

Picturescope. Washington, D.C.: Special Libraries Assn., Picture Division, 1953–1987.

Pollard, Nik. "Printed Ephemera." In *Art Library Manual*, edited by Philip Pacey, 316–36. London, Eng., and New York: Bowker in association with the Art Libraries Society, 1977.

Roberts, Helene E. "Visual Documentation: Engravings to Videodiscs." *Drexel Library Quarterly* 19 (Summer 1983): 18–27.

Samuel, Evelyn. "Microforms and Art Libraries." *Microform Review* 10 (Summer 1981): 141–47.

Schuller, Nancy S. *Management for Visual Resources Collections.* 2d ed. Englewood, Colo.: Libraries Unlimited, 1989.

Sisson, Jacqueline D. "Microforms and Collection Development in Art Research Libraries." *Microform Review* 8 (Summer 1979): 164–72.

Smith, Virginia Carlson. "Microforms." In *Art Library Manual,* edited by Philip Pacey, 236–55. London, Eng., and New York: Bowker in association with the Art Libraries Society, 1977.

_____, and William Treese. "A Computerized Approach to Art Exhibition Catalogs." *Library Trends* 23 (Jan. 1975): 471–82.

"Special Issue on Professionalism." Special issue of *Visual Resources: An International Journal of Documentation* 6, no. 4 (1990).

Stam, Deirdre C. *The Information-Seeking Practices of Art Historians in Museums and Colleges in the United States 1982–83.* D.L.S. thesis, Columbia University, 1984. Ann Arbor, Mich.: University Microfilms International, 1985.

Sutherland, John. "Image Collections: Librarians, Users and Their Needs." *Art Libraries Journal* 7 (Summer 1982): 41–49.

Tansey, Luraine. "Classification of Research Photographs and Slides." *Library Trends* 23 (Jan. 1975): 417–26.

"Visual Arts Issue." *Microform Review* 8 (Summer 1979).

Visual Resources: An International Journal of Documentation. London, Eng.: Gordon and Breach, 1981– .

Walker, William. "Art Books and Periodicals: Dewey and LC." *Library Trends* 23 (Jan. 1975): 452–70.

_____. "Art Libraries: International and Interdisciplinary." *Special Libraries* 69 (Dec. 1978): 475–81.

Walter, Nadine. "Computerization in Resarch in the Visual Arts." *Art Documentation* 10 (Spring 1991): 3–12.

CHAPTER 2

History

Nancy C. Cridland

History is the written record of humankind's past, and our attempt to study that past. The time prior to the advent of writing is usually designated as prehistory and is usually the province of anthropologists and archaeologists, although materials on prehistory are sometimes considered part of the historical collection.

History has been described in many ways. It has been defined as collective autobiography and as the study of what survives of the past. Henry Ford called it "bunk," and Voltaire once defined it as "a pack of tricks that we play on the dead." Each age writes its own history, interpreting the past in the light of the present; each age makes its own contribution to the accumulation of historical knowledge; and each age asks its own questions of the past, often seeking lessons from the past to throw light on contemporary problems.

Profile of History

The study of history is sometimes defined as the study of change over time. Early written histories dealt largely with rulers and with wars, because only rulers were seen to change in a largely static society, and war was the usual process of change. For many years, history meant primarily political and military history, with some attention to diplomatic affairs. After the Industrial Revolution, economic history took shape. Later, social history appeared, expanding to include many specialities, and intellectual and cultural history claimed their place. By common consent, historical studies do not include (or touch only very lightly on) the history of music, art, and literature, these topics being left to their own specialists. The history of science and technology is also sometimes regarded as a separate sphere of scholarship. But almost every other aspect of human life on this planet is regarded as fair game for the historian: political activity of all kinds; economic structures and activities; religion; the interaction between humans and the physical environment over time; cultural and intellectual developments; the history of racial and ethnic groups, of social classes, and of the interaction between groups; and, in short, nearly any human activity or interest that can be traced over a significant time period.

With virtually everything that has ever happened, anywhere, in any time frame, included in its compass, history is a very broad discipline with many, many fields of specialization. While teachers of survey courses are of necessity generalists, and amateur history buffs may or may not be, historians involved in research make no pretense of "keeping up" (on more than the most casual basis) with fields other than their own. The literature and the subject material are simply too vast.

Historical research and writing was not regarded as a separate vocation until quite recently. History and literature were virtually inseparable for centuries, with historical writing being regarded as simply a literary genre that might in some cases include elements of fiction and that had no purpose other than to provide enjoyment, inspiration, and perhaps, information to the general reader. The serious collection and preservation of historical documents began in the sixteenth and seventeenth centuries, but the Enlightenment historians of the eighteenth century were still very much men of letters. "Woe unto details," said Voltaire. (Modern readers of some esoteric historical monographs might wish for a similar triumph of style over nitpicking.) History, as such, was not yet taught as an academic discipline in the great universities.

History as a profession really began in nineteenth-century Germany with Leopold von Ranke and his colleagues. Ranke virtually invented modern academic history with his stress on precise fidelity to fact and on the primacy of source materials. The teaching of history by means of seminars also developed in Germany during this period. American universities imported these techniques enthusiastically in the late nineteenth century.

Most historians before the twentieth century would have agreed with E. A. Freeman that "History is past politics, and politics is present history." Nineteenth-century historians wrote primarily about governments, and about relations between nations. Today a considerably broader approach is taken. Historical research is the process of examining and interpreting the primary sources: the records (of whatever nature) surviving from the time of the actual event. The historian must master and take into account all the existing literature on the topic; the final product (a book or article) will document both this literature search and the historian's own sources and will contribute new information, new interpretations, or both, for future historians to build upon.

Early History

The earliest forms of historical literature that survive are lists and records carved on stone or clay. Written historical accounts developed gradually from the mythology and epics of earlier times, and for many centuries history was written about contemporary or very recent times only, with no serious attempt to reconstruct earlier periods. When the early writers did describe the past, it was usually to point out the tradition of glory their own rulers were maintaining or, on the contrary, to indicate the evils and darkness that existed before all was righted by their sovereigns.

The histories of the classical world were polished literary efforts. Herodotus (484–425 B.C.) is usually credited with being the first historian, or at least the first identifiable historian whose works have survived. The earliest Greek and Roman historians made lavish use of myth in their accounts, but Thucydides and Tacitus, who followed, were for the most part soberly factual narrators who compared sources carefully. A prime purpose of the writings of the classical historians was to celebrate the moral values and virtues demonstrated therein. Indeed, the classics were still deemed useful for inculcating moral values well into the twentieth century.

The early Christian historians (such as Eusebius) represented a step backward in the development of historical method, with a strong antipagan bias and some reversion to the mythical. While often inferior to late classical history both in methodology and in literary merit, the Christian histories did systematically preserve the historical record.

The chronicles surviving from the early Middle Ages were often composed by monks conscious of their mission of preserving the historical record (though by no means necessarily above slanting or doctoring the record to advance their own careers, to make the desired didactic points, or to enhance the literary value of the product). The early chronicles, usually written in Latin, were strictly chronological in form. The chroniclers often made industrious, if not discriminating, use of the available source material and cheerfully wove myth and miracle into their narratives as it suited their purposes. The Venerable Bede's *Historia Ecclesiastica Gentis Anglorum* is a landmark document of eighth-century history; the *Anglo-Saxon Chronicle* is an important late ninth-century compilation. Some notable medieval chronicles are the *Gesta Regum Anglorum* of William of Malmesbury (c. 1096–1143), the *Historia Ecclesiastica* of Ordericus Vitalis (1075–1143), and the

Chronica Majora of Matthew of Paris (c. 1200–1259). Historical writing was also developing at this time in other parts of the world, notably in China and in the Islamic world.

In the thirteenth and fourteenth centuries, the mythical and the religious elements were gradually disappearing from historical writing. Several factors contributed to the change. The decline of the monasteries meant that there were fewer scholar-monks. (The monks in the remaining monasteries often had a secular education, after the decline of many of the schools that had been associated with monasteries.) While the developing universities did not teach history as a discipline or contribute much to its development, still the growth of the universities meant the appearance of an educated lay population with secular interests. During the same period, the increasing power of princes and kings offered an alternative source of support to fledgling writers who in earlier generations would probably have turned to the monasteries. The secular histories of the Renaissance period appeared first in Italy, home of the Renaissance and a land where there had always been a variety of lay professionals. From Italy, Renaissance history spread in the fifteenth century to France and later to England. The growth of cities in Tudor England spurred the development of town chronicles as an alternative to monastic chronicles.

The secular history that resulted from all these developments was largely political and military history. (The religious history that did survive was also institutional history, being predominantly ecclesiastical.) Geoffroy de Villehardouin's *Conquete de Constantinople* is usually cited as the first important vernacular history to appear during this period. Secular, vernacular chronicles became increasingly common; they were still, above all, literary productions.

Political History

For historians from the earliest times, the political structure has served as an organizing principle, and consecutive governments have formed the historical units. The kingdom or state was the unit described, and events were cast in terms of the role played by the monarch or of the effect of events on the monarch's government. Those who attacked the throne, from without or within, were the other principal actors. The successive reigns or governments served as obvious and structurally coherent historical units. War also featured largely in early histories; accounts of it often featured considerable battle detail and careful attention to the effect on the government but paid little heed to the impact on the larger and long-suffering nonparticipant population.

With the development of organized political activity and of democratic governments, the development and activity of all political parties, whether or not currently in power, became an important part of the historical record. Electoral activity and voting records also became objects of historical scholarship.

Political activity is carried on by identifiable actors on definite and often documentable dates. The relatively orderly accumulation of generations of political history led naturally to the traditional method of teaching history by stressing the memorization of names and dates. No one would have argued that all the names and precise dates thus taught were of earth-shaking significance, or that the ability to parrot them all constituted a grasp of the subject matter. But without familiarity with key personages and at least some sense of the relative sequence of key dates, the student was ill-equipped even to begin to consider the issues. New teaching methods and increasing emphasis on social history, however, have led to a de-emphasis of rote memorization.

Political history has always been well served by the acquisition of relevant monographs and journals, supplemented by newspapers, a wide range of government publications, and the archives and manuscripts that the scholar may have to travel to use. Political data (and the census data so basic to interpreting it) are increasingly available in computerized forms, however, and access to the computerized material has become vital.

Diplomatic History

Archival research, beginning with the opening of archives in the nineteenth century, led to an increasing interest in diplomatic history. Archival research lent itself perfectly to the application of Ranke's exhortation to write history *wie sie eigentlich ist* (as it actually is). Diplomatic history had always been an element of political history, of course, but the vast documentation available allowed for much more intensive research and led to reinterpretation of many events. In this country, Samuel Flagg Bemis's *Diplomatic History of the United States* was a landmark in the development of diplomatic history.

In recent years, much archival material has been microfilmed and is readily available either for purchase or on interlibrary loan. In addition to archives, of course, diplomatic historians use newspapers, private papers, published books by participants in events, and most of the other sources used by other historians.

Diplomatic historians, like all historians, will be increasingly hampered by the growing reliance on telephones and on electronic communication, which leave no paper trail. Methods of historical research must always change as the form of the historical record changes, but the passing of the day of extensive paper correspondence is frequently lamented by those who have come to depend on it.

Economic History

Economic history and business history grew up together and are often linked, but the terms are not at all synonymous; economic history considers all aspects of economic life, including labor, agriculture, consumption patterns, and so forth, while business history is not confined to economics but also considers the social and cultural aspects of the history of business. From the earliest times there were, of course, treatises on various aspects of economic life (such as various forms of agriculture), but modern economic and business literature had its beginnings in the early eighteenth century, when reference books and published compilations of data began to appear, along with the works of philosophers such as Malthus and Adam Smith who primarily were interested in economic thought. Collection and preservation of census data began in the late eighteenth century, with the United States playing a leading role. Governmental agencies have always played a prime, though not exclusive, role in the gathering and maintaining of economic data. Over time the accumulation of many kinds of reliable data has been a considerable boost to the study of economic history.

Biographies of business figures also began to appear more frequently in the eighteenth century, and by the early nineteenth century periodicals and annuals dealing with business activity, such as *Niles' Register, DeBow's Review, Poor's Manual of Railroads*, and magazines devoted to specific businesses, also began to appear with increasing frequency. Histories of individual companies also began to appear more frequently during the nineteenth century, though these were usually commissioned by the company and made no pretense of objectivity.

Narrative histories dealing primarily with economic activity were rather uncommon before the twentieth century. There was of course the "muckraking" journalism during the Progressive period (which took a very different point of view from that of previous company histories). For example, Ida Tarbell's *The History of the Standard Oil Company* was a dramatic departure from the uncritical admiration accorded by earlier writers. But the interest of professional historians in studying economic and business history, bringing to it the scholarly tradition of careful documentation of sources and a formal attempt at objectivity, was really a phenomenon of the very late nineteenth and the early twentieth centuries.

Economic history advanced very rapidly with the development of sophisticated statistical techniques and of computers permitting rapid, large-scale manipulation of data. The scarcity of reliable data for earlier periods has made it impossible to develop statistical manipulation in those fields to quite the degree to which it is done for modern history, but an impressive amount of data collection has been accomplished nonetheless, using such sources as city archives and parish registers. Economic historians often make more use of collections of data than of narrative sources of any kind. Those who deal almost entirely with manipulation of data are sometimes called *cliometricians,* a word coined to indicate the combination of history and measurements.

Not all economic history is written by historians, of course. Economic history also flourishes as a specialty (or rather, as many specialities) within economics. Economic history as written by economists is typically much more statistically dense, deals more with economic theory, and is less narrative in form than that produced by historians. It is also usually more narrowly focused on economic aspects of the topic at hand, and sometimes historians believe that noneconomic factors are not sufficiently taken into account.

There has been considerable controversy among historians over some of the economic history produced by economists. The thesis of Robert W. Fogel's *Railroads and American Economic Growth,* which questioned the received wisdom that railroads were critical to nineteenth-century economic development, was vigorously contested. Even greater controversy surrounded Fogel and Engerman's later *Time on the Cross,* which made use of statistics to demonstrate that the slaves were better off under slavery than they were after emancipation. The methodology of Fogel and Engerman came under intense attack by scholars in many disciplines, and the carefully chosen title of their work did not deter its critics from accusing them of moral callousness.

Such heated controversy, however, is unusual. Economic historians employing the differing approaches of history and economics belong to some of the same professional associations (such as the Economic History Association and the Business History Conference) and often work in very similar ways.

Popular works of economic and business history do appear, and they are sometimes of interest to scholars, if only because such works are influential. John Kenneth Galbraith's *The Great Crash: 1929,* for example, is often assigned in the classroom. In general, however, the gulf between the popular and the scholarly is wider for economic history than it is for most other fields. The more technical works would be unreadable to most of the lay public.

Social and Intellectual History

Social history is a very elastic concept. It is often defined as "history with the politics left out." Many social histories of a time period and/or a region follow this prescription precisely, skipping very lightly over political aspects that are presumed to be known to the reader or readily accessible in other sources. Social history obviously overlaps with economic history and with sociology, and many social historians find much of the relevant literature outside the mainstream of historical writing.

Social history, even that written by scholars and based on extensive research, is often very popular with that much-maligned figure, the "general reader," and is likely to be found in all types and sizes of libraries.

Immigration history is a prime example of an influential development in social history, and it is largely a twentieth-century development. The pioneering works, such as Marcus Hansen's *The Atlantic Migration, 1670–1860* and Oscar Handlin's *The Uprooted; the Epic Story of the Great Migration That Made the American People*, were general, but there are also many studies that follow emigrants of a particular nationality or ethnic origin from their origins in the Old Country to their fate in the new. Ethnic history is distinct from immigration history since in ethnic history groups are also studied in their native area. Obviously, ethnic history attracts those whose own background is that of the group being studied, and earlier ethnic histories were nearly always written by members of the group, with or without academic standing. But like other specialties, ethnic history has now become professionalized, attracting scholars regardless of personal origin.

Many of the currently popular topical specialties are usually categorized as social history: Black history, urban history, family history, the history of women, and so forth. Strictly speaking, of course, such specialties rarely "leave out the politics" or the economics.

There is also overlap between social and intellectual history, since the latter often deals with ideas held by particular groups and with the sources of these ideas. Intellectual history is also pursued on a more theoretical plane, with the history of ideas being traced for its own sake; this kind of intellectual history overlaps more with philosophy than with social history. Intellectual history may also overlap with literature. Vernon L. Parrington's *Main Currents in American Thought* was a landmark work that treated literature and political writing within a single framework. Though intellectual history as a specialty within history was a relatively late development, the study of the history of ideas is of course by no means new. Pursued by historians, it usually involves studying ideas within their historical setting, including related developments in literature, the arts, music, philosophy, psychology, sociology, and other fields.

Current literary theory has had a major impact on history as on other disciplines. Poststructuralism, with its assault on narrative, has attracted much attention in historical circles, but the writings of its critics have also been influential. Historians working in many areas and fields acknowledge debts to literary theorists who have helped shape their thinking.

History in the Twentieth Century

Ancient history (that is, the history of the classical world) was a major portion of the history curriculum in this country well into the early twentieth century. Most American students also studied American history, perhaps British history, and a "world history" course that focused almost entirely on Europe. Other parts of the world came into play as they became objects of European colonialism, but the non–European world was rarely studied for its own sake until well into the twentieth century. Today, however, many students in survey courses (now usually designated as "European civilization" rather than as "world history") never study the classical period at all since the survey courses often start at about A.D. 1500. Study of the non–European world, on the other hand, has become quite common and is often required of history majors.

The great historians of the Annales school in France early in this century were influential in broadening historical study to include geographic, environmental, and social developments. A typical study might examine a small area over a short time span and paint a broad canvas covering all aspects of life in that place and time. Lucien Febvre's *Philippe II et la Franche-Comté* and his *Le Problème de l'Incroyance au XVIe Siècle*, Marc Bloch's *Les Caractères Originaux de l'Histoire Rurale* and *La Société Féodale* were key works; Fernand Braudel, author of *La Méditerranée et le Monde Méditerranéen à l'Époque de Philippe II*, was an influential later exponent. The influence of the Annales school spread slowly, but today it is taken as a matter of course that history includes all of these things and more. Interdisciplinary history has become commonplace, with historians studying and borrowing from the techniques of economics, geography, anthropology, psychology, and other disciplines. Courses in constitutional history, military history, legal history, educational history, and so forth, have become very common in history departments.

In the early to mid–twentieth century, there was considerable debate over the question of whether history is a science. History was usually classified as a social science for many years. The narrative style of writing fell somewhat out of favor as historians learned from and allied themselves with social scientists, with objectivity as a key value. Development of statistical techniques (and later of computers) made possible a great expansion of quantitative and demographic studies, which historians pursued in common with economists, political scientists, sociologists, and others. All kinds of census, electoral, economic, and attitude-survey data have been well used.

During the 1960s and 1970s, however, the presumed objectivity of the historians of the day was strongly attacked by many young historians who advocated taking a stand on moral issues, and who revived the old approach of "doing history" by focusing on conflict and taking sides. These scholars denied the possibility of objectivity and urged that historians state their position and make their biases explicit rather than implicit (as the young historians believed had been the case). There grew up what was commonly called the "new social history," though very little in history is entirely new. It was strongly influenced by the New Left (which, however, had no monopoly) and often studied history "from the bottom up instead of from the top down," focusing on the disadvantaged and those outside the mainstream of culture, rather than on the elites. Jesse Lemisch's famous essay, "The American Revolution Seen from the Bottom Up" appeared in *Towards a New Past: Dissenting Essays in American History*, edited by Barton Bernstein. The ordinary people in many societies were examined in studies such as Philip Greven's *Four Generations: Population, Land and Family in Colonial Andover, Massachusetts* and Jeffrey Kaplow's *The Names of Kings: Parisian Laboring Poor in the Eighteenth Century*. Ground-breaking studies of socioeconomic structure and of distribution of wealth and income, such as Jackson Turner Main's important *The Social Structure of Revolutionary America*, appeared during this period. Social mobility became a popular focus of research; Stephen Thernstrom's *The Other Bostonians: Poverty and Progress in the American Metropolis, 1880–1970* was a landmark work.

After a recent period of wobbling between the social sciences and the humanities, history seems once more to be turning up often in the humanities column. Many people still do regard history as a social science; obviously, historians have much in common with both groups. Certainly the writings of quantitative historians, which are dense with statistics and statistical manipulations, are more congenial to social scientists than to humanists, but other approaches, such as intellectual and cultural history, fall squarely into the tradition of the humanities.

Until well into the twentieth century, the teaching of history was usually a matter of straight-line, chronological presentation of whatever period and area was being studied. The political history of the time was used as the framework, whatever else might be worked in along the way. The popularity of interdisciplinary approaches and the development of scholarly specialties such as Black history and the history of women have changed the curriculum radically. Many specialized courses on focused topics are offered today (the Black Death, environmentalism in American history, the history of warfare, Puritanism in England and the colonies), changing the shape of library collections as they lead to much greater use of materials focusing on a topic rather than a chronological or geographic entity.

In addition, in recent years some social historians have been interested in exploring the history of fields once left to others, such as the history of sports, the history of homemaking, the history of aging, the history of education, and the history of medicine. Trained historians have brought new insights and approaches to the fields they study and, in turn, have acquired new understandings of the changing role of these enterprises in society as a whole over long time spans. Librarians must respond to these changing approaches. They must provide the new literature that crosses disciplinary lines and assist their patrons in locating needed information or material that may be in the literature of history but is likely to be in the literature of the field being studied (in the medical or education literature, for example) or even in the literature of another social science such as sociology or psychology.

Use of Historical Collections

Most historians are bibliophiles. Historians are usually regular and enthusiastic users of libraries. Along with the literary scholars, they are usually regarded by librarians as the researchers most interested in the collections and the most supportive of the library.

Historians expect very high standards of service and may not be very tolerant of what they perceive as excessively slow action. Walter Rundell suggests that because historians are so enthusiastic about their own research, they have not grasped the fact that *work is not play* and, therefore, have an abnormally low tolerance for frustrations or difficulties that they encounter in their workplace.[1] But they are never indifferent to libraries; they are correspondingly appreciative and quick to notice when their needs are met. Since librarians *like* patrons who regard libraries as important and who make good use of the collections they have so painstakingly selected, acquired, and prepared for use, historians and librarians usually enjoy a very good, mutually supportive working relationship.

---

1. Walter Rundell, "Relations between Historical Researchers and Custodians of Source Materials," *College and Research Libraries* 29, no. 6 (Nov. 1968): 466.

In addition to being the mainstay of historians and history students, historical literature is used heavily by patrons working in literature, political science, religious studies, classics, sociology, and from time to time by patrons from nearly all fields of study. In fact, there are in most disciplines some scholars specializing in a historical approach who will be using the historical collections intensely. While historians themselves are heavy library users and often require little assistance, these secondary users need and appreciate considerably more guidance in finding their way around historical material. A history reference librarian may often spend more time with, and be of more help to, these users than to the primary clientele.

A history collection for general readers or to support undergraduate instruction can be relatively compact. Book reviews and excellent bibliographies abound to assist in the development of such a collection, which with careful planning can readily be tailored to the desired size and scope. Any collection for research purposes, however, will need to be large enough to contain a critical mass of material in any area for which research is being supported and will contain a great proportion of retrospective material, some of which will be expensive in proportion to the frequency of use but is nevertheless vital. Even the largest and best-planned collection is unlikely to cover all of a researcher's needs.

The typical use studies focusing on materials in other disciplines, and suggesting a very short half-life, can be alarming to librarians who work with historians. They would be even more alarming to historians, if they read about them, because of the tremendous importance to them of retrospective materials. Because history is such a specialized field of study, materials on a particular topic may be completely unused for a long period of time and then become very much in demand again when someone in that field comes to the institution or when that topic once more becomes a major focus in historical research. Of course, some books, particularly works of synthesis which were not among the best to begin with, do become dated and will be relatively little used in their later life. But physical fragility, not obsolescence, is the great enemy in history collections.

History Collections in Libraries

A separate history library is a rather rare thing, though some large library systems do have a history reading room or collection (which does not purport, however, to hold all the history materials the library owns). It is usual for historical materials to be included in the general humanities and/or social science collections, acknowledging the major overlaps between history and archaeology, classical studies, political science, economics, sociology, anthropology, geography, religious studies, and other disciplines. Any general collection, of course (and particularly any academic collection) will have a sizable collection in history.

Many special collections also include historical materials on a particular topic. Archives of all kinds, rare book and manuscript collections, and state and local historical society collections are also prime sites for historical research.

A large academic library collects historical material extensively in most fields of history, though institutional specialties usually define the collection. Even the largest libraries do not collect comprehensively in every field of history. Smaller college libraries usually collect primarily or solely in English, and they collect selectively, tailoring the collection to support the teaching program. They will buy many of the same broad works of synthesis as the larger libraries do but will buy highly specialized monographs much more selectively.

Public libraries usually buy many biographies and narrative histories and may stock a large number of books on royalty and on military history, both of which are popular with history buffs. In addition, they may buy many of the highly illustrated, part-travelog histories aimed at a popular audience. The very largest public libraries build substantial research collections, including the same types of source materials and analytical monographs that an academic library collects, though perhaps in more limited areas than those an academic library will try to cover. But the smaller libraries will buy the analytical monographs sparingly, if at all. Public libraries large and small often do maintain special collections, covering local or regional history or perhaps built around some special aspect of local history, and such collections will often include manuscripts, artifacts, ephemera, and other formats that the library might not otherwise collect. A state library will usually have substantial holdings in the history of that state and may provide special services related to state history, particularly for genealogists.

The collections of a historical society library reflect the primary commitment of the society, covering and usually limited to the history of the state or locality concerned. Such collections nearly always include materials in many formats.

Library Facilities for History

Because of its heavy dependence on books, history has thus far not created as many demands on the library for special facilities as many other disciplines have. However, the need for more and more shelf space is the principal strain history puts on the facilities. The historical literature continues to grow, the areas of history in which a library collects tend to expand, and yet historians are virtually never willing to part with anything. Because some of this very bulky literature is used infrequently, older historical material (and old periodicals and newspapers used primarily by historians) may be among the first materials selected for shelving in a remote storage area, should the library develop such an area. This may work reasonably well if service from the storage area is reliable. But it is inconvenient and inevitably will handicap students, who often postpone their research until too late to wait for special service. A more serious problem is that as research projects and even historians come and go, what was last year's low-priority, never-used material may often become this year's *sine qua non*, causing considerable hardship for the historian who cannot understand why his or her material has been singled out for storage. Shifting materials as interests change is unlikely to be practical, so great care should be taken in selecting materials for storage.

Replacing bulky sets with microform is unlikely to be a popular option (with historians) and is seldom financially possible in any case. When microform replacement is possible, however, the space savings are substantial, and microform is often the best answer to problems with deteriorating material. Certainly when new material is being added, both cost and space considerations may suggest the purchase of microforms. Relying on the Center for Research Libraries or on other nearby libraries is another alternative to purchasing the big space-eaters, and often it is a perfectly practical alternative in the case of little-used material. Nevertheless, remember that historians will require dependable, continuing quick access (that is, in most cases, local access) to a wide variety of research materials for perfectly valid reasons relating to their research techniques, which often involve extended use moving back and forth, between materials. Both effective service to historians and good public relations require consultation when major changes in accessibility loom.

Historians also use slides, films, videotapes, sound recordings, and so forth, in their teaching, and they share with other disciplines a need for facilities for use of all these materials. (Indeed, they may be heavy users.) For research collections, access to online databases must also be provided. The increasing use of computers for the storage and manipulation of historical data is leading to a need for more computer facilities, equipment, and computer links. Increasingly, much historical data and even many historical texts will be accessed from remote locations.

Preservation of Materials

No discipline has a greater stake in the preservation of deteriorating library materials than has history. The history collections include many of the oldest volumes in most American libraries, since history is a long-established discipline and its retrospective materials must be retained. Some ephemeral material and popular literature can be freely discarded as it deteriorates, and few tears will be shed over the demise of third-rate secondary material as long as other copies are being preserved elsewhere. But all collections of source material and all of the significant secondary literature are enduring and necessary parts of the historical record, and the working historian needs to have much of it at hand. In addition, historians are deeply concerned about the preservation of many other materials (such as newspapers, popular magazines, and discussions of contemporary issues) that were not initially regarded as historical literature but that have great historical importance.

Both source materials and the classics of historical literature are reprinted (or offered on microfilm) with fair regularity. For some valuable older material, facsimile reprints are sometimes offered, preserving at least in essence the original typography and appearance.

However, at any given time a particularly needed item is unlikely to be available (even if it is listed as being in print) and in the case of large sets (and sometimes in the case of individual titles) is likely to be extremely expensive because the sales market for specialized history volumes is confined to large libraries and, therefore, is very small. The out-of-print market is often heavily used by libraries to replace worn-out or missing books, but unless the item being replaced has been subjected to exceptional abuse, the likelihood is that the replacement copy will be nearly as worn as the library's own. These are often the very items that other libraries are unwilling to lend because their copies are in seriously deteriorating condition also.

In many cases it would be advisable to purchase replacements of key works as they become available, lest the opportunity be gone when the library's original copy finally falls apart. A systematic program of making such replacements is very costly indeed, both in staff time and in money, and in most libraries it is possible only on a very limited scale and in cases of severe and apparent need. The current interest in developing and implementing new techniques for preserving library materials is a great blessing for historians, who can be among the library's strongest allies in seeking the funding, staffing, and environmental conditions necessary for a sound preservation program.

Though historians often value the ambiance of the original format—

the ancient binding, the real, if yellowed, newspapers—for most materials historians are concerned primarily with the preservation of the content rather than of the physical book or journal. Therefore, many historians are very much interested in all the technological advances that help to preserve valuable material—from photocopy to microfilm to computerization—and in other preservation efforts both local and cooperative. Librarians who serve historians will also need to look to the future as well as to the past, making every effort to preserve and to provide access to the historical record that is the story of our civilization.

The Literature of History

Historians work with two kinds of literature: primary sources and the secondary literature. Much source material is available in libraries, of course: printed or microfilmed collections of documents of all kinds, compilations of statistical data, manuscript collections, newspaper back files, and so on. But historians usually need more than their local collections for their research: Historians are heavy users of interlibrary loan, and historical research often involves travel.

The primary mode of communication for historians is the scholarly monograph, with journal articles running a rather distant second. Not much research has been done on the use of library resources by historians, but the few studies that have been done, in the United States or in Britain, at large universities or at smaller polytechnic colleges, all confirm what common sense and casual observation suggest: books are most often used, with lesser but steady use of periodical articles. Dissertations, newspapers, manuscripts, and archives are also used regularly. Videotapes and films are used for teaching purposes but infrequently for research. Computers were early embraced by quantitative historians as an essential tool for their own gathering and manipulation of data, but sharing of computerized data has developed more slowly.

A prime characteristic of the literature of history is that much of it retains its value as it ages. Primary source material is of permanent value to historians, of course, but even in use of the secondary literature, historians are far more likely to use older materials than most of their academic colleagues in other disciplines. Hence, a good standard bibliography in history retains its value and may be in regular use even when it is very old and must be heavily supplemented with newer sources.

A research collection in history will contain a large proportion of foreign language material. British historical literature is no problem, of course; many English language publications are distributed in both countries, and most of the important review sources for scholarly literature cover both. A great deal of important historical literature is published in German. Historical materials in Spanish and French are also important in most American research libraries. Collecting in other languages varies with the curriculum and the scope of the collection, but in a large library it will be extensive. Source materials and very important monographs may well be held both in the original language and in an English translation, where both are available; the translation is necessary for students with limited language competence, but the scholar often must have the original.

Unfortunately, some types of historical literature are very easy for libraries to acquire but almost impossible to keep. These materials are frequently (and sometimes very ingeniously) stolen, not only out of greed but because the patron does not know how else to acquire the material—or would be embarrassed to—or because he or she does not want the material to be available to other patrons. Materials on certain currently controversial political, religious, social, and sometimes international controversies; some types of illustrated military materials; and some sexually oriented materials tend to evaporate like the dew when they are shelved in the stacks. The vulnerable topics will vary considerably over time and will differ somewhat across libraries, but some materials can be kept only by eternal vigilance or by restricted access. Resignation to loss for the time being is a frequent approach to this problem; unless the budget is extremely generous, it may be fiscally wiser to make replacements later if interest is transient.

Primary Source Material

Primary sources in history are the records made at the time of the event (or somewhat later) by the participants or by firsthand observers. These may take many forms, including but not limited to edited or unedited versions of ancient texts, surviving diaries and correspondence, the writings of participants in events and their written accounts of events, parliamentary proceedings and many other kinds of government reports and proceedings, governmental and organizational archives, and manuscripts of many sorts.

Primary sources for the history of ancient Rome, for example, would include the archaeological evidence of all kinds: remains of buildings and of cities, coins, surviving art that depicts the life of the time, inscriptions, surviving tools, and other material objects. It would also include such surviving texts that are records created at or near the time of the event: letters, autobiographical material such as Caesar's *Gallic Wars*, and the like. (Surviving literary and historical texts, of course, are secondary sources.)

Primary sources for the Watergate crisis, on the other hand, would include the newspapers of the time; the *Congressional Record;* the proceedings of committee hearings; the relevant records of the FBI, the CIA, the Attorney General's office, and many other government agencies; the Nixon papers and tapes now in the National Archives and any other surviving White House records; the memoirs of Nixon, Kissinger, and a host of other participants; any surviving relevant documents created by any of these participants; and so forth. Note that some of these sources are not currently available to the researcher. Historians often face problems in research due to source materials that are sealed or in private hands.

All types of source materials are collected in libraries when they appear in published form; unpublished materials are usually held by special collections. Almost any written material may become a primary source for some purposes when the literature itself is studied: popular magazines as a reflection of popular culture, novels as conveyors of ideology, the secondary literature of history itself in the pursuit of historiography (the history of historical writing).

A great deal of source material exists in the form of large sets, original documents painstakingly collected by individuals or, more often, by scholarly organizations (sometimes government agencies). The various Monumenta Germaniae Historica series, the Loeb Classical Library, the Collection de Documents Inédits Relatifs à l'Histoire de France, and the British Public Record Office publications such as the Rolls Series all fall into this category, as do many other compilations in almost every field of history.

Many large microform sets are also compilations of source material, ranging from the papers of an individual to the *Short Title Catalogue* sets that include published titles selected from A. W. Pollard and G. R. Redgrave's *A Short-Title Catalogue of Books Printed in England, Scotland, & Ireland and of English Books Printed Abroad, 1475–1640* (2d ed., London, Eng.: The Bibliographical Society, 1976–1991) and from Donald Wing's *Short-Title Catalogue of Books Printed in England, Scotland, Ireland, Wales, and British America, and of English Books Printed in Other Countries, 1641–1700* (2d ed., New York: Modern Language Assn., 1972–). Major and inclusive collections such as the latter are useful to scholars in any field of research that concerns itself with the past, but historians are prime users and are usually instrumental in getting such a collection into the library.

A considerable amount of archival material is available in microform. Whether local ownership is necessary depends on the scope of the collection and the research needs of its users. Needed materials can often be borrowed from the Center for Research Libraries or from other libraries if use will be very infrequent. For small, easily identifiable material it is often possible for either the library or the researcher to obtain photocopies or film by mail directly from the archive in question.

Microfilmed archival material is extremely convenient for the scholar and makes many previously inaccessible materials available for student use. But microfilmed material has its limitations. The quality of the microfilming is sometimes poor, and there are often questions about the criteria by which documents were selected or arranged for filming. Therefore, serious scholars making extensive use of any archive usually must do their research on site.

Primary source material for historians presents two major problems for libraries. First, it retains its importance far beyond the life expectancy of the physical format in which it appears, leading inevitably to the existence of shelves full of shockingly deteriorating books that can be neither discarded nor replaced. These books are often so absolutely crucial that their absence (either temporarily for repairs or permanently due to theft or disintegration) can precipitate serious crises for researchers. Second, newly available source material will be published in large sets or microform collections that are exceedingly expensive and very difficult to fit into the library's budget. But often there is genuinely an urgent need for the material: it has been little exploited in its unavailable past and, thus, is prime grist for research; now that it is available, it is no longer possible to conduct related research without taking account of it.

When important older materials are worn out or missing, interlibrary loan is usually the first resort. Many libraries are surprisingly generous in lending fragile older materials, and it is important to be sure the patron respects that generosity. Basic source material must often be replaced for the library's own collection as promptly as possible, however. Reprint and microfilm editions of source materials may be available, though not necessarily affordable. When the material is not available on the market and copyright is no longer a consideration, it is sometimes possible to obtain a microfilm or photocopy from another library. In fact, the library's own deteriorating volume often can be copied, and this may be the best solution if the material is not otherwise obtainable.

Libraries belonging to the Center for Research Libraries can often rely on Center ownership of the very expensive collections of primary source material. Newspapers, state documents, archival microfilms, and major microform projects like the papers of the eighteenth-century Prime Ministers are typical examples. The Center's purchase decisions are based on polls of the membership, and members can propose purchases. Where the source material is central to the institution's curriculum, or where heavy and continuing use is expected, this will not be a satisfactory solution. But for material to be used infrequently, or perhaps by one scholar for personal use only, it can be a very good solution—particularly as opposed to not having access at all. Research libraries in a particular area often cooperate with one another in the purchase of very expensive items, relying on one another for access and avoiding costly duplication.

Many primary sources are not held in libraries at all, and the historian must travel to use them. Manuscript collections, in particular, are often privately held, and museums often hold significant source material. Historians also use the files and archives of many organizations, including, but not limited to, governmental units at all levels, businesses, trade and professional associations, churches, and voluntary associations of all kinds.

The interest of historians and others in using archival material has led in many cases to the upgrading of the organizational status and physical facilities of archives, to more systematic preservation of material, and to improved access to archival material. In the United States, for example, the American Historical Association established a Public Archives Commission in 1899 to create and publish inventories of and guides to archives, and in 1910 the association petitioned Congress to establish a proper archive depository. Congress authorized the development of building plans in 1913, but World War I intervened. After further delays, the National Archives and Records Service was actually established in 1934. Energetic efforts by the National Archives staff, supported by historians and other interested parties, have gradually led to the systematic deposit, management, and preservation of records of a wide range of governmental agencies. Increasingly, both governmental units and private organizations have responded to the interests of researchers with a serious effort to organize and make accessible the files that document their history.

Secondary Sources

Monographs

The monograph (a book-length treatment of a single subject) is the primary mode of scholarly communication among historians. The scholarly monograph with its distinctive apparatus including footnotes, bibliographies, and indexes was a nineteenth-century product.

In this country university presses publish much of the contemporary monographic literature in history, but there is also a steady flow from the trade presses. In Europe much of the output comes from commercial presses. In addition, many historical organizations and institutes such as the Medieval Academy of America, the Pontifical Institute in Toronto, the Hakluyt Society, the Deutschen Historical Institute in London, to name a few examples, publish monographic series.

A common pattern is for research on a topic to accumulate for a period of years in the form of monographs and sometimes articles on specialized aspects of that topic. When enough research has accumulated to suggest a new interpretation, a synthesis (or several) will appear using the accumulated data to produce a broad interpretation that will serve as the standard work for some years, while further research (perhaps suggested by the new interpretation) takes place. Such a work of historiography will focus on the historical literature rather than the historical events.

Today most of the serious historical writing is done by academics, though in earlier centuries this was not the case. There are also academically trained professional historians who work for other agencies and who contribute to the scholarly literature, of course, and there are unaffiliated scholars such as James Flexner and the late Barbara Tuchman who command respect in the academic world. In the case of recent history, works by participants are regarded as source materials and are very much in demand, and works by journalists are also sometimes accepted as having considerable value where the author is knowledgeable and brings to bear a real depth of experience and understanding. However, in fields of history where personal experience is not a factor, it is rare these days to find a highly regarded work not written by a professional (most often an academic) historian.

Biography

Biography is an integral part of history that seems to be enjoying something of a revival these days as a form of historical writing. Biographies are certainly the historical genre most popular with the general reader. There has been considerable scholarly controversy over the relationship between biography and history. Biography has sometimes been viewed as a "lazy" approach for both the writer and the reader, no doubt interesting and perhaps even of literary merit but still a genre entirely distinct from history. But more often it is seen as a necessary (if limited) contribution to historical understanding.

Scholarly biography has developed much as history has over the centuries, starting with literary works incorporating elements of myth and gradually incorporating scholarly research methods. Plutarch's *Parallel Lives* and Suetonius's *Lives of the First Twelve Caesars* are distinguished biographical writing surviving from classical times. Biography during the early Christian era was largely hagiographical. Einhard's *Life of Charlemagne*, written in the early ninth century (in Latin, of course), marked a return to the classical tradition. Asser's late ninth-century *Life of King Alfred* (there is some dispute about the date and authorship) is another notable early medieval contribution. Joinville's *Vie de St. Louis*,

appearing at the beginning of the fourteenth century, is a landmark vernacular biography. Like history, biography gradually shed its miraculous
elements during its medieval development. By the time of the seventeenth
century, even the lives of the saints were being rewritten in an effort to
assess the sources and eliminate the fictional.

A recent trend in historical biography has been the appearance of
"psychohistory," biography that applies the insights developed by
psychologists to historical figures. Erik Erikson's *Young Man Luther*
was a pioneering work in this genre, written by a psychologist and highly
controversial because many historians believed Erikson lacked sufficient
understanding of the historical context. Psychohistory later attracted a
number of scholars trained as historians but interested in learning about
and using the tools that psychology has to offer. Fawn Brodie, for example, has applied the techniques of psychohistory in *Thomas Jefferson:
An Intimate History* and *Richard Nixon: The Shaping of His Character*.

Biography has always been written on many different levels and with
many differing intentions. Not all biographies of historical figures serve
a serious historical purpose. Many are intended purely as light entertainment; they may contain elements of historical fiction, such as supposi-
tious dialogue. Others, while more serious, are personal biographies
that shed little or no light on the historical context. Some entirely serious and thoroughly researched biographies are written about figures
who played such a minor role in history that it would scarcely occur to
anyone to consult them in the course of historical research unless in
the process of trying to develop a "feel" for the period in question. Biographies of musicians, artists, and so forth, have been traditionally considered
to be part of the literature of those disciplines rather than of history.

Not all biographies cover the whole of the subject's life. When only
a brief period is covered, or only one aspect of the life in question, it is
difficult to draw a firm line between works that are biographies and
those that are simply historical or topical works. On the other hand, an
interpretative study written by a gifted biographer who has done his or
her homework can add much to an understanding of historical events.
Well-done biographies such as Catherine Drinker Bowen's *John Adams
and the American Revolution*, Elizabeth Longford's *Victoria R.I.*, and
James Flexner's multivolume *George Washington* are probably better
accepted and used by historians (especially in teaching) than are any
other secondary works by nonhistorians.

Local History

Much local history is published by local or regional historical societies.
Some of it is aimed primarily at a local audience, and local history is

particularly prone to what historians call "antiquarianism," by which they mean an uncritical accumulation of detail for its own sake to be admired because it is "old" rather than because it is significant and has been competently evaluated. Nevertheless, enthusiastic amateurs have been responsible for the recording and preservation of much of value that would otherwise have been lost.

Some of the local history that finds its way into print will be basic source material for the future: memoirs, maps, lists of residents and of businesses, and so forth. More often, however, it is secondary literature, as the history of the area is reconstructed using whatever sources lie at hand.

Many state historical societies have a publications series of some sort. Many have published collections of primary documents. Some publish serious historical research, and others aim almost entirely at a popular audience. The regional historical societies of other nations also vary considerably in the nature, quality, and intended audience of their publications. Some (such as some of the Record Societies in England) focus on the publication of primary documents, and others publish a variety of monographs on local or regional history.

The publications of small, local historical societies are more likely to be one-shot efforts. They are usually less suitable for academic library collections, except perhaps collections in the immediate area, but a few are of wider usefulness.

Most libraries, including academic libraries for the most part, do give special attention to their own (variously defined) locality in collection building and cast a more critical eye on local history for other areas. Intensive collection of local history for a given area can be surprisingly time-consuming, since much of the material is quite elusive.

Local history is also sometimes written by scholars who use the locality as a case study, where the real focus is on the subject matter being examined and not on the locality itself.

Oral History

Though participants in many historic events may seem indecently eager to rush into print with their reminiscences and observations, much of the historical record is lost to us (or distorted) because a majority of participants do not record their experiences. This is obvious in the case of obscure figures, of course, but it is also true of many public officials and other key figures who never get around to recording their experiences. Interviews have always been used to some extent to preserve the comments of those who do not write. The advent of the portable tape recorder has made it much easier to record personal observations and has contributed greatly to the accuracy of the record. Recorded interviews are later transcribed for use and for preservation, though the original is often preserved, too.

The Columbia Oral History Collection is probably the largest existing archive. It has collected interviews with thousands of individuals in many fields of endeavor. It is particularly strong on the New Deal period but also includes a large number of interviews of participants in the Eisenhower administration. Also significant are the collected interviews with leading and pioneer figures in advertising, the arts, aviation, journalism, public health, radio, and so forth. These collections of memoirs have been transcribed and microfilmed and made available for purchase by libraries, either complete or as individually purchased subject sets. There are many other oral history projects in progress, some available for purchase. (The format may be anything from a typeset book to a microfilm to a photocopied typescript.) Oral interviews are sometimes also available on video- or audiotape.

Many local history projects are making good use of oral history techniques to record the early history of their community (or another significant period) while the participants are still available to share their recollections. Institutional and organizational histories are also frequently gathered partly or largely by means of oral history strategies. The accumulated material often is transcribed and deposited in a library and sometimes reproduced for acquisition by other libraries. In time, development of better coordination and bibliographic control of oral history products should improve access to these materials and increase their usefulness to historians.

Government Publications

Historians are among the prime users of a government publications collection, making extensive use of parliamentary proceedings, published archival materials, departmental reports, committee and commission reports and proceedings, census and other statistical data, and other official publications of many sorts. Government documents form a significant part of the historical record of any age.

Though nearly all American libraries regardless of size hold at least some United States government publications, only the large and medium-sized academic libraries and the larger public libraries are likely to hold much that is useful to historians. The *Congressional Record* may come first to mind, along with such things as presidential papers, but congressional hearings form another important part of the legislative record, and governmental agencies and departments produce a very sizable literature of immense historical value. The United States census offers a wide variety of statistics, covering many topics and broken down

in many useful ways. Government publications collections are in particular need of knowledgeable librarians to help the patron find the relevant material, since the size and complexity of the collections is apt
to defeat the uninitiated. (Of course, some government documents also
are available in various compilations created by trade publishers and are
shelved in the general collection—collections of treaties, key Supreme
Court decisions, and so forth.)

In the United States many large research libraries are designated
as depository libraries and automatically receive publications of the
federal government. (Materials are issued by category, and the categories
a depository library will receive are agreed on by contract.) Depository
libraries are required to make the deposited materials available for use
and must agree not to dispose of the material. Nondepository libraries
may purchase government publications (and depository libraries may
purchase nondeposited material) by selecting from the *Monthly Catalog of United States Government Publications* (Washington, D.C.:
USGPO, 1951–). State and local documents are also collected extensively
by libraries, though the depth and range of collecting varies considerably
from library to library.

In the second half of this century, collection of foreign government
documents by American libraries has expanded enormously. Large
libraries also collect the publications of international organizations such
as the United Nations and the European Economic Community.

Government publications have always come in a variety of formats,
including many small pamphlets and paperbound volumes as well as
ponderous and durably bound sets. For some time there has also been
substantial publication in microform, and in recent years computerized
material has appeared. (Important indexes to government publications
have also appeared in computerized form.) Sometimes there is a choice
of format for materials, and sometimes there is not. As the old "serial
sets" that contain congressional documents back to the early days of
United States history begin to wear out, libraries are beginning to replace
them, or at least to provide a backup, in microfilm.

Government publications are housed and serviced in libraries in
various ways. Sometimes they constitute a separate department; sometimes they are shelved near and serviced by the general reference
department. Where the collection is not large, it may be fully cataloged
and simply shelved in the stacks. On the other hand, where there is
a separate department, records may be maintained there, with no actual
cataloging for the main catalog at all. The disadvantage of cataloging
is that there are many very small pieces and there will be many, many
entries under the name of an agency (perhaps more of a drawback with
card files than with online catalogs); the disadvantage of an uncataloged

system is that even experienced library users sometimes forget to consider the likelihood that a particular item needed is a government publication. Online catalogs may include records for government publications even where the card catalog did not, with computer searching easing the burden of looking for what previously seemed to be a needle in a haystack.

It is important not to lose sight of the fact that many government agencies (both in the United States and elsewhere) publish significant amounts of history proper—that is, secondary literature based on historical research, as opposed to contemporary material destined to become part of the historical record. Such material may appear in the form of monographs, pamphlets, or periodicals. Often the patron is best served if these historical works can be integrated, at least bibliographically, into the general collection.

Journals

There are many historical journals, some general in coverage and some very specialized. Virtually all carry articles, but the commitment of the major journals to thorough review coverage of the literature is valued as much or more by readers.

A number of the important historical journals date from the late nineteenth or early twentieth century, but the number of titles proliferated rapidly from about 1945 to about 1975. (There are still new ones, but the rate of expansion has slowed down considerably.) The *American Historical Review* (begun in 1895) is the flagship and leading general journal in this country. There are major journals for general history in several other countries. Germany's venerable *Historische Zeitschrift* (1829–) is one of the most important and is particularly valuable for its coverage of ancient and medieval history. The *English Historical Review* (1886–), the (English) Historical Association's *History* (1912–), the French *Revue Historique* (1876–), and the Italian *Rivista Storica Italiana* (1884–) are among other important European general history journals.

Some specialized journals focus on the history of a particular country. The *Journal of American History* is the leading journal for United States history; Spain's *Hispania* and Sweden's *Historisk Tidskrift* are other examples. Other journals specialize in a region (such as the *Journal of Southern History*), and nearly every state historical society publishes a journal. Some journals focus on an approach (*Journal of Psychohistory*) or a topic (*Agricultural History*). Others—and these are often interdisciplinary—focus on a chronological period: the *Renaissance*

Quarterly, the medieval *Speculum*, *Victorian Studies*. Several journals focus on the teaching of history, *The History Teacher*, *Social Studies*, and *RALPH: Studies in Medieval and Renaissance Teaching* among them. There are also several popular history magazines, such as *American Heritage* and *The Civil War Illustrated*.

Very few historical journals in this country come from commercial publishers. Scholarly organizations sponsor many journals, which are either anchored at a particular academic institution or migrate as officers change. Such journals may depend heavily on individually contributed services and usually have budgetary problems, so it is not unusual for historical journals to be published rather irregularly and well behind the cover date. It is not unusual, either, for journals to cease publication and later resume.

Current issues of journals may not be heavily used in the library since many historians personally subscribe to those in their own specialty, and students (other than browsers) are more likely to use the journals after the articles are listed in periodical indexes or are cited in the literature. (Some historians, of course, do visit the reading rooms regularly to catch up on current periodical literature.) Improved bibliographic services such as online services have probably resulted in some increase in use of the current issues.

Maps

Historians use a variety of maps both for their own information and for teaching: it is often impossible to make sense of historical events without an appropriate map. Maps come to mind readily for distances or for evaluating military strategy, and the most senior of us remember maps of the world with all the British possessions shaded in red. But relief maps, population maps, maps showing the distribution of natural resources, and so forth, can be as important as political maps. Computer-generated maps are also becoming an invaluable tool.

A good basic historical atlas, such as the *Times Atlas of World History* (3d ed., Maplewood, N.J.: Hammond, 1984) or William Shepherd's *Historical Atlas* (9th ed. rev., New York: Barnes & Noble, 1980), is essential for all reference collections. Specialized maps, such as Richard Talbert's *Atlas of Classical History* (New York: Macmillan, 1985), the *Historical Atlas of Africa* edited by J. F. Ade (New York: Cambridge University Press, 1985), or Stanley J. Parsons's *United States Congressional Districts, 1883–1913* (New York: Greenwood Press, 1990), will answer many otherwise intractable reference questions in the field of history.

Literature Outside the Historical Collections

There are many library materials that are commonly regarded as general rather than subject-specific, but that may be used more by faculty and students in history than by any other department. Newspaper back files and indexes, many government publications such as congressional and parliamentary proceedings, biographical dictionaries of all kinds, handbooks such as the *Statesman's Year-book*, atlases, and gazetteers fall into this category.

Many current surveys also fall inexorably into the history area as they age. So far only recent history benefits from many of these, but the steady accumulation becomes increasingly valuable. All sorts of statistical compilations, all the opinion poll reports, the television news indexes, and the current chronologies such as *Facts On File* and *Keesing's Contemporary Archives* are becoming increasingly rich resources.

Writings on a wide range of current issues, factual or expression of opinion, are historical treasures, and the popular press (including magazines) is very important to historians. In fact, the social significance of many varieties of trivia leads to increasing respectability as the material ages. Advertising, handbills, caricatures, pamphlets, popular sheet music, sermons or tracts produced by small religious groups, comic books, political posters, and pornography have all been found useful by historians. Of course, the overlap of history with economics, political science, religion, classical studies, and so forth, means that much of the literature of those disciplines will be equally useful to historians.

Reference Tools

Bibliographies, dictionaries, atlases, indexes, handbooks, encyclopedias, and handlists devoted to history constitute a vast literature in themselves since the discipline is so broad and includes so many specialties. Many of the more general dictionaries, directories, and encyclopedias are especially useful to historians also. As in any discipline, historical reference materials soon become dated in the sense that newer publications and information sources will not be included. But since older material is so much used in history, some of the classics are still in heavy use although two or three generations have elapsed since their publication. They may need to be supplemented with newer resources, but they are still invaluable.

Good basic bibliographies and guides to historical literature, such as the American Historical Association's *Guide to Historical Literature* (New York: Macmillan, 1961) and the American Historical Association and Royal Historical Society of Great Britain's six-volume Bibliography of British History series, have a long life and continue to be useful for

many years—to some extent, permanently. While relying on these standard works, many historians tend not to make much use of uncritical,
inclusive bibliographies that contain many titles irrelevant to their purpose and of little scholarly value. They usually prefer to seek recommendations from colleagues or to turn to works cited or favorably reviewed
by scholars they trust.

The most useful overall guide for beginners, though it is now in
serious need of updating, is Helen Poulton's *The Historian's Handbook:
A Descriptive Guide to Reference Works* (Norman, Okla.: University
of Oklahoma Press, 1972). William Langer's *Encyclopedia of World
History: Ancient, Medieval and Modern* (Boston, Mass.: Houghton Mifflin,
1972) is a handy one-volume chronology organized by country, useful
for retrieving dates and for ready-reference use in answering quick
queries. The multivolume *Cambridge Histories*—the *Cambridge
Medieval History*, the *Cambridge Modern History*, and others—are also
useful for reference purposes. *Historical Atlas* edited by William R.
Shepherd (9th ed. rev. and updated, New York: Barnes and Noble, 1980,
1964) is a standard tool. In addition, there are many historical atlases,
both general and specialized.

The first volume of the *Directory of American Scholars: History*
(New York: Bowker, 1982) serves as an informative directory of histor-
ians, while Warren Kuehl's *Dissertations in History* (three volumes
covering 1873–1980; vols. 1, 2, Lexington, Ky.: University of Kentucky
Press, 1965, 1972; vol. 3, Santa Barbara, Calif.: ABC-Clio, 1984) has served
as an easier-to-use, subject-indexed adjunct to *Dissertation Abstracts*.
Now that *Dissertation Abstracts* is available on CD-ROM, however,
searching it can be much easier and more effective than before. The
American Historical Association's *Doctoral Dissertations in History*
(Washington, D.C.: The Assn., 1973–) lists dissertations in progress.

Many periodical indexes are useful for historical research. Due to
history's precarious position straddling the social sciences and the
humanities, both the *Social Sciences Index* and the *Humanities Index*,
as well as the *Social Sciences Citation Index* and the *Arts and Humanities Citation Index*, must be checked for many historical topics. Many
other indexes, both printed and online, may be useful at times depending on the topic. The American Historical Association's *Recently Published Articles* lists periodical articles arranged by topic. *America, History
and Life* (Santa Barbara, Calif.: ABC-Clio, 1964–) is the standard
abstracting service for American history, and *Historical Abstracts*
(Santa Barbara, Calif.: ABC-Clio, 1955–) for the rest. Both now include
dissertations and selected books. However, the *International Bibliography of the Historical Sciences* (Munich, Ger.; London, Eng.; Paris, Fr.;
and New York: Sauer, 1926–) has much broader (though rather slow)

international coverage of journals, and *Writings on American History* (Millwood, N.Y.: Kraus, 1902–) is also useful. The *Combined Retrospective Index to Journals in History 1838–1974* (Washington, D.C.: Carrollton Press, 1977) offers extremely useful, though not complete, coverage. There is also a multivolume directory of historical journals, the *Historical Periodicals Directory* (Santa Barbara, Calif.: ABC-Clio, 1981–1986).

The *Harvard Guide to American History* (rev. ed., Cambridge, Mass.: Belknap Press of Harvard University Press, 1974) is the basic guide to American history, offering both general guidance to research resources and extensive lists (by topic) of books and sometimes journal articles. Though now dated, it is an indispensable starting point. Richard Morris's *Encyclopedia of American History* (6th ed., New York: Harper and Row, 1982) is perhaps the best one-volume reference tool in American history.

The multivolume *Dictionary of American History* (New York: Scribner, 1976) and the *Dictionary of American Biography* (New York: Scribner, 1928–1937; supplements, 1944–) and their supplements are basic and complementary reference tools. The *Dictionary of National Biography* (London, Eng.: Smith, Elder, 1885–1901; supplements, 1903–) is the British counterpart for biography and is equally basic. These sets include substantial, often column-long biographies or articles accompanied by a brief bibliography. All articles are written by specialists and signed by their initials; a key to the initials is provided. The *Dictionnaire de Biographie Francais* (Paris, Fr.: Letouzey et Ane, 1933–), the *Allgemeine deutsche Biographie* (Leipzig, Ger.: Duncker & Humblot, 1875–1912), and *Neue deutsche Biographie* (Berlin, Ger.: Duncker & Humblot, 1952–) are invaluable for their respective countries. There are many other biographical dictionaries, both general and specialized, that are useful for historical figures.

Many guidebooks that may include considerable material on history are available for specific areas of history as well as for the study of particular countries. Hermann Bengtsen's *Introduction to Ancient History* (Berkeley, Calif.: University of California Press, 1970) is an excellent example of an all-purpose introduction to the field, describing journals, academies, manuals, and so forth, as well as offering bibliographic guidance. (There are also a number of other good handbooks on the classical world.) Many of the standard guides are purely bibliographic in scope, but they are highly useful for their coverage of the basic source materials and the literature. Louis Paetow's long-standard *Guide to the Study of Mediaeval History* (rev. ed., New York: Crofts, 1931) is a prime example. Like all guides and bibliographies, it must be supplemented with sources for newer materials.

Historical statistics of varying degrees of reliability fill many ponderous volumes, many reels of microfilm, and many megabytes of computer space; they also lurk in many unsuspected corners of the literature and can take hours to track down. Fortunately, there are several one-volume compendia that can answer a substantial number of the common reference questions. *Historical Statistics of the United States, Colonial Times to 1970* (Washington, D.C.: USGPO, 1984) is a key resource. Brian Mitchell's various publications including *Abstract of British Historical Statistics* (New York: Cambridge University Press, 1988) and its supplement, *European Historical Statistics 1750–1975* (New York: Facts On File, 1980), *International Historical Statistics: The Americas and Australasia* (New York: Cambridge University Press, 1983), and *International Historical Statistics: Africa and Asia* (New York: New York University Press, 1982) are extremely helpful reference tools. The *Statesman's Year-book* (London, Eng.: Macmillan; New York: St. Martin's Press, 1864–) is invaluable for modern history.

Guides to Manuscripts and Archives

Manuscripts are normally acquired by special collections departments, and archival material by definition is housed in archives, though compilations of such material may appear in printed form. However, guides to manuscript and archival collections (both general guides and those listing the holdings of a specific collection) are important purchases for general collections in research libraries, as a starting point in planning research. The general guides to manuscripts and archives, such as the *National Union Catalog of Manuscripts* (Washington, D.C.: Library of Congress, 1962–), the National Historical Commission's *Guide to Archives and Manuscripts*, and the part-bound, part-microfiche *National Inventory of Documentary Sources in the U.S.* (Teaneck, N.J.: Chadwyck-Healey, 1985–) are usually housed in the reference collection. Subject-specific guides and guides to specific collections or archives range from brief, stapled, privately printed handlists to multivolume sets, with prices ranging from gratis to very expensive. They are collected extensively only where there are researchers who use them.

Access to state and local archives and to archives in other countries varies considerably. Guides, handbooks, and directories for all kinds of archives in this country and abroad are published regularly but by no means are all archives represented. At many locations, even on-site documentation may be sketchy.

Microforms

Historians are heavy users of microforms because many of the basic source materials are available in no other format. Newspapers, archival materials, and an increasing number of government documents are more durable, are less expensive, and consume less shelf space in microform. Microform is also often a feasible way of obtaining from another institution a copy of a bulky item needed by a local patron.

Many of the large, heterogeneous microform sets assembled from various collections and focused on a single topic are historical in nature. Such sets can be very useful for teaching purposes or for research if there is adequate bibliographic access. All too often, however, the kind of cataloging that would make individual components of the set accessible to users is simply not possible. (The physical quality of the filming is variable, also.) Even if the publisher furnishes catalog cards for the individual pieces within the set, the necessary editing and filing of the cards has often been too costly for the library to undertake. Fortunately the library community has been at work in recent years developing cooperative or grant-funded projects to provide cataloging for some of the most valuable sets, and tapes of the cataloging for many sets are available to purchase and load. Without this access, however, such a set is apt to be an expensive white elephant unless an enthusiastic faculty member takes a hand and directs students to it.

Some materials are not very well suited to microform, and librarians with some concern for historians are well advised to resist acquiring the microform if hard copy is at all available. The old German *fraktur* type; interrelated documents that will require a lot of flipping back and forth; detailed graphics, such as finely drawn maps; and copies of holograph manuscripts are examples of materials that can be painful at best to spend long hours with.

Nonprint Materials

Thus far, historians have not been heavy users of nonprint (other than microform) materials, at least in their research. They tend to prefer the book to visual or auditory presentations of the same material and to scorn popularization. Many do like to use audiovisual materials in their teaching, though even in teaching they probably use books more than most disciplines.

There are many attractive films, slides, and videotapes available for the teaching of history. These include films or tapes of the actual events and historical personages as well as purely instructional reenactments and other materials. Computer programs and games for teaching history are also commercially available; some instructors develop their own.

Videotapes, currently primarily a teaching tool, will become increasingly useful for historical research as the historical record accumulates on tape. Begun in 1968, the Vanderbilt Television News Archive has been the most comprehensive record of network news to date. This project has been only a start of what will surely be broadly retained and available video records of events.

Computer Databases

Libraries are moving rapidly into providing access to computerized databases, online and otherwise. Historical materials have not been in the forefront of this movement, for obvious reasons: most of the historical record has never been computerized. The relatively skimpy funding undergirding historical research is also a retarding factor.

Historical statistics are highly amenable to computerization, and historians who use statistics are apt to be computer enthusiasts. Computerized compilations of data are becoming increasingly well organized and accessible. The Inter-University Consortium for Political and Social Research at Ann Arbor provides to member institutions machine-readable data including United States election data, congressional roll-call votes, a variety of census and legislative records from many countries, and widely assorted attitude surveys. Census data from all countries, until now available in printed and sometimes in microfilm cumulations, is increasingly moving to the greater flexibility of computer formats. The Medieval and Early Modern Data Bank, developed at Rutgers and now working also through European offices, is a center for the collection and distribution of databases for the medieval and early modern period, to be available to scholars through Research Libraries Information Network (RLIN).

Bibliographic data is particularly suited to online access. ABC-Clio is a primary supplier, offering Historical Abstracts and America, History and Life online through Dialog and BRS. Many other databases can be useful to historians, and the number will increase as databases grow to include longer timespans. In theory, at least, online databases offer an ideal approach to the complexities of historical research, making it possible to follow a topic (or the interrelationships of two or more topics) through extended time frames and multiple formats much more easily and efficiently than by using printed indexes.

In practice, of course, many hindrances and problems are encountered in use of online access. The first is the continuing importance of the vast retrospective literature, most of which has never been electronically indexed and much of which may never be because of the cost. Second, indexing by date or chronological period has thus far been as unsatisfactory online as it is in the manual files of the card catalog. The problem of searching for information on varying time periods and, to a lesser extent, that of searching for information on various geographical entities will probably never be entirely solved. In time, however, more sophisticated computer programming may improve the effectiveness of such searches. A third problem with online searches for historians is the number of databases that must be accessed, especially for contemporary history, if the search is to be a thorough one. Databases that cover only selected historical journals will include only the citations likely to be known already. Historians may be particularly anxious to locate relevant research by political scientists, sociologists, economists, scholars in religious studies or literature, and others. The need to cover many databases will grow steadily over time as existing databases grow to cover longer historical periods. But the cost can be very substantial. Periodical indexes on CD-ROM are a help but, thus far, do not offer sufficient retrospective coverage and are useful only as an updating technique.

In common with all researchers, historians are hindered by the lack of standardization both of computer equipment and of database formats and by the lack of bibliographic control over machine-readable data. In common with their colleagues in other fields, historians also now find themselves (or worse, never find out they are) duplicating individual efforts to collect and key-in historical data of various sorts.

Finally, establishment of adequate databases for historians is hindered by chronic underfunding of historical studies. Historians do not obtain many large grants, have few or no counterparts doing well-funded research in private industry, and are rarely sought out to conduct contract research for industry or other outside funding sources. History is an impecunious discipline and is likely to remain so.

Cataloging and Classification

Historians learn early to be active rather than passive library users because their material is so scattered. The basic classifications for history in the Library of Congress system are C for the history of civilization and the "auxiliary" topics such as archives and numismatics; D for general, European, Asian, African, and South Pacific history; E for the United States; and F for local United States history and for Latin American history. In Dewey the basic classification is 900, subdivided for various areas. But much historical literature is found in almost every other classification. In the Library of Congress system, religious history is in the B classification, economic and social history in H, political history in J, legal history in K, and so on. The same is true of the Dewey system, with religion in the 200s, the social sciences in the 300s, and technology in the 600s—all containing history. With the Dewey system, a further complication is that biography has its own 920 classification apart from the topics or historical events with which the biographees are associated. But at least in the Dewey system the biographies are all shelved together. Under the Library of Congress system, books about Henry Ford or Lord Louis Mountbatten or Desiderius Erasmus can be found in several widely separated locations.

Users often complain because "their" material is not shelved together. But history can be (and is) approached from so many standpoints that putting a "subject" together is impossible. Is a monograph on a railroad strike "about" railroads, labor history, United States history in the early twentieth century, or Illinois history? It might even be seen as part of the history of Poles in America if the workers were predominantly Polish and Polish culture played a part in or was affected by the event. The difficulty is, of course, an intrinsic factor of cataloging, applicable to nearly every discipline. However, it is exceptionally troublesome in historical studies, where chronology and geography are such crucial factors, and a mix of economic, diplomatic, political, religious, and ethnic factors may be equally important. The sheer bulk of historical literature (and of other related literature) greatly exacerbates the problem.

Subject headings are easy to use for a very specific name or event in history, such as Bismarck or the Treaty of Versailles, but such is not the case when a more abstract concept is involved. What does one look up for material on the effects of the depression in the Midwest or on the role of women in medieval France? Even for the experienced catalog user, it will take some guesswork to get started. For the neophyte or for anyone who does not work daily in libraries and who, therefore, does not habitually think in subject heading terms, very general terminology is difficult even to guess; there is nothing obvious about "U.S.—Social conditions, 1945– ."

Online catalogs with keyword searching can do much to cut across catalog structure and solve, or at least ameliorate, such problems. Carefully constructed keyword searches can provide access to many of these topics more easily than the card catalog can. But a price is paid for this facility: it is difficult to be sure enough alternative and variant terms have been included to elicit everything important. Dates and geographical areas are still elusive in many online catalog systems, and it is very easy to overlook some of the possibilities.

A persistent problem in traditional cataloging is that much of the terminology used is obsolete: "European War" is an exceedingly obscure designation for World War I. In time, online catalogs will make it much easier to update terminology. However, many large research collections will probably rely, at least partially, on card catalogs for their older materials for many years to come, and cannot afford to recatalog these materials when subject headings change. Consequently, even efforts to

update terminology may make things more confusing for patrons, requiring them to use one subject heading in the online catalog and another
in the card catalog because large libraries cannot afford to complete
conversion of card catalogs to machine-readable form.

Geographic terms, in particular, become outdated as national boundaries shift and new names are adopted; these changes affect both classification and subject headings and can be costly to implement. Moreover,
implementation of new terminology can hinder rather than help historical research. Decisions about when to make changes and how far to
go with the adjustments sometimes invoke political sensitivities; there
has been controversy for some years over changes in East European
classification and nomenclature. A major adjustment in this area was the
introduction of the DJK classification for Eastern European history.
Eastern Europe was not frequently viewed as an entity at the time of the
creation of the Library of Congress system, when the Austro-Hungarian
empire sprawled across the continent and the Soviet Union had not yet
come into being; later, the Eastern bloc became a necessary concept for
categorizing a substantial literature. Today, further changes are occurring
and will once again alter our perceptions on categorizing.

Dislocations also occur as political ties linking distant areas are sev-
ered or entered into. The literature on the colonial administrations of
France, Germany, and Britain can be widely separated from that on the
same areas after independence, while the history of Hawaii is in DU (for
the South Pacific) under the Library of Congress classification rather than
in F with United States state and local history (where it would be if the
classification system were being drawn up today).

Outdated general terminology may seem to matter less than outdated
classification, the cost of changing it being what it is, but over time the
old terminology becomes quaint if not obscure. Changing from "Spanish
America" to "Latin America" some years ago was a massive and extremely
expensive effort, but one that was long overdue.

The subject catalog is extremely difficult to use when time frames
or geographic locations are involved, as is usual in history. Again, sheer
bulk is a major problem. Thumbing through literally hundreds of cards
under headings such as "U.S.—Economic conditions—1865 – 1918" can
be a very time-consuming and unproductive exercise, particularly if one
suspects that "U.S.—Economic conditions—1865 – 1921" might be a
better choice and should be checked also. Fortunately, many of the relevant materials will be represented by cards under both headings.

The hierarchical structure of the subject catalog can make level of
specificity a very real problem. If "Jews—Paris" has been assigned to a
book as a subject heading, "Jews—France" often will not be. Furthermore,
the separation in the catalog between the two is the same as the shelving

separation imposed by the classification system, possibly causing the researcher to miss relevant literature. It is important to guide users of the catalog to seek the most specific heading possible and to be aware of varying possibilities. Again, keyword searching can help, but it will become less efficient as databases grow larger.

Subject entries are often used by experienced researchers primarily to compile a list of classification ranges suitable for shelf browsing, with culling of individual items to take place at the shelf. (The most promising citations will be copied in full, lest these items not be on the shelf at the moment.) But students should be reminded to use the subject catalog, bibliographies, and bibliographic notes of key works to develop their own bibliographies, rather than limiting themselves to what they see on the shelf. Experienced historians usually need no reminder.

Profile of History Librarianship

Professional Associations

Librarians interested in history are active in a number of professional organizations. There is no single umbrella organization, partly because libraries are organized so differently in their handling of history and partly because interests are often relatively specialized. Of course, many librarians interested in history are active in the American Library Association (ALA) and other groups focusing on all areas of library activity and service.

Both history specialists and other librarians with a special interest in history are members of the History Section of ALA's Reference and Adult Services Division (RASD). ALA's Association of College and Research Libraries' Western European Specialists section (WESS) has become the center of activity for many academic librarians who work with the history of Western Europe. Originally focused primarily on twentieth-century Europe, WESS now has a flourishing classical, medieval, and Renaissance studies contingent and has members interested in all historical periods. WESS sponsors both programs at ALA and special conferences, frequently outside the United States, for Western European specialists.

The Association for the Bibliography of History, which is affiliated with the American Historical Association and meets just prior to and in conjunction with its annual meetings, includes both historians and librarians. Reports on bibliographic projects are presented at the meetings, and committees of the organization serve as liaisons with related organizations. The organization maintains the National Registry for the Bibliography of History and publishes a newsletter.

The American Association for State and Local History (AASLH) is the primary organization for those who are working with state and local historical societies. AASLH holds annual conferences and sponsors workshops; its publication series includes material on historical preservation.

Librarians who work with area studies programs are commonly active primarily in the scholarly associations related to their area of specialty rather than in library organizations. The American Association for the Advancement of Slavic Studies, the African Studies Association, the Asian Studies Association, the Middle East Studies Association, and the Classical Studies Association each have a subgroup composed of librarians, and there is an independent organization for Latin American Studies librarians, the Seminar on the Acquisition of Latin American Library Materials (SALALM). In addition, librarians are active in many other scholarly associations related to individual specialties.

Training and Continuing Education

Though the number of positions for librarians working exclusively with history is relatively small, librarians in many nonspecialist positions find that historical queries or materials make up a large (or even predominant) part of their work. General reference desks make considerable use of expertise in history. Government documents collections, manuscript collections, newspaper collections, public and private archives, and rare book and other special collections are heavily used for historical research and, therefore, need historically knowledgeable staff. Academic and large public libraries, historical societies, many special collections, and some government agencies employ librarians with training in history.

A strong background in history is useful in any humanities or social sciences collection. Knowledge of the field, of course, is important to librarians who are selecting historical materials, but it is also important for reference service to patrons from other disciplines who are interested in historical topics. Librarians who are knowledgeable know their way around the literature, understand the difference of approach in different fields of history, and know what other disciplines are applicable and what kinds and formats of literature are currently in use (including computerized material).

For a librarian who wants to specialize in history in an academic library setting, foreign language skills are almost as important as a background in history, at least in the larger institutions. For most positions, bibliographic competence in the major West European languages is a minimal necessity, perhaps with stronger abilities in one or two key languages. Classical, Russian and East European, African, or Asian languages may be needed for specialized positions. Librarians with some background in history are so plentiful that a second master's degree in the relevant discipline and some library experience are usually necessary for any position with a special focus on history.

Providing reference service in history to serious researchers requires bibliographic knowledge of many languages, knowledge of the basic reference tools, and some familiarity with government publications and with sources of information about archives and manuscripts. Keeping abreast of available computer databases is also important.

Perusal of the major historical journals (especially the book reviews) is one of the best ways to keep up with new trends and developments in historical research. In addition, publications such as *Historical Methods* (Pittsburgh, Pa.: University of Pittsburgh, 1967 – 1977; Washington, D.C.: Heldref Publications, 1978 –) help maintain awareness of new research. Furthermore, talking to historians and their students about their research helps librarians spot new trends and also makes it easier to provide good service. The library literature occasionally includes articles specifically about history collections or their users, and history accounts for such a substantial portion of general collections and of their clientele that many articles in general library literature have substantial application to history.

Pursuing historical research of one's own, or an advanced degree in history, helps to keep apace of the library needs of researchers and to maintain communication with patrons in history. However, specialized research does not substitute for a general awareness of the trends and publications in many aspects of history. A lively curiosity about anything and everything in historical scholarship pays dividends on the job. Perhaps the best advice is to read, participate in organizations, talk to historical researchers, and read, read, read.

Professional Readings

Bailey, Herbert S., Jr. "The Professional Historian and His Readers." *Scholarly Publishing* 1, no. 3 (Apr. 1970): 275–79.

Bath University Library. *Investigation into Information Requirements of the Social Sciences.* 2 vols. Information Requirements of Researchers in the Social Sciences, Research Report 1. Bath, Eng.: Bath University Library, 1971.

Bebout, Lois, Donald Davis, Jr., and Donald Oehlerts. "User Studies in the Humanities: A Survey and a Proposal." *RQ* 15, no. 1 (Fall 1975): 40–44.

Bowen, Catherine Drinker. *Biography and the Calling.* Boston, Mass.: Little Brown, 1969.

Brogan, Martha. "Charting the New Atlantic: WESS in Its Second Decade." *WESS Newsletter* 10, no. 2 (June 1987): 7–17.

Clifford, J. Garry. "Yale 14, Harvard 0." *Newsletter of the Society of American Foreign Relations* 11, no. 1 (Mar. 1980): 7–11.

Falk, Joyce Duncan. "Computer-Assisted Production of Bibliographic Databases in History." *Indexer* 12, no. 3 (Apr. 1981): 131–39.

———, ed. "Computer-Assisted Reference Service in History." *RQ* 21, no. 4 (Summer 1982): 342–63.

———. "Librarians and Historians at the American Historical Association"; Stoan, Stephen K., "Historians and Librarians: a Response." *College & Research Libraries News* 47, no. 8 (Sept. 1986): 501–3.

Fyfe, Janet. *History Journals and Serials: An Analytical Guide.* New York: Greenwood, 1986.

Garfield, Eugene. "Is Information Retrieval in the Arts and Humanities Inherently Different from That in Science?" *Library Quarterly* 50, no. 1 (Jan. 1980): 40–57.

Hernon, Peter. "Information Needs and Gathering Patterns of Academic Social Scientists, with Special Emphasis Given to Historians and Their Use of U.S. Government Publications." *Government Information Quarterly* 1, no. 4 (1984): 401–29.

Jones, Clyve. "The Characteristics of the Literature Used by Historians." *Journal of Librarianship* 4, no. 3 (July 1972): 137–56.

Kammen, Carol. *On Doing Local History: Reflections on What Local Historians Do, Why, and What It Means.* Nashville, Tenn.: American Assn. for State and Local History, 1986.

MacAnally, Arthur Monroe. "Characteristics of Materials Used in Research in United States History." Ph.D. thesis, Graduate Library School, University of Chicago, 1951.

McWhinney, Grady. "Documents and the Historian." *Alabama Historian* 28, no. 1 (Jan. 1977): 2–6.

Morgan, Dale O. "The Archivist, the Librarian and the Historian." *Library Journal* 93 (15 Dec. 1968): 4621–23.

Morill, J.S. "Microform and the Historian." *Microform Review* 16, no. 3 (Summer 1987): 203–12; Hill, Lamar M. "Additional Reflections on Microforms and the Historian." *Microform Review* 17, no. 2 (May 1988): 87–89.

Morrow, Carolyn Clark. *The Preservation Challenge: A Guide to Conserving Library Materials.* White Plains, N.Y.: Knowledge Industry Pubs., 1983.

Morton, Bruce. "U.S. Government Documents as History." *RQ* 24, no. 4 (Summer 1985): 474–81.

Perman, Dagmar Horna, ed. *Bibliography and the Historian: The Conference at Belmont of the Joint Committee on Bibliographical Services to History, May 1967.* Santa Barbara, Calif.: Clio, 1968.

Peterson, Agnes F. "Collecting Sources Today for the Scholars of Tomorrow." *Collection Management* 6, no. 1–2 (Spring–Summer 1984): 145–55.

Piehl, Charles. "Historical Research and Medium-sized Public Libraries: The Potential." *RQ* 21, no. 3 (Spring 1982): 250–53.

Richey, Elinor. "One Biographer's Indispensibles." *Pacific Historian* 21, no. 3 (Fall 1977): 294–99.

Rodney, Joel. "Such Are the Joys . . . (With Apologies to the Late George Orwell)." *Record* 30 (1969): 97–103.

Rundell, Walter. "Relations between Historical Researchers and Custodians of Source Materials." *College and Research Libraries* 29, no. 6 (Nov. 1968): 466–76.

Shepherd, John. *The Information Needs and Information Seeking Behavior of Polytechnic Lecturers in the Subject Area of History.* British Library Research and Development Department Report 5743. London, Eng.: British Library, 1983.

Stannard, David. *Shrinking History: The Failure of Psychohistory.* New York and Oxford, Eng.: Oxford University Press, 1980.

"The State of the Art of Bibliography and Indexing of American History." *RQ* 15, no. 3 (Spring 1976): 219–21.

Stern, Peter. "Online in the Humanities: Problems and Possibilities." *Journal of Academic Librarianship* 14, no. 3 (July 1988): 161–64.

Stieg, Margaret F. "The Information of Needs [sic] of Historians." *College and Research Libraries* 42, no. 6 (Nov. 1981): 549–60.

_____. *The Origin and Development of Scholarly Historical Periodicals.* University, Ala.: University of Alabama Press, 1986.

Stoan, Stephen K. "Research and Library Skills: An Analysis and Interpretation." *College and Research Libraries* 45, no. 2 (Mar. 1984): 99–109.

Thompson, Paul. *Voice of the Past: Oral History.* Oxford, Eng., and New York: Oxford University Press, 1981.

Tilly, Louise A. "People's History and Social Science History"; "Between Social Scientists: Responses to Louise A. Tilly"; "Louise A. Tilly's Response . . . with a Concluding Comment by Ronald J. Grele." *International Journal of Oral History* 6, no. 1 (Feb. 1985): 3–46.

Tucker, Melvin, et al. "Historians and Using Tomorrow's Research Library: Research, Teaching and Training." *History Teacher* 17, no. 3 (May 1984): 385–444.

Zink, Steven D. "Journal Publishing in the Field of U.S. History." *Scholarly Publishing* 11, no. 4 (July 1980): 343–59.

3

Literature

James K. Bracken

Any attempt to define or describe the place of literature in libraries or to identify, specifically, the librarian responsible for literature is quickly foiled by the task's apparently simultaneously procrustean dimensions and protean dimensionlessness. Certainly, the task seems as formidable as answering the question at its base, "What is literature?" The fact that few academic or public library systems maintain separate facilities denoted as "literature" libraries suggests that a "literature" librarian might not exist at all. At the same time, however, the certain knowledge that significant portions of the collections in the majority of academic and public libraries consist of what is commonly acknowledged as literature implies that somewhere out there are librarians who have been about the business of acquiring, cataloging, maintaining, and otherwise servicing literature. Nearly all American libraries own literature; few, however, handle it in special ways. This makes literature distinct from other subjects where the subject material demands special location, treatment, or collection practices, and means that the literature librarian may be concerned with distributed collections of materials distinguished by their contents rather than form, location, or handling.

At the outset it might be worthwhile to indicate what the literature library is not. Some distinctions need to be made between what is meant by libraries with literature and those library units that are concerned with publications in languages other than English, some of which might be regarded as literature. In American academic and research libraries, literature is usually understood to mean British and American literature or, perhaps more accurately, literature in the English language. Literature in languages other than English is equated with "area studies," or "area specialists"—specialized units in libraries that collect and maintain materials from and/or about specific geographical or political regions. This is especially common in major academic or research libraries. Many include special "area studies" libraries for materials from Latin America, east Asia, Eastern Europe, and the like. These collections are equivalent in many ways to special collections. The linguistic and bibliographic problems inherent to efforts to collect and service materials in languages other than English make area studies librarianship more akin to rare books and special collections work. While the literature of a particular country or region is usually contained in an area studies library's collection, that literature typically represents only one of the area studies library's subject interests.

Neither should the literature library be confused in any way with the rare books or special collections library that collects literature in English. Certainly, numerous specific special collections consist entirely of literature. Venerable private institutions like the Folger Shakespeare Library, the Huntington Library, and the Newberry Library maintain extensive collections of original editions and manuscripts of literary works as well as contemporary and more recent secondary materials about literature. Similarly, many of this nation's academic and public library systems contain units renowned for their vast rare and special literary collections. At the same time, however, many of these collections also contain much more than what is understood to be literature. The common feature of these special collections and libraries, and the one that distinguishes them from other libraries that also contain literature, is that rare books and special collections units acquire, catalog, maintain, and service materials based on their "specialness," that is, conditions of scarcity or rarity, physical attributes or qualities, significance as integral components of the collection, or similar criteria. Their reasons for existence, underlying concerns, and day-to-day operations are based on principles that are fundamentally different from those of other libraries that also contain literature.

In contrast to area studies or rare book and special collections libraries, libraries (or perhaps, more accurately, the particular unit or units in library systems) that collect what is usually meant by "literature" might best be described as a generic "every library." It certainly includes portions of the stacks of both undergraduate and research collections as well as those caches of literature commonly referred to as the "browsing" collection (of popular fiction, biography, essays, and the like). It also consists of significant portions of most reference, serial, microform, and audiovisual media collections. Are there area studies collections that specialize in the literary works of Great Britain and the United States or other libraries that serve as specialized reference, reserve, or reading collections for English-language literature? Most assuredly, there are numerous examples, existing mainly in major academic and public libraries. On the other hand, few of these can account for more than small portions of a library system's total literature collection.

Few libraries will claim that they are literature libraries. The diversity of their holdings and services as well as the sensibilities of their various constituents prohibit this. On the other hand, identify on any American campus the library facility named "general library," "humanities library," or "main library," or the public library in any city or town, and you will locate a library in which a significant portion of the collection likely consists of literature. And as it is—all at once—both with and without a specific identity, it is also both with and without a specific constituency. It is the place where august scholars and ambitious readers still vie for the opportunity to obtain the circulating copies of James Joyce's *Ulysses*, J. D. Salinger's *The Catcher in the Rye*, and, more recently, Salman Rushdie's *The Satanic Verses*. What each might want with a work of literature is as different as the individual would-be users—or as different as each person's definition of literature. One might wish to analyze its symbolism, another might need it for a course of study, and still another might want to read it, as a good book, purely for recreation. The potential uses of any work are many. This cannot be said of the literature of pharmacy, engineering, or chemistry, or even of the literature of sociology or economics; the central literatures of these fields are really only intended to be intelligible to their practitioners. While, of course, the same might be said to be true of what could be called the "professional literature of literature" (that is, critical studies of literature, such as the numerous interpretations of Hamlet's madness or Moby Dick's whiteness), this does not apply to the works that are literature, such as novels, short stories, poems, plays, essays, autobiographies, and so forth. This literature belongs to all of us.

Literature's librarian, by extension, would seem to be a rather mythical creature. In that "literature" is not rare, special, unique, or remote, neither is the particular type of librarianship that is responsible for literature particularly plagued or concerned with the problems associated with efforts to collect, maintain, and service it. At the same time, the literature librarian's constituents are both the advanced scholar and the inquisitive and curious reader who, on some occasions, are distinct individuals, while in many other instances, they are one and the same.

This essay will address the handling of English-language literature and the practice of literature's librarianship largely from the perspectives of American academic libraries. Some attention is also given to literature in public libraries. Despite these limitations, the topic remains amply unwieldy. Although there is very little that is rare or special about literature in American libraries, the fact of literature's common place and centrality in both academic and popular cultures—its very "generalness" or, perhaps, even "genericness"—indicates its importance. The implications of acquiring, maintaining, and servicing literature are at once both transparent and predominant. The handling of literature is likely to be distributed among many units and individuals within libraries. Some will certainly be consciously concerned with its identity as literature; many others, however, will not share this concern. At the same time, literature's most prominent users—those august scholars and avid readers—are at once both a library's staunchest supporters and most vociferous critics. This essay will suggest that such is the wonderfully inevitable and unavoidable fortune of English-language literature in American libraries and, furthermore, that this is the way it will probably remain. The implications of this situation are both profound and comic for the professional who decides to specialize in the field (or, rather, the un-field) of literature librarianship.

Profile of Literature

To paraphrase Horace in *Ars Poetica*, the aim of the poet is either to teach or to delight, or to teach and delight at the same time. What constitutes literature and its uses can be most conveniently characterized along similar lines. Literature can be used in scholarship, the activity of trying to learn more about the human condition by examination of humankind's literary creations; and it can be used in recreation, the activity of appreciating humankind's literary creations for no more than the pleasure that appreciating provides. When scholarship and recreation conjoin, there is pleasure through learning or learning through pleasure. What specifically constitutes literature used in scholarship and recreation on a title-by-title basis, or, to phrase it another way, what literature literally and physically encompasses *is* whatever its scholars and readers use. The distinctive uses by literary scholars and literary readers, in general, identify literature.

The "literature" of literature consists entirely of works of literature and works about literature. In general, it is use alone that distinguishes one from the other. *Works of literature* is most readily understood to mean primary works. An acceptable contemporary definition of a primary work of literature would be that it is a "document" that is put to the uses that are appropriate to works of literature; that is, the work that is studied by scholars or read by readers for the qualities that are restricted to the contents of its physical form. Its most commonly identifiable characteristic is that it is creative. This creative aspect is shared by both fictional and nonfictional works. Its most frequent and recognizable manifestations include, but are not limited to, such things as novels, short stories, plays, and poems. The criterion of creativity is not an exclusive one, however. Works such as essays, autobiographies, letters, and correspondence are also regarded as literature. While literature is typically identified as published writings, it in fact also includes unpublished and unwritten works. When scholars study or readers read primary works, they are ultimately concerned with works *by* individuals. Regardless of the particular manner of composition, which might have been single-handedly or collaboratively accomplished at one point in time or over its expanse, the primary work is always that work *by* someone, even if that someone is unknown. Emphasis here is on the word *by*.

Works about literature, in contrast, is most readily understood to mean secondary works. An acceptable definition of a secondary work of literature would be that it is a "document" that is put to the uses that are appropriate to works about works of literature; that is, the work that is studied by scholars or read by readers for what it says or suggests about the qualities in works by someone. Its most recognizable characteristic is that it is factual, as opposed to creative, and typically nonfictional. Its most frequent and recognizable manifestations are works such as book- and essay-length analytical, evaluative, and interpretive studies and commentaries that directly or indirectly focus on a particular work, or works, by others. Most commonly, but not exclusively, these are written and published works, such as scholarly and popular monographs, articles, reviews, and dissertations. Secondary works, however, might also be unpublished or unwritten. That a secondary work is explicitly or implicitly critical is largely a matter of interpretation on the part of its user. The characteristic that all these secondary works share is that they are used for what they say *about* other works.

There is little confusion when a primary work is a poem or a novel or when a secondary work is an analysis or explication of these works. Sometimes, however, the distinction between a primary work and a secondary work is more difficult to make. James Boswell's famous *Life of Samuel Johnson* is, on the one hand, a secondary source for research on Johnson while, on the other, the primary work upon which rests Boswell's reputation as a writer. Recorded footage of Robert Frost reading his poetry at John F. Kennedy's inauguration is an invaluable primary record. A recording of Frost's comments on T. S. Eliot's poetry is at once primary documentation of Frost's critical thinking and also a secondary work for its criticism of Eliot. The PBS series *Voices and Visions*, featuring American poets reading their works or commenting on the works of others, is an example of literature's extension beyond traditional formats that suggests the difficulties of attempting to distinguish primary and secondary works. Recent trends toward the expansion of literature's canon and, furthermore, the study of literary criticism (that is, the study of the works of the critics about the works of other authors) has some-what clouded these distinctions. The writings of members of particular critical schools or movements, such as "new" critics like I. A. Richards or Cleanth Brooks; deconstructionist critics Jacques Derrida or Paul de Man; feminist literary critics Julie Kristeva or Elaine Showalter; Marxist literary critics Georg Lukacs or Terry Eagleton; or reader-response critics Wolfgang Iser or Stanley Fish, among many others, are at once both primary and secondary works. On the one hand, writings by these critics constitute the "sacred texts," so to speak, of their movements and are scrutinized by disciples and detractors alike in much the same way that scholars study the Bible, Qur'an, or Vedas; on the other hand, undergraduates stumble upon works by these same critics in their litera-ture searches and seek them out for what they might reveal about the likes of Shakespeare and Melville. Readers are encouraged to use the navigational points of "by" and "about" to maintain a reasonably consis-tent course.

No clearer or less circular definitions of works of literature and works about literature, except those based on appropriate uses, are really possi-ble. Their validity depends exclusively on the willingness of the users of literature to accept a rather descriptive, as opposed to prescriptive, conception regarding both literature's canon and its potential forms. What one scholar or reader might use as a primary work, another will use as a secondary work, and vice versa. As we quickly approach the century's end, the accepted canon of literature is as inclusive, wide, and varied as the interests of scholars and readers. Likewise, literature's physical manifestations are only restricted by the limits of innovative technology. Just as literature's original "documents" were oral, its future ones are likely to be electronic.

Literature in Libraries

How much primary literature and how much secondary literature a library collects says a great deal about a library's purpose. Indeed, public and academic libraries can be separated along these lines, reflecting Horace's description. In "The Function of the Library in Graduate Study in English,"[1] F. W. Bateson indicated the varieties of primary and secondary literary works that should be in academic collections intended to support literary research, or literature as a source of instruction. These included

---

1. F. W. Bateson, "The Function of the Library in Graduate Study in English," *Journal of General Education* 13 (April 1961): 5–17.

facsimiles or reproductions of manuscripts and printed texts, standard editions, biographies, bibliographies and reference works, book-length critical studies, and creative and critical periodicals. Although, in contrast to Bateson's day, these kinds of resources are now likely to be represented by their various electronic versions, emphasis remains on the standard and canonical. The exact proportions of these materials are dependent both on a particular library's perception of its needs and, of course, on its fiscal abilities to meet them. But whether divided into eight different kinds of literary resources or eighty, all classifications boil down to the two already discussed—the works themselves and the works about them.

Public Libraries

Literature collections in public libraries are generally intended to support literature as a source of delight. Interest is on the primary works and their appreciation. The concept of canonical and noncanonical literature is not nearly so relevant as in the academic library. Instead, what a public library collects is largely determined by its perception of what its patrons wish to read. In general, primary materials—in particular, works of fiction— are collected broadly. Lists of literary works included in such guides as *The Reader's Adviser: A Layman's Guide to Literature* (13th ed., New York: R. R. Bowker, 1986) are intended to guide readers' tastes and interests. Other cumulations—like Juliette Yaakov's *Fiction Catalog* (New York: H. W. Wilson, 1986), now in its eleventh edition, and Marilyn E. Hicken's *Cumulated Fiction Index, 1980–1984* (London, Eng.: Assn. of Assistant Librarians, 1985), and earlier volumes; as well as more specialized bibliographies, like Oatis Welton Coan and Richard Gordon Lillard's *America in Fiction: An Annotated List of Novels that Interpret Aspects of Life in the United States, Canada, and Mexico* (5th ed., Palo Alto, Calif.: Pacific Books, 1967) and Everett F. Bleiler's *The Guide to Supernatural Fiction: A Full Description of 1,775 Books from 1750 to 1960, Including Ghost Stories, Weird Fiction, Stories of Supernatural Horror, Fantasy, Gothic Novels, Occult Fiction, and Similar Literature* (Kent, Ohio: Kent State University Press, 1983)—reflect the scope of this advisory function, at least with regard to the novel.

The appetite of public libraries for drama, poetry, short fiction, and essays is less voracious. Works of these kinds are obtained in less substantial quantities. Nonetheless, the longevity of such basic guides as *The Play Index* (New York: H. W. Wilson, 1953–), *Essay and General Literature Index* (New York: H. W. Wilson, 1934–), and *Granger's Index to Poetry* (8th ed., New York: Columbia University Press, 1986), as well as that of the *Short Story Index* (New York: H. W. Wilson, 1953–), indicates the popularity of these genres beyond academic circles.

Public libraries collect secondary materials on a less substantial scale. As in most academic libraries, it is important in public libraries to have a solid reference collection to support both the acquisitions and reference functions. There is little interest in obtaining substantial holdings of critical works on even the most popular writers. Biographical works are as likely to be obtained to satisfy patrons whose interests are biography as they are for secondary values.

It is inaccurate, however, to presume that a public library buys only popular fiction and, furthermore, that research does not take place in public libraries. In fact, the widest range of academic work also occurs in literature collections in public libraries. Elementary and secondary school writing and literary research exercises as well as research activities of independent scholars require both basic and advanced biographical and bibliographical support. Indeed, the largest public libraries support the levels and types of research that are identical to those of major academic libraries. Just as frequently, the local public library is more likely in tune with the works of regional writers than are academic libraries in the same areas.

Two problems have dominated discussions of literature in public libraries. The first is duplication of materials in demand. How many copies of a best-selling novel or biography are required to satisfy the expectations and appetites of patrons? Anecdotal evidence suggests that a library needs an exceedingly great number of copies of a popular title, such as Margaret Mitchell's *Gone with the Wind*, to ensure that a copy is available.

The second matter of perennial concern in public libraries is the classification of fiction. Like the duplication of titles, the classification of fiction has been discussed for nearly a century. Various schemes have called for alphabetical classification by authors with subdivisions for broad subjects, genres, formats, or literary quality. The fundamental intention of all fiction classification schemes, as S. L. Baker and G. W. Shepherd, S. S. Intner, and others have noted, has always been to increase the user's access to the collection so that works can be selected according to reading interests; that is, as Baker and Shepherd put it, "fiction classification should make it easier for library users to find the types of fictional works they want—whether it be a Harlequin romance or the latest work by Barbara Pym."[2] This is in keeping with the public library's advisory function and general commitment of making available to readers the varieties of literary works that will bring the most pleasure (and encourage support of the next library bond issue).

---

2. S. L. Baker and G. W. Shepherd, "Fiction Classification Schemes," *RQ* 27 (Winter 1987): 246.

Academic and Research Libraries

In contrast, in academic libraries, greater attention is given to acquiring secondary materials that offer interpretations of a selected number of primary works. Indeed, the kinds of primary materials that are commonplace in the public library's literature collection are just as likely to be restricted to a specific part of the academic library's collection, usually referred to as the "browsing" collection, as they are to be recognized as part of the research collection. Many academic libraries disregard popular literary works as literature and routinely advise patrons who request them to go to the local public libraries (just as often to the approval as to the chagrin of members of the English-language literature department's faculty).

In the academic library's literature collection, the concept of literature's canon is everything. The focus of its literature collection is on the literature, its making and interpretation. Charles B. Osburn has noted that all literature collections in academic libraries support three kinds of activities: "scholarship in literary history," employing biographical, source, and analogue studies that focus on writers; "the criticism of the literary texts," focusing on specific texts of works; and "the appreciation of literature."[3] The acquisition of general or popular literary works is of secondary importance. (Ironically, several notable rare books and special collections units within academic libraries are devoted to the collection of just this.) The acquisition of literary scholarship, on the other hand, is foremost. Its primacy is evidenced by collections numbering in the hundreds of thousands of volumes in major research libraries. It is absolutely safe to say that secondary works about literature are far more numerous than the primary literary works themselves. One *Hamlet* has generated volumes of commentary about it. It is equally safe to point out that, more often than not, both the *Hamlet* specialist and the undergraduate student interested in writing a term paper on the Dane's madness may want access to every potentially relevant work about their subject and may expect that the academic library will be able to accommodate them.

No field is more book-conscious than literature as practiced in American colleges and universities. Osburn notes that literature and language, and humanities in general, are book driven, that they have a "strong bibliographic orientation," and suggests that literature and history are "stereotyped as heavily library-dependent areas of scholarship."[4] This is attributable to the literal centrality of the book in the study of

---

3. Charles B. Osburn, *Academic Research and Library Resources: Changing Patterns in America* (Westport, Conn.: Greenwood Press, 1979), 78.
4. Osburn, *Academic Research and Library Resources*, 66.

literature. While the primary materials of other disciplines in the human-ities, specifically the fine arts and music, are not bibliographic, the primary resources of literature are books, books, and more books. Similarly, while the primary laboratory of fine arts or music scholars must necessarily be where the primary resources are located—the gallery and museum or the concert hall—the laboratory for the literary scholar is the library.

Just how librarians handle literature—that is, acquire, catalog, and service it—is to a great extent determined by the size and sophistication of individual library systems. (In small academic or public libraries, the librarians responsible for all aspects of literature librarianship might be solitary individuals.) The responsibilities for acquiring, cataloging, maintaining, and interpreting works of and about literature might be inextricably integrated into normal technical and public service routines. In a major academic or public research library, at the opposite end of the spectrum, these responsibilities are likely to be distributed among several professionals in different units. Only the most rigidly decentral-ized system would leave the technical processing of literature to those responsible for selecting it, on the one hand, or interpreting it, on the other. In general, the technical processing of literature is likely to be handled in separate acquisition and cataloging departments whose per-sonnel are far too busy—indeed, overwhelmed by the sheer volume of material—to distinguish anything more than books from journals regard-less of subjects. Although specially trained personnel might be employed for the technical processing of literary works or works about literature that are designated as rare or special, this will not be the case for litera-ture in general.

Those who work as English-language literature librarians basically occupy two different camps or, perhaps more accurately, wear two differ-ent hats. Some select and acquire literature; others interpret it in the course of public services. In many cases the librarian is responsible for both literature's selection and its interpretation. Logic and efficiency sug-gest that a single selector would coordinate the selection of materials for an individual collection or for all of the units containing literature within a library system. More often than not, however, selection decisions are made unilaterally on the basis of a particular unit's perception of its needs.

Selection

The building of a literature collection might appear at first to be among the most romantic responsibilities of the literature librarian. This certainly was the case in former times when Sir Thomas Bodley forbade his librar-ian, Thomas James, to collect works of vernacular literature. Thank goodness that Sir Thomas relaxed his strictures or today there might be substantial black holes in English literature. William McPheron points out that the acquisition of literature in modern libraries is, as in Bodley's day, truly "a challenge of choice."[5] On the one hand, more primary and secondary literature is available than ever before. On the other hand, the expense of collecting it has skyrocketed. It is commonly held that, as McPheron puts it, the "decentering of cultural authority" since the 1950s that has "revolutionized the literary canon and diversified the methods of its analysis"[6] has liberated the literature librarian from the responsibility of trying to collect all of the possibly relevant books. For the conscientious literature librarian, the price of such liberation is anxiety.

In general, until quite recently, the selection of materials for academic library collections was left to either the librarian or the teaching faculty, or to the librarian in consultation with the teaching faculty. What was acquired was based on the selector's knowledge of the literature and of its potential local users. It involved the time-consuming scanning of reviews for new titles and the checking of bibliographies for retrospective ones. Although arduous, the process resulted in a collection that the librarian or faculty selector knew very well, having built it on a title-by-title basis. The currently advocated method for developing literature collections, as neatly detailed by Eric Carpenter, seems radically different from the traditional methods in that it is, on the one hand, more systematized while, on the other, more removed from the literature. Carpenter's process includes assessing the needs of the local department; evaluating the collection versus the needs; writing a collection policy in the context of the library's situation; implementing the policy; managing the collection through replacement, preservation, storage, weeding, and other activities; and sharing resources with other collections as appropriate.[7] Some other related activities in the collection development process, as identified by James A. Cogswell, Robert N. Broadus, Susan J. Steinberg, and Marcia Pankake, among others, include fiscal management as well as user liaison in all areas, that is, user education, online searching, and reference services.

Whether broken down into two or two dozen components, the processes involved in acquiring literature require enormous quantities of time and effort and are only likely to yield highly subjective results. In that more literature, both primary and secondary works, is available

5. William McPheron, Stephen Lehmann, Craig Likness, and Marcia Pankake, eds., *English and American Literature: Sources and Strategies for Collection Development*, ACRL Publications in Librarianship, no. 45 (Chicago: American Library Assn., 1987), viii.

6. McPheron et al., *English and American Literature*, ix.

7. Eric Carpenter, "Collection Development for English and American Literature: An Overview," in McPheron et al., *English and American Literature*, 1–19.

than ever before, the selector is always compelled to choose not merely between good titles and bad titles but rather between good works by or about Shakespeare, say, and others by or about Hawthorne. Here selectors are in no-win situations. In many cases, the quality of the title is not as important as the known need for the title by students or faculty. In other cases, the quality of the title, judged by help from reviews, critiques, discussion with on-campus faculty, or the independent knowledge base of the selection librarian, is truly of greatest value and is central to the proper and rational expenditure of a collection budget. Depending on the size of the materials budget, the realities of the range of selection responsibility, and the politics or the influence of the requesting faculty members, the quality of a title (determined somehow or another) may or may not be as heavily considered in selection decisions as audience, research level, funding level, and other less subjective factors.

Approval and similar gathering plans that employ more mechanical methods of selection are now widely used to help the selector deal with the bulk of primary and secondary literature that would have been previously selected on a title-by-title basis. These allow the selector to more systematically gather materials according to a particular library's needs by permitting the specification of subjects, academic levels, formats, publishers, and so forth, of the works to be provided. An effective approval plan will provide methods for the selector to obtain, let us say, editions of works of or studies about the literature of the eighteenth century at the upper division undergraduate level from a selection of university presses and, at the same time, works by or about Shakespeare at the professional or graduate level from a comprehensive list of publishers. Similar gathering plans can be designed to obtain contemporary novels, poetry, and the like. Adjustments in the plan's profile can be made in response to changes in the programs that the collection is intended to support. Approval plans effectively reduce the amount of time that selectors need to spend reading reviews and checking bibliographies, initiating firm orders, and the like. These activities are now only necessary to obtain materials that for one reason or another are not provided by the gathering plan. On the other hand, while in the old model the collection was only as good as the selector's knowledge, in the new it is only as good as the approval plan's profile and its vendor's responsiveness.

As effective as approval plans are for gathering the bulk of literature, the selector nevertheless must be vigilant about making certain that what should be automatically received is actually obtained. One constant and nagging problem for the literature librarian is keeping up with the publication of scholarly editions, such as *The Centenary Edition of the Works of Nathaniel Hawthorne*, published by The Ohio State University Press; the University of Florida Press's edition of *The Works of Laurence Sterne*;

and the Cambridge University Press's edition of *The Writings of D. H. Lawrence*. Many libraries will permit establishing standing orders with series publishers to ensure timely receipt of all volumes. Such is always desirable. However, maintaining a standing order typically means that duplicate volumes will be received on a library's approval plan and will have to be returned. On the other hand, attempting to exclude such series from the approval program will necessarily exclude other wanted titles that cannot be obtained through standing orders. The problem is partially attributable to the fact that most editorial projects involve years of work, and institutional memories—both of libraries and publishers— are short. The definitive edition of the works of Hawthorne, for example, began in the 1960s and is just now nearing completion. Keeping up with editions is a problem with the only real solution being the selector's vigilance.

A larger issue has to do with the selector's obligation. The librarian or faculty member who is responsible for collection development—either by selecting materials on a title-by-title basis or by some strategy that combines selection via an approval plan and firm ordering—must make choices that affect the research of faculty and students as well as the overall literature collection. To whom is the collection manager obliged: the library, the faculty, the students, or literature itself? Professional opinions are not in agreement. Carpenter suggests one response: "It is, therefore, finally the English bibliographer's responsibility to insure that the clientele's expectations are satisfied, both within the field and in related areas. If the psychology department, for example, has no interest in psychoanalysis but English does, books in psychoanalysis should be purchased from the English funds."[8] Without indicting Carpenter, it must be suggested that selectors are in the tough business of making decisions about the appropriateness of requests for materials. Sometimes popularity must be sacrificed to maintain integrity.

Cataloging and Classification

Cataloging and classifying literature has none of the glamour of its selection. Its typical problems, like those in acquisitions, however, are just as troublesome. As James E. Ross suggests, a fundamental and common problem in the cataloging of literature revolves around the choice of entry; that is, the establishment of the author's name.[9] This basic authority work is most associated with primary literary works, but the problem,

---

8. Eric Carpenter, "Collection Development," in McPheron et al., *English and American Literature*, 14.

9. J. E. Ross, "Artists and Poets Online: Issues in Cataloging and Retrieval," *Cataloging and Classification Quarterly* 7 (Spring 1987), 91–104.

of course, is common with all creative works—whether musical, artistic, or literary. Literary scholars, like historians and scientists, are typically interested in attaching their names to their writings. Their tenure and promotion, in addition to their reputations among colleagues, are dependent on the ready identification of their works. This logic is not always applicable to works by creative writers; indeed, history is full of examples in which the writer's survival has depended on anonymity and disassociation with religious, political, or social causes and turmoils. The pen names that baffled the officers of the Star Chamber from late Tudor and Stuart reigns have had similar effects on modern catalogers. Likewise, assumed names in less tenuous circumstances have been nonetheless bewildering. Examples are legion. Some, like George Eliot and Mary Anne Evans, are readily resolved: Evans only published under George Eliot. Others, like Mark Twain and Samuel Clemens, are more insidious. The problems can only be resolved by time-consuming research and comparison of records.

A singular problem typically associated with the Dewey decimal classification of literature is similarly needling. The Library of Congress and the Dewey decimal classification systems approach literature in fundamentally different ways. Whereas the Library of Congress system attempts to pull together works by individual writers under a single class number, the Dewey decimal system can actually segregate a writer's works by genres. It is not at all unusual to discover that Emerson's poetry is assigned the Dewey decimal classification 811 (for American poetry) and his essays 814 (for American essays). Likewise, Ben Jonson's poetry will be located in 821 (for English poetry), plays in 822 (for English drama), and prose writings, such as *The English Grammar*, in 228 (for English miscellaneous writings). To make this cumbersome situation even more exasperating, an author's autobiographical writings are occasionally assigned to the 900s (for biography). The awkwardness of Dewey's classifications for literature can be lived with as long as all the volumes in collected editions are assigned to one class or another. At the same time, the superiority of the Library of Congress classification for literary research is debatable, and the use of either system has unknown effects on the quality or quantity of work in those collections—researchers associated with the libraries of the University of Illinois at Urbana–Champaign and the University of Michigan, which use the Dewey classification, appear to have published as prolifically and as prestigiously as those at Indiana University and The Ohio State University, which use the Library of Congress system.

Public Services and Literature

Collection management is the interface of technical processes of acquisition and cataloging and classification and of public services, such as reference services, user education, and liaison with academic departments. Paul Mosher defines collection management as "the systematic, efficient, and economic stewardship of library resources."[10] The term, in its fullest implications, is most appropriate for the activities of the literature specialist in the modern academic or public library. Osburn has observed that the "treatment of literature in American universities of the twentieth century presents perhaps the most complex academic phenomenon of all."[11] Similarly, literature's treatment and handling in American academic libraries is just as much a complex of extremes. The enormity of the task has been emphasized throughout this survey. Too many variables must be reckoned with. More primary and secondary works are published annually in literature than in any other field. Libraries typically contain more works of literature than works in any other subjects. Departments of English in American universities include more faculty and graduate students and offer more courses with greater total enrollments than departments in other fields. But even more significant, no faculty members are traditionally more vocal about the library and libraries than those in English-language literature departments.

The responsibility for providing for the needs of these faculty and students falls squarely on the shoulders of the librarian who develops, maintains, and interprets the literature collection. Where these responsibilities are separated, the faculty and students sometimes fall through the cracks. As the previous discussions of the acquisition, cataloging, and classification of literature suggest, this responsibility is, thank goodness, typically distributed among several individuals in all but the smallest libraries. On the other hand, in these matters of technical processing, including the processes involved in acquisitions, the literature librarian has little more than an advisory function. Acquisitions librarians actually acquire; cataloging librarians actually catalog. Here collection managers can only hope that their intentions and instructions are sufficiently lucid to be adequately interpreted. In the various activities of public services, on the other hand, the literature librarian gets to exercise full authority and expertise in the field.

Many major academic library systems maintain facilities for undergraduate needs. As the undergraduate library's collection is usually intended to support the curricular activities of lower-division students, it will certainly contain literature. How much literature this collection might or should include, however, are difficult questions to answer. Some undergraduate libraries have attempted to imitate the collections of

---

10. Paul H. Mosher, "Collection Development to Collection Management: Toward Stewardship of Library Resources," *Collection Management* 4 (Winter 1982): 44.

11. Osburn, *Academic Research and Library Resources*, 77.

small academic libraries, including the core materials of both lower- and upper-division levels of literary study. Others have been known to exclude (to the pleasure of many teaching faculty) such basic materials as the various Magill's Masterplots, like *Critical Survey of Drama: English Language Series* and *Masterplots II: Short Stories Series*, and Gale's Literary Criticism series, like *Contemporary Literary Criticism* and *Twentieth Century Literary Criticism*. Lists of basic literary resources, such as those included in *Books for College Libraries* (3d ed., Chicago: American Library Assn., 1989) and *The Reader's Adviser*, provided good bases for collection development.

Compounding the difficulty of determining the appropriateness of literary materials in the undergraduate library is the instability of literature's place in the undergraduate curriculum. Trends in undergraduate instruction in English departments suggest that few lower-division courses require the study of literature. Many courses are exclusively intended to teach the basics of written composition. Here, analyses of contemporary manifestations of social problems or events are more likely to be the foci of library user education than comparable literary examples, such as irresponsible sexual behavior as illustrated in Shakespeare's *Romeo and Juliet*, or hunger in America as experienced by the Joads in Steinbeck's *The Grapes of Wrath*. In such courses, analysis of literature serves as little more than a pretense for writing. As James E. Ford has indicated, library user education has been considered most appropriate and, furthermore, successful, in English courses that required research papers.[12] The irony here, of course, is that the instruction has little to do with literature or, for that matter, in light of the recent efforts to integrate writing across the curriculum, with the traditional, central interest of most English-language literature departments—literature. The bottom line is that library user education is appropriate wherever research paper writing is taught and is not the exclusive responsibility of literature departments. Indeed, analyses of the English curricula at various American colleges suggest that the serious study of literature typically begins at the upper-division (300-course) level, whose support is usually the responsibility of the academic library's research collection.

On the other hand, it is typical for the undergraduate unit in the major academic library system to physically contain the notorious "browsing" collection. Sometimes occupying an entire wing of a library building and just as often, in the small college library, taking up the space of a few shelves, this collection usually offers varieties of best-selling fictional and

12. James E. Ford, "The Natural Alliance between Librarians and English Teachers in Course-Related Library Use Instruction," *College and Research Libraries* 43 (Sept. 1982): 379–84.

nonfictional works and is intended to provide opportunities for popular, noncurriculum-related reading. In short, it offers the academic community an alternative to membership in the local public library. (On the other hand, academic libraries that forgo collections for this purpose typically actively direct their communities toward the resources for popular reading that are available in public libraries.) Here the most recent works by Graham Greene, Robert Penn Warren, and Edward Albee are as likely to be found as those by Danielle Steele, Stephen King, and Louis L'Amour. These collections commonly contain the widest possible range of literature—romances, mysteries, historical fiction, science fiction and fantasy, and the like. As these copies are intended to be consumed, they are usually not considered to be part of a library system's research collections. Whether these materials are duplicated in the segments of the collection that are intended to support research, or ultimately transferred to that part of the collection—along with the works by Greene, Warren, and Albee—after their currency has waned is another question. Major libraries intent on maintaining research-level collections in literature will duplicate substantial portions of the browsing room's collections according to individual collection policies and interests. Other works will be routinely weeded and withdrawn.

The widest variety and most significant volume of library activities related to literature will be concentrated in the unit of a library system that contains the research collection. Here the fullest kind of literature librarianship will be practiced. Whether the reference division of that collection includes a professional librarian with specialized training or developed expertise in literary reference depends on the institution. Many institutions, of course, appoint librarians who hold advanced subject degrees in addition to an MLS degree. An advanced degree, however, does not automatically indicate a capacity for the provision of public services involving literature. In some systems, in addition, the same reference librarians might also serve as literature's "collection managers," the currently fashionable job title for subject bibliographers or subject specialists. This puts upon the incumbent the responsibilities for the development of the research collection in literature as well as liaison with the faculty members of an academic department (or departments) who have curricular and research uses and needs for the collection, in addition to the basic services provided by reference librarians, such as online searching and user education. The consolidation of these activities in a lone collection manager greatly facilitates faculty and, by extension, student access to these services. On the other hand, it also spreads the librarian very thin, compelling the trading-off of one kind of service for another. As Carpenter has noted: "Many libraries now combine public service and collection development on the assumption that public contact improves book selection decisions."[13] The combination of responsibilities, however, frequently results in draining the collection manager's energies and leaves little time for effective work at one responsibility or the other. Carpenter's research and the personal experience of anyone who has ever worked as literature's collection manager bear this out. English-language literature departments, along with history departments, are likely to possess both the largest and most diverse membership at even the smallest colleges. Ten to twenty percent of the faculty of the liberal arts college will be in the English department. The English departments of the largest universities include fifty to seventy tenured and tenure-track faculty, various emeriti and visiting appointments, nontenure-track instructors, and hosts of graduate research and teaching assistants. This community, coupled with its appetite for books and journals and, more important, its disposition steeped in a tradition that sees English-language literature at the center of the university, makes liaison, or public relations, with faculty the literature collection manager's predominant task.

The importance of public relations with the literature faculty goes right to the heart of the matter and the real practice of literature librarianship in academic libraries. All discussions of humanistic scholarship and the library center on access to the "book." To quote Karl J. Weintraub, "Humanists are probably the most book-bound creatures in the world of scholarship."[14] James Holly Hanford suggests that this bibliophilia is most deeply inscribed upon the hearts of literature faculty. "Nothing," he notes, "is more widely true about the teacher of modern languages, take him where you will, than that he is or has been a book lover."[15]

Running counter to this tradition of the literature scholar as book lover is another tradition—the "dark side," as it were—and one of which all English faculty members and their graduate research assistants, but few librarians, are cognizant. It is the tradition that depicts librarians, to quote Randolph G. Adams's infamous essay, as "enemies of books."[16] Any recent evidence of a "natural alliance" between librarians and English faculty is belied by a deeply instilled sentiment that librarians are afflicted with an enumerative mind-set that asserts that one text is as good as another, that a reprint, or a facsimile, or a photocopy is as good as the original. Recent analytical bibliographers (typically English-

13. Carpenter, "Collection Development," in McPheron et al., *English and American Literature*, 8–9.

14. Karl J. Weintraub, "The Humanistic Scholar and the Library," *Library Quarterly* 50 (Jan. 1980): 25.

15. James Holly Hanford, "The American Scholar and His Books," *PMLA* 74 (May 1959): 34.

16. Randolph G. Adams, "Librarians as Enemies of Books," *Library Quarterly* 7 (July 1937): 317.

language literature faculty) have been more diplomatic in expressing this basic indictment. In "Bibliographers and the Library" (with "bibliographers" used here as defined by humanistic scholars), G. Thomas Tanselle points out that "Librarians are not usually enemies of works . . . but they are often enemies of books, for they are frequently careless of the physical forms in which works are presented."[17] Tanselle, among others, would believe that librarians have consistently publicly demonstrated to bibliophilic literature faculty that books might be better left out ·of their reach.

A brief illustration from a review published in *American Reference Books Annual* suffices as an illustration. Of Michael Hargraves's *Harry Crews: A Bibliography*, the librarian-reviewer wrote: "*Harry Crews* is one of the most unusual bibliographies this reviewer has ever seen. After spending several weeks reading books and articles by and about Crews, I then felt capable to review this book. Unfortunately, it was only then I discovered that this was not an annotated bibliography, but a bibliography giving actual physical descriptions of Crews's works."[18] In the mind of the literature scholar, who practices descriptive bibliography as a form of reverence for the book as the physical evidence of literature, modern library science's seeming obliviousness to the significance of a work's physical form in favor of its function almost automatically classifies librarians as philistines and disqualifies them to practice literature's stewardship. To describe librarians as bibliographic illiterates is perhaps to overstate the issue.

Whereas, to the librarian, bibliographic description is cataloging—that is, the necessarily routine matter of accurately and efficiently recording selected physical characteristics of a work in order to locate it in a collection of hundreds or perhaps millions of other books—to the bibliographically conscious literary scholar it is something vastly different: Bibliographic description aims through systematic analysis to distinguish a particular copy of a book from all other copies, including the ideal copy, and thereby indicate the status, or authority, of its contents. "In my opinion," remarked the noted literary bibliographer Fredson Bowers, "this highest form of bibliography should offer a definitive account of a book or else should differentiate itself as belonging to a somewhat lower genre"[19]—genres which, it should be noted, include library catalogs. It is not at all surprising, as Ford has so wonderfully indicated, that

17. G. Thomas Tanselle, "Bibliographers and the Library," *Library Trends* 25 (Apr. 1977): 749.

18. Janet R. Ivey, "Review of Michael Hargraves's *Harry Crews: A Bibliography,*" in *American Reference Books Annual* 18 (1987): 447–48.

19. Fredson Bowers, *Principles of Bibliographic Description* (Princeton, N.J.: Princeton University Press, 1949), 5.

librarians and English faculty have a "natural alliance"—in situations that typically have nothing to do with literature.[20] The librarian who can dispel the profession's images of bibliographic carelessness and mindless bibliometricism by appealing to humanistic scholarship's bibliographic and bibliophilic sensibilities will score a public relations victory, not only winning the faculty's confidence and acceptance as one of their number but also restoring to a degree its confidence in the library as something more than a receptacle or depository for materials that they would otherwise keep in their offices.

Profile of Literature Librarianship

Education of the Literature Librarian

In that the most fundamental responsibilities of the literature librarian are more in the area of public services than technical services and as much public relations work as bibliographic, debating whether or not the literature librarian needs an advanced degree in literature is really quite mindless. Not surprisingly, noteworthy English-language literature scholar bibliographers such as Fredson Bowers and Arthur Brown have indicated that those who would be literature's stewards could benefit from course work in literary studies. Richard L. Hopkins and Roy Stokes, on the behalf of library science education, have suggested that would-be subject specialists need more than mere knowledge of bibliographic resources and that responsible professional programs should provide it. To adapt Pope's argument from his "Essay on Criticism," "a little learning" about the subject is advantageous, if for no other reason than to show the would-be literature librarian just how much remains to be known, and, of course, drinking deep from "the Pierian spring" by taking an advanced degree is always preferable. The librarian who can distinguish unassisted some of literature's myriad Dromios is simply several steps ahead of another who needs to consult the numerous dictionaries of literary characters to provide the same information; in other words, knowledge of literature itself is to a degree counterbalanced by willingness to learn literary reference sources and persistence in using them. Similarly, an advanced degree (or degrees) certainly facilitates use of networks that might not be available otherwise. Sharing mutual academic or research experiences and the like can break the ice and initially win acceptance for an incumbent. But, on a day-to-day basis over time, the literature librarian's survival tools are interpersonal

---

20. Ford, "The Natural Alliance," 379.

communication skills. These include the abilities to say "no"; to serve as an effective mediator in conflict resolutions; and not only to empathize with problems that are the ultimate concerns of others but also to adopt them as your own.

Literary Bibliography Courses

Those who have achieved the Ph.D. in literature will say that the specialized bibliographic preparation of literature scholars for their careers is more intensive and sophisticated than for scholars in other academic fields and, furthermore, than for many professionals, including doctors and lawyers. This is only in keeping with literary scholarship's perception of the library as literature's laboratory. For the last several decades most English departments have required their graduate students to take courses that explored the resources and methods of literary research. Indeed, until the last decade, many departments employed this course as an ordeal or rite of passage that weeded the graduate program of students who were not committed to careers of research. The bibliographic intensiveness and depth of these courses is immediately evident in some of the various enumerative bibliographies that continue to serve as textbooks, including Richard D. Altick and Andrew Wright's *Selective Bibliography for the Study of English and American Literature* (6th ed., New York: Macmillan, 1979); Arthur Garfield Kennedy, Donald B. Sands, and William E. Coburn's *A Concise Bibliography for Students of English* (5th ed., Stanford, Calif.: Stanford University Press, 1972); and James L. Harner's *Literary Research Guide* (3d ed., New York: Modern Language Assn., 1989), formerly by Margaret C. Patterson. Emphasis in these guides is on research in libraries. Altick and Wright cover about 650 basic resources; the other guides each cover several thousand sources. Similarly, the pedagogy of literary research as well as the field's research methods are also routinely examined by its scholars. The journal, *Literary Research* (College Park, Md.: Literary Research Assn., 1986), formerly *Literary Research Newsletter* from 1976 to 1985, presents syllabi, exercises, and other assignments, as well as enumerative bibliographies of new resources that define the state-of-the-art. Problem sets and "pathfinders" remain the common instructional instruments of the literary research course. In short, by the end of a quarter- or semester-long course literary graduate students have had substantial hands-on experiences with the full range of general and humanities and social science resources, including such works as Sheehy's *Guide to Reference Books*, Walford's *Guide to Reference Materials*, *National Union Catalog*, *British Museum Catalogue*, *National Union Catalog of Manuscript Collections*, *Books in Print*, *British Books in Print*, *Union List of Serials*, *Ulrich's International Periodicals Directory*, *The Annual Register of World Events*, *The*

Literary Marketplace, The Oxford English Dictionary, Dictionary of National Biography, Dictionary of American Biography, Readers' Guide to Periodical Literature, Humanities Index, Poole's *Index to Periodical Literature, The British Humanities Index, New York Times Index,* and *Palmer's Index to the Times.* Recent versions of the introductory literary research course have included significant coverage of electronic resources, including OCLC, RLIN, and databases available on DIALOG, BRS, and other services. Harner's textbook, *Literary Research Guide,* discusses these and other specialized electronic resources in detail. The rigorousness of coverage is analogous to that offered in the library science curriculum's general reference courses as represented by editions of volume I of William Katz's *Introduction to Reference Work.*

On the other hand, the introductory literary bibliography course coverage of the range of specialized research resources commonly used in literary research is far more intensive than the coverage of any one field typically presented in library science courses in humanities or social science reference. Indeed, literary graduate students have commonly been expected to use the full range of tools that constitute the national bibliographies of Great Britain and the United States as well as the major primary and secondary bibliographies, reference works, and other resources for the particular literary genres and periods. Exercises routinely require the use of such resources as the *MLA International Bibliography* (New York: Modern Language Assn., 1921–), *New Cambridge Bibliography of English Literature* (Cambridge, Eng.: Cambridge University Press, 1969–1977), *A Short-Title Catalogue of Books Printed in England, Scotland, & Ireland and of English Books Printed Abroad, 1475–1640* (2d ed., London, Eng.: The Bibliographical Society, 1976–1991), Charles Evans's *American Bibliography* (1903–1934; reprint, New York: Peter Smith, 1941), and *The Wellesley Index to Victorian Periodicals, 1824–1900* (Toronto: University of Toronto Press, 1976–). By comparison, in the library science curriculum, only specialization in medical or legal librarianship offers comparable experiences.

In addition to this intensive introduction to general and specialized bibliographic resources and research methods, introductory literary bibliography courses have also traditionally included instructional units covering the principles and techniques of descriptive bibliography and textual studies. Typical instructional instruments, such as the transcription of a manuscript in Elizabethan secretary hand, the physical description (title page transcription, signature collation, and analyses of the printing and publishing histories) of a copy of a Victorian novel, or the evaluation of the authority and integrity of a critical edition, emphasize the significance of the book (the literal and physical format of literature) that was, until quite recently, central to the field. Standard works that have commonly served as textbooks for these introductions to descriptive bibliography include Ronald Brunlees McKerrow's *An Introduction to Bibliography for Literary Students* (London, Eng.: Oxford University Press, 1928) and Philip Gaskell's *A New Introduction to Bibliography* (New York: Oxford University Press, 1972).

To be honest, most recently the introductory research courses offered in many English-language literature departments have reduced the earlier emphasis on descriptive bibliography in order to include units on such topics of current interest and opportunity as the teaching of composition and women's and ethnic studies. In the early 1980s, indeed, T. H. Howard-Hill found little consistent interest in bibliography in American graduate programs in either literature or library science. At the same time, however, Howard-Hill found it desirable to encourage greater attention to bibliographical education in both.[21]

As it is in the library science curriculum, the literary bibliography course is oftentimes as much professional indoctrination as bibliographic introduction. Not surprisingly, as evidenced in the remarks of Adams, Bowers, Brown, McCorison, and Tanselle, among others, it is literary scholarship's specialized and particular orientation that frequently puts it at odds with librarianship. Bowers's explicit plea that "more young men and women . . . take a liberal arts M.A. or Ph.D. in literature and history as preparation for librarianship,"[22] however, obscures the fact that the issues dividing literary scholars and librarians are perhaps more philosophical than professional. Indeed, within library science's curricula it is possible to obtain both the formal philosophical introduction and practical bibliographic training that are needed not merely to work but to be accepted as a literature librarian. Although subject training may be preferable, the only true prerequisite is a candidate's sensitivity to bibliophilia.

Although nothing in library science's curriculum (short of intensive independent study outside the field) is comparable to the introductory literary bibliography course, much in the curriculum is complementary. As already indicated, the basic resources of literary research are identical to many of the basic resources covered in courses on general, humanities, and social science reference work, although the literary applications of these resources are not usually emphasized in library science courses. In addition to covering the most broadly applicable literary resources, library science reference courses introduce interdisciplinary resources, such as *Arts and Humanities Citation Index* and *Current Contents: Arts*

---

21. T. H. Howard-Hill, "The Place of Bibliography in the Graduate Curriculum: Introductory Remarks," *Literary Research Newsletter* 9 (Fall 1984): 45–52.
22. Fredson Bowers, "The Function of Bibliography," *Library Trends* 7 (Apr. 1959): 510.

and Humanities, as well as resources in other specific disciplines that are particularly valuable in literary research. These only the most experienced literary scholars will know. For an authoritative introduction to Christian images in *Beowulf*, for example, few literary handbooks surpass that included in *The New Catholic Encyclopedia*. Other basic disciplinary resources like *America History and Life*, *Historical Abstracts*, *Communication Abstracts*, *ERIC*, *LLBA: Linguistics and Language Behavior Abstracts*, *Psychological Abstracts*, *The Encyclopedia of Philosophy*, *The New Grove Dictionary of Music and Musicians*, and the McGraw-Hill *Encyclopedia of World Art* can also be useful in literary research. Similarly, library science courses cover the national and trade bibliographies of Great Britain and the United States, as well as those of other countries. Knowledge of the bibliographies of Italy, France, and Germany is complementary. Courses on the history of the book, which emphasize both the ancient and continental antecedents of writing, illustration, and printing in England, neatly complement the coverage of paleography, analytical bibliography, and textual studies provided in the literary curriculum. An understanding of the interdisciplinary uses and resources of general, humanities, and social science research and an appreciation of the centrality of the book to humanistic and, in particular, literary scholarship are adequate preparation for work in literary librarianship. Specialized knowledge of literary resources comes with practice in the field.

Professional Associations

No professional organization presently exists to support English-language literature librarians in the full range of their activities. Indeed, the notion that any particular aspect of the practice of literature librarianship is an area of specialization, analogous to medical or legal librarianship, is a rather recent one. Not surprisingly, specialization emerged from that aspect of the job that is most intimately related to money—selection and acquisitions. In 1982, the English and American Literature Discussion Group of the American Library Association's Association of College and Research Libraries (ACRL) was established, ostensibly recognizing "the emerging maturity of the subject specialty of English-language literatures in American libraries."[23] More specifically, however, it reflects the reality that while more literature is available than ever before, academic libraries are increasingly unable to obtain it at the levels to which they were formerly accustomed.

---

23. McPheron et al., *English and American Literature*, vii.

The English and American Literature Discussion Group has sponsored several conference programs as well as the publication of McPheron et al.'s collection of essays, *English and American Literature: Sources and Strategies for Collection Development*, that have addressed a variety of issues of both immediate and remote interest to academic librarians responsible for the collection of English-language literature. This ACRL publication represents the state of the art on the selection and acquisition of current and retrospective, primary and secondary literary works (including reference works and rare books), serials, and nonprint media. The important topic of literature's selection for public libraries is outside the scope of the essays.

In that many more librarians provide literary reference and advisory services than actually select literature for collections, it would seem that English-language literature librarians are indeed a specialized group in need of a forum. The "genericness" of literary librarianship in both academic and public libraries probably prevents this, however. Librarians who are responsible for answering literary reference questions or providing user education lectures in courses offered by English departments are more likely to see themselves as reference librarians or bibliographic instruction librarians and continue to align themselves with such professional organizations as the Reference and Adult Services Division and ACRL's Bibliographic Instruction Section, or the Bibliographic Instruction Round Table of the American Library Association rather than recognize the specialness of literature librarianship.

The Literature of Literature

Primary Bibliographies

Librarians are far less familiar with primary than with secondary bibliographies. Primary bibliographies account for the works by individual writers or the works that constitute the literature of a specific genre, period, or subject. The best primary bibliographies are also known as descriptive bibliographies. Classic examples include W. W. Greg's four-volume *A Bibliography of the English Printed Drama to the Restoration* (London, Eng.: Bibliographical Society, 1939) and B. C. Bloomfield and Edward Mendelson's *W. H. Auden: A Bibliography, 1924–1969* (2d ed., Charlottesville, Va.: University Press of Virginia, 1972). Emphasis is on identifying, by means of description of the actual physical pieces, the works that constitute the canon of a period, genre, author, subject, or other limited area. Typical features include facsimiles or transcriptions of the title and copyright pages and substantial details about a work's format, pagination, contents, typography, paper, binding, dust jacket, and printing and publishing history, including data about the size of its press run, the price of a copy, and the like. Locations of the copies upon which the descriptions are based may be provided. Notable series of primary bibliographies include the University of Pittsburgh Press's Pittsburgh Series in Bibliography for such authors as Ralph Waldo Emerson, Nathaniel Hawthorne, Margaret Fuller, and Eugene O'Neill; Oxford University Press's Soho Bibliographies for Henry James, Katherine Mansfield, Arthur Conan Doyle, and George Bernard Shaw; the University of Texas Press's Tower Bibliographical Series, for Elizabeth Bowen and Edward Dahlberg; and Dawson's Pall Mall Bibliographies, for Thomas Dekker, Abraham Cowley, and Robert Greene, among others. In addition, there are many other primary bibliographies that have been published by various university presses as individual works of scholarship.

A significant number of other primary bibliographies also traditionally associated with literature are typically regarded as reference works. These include Donald Wing's *Short-Title Catalogue of Books Printed in England, Scotland, Ireland, Wales, and British America, and of English Books Printed in Other Countries, 1641–1700* (2d ed., New York: Modern Language Assn., 1972–); Lyle Henry Wright's *American Fiction, 1774–1850* (2d ed., San Marino, Calif.: Huntington Library, 1969); and G. William Bergquist's *Three Centuries of English and American Plays* (New York: Readex Microprints, 1963). Offering less bibliographic detail than many other descriptive bibliographies, bibliographies of this variety cover wider and deeper ranges of works in addition to serving as finding aids to microform collections that reproduce the full texts of the actual works. Similarly, the numerous published catalogs of library collections, such as *The Catalog of Printed Books of the Folger Shakespeare Library* (Boston, Mass.: G. K. Hall, 1970), also function as important aids in research.

Where primary bibliographies are located in the library collection is also subject to local perceptions of their uses. Rare book or special collection units will necessarily want to own selected descriptive guides to the kinds of works that are collected. These will be used in routine acquisitions, cataloging, and reference services. Scholars and collectors, similarly, will also require ready access to primary bibliographies. Their uses and value, on the other hand, will mainly only confuse those library users to whom one copy of *Huckleberry Finn*, say, is as good as another— that is, most students and, embarrassingly, many librarians. In fact, Geoffrey Keynes's exquisite descriptive bibliography of the works of John Donne, *A Bibliography of Dr. John Donne, Dean of St. Paul's* (4th ed., Oxford, Eng.: Clarendon Press, 1973), will be of little help to the student who needs critical studies of "The Canonization" or "Air and Angels."

Similarly, the library unit containing such microform collections as University Microfilms International's *American Periodicals*, Readex Corporation's *English and American Plays of the Nineteenth Century*, and Research Publications' *American Literary Annuals and Gift Books* will want to have the corresponding finding aids. When this is a library system's specialized microform unit, duplicate copies of these catalogs are typically required in the reference collection. Although machine-readable tapes of many major catalogs are available for loading onto a library's online system, it should be remembered that scholars read and study guides of this variety. Online access seldom means that printed copies of primary bibliographies can be dispensed with.

Secondary Bibliographies

For the majority of literary reference questions, secondary bibliographies are unquestionably the most useful reference resources. These include writings and other materials about literature—that is, works about the writings of a specific writer or group of writers, or of forms (genres), periods, or subjects. The range of secondary bibliography formats and scholarly contributions is enormous. The best ones are comprehensive, covering works of all types in all languages and from all periods about their subjects. In addition, the best secondary bibliographies include annotations that are descriptive, offering specific information on the scope and contents of sources, as well as evaluative, indicating the significance of sources in the field.This latter aspect is the real scholarly contribution of a secondary bibliography. The merely mechanical cumulation and description of sources is mindless.

The arrangement of entries in secondary bibliographies varies. Chronological arrangement seems to offer the most useful access to sources, allowing researchers to readily gauge an author's or work's critical reputation at particular times. A strict subject arrangement presumes that critical studies are limited to one work or another. Works that duplicate entries or offer cross references in order to compensate for the coverage of different subjects tend to inflate the bibliography's size and the researcher's expectations.

Equally important as a secondary bibliography's annotations is its indexing. Subject indexing is essential. The usefulness of numerous secondary bibliographies is greatly enhanced by the provision of nominal headings for such topics as bibliography, biography, allusions, sources, and characterization. The best topical indexing, however, will most accurately reflect the secondary literature itself, offering subject headings for individual works, the names of individual characters, particular allusions, the names of other authors, and the like.

As in all things, the use of scholarly judgment in the production of a secondary bibliography is everything. To include entries for every article in an *Oxford Companion* or the *Encyclopaedia Britannica* but omit ones for dissertations or for works in German, for example, is a disservice to scholarship. Likewise, to describe sources by paraphrasing their titles without evaluation of usefulness or to fail to provide a volume with subject indexing is to neglect scholarly responsibility.

Secondary bibliographies in literature are by-products of modern scholarship. Comparatively few were available through the mid-twentieth century. In contrast, David Nordloh has referred to the decade of the 1980s as "the age of the reference work."[24] Series of secondary bibliographies, such as Scarecrow Press's Scarecrow Author Bibliographies; Kent State University Press's The Serif Series: Bibliographies and Checklists; G. K. Hall's Reference Guides to Literature, Reference Publications in Literature, and Masters of Science Fiction and Fantasy; Garland's Garland Reference Library of the Humanities; Northern Illinois University Press's (and now Garland's) Annotated Secondary Bibliography Series on English Literature in Transition, 1880–1920; and Borgo Press's Bibliographies of Modern Authors, among many others, today continue the flood begun in the 1960s.

Where secondary bibliographies are located in a library's collection is a matter of local perception. Some institutions have adopted hard-and-fast policies, while others have remained more flexible, shelving in the reference collection author and other specialized bibliographies relevant to current teaching and research needs. The secondary bibliographies for Shakespeare, such as Gordon Ross Smith's *A Classified Shakespeare Bibliography, 1936–1958* (State College, Pa.: Pennsylvania State University Press, 1963) and selected volumes of the Garland Shakespeare Bibliographies (1980–), are most commonly kept in reference collections. Although the sheer quantity of secondary bibliographies for even the major individual authors prohibits maintaining them in any single collection, in one way or another as many as are affordable should be at hand. Use of such general and specialized bibliographies of bibliographies, such as the *Bibliographic Index*, T. H. Howard-Hill's *Index to British Literary Bibliography* (New York: Oxford University Press, 1969–), and Alan R. Weiner and Spencer Means's *Literary Criticism Index* (Metuchen, N.J.: Scarecrow Press, 1984), allow the literature librarian to confidently identify the availability of these specialized sources without contending with an unwieldy collection. Unfortunately,

---

24. David Nordloh, "General Reference Works," *American Literary Scholarship* (1986): 481.

this typically prohibits the literature librarian from seeing the faces of researchers when, secondary bibliographies in hand, they discover references to the myriad critical books and articles on authors, works, and subjects about which they were sure no one had ever written.

Online Resources

Although neither so important nor imperative as in the sciences and "harder" social sciences, access to electronic information technologies is nonetheless attractive to literary scholars. This is most understandable. Until very recently, literary researchers were obliged to *read* the likes of the *MLA International Bibliography* and *Oxford English Dictionary*. The prospect of obtaining fingertip access in the near future to a single database that will include the contents of Pollard and Redgrave's and Wing's short-title catalogs (covering, respectively, works from 1475 to 1640 and 1640 to 1700), Evans's *American Bibliography, The Eighteenth Century Short-Title Catalogue*, and *The Nineteenth Century Short Title Catalogue* is cruelly tantalizing. (Henry L. Snyder has described a proposed short-title catalog of works from 1475 through 1800.[25]) In that literary scholars, like chemists and attorneys, know that electronic information technology can facilitate research, they usually consider the librarian who is knowledgeable of its specialized uses and products as a valuable resource. The politic, public relations-minded literature librarian will see this interest as an advantage and put it to use. Indeed, whereas literary scholarship's interest in the printed versions of such resources as the *MLA International Bibliography* and *Oxford English Dictionary* was formerly considered proprietary, it is now just as likely to recognize an instructional and research partnership with librarianship when electronic versions of these resources are available. Differences in opinion that centered on the book evaporate, it seems, when books are transmogrified. This thesis will, doubtless, be more severely tested when literary resources are produced exclusively in electronic formats and their quotation is required. In the meantime, the increasing availability of these and other traditional literary resources in electronic formats have provided librarians with excellent opportunities to teach both literature faculty and students.

Research Guides

Research guides are a specialized type of secondary bibliography, intended to highlight the most significant or essential research resources for

---

25. Henry L. Snyder, "The English Short-Title Catalogue," *Papers of the Bibliographic Society of America* 82 (1988): 333–36.

literary study. The variety of guides is enormous. Guides can be distinguished as being either general or specialized. General guides typically cover resources for either or both English and American literature. Perhaps the most highly respected general guide is Richard D. Altick and Andrew Wright's *Selective Bibliography of the Study of English and American Literature* (New York: Macmillan, 1979). Now in its sixth edition, Altick and Wright's guide continues to be used as a textbook in the basic bibliography courses offered in graduate programs in English and American literature. By comparison, Nancy L. Baker's *A Research Guide for Undergraduate Students: English and American Literature* (2d ed., New York: Modern Language Assn., 1985) provides a discursive guide to a more selective and less demanding list of basic resources, such as the *Oxford English Dictionary* and *MLA International Bibliography*. Other research guides, such as James L. Harner's *Literary Research Guide* (New York: Modern Language Assn., 1989) and Michael J. Marcuse's *A Reference Guide for English Studies* (Berkeley, Calif.: University of California Press, 1990), literally cover thousands of research resources of all varieties.

Specialized research guides usually restrict coverage to primary and secondary resources for particular literary forms, periods, or subjects in either English or American literature. Other specialized guides survey particular areas, such as the collections of particular libraries. The classic example is Floyd Stovall's *Eight American Authors: A Review of Research and Criticism*, first published in 1956, and available in an edition revised by James Woodress (New York: Norton, 1971). This work is a collection of essays by different subject specialists that survey the literary contributions and critical reputations of Edgar Allan Poe, Ralph Waldo Emerson, Nathaniel Hawthorne, Henry David Thoreau, Herman Melville, Walt Whitman, Mark Twain, and Henry James. A succession of similar specialized guides has followed the model of Stovall's work. Many of the best specialized guides have been sponsored by the Modern Language Association, including John H. Fisher's *The Medieval Literature of Western Europe: A Review of Research*, David J. DeLaura's *Victorian Prose: A Guide to Research*, Richard J. Finneran's *Anglo-Irish Literature: A Review of Research*, and Joel Myerson's *The Transcendentalists: A Review of Research and Criticism*, with some bearing the series title Modern Language Association of America Reviews of Research.

Trade publishers have also produced different series of specialized research guides intended to offer comprehensive survey coverage. Appleton's (and later AHM Publishing's) Goldentree Bibliographies in Language and Literature included more than twenty paperbound, unpretentious volumes designed as checklists of selected primary and secondary resources for major and minor authors in most literary periods.

Annotation was minimal and cryptic at best; in many of the guides, especially important works were simply marked with asterisks. The Gale Information Guide Library: American Literature, English Literature, and World Literatures: An Information Guide Series was more ambitious in scope. Some thirty volumes in this series provided annotated entries for primary and secondary works for authors in particular literary periods and genres. Although publication of the series was suspended before all of the projected volumes were completed, nevertheless, the Gale series succeeded in offering more comprehensive specialized guidance for more literary periods than was previously available elsewhere. Publishers have more recently devoted attention to providing specialized guidance for authors who were not previously recognized in literature's canon. Thomas M. Inge, Maurice Duke, and Jackson R. Bryer's *Black American Writers: Bibliographical Essays* (New York: St. Martin's, 1978) and Duke, Bryer, and Inge's *American Women Writers: Bibliographical Essays* (Westport, Conn.: Greenwood Press, 1983) are designed to complement the specialized guides modeled on Stovall's work.

Reference Tools

The reference literature of literature is voluminous, elaborate, and commonplace, encompassing all of the commonly known varieties of reference works and none that is unique to other disciplines in the humanities. In general, literary reference works can be most conveniently distinguished according to their two main uses. The first kind is used to identify literary works, the second to identify works about literature, including works about those who produce it. Locating works by Samuel Clemens or works about Clemens's writings are distinctly different activities, usually requiring unique sets of resources for success. These activities, however, as Budd, Heinzkill, and Stern, among others, have shown, underlay nearly all of the academic uses of literature. Actual reference work in literature resists ready classification or categorization. Richard Altick illustrates research as a fluid process, involving varieties of different and similar resources. A researcher requires access to a repertoire of sources, since in the process of verifying a particular detail, within a bibliography, let us suppose, other queries will naturally surface calling for biographical sources, dictionaries, handbooks, indexes, and the like.[26] Altick's descriptions sharply contrast with those provided by Roland Stevens and Linda Smith, who distinguished the different needs of various academic library users. Undergraduates most frequently need plot summaries,

---

26. Richard D. Altick, *The Art of Literary Research,* 3d ed., rev. by John Fenstermacher (New York: Norton, 1981).

critical analyses of particular works, and dictionaries of literary terms, whereas "the predominant reference needs of graduate students are similar to those of undergraduates but usually are of a more advanced level." When faculty need help in their subject fields, concluded Stevens and Smith, they generally require bibliographies, directories, or sources to verify complex citations.[27] In truth, the distinction of neophyte and veteran researchers belies the complexity of research in a field in which the primary and secondary literature are constantly expanding.

The literary content of reference collections varies among differing types of libraries as well as in libraries of the same types. The great number of volumes in a literary reference collection typically makes it impossible to house in a single location. The collection consists of at least the following major kinds of frequently used materials: primary and secondary bibliographies, including general and specialized research guides and bibliographies for genres, literary periods, and subjects; dictionaries, encyclopedias, and handbooks, including companions, historical surveys, annals and chronologies, dictionaries of critical terms, dictionaries of fictional characters, anonyma and pseudonyma, gazetteers and atlases, plot summaries and digests, and dictionaries of vocabulary and allusions; biographical sources; directories; and indexes and abstracts, including yearbooks and annual reviews.

Additionally, the reference literature of literature, if not the reference collection, also includes two other disparate types of sources: journals and concordances. Although not usually shelved in reference collections, many critical and creative literary journals include important features, such as book reviews, bibliographical addenda, and checklists of critical studies, that complement reference works and keep them up-to-date. In contrast, although typically associated with individual authors and works and, therefore, not usually shelved in reference collections, concordances and other textual indexes are reference works almost by definition.

Compounding the volume of literature's general reference literature is the vast array of works devoted to genres, periods, and individual authors. Indeed, each author is likely to have his or her own reference literature that consists of all of the varieties of reference works that might support a literary genre or period, including journals and concordances. Even with the most ideal facilities, the best reference collections, including those in the special "libraries," "reading rooms," or "collections" devoted exclusively to English-language literature, can do little more than attempt to maintain the basic sources to support immediate or more frequent needs. To do more in general reference collections would

27. Roland E. Stevens and Linda C. Smith, *Reference Work in the University Library* (Littleton, Colo.: Libraries Unlimited, 1986), 4–5.

necessarily displace works in other disciplines. Literature librarians should take consolation in the fact that literary scholars cannot restrict their research activities to the reference collection. Most will be satisfied so long as needed materials are available somewhere within a library system. Astute and judicious decision-making by the collection managers can minimize some problems: needs can be satisfied. On the other hand, only the most ideal levels of funding can permit collection managers to obtain materials to their levels of expectations.

Literary reference works of all varieties are presently available both in traditional printed (or microform) formats and in electronic formats (online, CD-ROM, and diskette). The majority of the electronic resources, such as the MLA Bibliography database and the *MLA on CD-ROM*, represent digitized versions of printed works with augmented search capacity. Only a few literary reference works, like The Eighteenth Century Short-Title Catalogue, are exclusively available electronically, although the numbers of such works are increasing.

The following sections are not intended to serve as a comprehensive survey of literature's reference literature, but rather to delineate its present shape and extent. Learning to live and work with literature's reference literature is a formidable task. It should be noted that the literature used in literature's selection and acquisition is but a small subset of literature's reference literature. The slim acquisition budgets of many modern academic libraries and the convenience of approval plans seldom require the literature selector to venture beyond *Choice, American Reference Books Annual, TLS: Times Literary Supplement*, and *New York Review of Books*. The days when subject specialists employed such retrospective guides as the *New Cambridge Bibliography of English Literature* to select desiderata appear to be in the past.

In their survey of reference works and resources in the humanities, Stevens and Smith suggested that the most frequently asked questions in literature can be answered satisfactorily with a variety of dictionaries, encyclopedias, and handbooks: the "most frequent of the types of literary questions are those dealing with a particular writer or a particular work, as contrasted with those of a broader literary topic." Stevens and Smith found that "undergraduates who are taking a literature course" frequently need a "critical analysis of a particular work" or a "definition of a literary term."[28] Plot summaries and dictionaries of critical terms, Stevens and Smith noted, served as basic sources. As accurate as their conclusions might be, this assessment truly minimizes the variety of literary dictionaries, encyclopedias, and handbooks that are now available to

28. Stevens and Smith, *Reference Work in the University Library*, 92–93.

assist both the novice and seasoned literary researcher. Companion-type handbooks, historical surveys, annals and chronologies, dictionaries of critical terms, dictionaries of pseudonyms and fictional characters, atlases and gazetteers, plot summaries and digests, and dictionaries of vocabulary and allusions are perhaps the most readily identifiable types.

One-Volume Handbooks

The most familiar one-volume handbooks of literature are certainly the numerous Oxford Companions, including Margaret Drabble's *The Oxford Companion to English Literature* (5th ed., New York: Oxford University Press, 1985) and James D. Hart's *Oxford Companion to American Literature* (5th ed., New York: Oxford University Press, 1983). As different as the most recent editions are, each shares the purpose of attempting to cumulate brief explanatory entries for authors, works, schools, movements, periods, and topics. Most recently, Cambridge University Press has tried to challenge Oxford with its own series of companions, including Michael Stapleton's *The Cambridge Handbook to English Literature* (New York: Cambridge University Press, 1983) and Jack Salzman's *The Cambridge Handbook of American Literature* (New York: Cambridge University Press, 1986). The coverage of these younger works, unfortunately, pales by comparison with the old favorites.

Historical Surveys

Much the same is the case of historical surveys. The old favorites, like Albert C. Baugh's *A Literary History of England* (2d ed., London, Eng.: Routledge & K. Paul, 1967) and Robert E. Spiller's *Literary History of the United States* (4th ed., New York: Macmillan, 1974), continue to stand as standard resources as much for their familiarity as for their critical and bibliographical information. Although Emory Elliot's anxiously awaited *Columbia Literary History of the United States* (New York: Columbia University Press, 1988) offered authoritative surveys of authors not included in Spiller's history, it lacked the bibliographic apparatuses that have made the older work an important reference resource.

Significant multivolume encyclopedic surveys of English and American literature include A. H. Ward and A. R. Waller's *Cambridge History of English Literature* (Cambridge, Eng.: The University Press, 1907–1933), usually referred to as the *CHEL*, and William Porterfield Trent et al.'s *Cambridge History of American Literature* (Cambridge, Eng.: The University Press, 1917–1921). As in specialized guides, in these works different experts contributed specific essays on the full range of individual authors, works, and topics. Several volumes in the more readable *The Oxford History of English Literature*, usually referred to as the *OHEL*, remain to be completed.

Specialized handbooks and encyclopedias for individual authors have also become increasingly numerous. Handbooks for such major authors as Geoffrey Chaucer, William Shakespeare, and Edmund Spenser have long been available. Macmillan's Literary Companions have appeared for Rudyard Kipling, D. H. Lawrence, and George Orwell. More recently, Greenwood Press has published handbooks and encyclopedias for John Donne, Henry James, Kate Chopin, Eugene O'Neill, Thomas Wolfe, James Joyce, and H. P. Lovecraft. Finally, works like the several Gale Literary Criticism series, such as *Nineteenth-Century Literature Criticism* and *Shakespearean Criticism*; Magill's Masterplots and its Critical Survey series, such as *Masterplots II: American Fiction Series* and *Critical Survey of Poetry: English Language Series*; Ungar's Library of Literary Criticism series, such as *Modern Black Writers* and *Modern British Literature*; and Harold Bloom's Chelsea House Library of Literary Criticism, such as *The Critical Perspective* and *Twentieth-Century British Literature*, represent new species of encyclopedias that combine the qualities of secondary bibliographies and summaries and digests.

Chronologies

As in historical research in general, chronologies are useful in literary research for putting authors and their works in the perspectives of the concurrent political, social, religious, artistic, and scientific activities. Comprehensive literary chronologies, such as Richard M. Ludwig and Clifford A. Nault, Jr.'s *Annals of American Literature, 1602–1983* (New York: Oxford University Press, 1986) and Samuel Rogal's *A Chronological Outline of British Literature* (Westport, Conn.: Greenwood Press, 1987), cover the entire history of a literature. Chronologies that are more specialized and restrictive in scope are perhaps even more useful in research in that they tend to cite extensive primary and secondary resources, such as printing records, letters and correspondence, and biographical works. Alfred Harbage's *Annals of English Drama, 975–1700* (rev. by Samuel Schoenbaum, London, Eng.: Methuen, 1964) is a classic example. The work ostensibly serves as an index to plays included in such primary resources as Edward Arber's *Transcripts of the Registers of the Company of Stationers of London, 1554–1640* as well as the period's major descriptive bibliographies, like W. W. Greg's *A Bibliography of English Printed Drama to the Restoration*.

Like companions and handbooks, specialized chronologies for the lives of major individual writers have long been available for Shakespeare and other major authors. G. K. Hall and Macmillan's recently initiated Macmillan Author Chronologies, however, includes chronologies for the lives and careers of a range of authors that many veteran researchers might consider luxurious. Volumes are available for George Gordon, Lord Byron;

Charles Dickens; Joseph Conrad; George Eliot; Anthony Trollope; Virginia Woolf; and William Wordsworth, among others. The real value of an individual author's chronology to the researcher, it must be emphasized, depends on its references to standard primary sources. A chronology that includes detailed indexes for persons, places, and subjects is an invaluable guide to these resources.

Dictionaries

The critical terminology of literature is, like Latin or Greek, an arcane and foreign language that must be acquired through practice. "Companions" and other handbooks and encyclopedias can be counted on to note that William Shakespeare and Edmund Spenser used distinctive sonnet forms. Literary dictionaries, on the other hand, are needed to explain and illustrate their differences. No single dictionary will be adequate to answer every potential literary reference question. Librarians are advised to hesitate (or balk) when asked to weed them.

The most familiar dictionaries of literary terms include C. Hugh Holman and William Hammon's *A Handbook of Literature* (5th ed., New York: Macmillan, 1986), M. H. Abram's *A Glossary of Literary Terms* (5th ed., New York: Holt, Rinehart and Winston, 1988), and Alex Preminger's *Princeton Encyclopedia of Poetry and Poetics* (Princeton, N.J.: Princeton University Press, 1975). Much time can be saved by consulting Laurence Urdang and Frank R. Abate's *Literary, Rhetorical, and Linguistics Terms Index* (Detroit, Mich.: Gale, 1983) before proceeding beyond these few standard dictionaries. Urdang and Abate provide a cross index to thousands of terms defined in some seventeen various general, genre, and period, critical-term dictionaries and compilations. Such potential time-savers should be cherished.

Similarly, dictionaries of fictional characters, anonyma, and pseudonyma are also particularly valuable in literary research. Such works as Samuel Halkett and John Laing's *A Dictionary of Anonymous and Pseudonymous Publications in the English Language* (3d ed., rev. and enl., Harlow, Eng.: Longman, 1980–) are used to identify real authors. Others, like Ebenezer Cobham Brewer's *Reader's Handbook of Famous Names in Fiction, Allusions, References, Proverbs, Plots, Stories, and Poems* (1899; reprint Detroit, Mich.: Gale, 1966) and William Freeman's *Dictionary of Fictional Characters* (Boston, Mass.: The Writer, 1974), are routinely used to identify fictional characters. Specialized guides to characters appearing in works of particular genres, such as Thomas L. Berger and William C. Bradford's *An Index of Characters in English Printed Drama to the Restoration* (Englewood, Colo.: Microcard Editions Books, 1975), as well as to those appearing in the works of individual authors are also useful. Taplinger Publishing Company (New York) and

Elm Tree Books' (London) Who's Who in Literature series includes dictionaries of characters in the works of Charles Dickens, Thomas Hardy, D. H. Lawrence, and Henry James. Volumes in Archon Books' Plots and Characters Series identify the characters of Jane Austen, Charlotte and Emily Brontë, George Eliot, James Fenimore Cooper, Edgar Allan Poe, Herman Melville, Mark Twain, and Theodore Dreiser.

The many uses of dictionaries of English-language vocabulary for research on English literature are obvious. Contrary to what many may believe, however, not all problems can be resolved by consulting the *Oxford English Dictionary*. Coverage of antecedents of modern English is provided by Joseph Bosworth and T. Northcote Toller's *Anglo-Saxon Dictionary* (1882–1892, 1921; reprint, London, Eng.: Oxford University Press, 1972); by the more comprehensive, currently-in-progress *Dictionary of Old English* (now being released in microform sections by the Dictionary for Old English Project, Centre for Medieval Studies, University of Toronto); and by Hans Kurath, Sherman M. Kuhn, and John Reidy's *Middle English Dictionary* (Ann Arbor, Mich.: University of Michigan Press, 1952–   ). Similarly, the numerous well-known general dictionaries of English-language slang, usage, quotations, proverbs, and other "-isms" are complemented by myriad similarly specialized dictionaries for the vocabularies of periods, genres, and individual authors. Such works as *Stevenson's Book of Shakespeare's Quotations* (1937; reprint, London, Eng.: Cassell, 1969) and C. T. Onions's *A Shakespeare Glossary* (3d ed., New York: Oxford University Press, 1986) are classic examples likely to be found in every reference collection. Others like R. W. Dent's *Proverbial Language in English Drama Exclusive of Shakespeare* (Berkeley, Calif.: University of California Press, 1985), Norman Davis's *A Chaucer Glossary* (New York: Oxford University Press, 1979), and Jill B. Gidmark's *Melville's Sea Dictionary* (Westport, Conn.: Greenwood Press, 1982) will be located in reference collections according to particular needs.

The availability of the electronic version of the *Oxford English Dictionary* on CD-ROM, which includes the 1933 text of the first edition, presents enormous opportunities for literary research. The capacity to sort the *Oxford English Dictionary*'s approximately 415,000 entries by their various features, including the lemmas, etymologies, labels, and definitions, as well as by the dates, authors, cited works, and the more than 2 million cited texts potentially allows researchers to attempt to identify, for example, all of the words that Sir James A. H. Murray, the dictionary's editor, and other Victorian scholars believed to derive from Turkish, words that referred to women in the fifteenth century, or words that constituted the vocabulary of astrology.

Biographies

In general, biographies of writers are not reference works, although they are certainly essential resources for literary research. Research collections should attempt to acquire all biographical materials on major literary figures.

Works of collective biography serve as important reference resources. Basic general biographical encyclopedias that are useful in literary reference work and research include the venerable *Dictionary of American Biography*, or *DAB*, (New York: Scribner, 1928–37; supplements, 1944–) and *Dictionary of National Biography*, or *DNB*, (London, Eng.: Smith, Elder, 1885–1901; supplements, 1903–). In these works noteworthy scholarship can be found: C. H. Herford wrote on Ben Jonson, Mark Van Doren on Walt Whitman, F. O. Matthiessen on Hart Crane, and J. I. M. Stuart on Dorothy Sayers. Bibliographies, typically identifying depositories of letters and other primary materials, accompany the essays. For factual and authoritative accounts of the lives of writers these works are unsurpassed.

More recent specialized biographical works, such as the *Dictionary of Literary Biography*, or *DLB* (Detroit, Mich.: Gale, 1978–), and *Contemporary Authors* (Detroit, Mich.: Gale, 1962–), have attempted to pull together biographical materials on a far wider range of writers than either the *DAB* or *DNB*. The *DLB*, now exceeding one hundred hefty volumes, intends to present essays on writers from all periods of English and American literature. Emphasis is presently on American authors, although the *DLB* has already included volumes on Canadian, French, and German writers. Literature in the *DLB* is broadly interpreted, including works by children's writers, screenwriters, journalists, literary critics, and historians, among others. The scope of *Contemporary Authors* is even more inclusive. Here, a contemporary writer is defined as anyone who has written a book and is still actively writing. Coverage includes not only literary writers but also practicing literary critics and scholars. *Contemporary Authors* is a staple of general as well as literary reference work. It is a source on which a reference librarian can depend for reliable, comprehensive bibliographic information on both a contemporary writer's and a critic's writings.

Other general reference works, like *Biography Index, Personal Name Index to the New York Times*, and numerous "who's who" publications, are also useful in literary research. The latter variety includes such single-volume works as those in St. Martin's Contemporary Writers of the English Language series, including *Contemporary Dramatists*, 4th ed., and *Contemporary Poets*, 4th ed.; and H. W. Wilson's Wilson Author Series, including *American Authors, 1600–1900* and *World Authors,*

1975–1980. Very fortunately, these biographical dictionaries as well as the *DAB, DNB, DLB, Contemporary Authors, Biography Index,* and several dozen other works are indexed in cumulative editions and annual updates of Gale's *Biography and Genealogy Master Index.* Indeed, accessing the online version of this comprehensive index is oftentimes the most convenient reference strategy for locating information on an obscure author.

Directories

Many of literature's directories are biographical. Such works as *Contemporary Authors,* volumes in St. Martin's Contemporary Writers of the English Language series, and *The Writers Directory* (Chicago: St. James Press, 1971–) are typically used for locating particular authors as well as for biographical information. Other directories, such as *The International Directory of Little Magazines and Small Presses* (Paradise, Calif.: Dustbooks, 1965–) and *MLA Directory of Periodicals* (New York: Modern Language Assn., 1979–), are substantially used as bibliographies.

Perhaps literary scholarship's most useful directory actually appears as part of its journal literature. The fifth issue of each volume of *PMLA* (New York: Modern Language Assn., 1884–), "the voice" of English-language and modern literature's major professional association, lists its membership; administrators of academic programs; specialized programs of study (such as women's studies, ethnic studies, film studies, and so forth); sponsored prizes, awards, grants, and fellowships; humanities research centers; forthcoming meetings; and other useful information. This issue of *PMLA* should be kept in reference collections.

Indexes, Review Sources, and Current Bibliographies

As suggested previously, the full range of general indexes is used in literary research. *Readers' Guide to Periodical Literature* covers a variety of journals that feature contemporary poetry, plays, and fiction, as well as popular commentaries on literature and reviews of literary works. Likewise, both the *Humanities Index* and *Arts and Humanities Citation Index* are especially useful in literary research. Of the nearly 300 journals indexed in the *Humanities Index,* about a third are literary or literature-related. It offers excellent access to creative works in all literary genres, the subjects of literary criticism, and reviews of both primary and secondary works. Although far more complex and difficult to use, *Arts and Humanities Citation Index*'s "Permuterm Index" offers especially detailed subject access to literary criticism. Indexes in other disciplines, such as *The Philosopher's Index* and *ERIC,* are also routinely used.

By far, however, the *MLA International Bibliography* remains the single index that most English-language literature's teaching faculty want their students to use. Through the late 1970s and early 1980s, this desire was perhaps both a bit idealistic and sadistic, in that a vast array of specialized secondary bibliographies for genres, periods, subjects, and individual authors had become available that oftentimes provided equally comprehensive and far more humane and convenient access to criticism. This situation, although somewhat altered with the drastic restructuring of the *MLA International Bibliography*'s physical format in 1981, was certainly substantially (and perhaps permanently) reversed with the current wide availability of the *MLA International Bibliography* online and CD-ROM versions. Now that previous decades' secondary bibliographies have significantly grayed, the electronic *MLA Bibliography* appears to be the resource of choice in the 1990s to produce their customized updates and supplements. Indeed, the *MLA Bibliography* seems to have left English literature's other prestigious bibliography, the Modern Humanities Research Association (MHRA) *Annual Bibliography of English Language and Literature* (Cambridge, Eng.: Cambridge University Press, 1921–), struggling in its wake. This is a rather unfortunate perception, as the relationship of these comprehensive bibliographies is complementary. Although the *MLA Bibliography* covers criticism for a greater number of authors, the MHRA *Annual Bibliography* includes references to editions of literary works as well as book reviews, thereby offering somewhat deeper coverage for individual authors. Major academic libraries need to own both bibliographies to support advanced literary research.

Two annual publications, each perpetually a few years behind in publication, can be depended on to assess the states of English and American literary scholarship. These are *American Literary Scholarship* (Durham, N.C.: Duke University Press, 1965–) and *Year's Work in English Studies* (London, Eng.: Murray, 1921–). Their important contributions cannot be overstated. Each provides descriptions and evaluations of the primary and secondary works for genres, periods, and authors. Their contributed review essays by specialists can be used to bring up-to-date the coverage of specialized research guides. In addition to these general serial bibliographies and indexes, other specialized ones cover specific periods and genres. These, of course, include such well-known works as the *Essay and General Literature Index*, *Play Index*, *Short Story Index*, and *Granger's Index to Poetry*, as well as *The Eighteenth Century: A Current Bibliography* (Philadelphia, Pa.: American Society for Eighteenth-Century Studies, 1978–), *International Bibliography of Theatre* (New York: Theatre Research Data Centre, 1985–), *American Poetry Index* (Great Neck, N.Y.: Granger Book,

1983–), and *Index to American Periodical Verse* (Metuchen, N.J.: Scarecrow Press, 1971–).

Specialized indexes and bibliographies of criticism are also published as regularly featured articles in journals. *Bulletin of Bibliography* (Westport, Conn.: Meckler, 1897–) has published important checklists of primary and secondary works for such authors as Louise Bogan, Ellen Glasgow, John Dos Passos, Richard Wright, and Philip Roth, among many others, as well as for particular literary topics. The field's major review journals, *American Literature* (Durham, N.C.: Duke University Press, 1929–) and *Review of English Studies* (Oxford, Eng.: Clarendon Press, 1925–), include the tables of contents of selected major literary journals. Several other journals feature bibliographies that update other standard reference works. *Studies in Short Fiction* (Newberry, S.C.: Newberry College, 1963–), for example, annually publishes an index of short fiction appearing in anthologies as well as the feature "Annual Bibliography of Short Fiction Interpretation," compiled by Warren S. Walker, that updates Walker's *Twentieth-Century Short Story Explication* (3d ed., Hamden, Conn.: Shoe String Press, 1977) and its five supplements (1980, 1984, 1987, 1989, 1991) and index (1992).

Journals devoted to individual authors also publish important current bibliographies. *Shakespeare Quarterly* (Washington, D.C.: Folger Shakespeare Library, 1950–), for example, features a comprehensive bibliography of Shakespearean criticism, annually identifying as many as 4,000 items. *Thomas Hardy Annual* (Atlantic Highlands, N.J.: Humanities Press, 1983–), *James Joyce Quarterly* (Tulsa, Okla.: University of Tulsa, 1963–), *Keats-Shelley Journal* (New York: Keats-Shelley Association of America, 1952–), *Poe Studies* (Pullman, Wash.: Washington State University Press, 1967–), and *The Thomas Wolfe Review* (Akron, Ohio: University of Akron, 1977–) are just a few scholarly journals that regularly feature current bibliographies. William Wortman's *A Guide to Serial Bibliographies for Modern Literatures* (New York: Modern Language Assn., 1982) provides a comprehensive list of serial bibliographies published separately or as parts of journals. The point to be emphasized here is that a significant portion of literature's most up-to-date secondary bibliographies are not typically included in a library's reference collection, but rather in its current periodicals display area and in its periodical stacks.

Concordances

A reference work peculiar to the humanities and humanistic research is the concordance, a specialized comprehensive or selective index of the words that constitute a literary work or an author's canon. The usefulness of such a work continues to escape many librarians. For research that requires the close reading of the text, it is most valuable to be able to compare one part of the text with another. A concordance allows this by breaking a single text, such as that of Ralph Waldo Emerson's *Nature*, or even multiple texts, like the plays of William Shakespeare, into component elements—individual words (or, in the cases of Ezra Pound and James Joyce, particular symbols or characters)—and rearranging them by alphabetical or topical occurrences. It remains worthwhile to emphasize that a concordance's usefulness is relative to the authority of the text upon which it is based. A concordance to an unreliable text, no matter how well executed, can yield only unreliable information. As a result, the concordance is rather like the last frontier of primary research tools on an author. In general, a reliable text must precede its production.

The availability of electronic information technology in the 1970s radically multiplied the number of concordances that were produced. The recent advent of even more sophisticated and affordable optical scanning devices, on the other hand, suggests that the printed index may soon be rendered obsolete. Scholars and students can quickly scan and index the texts of their choice in ways that take little more time than making photocopies. Likewise, CD-ROM products like Electronic Text Corporation's *Wordcruncher Disk* conveniently contain both the transmogrified texts of selected standard editions of literary works, such as those of The Library of America editions of Mark Twain's *Huckleberry Finn* and Herman Melville's *Moby Dick*, as well as powerful concordance programs. Scholars and students need only choose among the CD-ROM's various indexing options to produce either comprehensive or selected concordances to particular texts.

Notwithstanding the availability of this technology, reference librarians will continue to need to invest in published concordances. Advanced research will always require the tedious reading of such works. Like Strong's prestigious *Analytical Concordance to the Bible*, concordances to the works of the most important or frequently studied authors or concordances that offer unique linguistic information are usually shelved in reference collections. These will include works like John S. P. Tatlock and Arthur G. Kennedy's *A Concordance to the Complete Works of Geoffrey Chaucer* (1927; reprint, Gloucester, Mass.: Peter Smith, 1963); Marvin Spevack's *A Complete and Systematic Concordance to the Works of Shakespeare* (Hildesheim, Ger.: Georg Olms, 1968–1980) or its abridgment, *The Harvard Concordance to Shakespeare* (Cambridge, Mass.: Harvard University Press, 1973); and Jess B. Bessinger, Jr.'s *A Concordance to the Anglo-Saxon Poetic Records* (Ithaca, N.Y.: Cornell University Press, 1978), a volume in Cornell University Press's well regarded Cornell Concordances. The latter series also includes concordances to the works of Ben Jonson, George Herbert, William Congreve,

Emily Dickinson, and e. e. cummings. Garland has published several series of concordances for the works of such authors as Daniel Defoe, the Brontës, Herman Melville, Henry James, and Joseph Conrad, among others, as well as individual volumes for the works of John Keats, George Meredith, Sylvia Plath, Alexander Pope, and Ezra Pound. Although other trade publishers have also produced concordances in the past (Scarecrow Press for E. M. Forster and Gerard Manley Hopkins, and Gale for Benjamin Franklin and Eugene O'Neill), the publication of a concordance has frequently been undertaken by its compiler. Others, for Robert Lowell and Edwin Arlington Robinson, have been completed as dissertations. On the other hand, as of this date no concordances have been published for the dramatic works of Ben Jonson or William Wycherley, or for the works of Mark Twain or W. D. Howells.

Conclusion

It is significant that rumblings against the usefulness of subject specialists seem to have become increasingly audible at the time when librarians who select literature (largely in major academic research institutions) have recognized themselves as specialists. William Katz observed that "As more and more information becomes topic- rather than discipline-oriented, the old argument that the librarian is better as a generalist than as a subject specialist is increasingly true." Such a "trained generalist," Katz suggested, can more readily cross disciplinary lines.[29] Meanwhile, Dennis W. Dickinson has argued that the subject specialist's days are numbered. The advent of innovative approval plans, publication on demand, and cooperative resource sharing, as Dickinson points out, certainly relieves the subject specialist in English-language literature of a great number of traditional collection development responsibilities, many of which (like religiously reading reviews) were somewhat tedious and some (like the typing of forms for firm orders) altogether unpleasant.[30] Dickinson's vision of a subject specialist's responsibilities is, however, a rather narrow one. Selection of materials is just one of a literature librarian's routine duties. Relief from one task will only allow the investment of greater effort in the larger and more user-focused activities of interpretation of the collection through traditional public services, such as reference work and user education (including those

29. William A. Katz, *Reference and Online Services Handbook: Guidelines, Policies, and Procedures for Librarians* Vol. 2 (New York: Neal-Schuman, 1986), 31.

30. Dennis W. Dickinson, "Subject Specialists in Academic Libraries: the Once and Future Dinosaurs," in *New Horizons for Academic Libraries*, ed. Robert D. Stueart and Richard D. Johnson (New York: Saur, 1979), 438–44.

taking advantage of innovative electronic information technologies), as well as permit a wider variety of opportunities for familiar and collegial interaction with the literature collection's constituents. Contrary to Dickinson's dark prediction, the future of the specialization in English-language literature librarianship remains as brightly certain as human-kind's interest in expressing itself. While subject specialists in disciplines in the sciences and social sciences might look at the future with concern, it is doubtful whether any variety of innovative technology will ever be capable of displacing the interpretive role of the subject specialist in any field of the humanities. Humankind's creative endeavors, whether in art, music, or literature, cannot be so readily mechanically accessed. In both American academic and public libraries, the subject specialist in English-language literature is, if nothing else, the consummate generalist.

Professional Readings

Adams, Randolph G. "Librarians as Enemies of Books." *Library Quarterly* 7 (July 1937): 317–31.

Baker, S. L., and G. W. Shepherd. "Fiction Classification Schemes." *RQ* 27 (Winter 1987): 245–51.

Bowers, Fredson. "The Function of Bibliography." *Library Trends* 7 (Apr. 1959): 497–510.

_____. *Principles of Bibliographical Description*. Princeton, N.J.: Princeton University Press, 1949.

Broadus, Robert N. *Selecting Materials for Libraries*. New York: H. W. Wilson, 1981.

Brown, Arthur. "The Text, the Bibliographer, and the Librarian." In *Otium et Negotium: Studies in Onomatology and Library Science Presented to Olaf Von Feilitzen*, edited by Folke Sandgren, 23–31. Acta Bibliothecae Regiae Stockholmiensis, vol. 16. Stockholm, Swed.: P. A. Norstedt and Soner, 1973.

Budd, John. "A Citation Study of American Literature: Implications for Collection Management." *Collection Management* 8 (Summer 1986): 49–62.

Calhoun, John C., James K. Bracken, and Kenneth L. Firestein. "Modeling an Academic Approval Program." *Library Resources and Technical Services* 34 (July 1990): 367–79.

Cogswell, James A. "The Organization of Collection Management Functions in Academic Libraries." *Journal of Academic Librarianship* 13 (Nov. 1987): 268–76.

Cudden, J. A. *A Dictionary of Literary Terms and Literary Theory*. 3d ed. Oxford, Eng.: Basil Blackwell, 1991.

Dickinson, Dennis W. "Subject Specialists in Academic Libraries: The Once and Future Dinosaurs." In *New Horizons for Academic Libraries*, edited by Robert D. Stueart and Richard D. Johnson, 438–44. New York: Saur, 1979.

Ford, James E. "The Natural Alliance between Librarians and English Teachers in Course-Related Library Use Instruction." *College & Research Libraries* 43 (Sept. 1982): 379–84.

Hanford, James Holly. "The American Scholar and His Books." *PMLA* 74 (May 1959): 30–36.

Heinzkill, Richard. "Characteristics of References in Selected Scholarly English Literary Journals." *Library Quarterly* 50 (1980): 352–65.

———. "Retrospective Collection Development in English Literature: An Overview." *Collection Management* 9 (Spring 1987): 55–65.

Hopkins, Richard L. "Perspectives on Teaching Social Sciences and Humanities Literatures." *Journal of Education for Library and Information Science* 28 (Fall 1987): 136–51.

Howard-Hill, T. H. "The Place of Bibliography in the Graduate Curriculum: Introductory Remarks." *Literary Research Newsletter* 9 (Fall 1984): 45–52.

Intner, S. S. "The Fiction of Access to Fiction." *Technicalities* 7 (July 1987): 12–14.

Katz, William A. *Introduction to Reference Work.* 5th ed. New York: McGraw-Hill, 1987.

———. *Reference and Online Services Handbook: Guidelines, Policies, and Procedures for Librarians.* Vol. 2. New York: Neal-Schuman, 1986.

McCorison, Marcus A. "Bibliography and Libraries at the Brink: A Jeremiad." *Papers of the Bibliographical Society of America* 78 (1984): 127–36.

McPheron, William, Stephen Lehmann, Craig Likness, and Marcia Pankake, eds. *English and American Literature: Sources and Strategies for Collection Development.* ACRL Publications in Librarianship, no. 45. Chicago: American Library Assn., 1987.

Marcuse, Michael J. "Special Issue: The Bibliography and Methods Course." *Literary Research* 12 (Spring-Summer 1987).

Mosher, Paul H. "Collection Development to Collection Management: Toward Stewardship of Library Resources." *Collection Management* 4 (Winter 1982): 41–48.

Nordloh, David. "General Reference Works." *American Literary Scholarship* (1986): 481–88.

Oppenheim, Rosa. "Computerized Bibliographic Searching in Literary Studies." *Literary Research Newsletter* 10 (Winter-Spring 1985): 17–34.

Orr, Leonard. *A Dictionary of Critical Theory.* Westport, Conn.: Greenwood Press, 1991.

Osburn, Charles B. *Academic Research and Library Resources: Changing Patterns in America.* Westport, Conn.: Greenwood Press, 1979.

Ross, J. E. "Artists and Poets Online: Issues in Cataloging and Retrieval." *Cataloging and Classification Quarterly* 7 (Spring 1987): 91–104.

Snyder, Henry L. "The English Short-Title Catalogue." *Papers of the Bibliographical Society of America* 82 (1988): 333–36.

Steinberg, Susan J., and Marcia Pankake. "English and American Literature, with Notes on Some Commonwealth Literatures." In *Selection of Library Materials in the Humanities, Social Sciences, and Sciences,* edited by Patricia A. McClung, 51–77. Chicago: American Library Assn., 1985.

Stern, Madeleine. "Characteristics of the Literature of Literary Scholarship." *College and Research Libraries* 44 (July 1983): 199–209.

Stevens, Roland E., and Linda C. Smith. *Reference Work in the University Library.* Littleton, Colo.: Libraries Unlimited, 1986.

Stokes, Roy. "The Teaching of Bibliography." *Library Trends* 7 (Apr. 1959): 582–91.

Tanselle, G. Thomas. "Bibliographers and the Library." *Library Trends* 25 (Apr. 1977): 745–62.

Weintraub, Karl J. "The Humanistic Scholar and the Library." *Library Quarterly* 50 (Jan. 1980): 22–39.

Wortmann, A. William, and David D. Mann. "The Introduction to Research and Bibliography Course." *Literary Research Newsletter* 10 (Winter-Spring 1985): 5–16.

Music

Elisabeth Rebman

Music is common to all cultures, but the emphasis of American libraries has traditionally been music of European-influenced Western cultures, concentrating on music of the high-art tradition. Such music is often referred to as classical music. Music of that long tradition has been notated and much has been written about it. These manuscript and printed resources have been the mainstays of library collections until the twentieth century, when the technological development of sound recordings added an important new dimension to library resources. In recent times, a proliferation of nonprint materials of relevance to music, including videorecordings and computer software, has expanded library resources and offered new possibilities for the study of music.

Music libraries may be found in public or private academic institutions, such as universities, colleges, or conservatories of music, and also in public libraries. Depending on the mission of the parent institution, they range in size and emphasis from research collections to collections of music for performance to general collections. Specialized research libraries with significant music collections may also be found in archives, historical societies, monasteries, and seminaries. Other special music libraries exist to serve a specific function for broadcasting companies, publishers, recording manufacturers, or performing groups such as orchestras and opera companies. Collection development efforts for these music libraries will reflect their specific functions and the constituencies they serve.

The collection's composition, its organization, and its available user services depend on the mission of the library and the needs of its users. Most general and large research music libraries contain a wide variety of materials. While they may differ in size and specialties, they share much in common in the issues of collection development and maintenance, organization of and access to materials, and service to users.

Profile of Music

The discipline of music may be divided into three main subfields: composition, performance, and the study of music. However, in the latter part of the twentieth century the areas of concern and the scholarly methods in the study of music have broadened considerably, blurring the traditional distinctions between subdisciplines.

Musical composition is the art of creating music. Musical compositions in the Western art tradition are captured by being notated for use by musicians who will perform them. Depending on historical context and relevant performance practices, a musical score gives a musician directions, with varying degrees of specificity, to bring the composer's intentions to life in sound. Because systems for musical notation vary substantially throughout the history of Western music, the modern performer re-creating a composition faces the challenge of understanding notational conventions, characteristics of sound, and a historical performing context. Traditional and modern notational systems also exist for music of the high-art traditions of non-Western cultures, such as those of some Asian countries, but these scores are rarely found in Western music libraries. Music of many cultures or subcultures, including that of national or folk tradition, is not notated for later performance; instead, composition and performance occur simultaneously, composer and performer being one. Western music of chiefly improvisatory composition, including much jazz and popular music, falls into this category. Musical compositions of this type may sometimes be notated after the fact of performance/composition, but they are more usually and completely captured for study through sound recordings.

Performance of music is the realization of a musical composition in sound and time. In a sense, a musical composition is brought to life only in performance, the notation of it being only a representation. To give meaning to their performance, musicians must develop a technical mastery of their instruments or voices as well as an artistic sense. They achieve these in part, by studying and communicating with other musicians, by listening to musical performances, and by studying music history and theory. Therefore, library resources are important for the development of the performer as well as the scholar. In the second half of the twentieth century, performance practice has become an important area of study for performers interested in re-creating music of an earlier era. To do so in a manner as close as possible to the way in which it was played and heard at the time of its composition, these performers apply historical study to inform their own performances. Originally of interest primarily to early music performers, historical performance practice is now also used by performers of music from the late eighteenth century through the early twentieth century.

The study of music involves a broad range of overlapping subfields and areas of investigation, including the study of composition and performance. The study of music as a scholarly discipline is called musicology, which comprises several major subdisciplines, including historical and systematic musicology, music theory, and ethnomusicology.

Historical musicology is a humanistic discipline whose traditions and methods are similar to those of history, art history, and literature. It divides music into historical style periods that parallel those from other disciplines, the broadest being antiquities, Middle Ages, Renaissance, baroque, classical, romantic, and modern periods. Historical musicology, which originated in the nineteenth-century German academic tradition and became established as a field of study in American universities in the post-war years, values and studies music of the past. Its object of study is the history of Western art music with its focus on composed, notated music of an assumed enduring value. The major concerns of historical musicology have been to establish the most reliable written texts (scores) possible, to correctly attribute works to their composers, and to study and document the lives of composers and their processes of composition. Having established authoritative texts and the related historical contexts, historical musicology seeks to analyze and classify works in order to define a genre, form, or style for a period, region, or composer. Thus, the areas of paleography, textual criticism, history of notation, and archival research play an important role in musicological research. The approach in traditional historical musicology has been objective, quasi-scientific, and objectively verifiable.

During the latter part of the twentieth century, areas of concern and scholarly methods of music historians have broadened. These new areas have included more critical investigations and speculative conclusions. Also, the historical performance movement has attempted to apply musicological research to influence the performance of music of previous eras with different performance traditions. Its objective is to re-create as far as possible the performing conditions of a composition's own time and place, including appropriate instruments and style of playing.

Only in recent years has criticism been developed as a part of traditional musicology. Academic music criticism is the study of meaning and value in musical works, which includes understanding them in their historical and cultural context. A partial, formalistic kind of criticism occurs with the analysis of an individual work, which has long been the concern of music theorists. A musician's interpretation of a work in performance is yet another type of criticism that transcends words.

Music theory is the study of the abstract principles embodied in music and the sounds of which it consists. It is a field with connections to physics and acoustics, cognitive psychology, mathematics, and computer science. Analysis is a branch of music theory that studies musical structure. Many analytical methods have been developed for the various methods of composition used both historically and currently. As an example, for an eighteenth-century western European piece of music, one might use a form of harmonic analysis that would not be appropriate for music from other periods or cultures. The discipline is also concerned with both the history of music theory through historical writings and the study and development of theories of existing repertoires. In the broad sense, it can be thought of as a part of musicology, but it is often perceived as a separate discipline with its own professional organizations, journals, and degree programs.

Ethnomusicology, an interdisciplinary study in music, is the study of music in its human context, specifically music outside the Western art tradition, and is concerned with music serving a variety of functions in a variety of cultural contexts. With a long and independent tradition of scholarship and method of investigation, ethnomusicology had its beginnings in the 1880s when the invention of the phonograph made possible the preservation of the disappearing music of non-Western cultures. Because it analyzes music with little or no written tradition, ethnomusicology applies much of the research methodology of anthropology, using fieldwork and recordings. First called "comparative musicology," ethnomusicology became a recognized academic field at the beginning of the twentieth century. In the 1920s and 1930s, scholars like Marius Schneider and Charles Seeger began to combine the concepts and methods of musicology (the study of music sound and structure) and anthropology (the study of music in culture). Since that time, scholarly organizations and academic programs in ethnomusicology have been established. From its beginning and to this day, ethnomusicological investigation has examined both the musical diversity of human cultures and the universality across all cultures.

Systematic musicology is the name sometimes given to the study of diverse topics in music that transcend historical and geographical boundaries or intersect with other disciplines. While there is no universal agreement on what systematic musicology encompasses, and while overlaps exist with ethnomusicology, historical musicology, and music theory, this area of study includes acoustics, aesthetics, psychology, physiology, sociology, pedagogy, iconography, organology (the study and classification of musical instruments), bibliography, and discography (bibliography for recorded sound). Music can be studied in relation to other arts. Musical iconography is the study of musical subject matter in works of art and depends on the critical tools of both music and art history. The value of artworks as musicological evidence has been recognized since the early part of this century, but it only recently has begun to be developed as a field in its own right. In addition, the disciplines of computer science and linguistics are of increasing importance in musical study. New interdisciplinary fields such as popular culture, ethnic studies, and gender studies include music among their subjects of study. The marked rise in interdisciplinary investigations in the latter part of the twentieth century has developed many of these fields, broadening the approach by adding new research materials and methodology and a new collaboration of music scholars with those in other disciplines. It is not surprising, for example, to find sociologists writing about music topics or musicologists writing from a sociological perspective in their respective professional literatures.

The Work of Composers, Performers, and Music Scholars

Composers draw upon their entire musical experience and education in the process of composition, and a background of library use may play a great role. While composers do not rely directly on the library for the creative process, they often use it for related needs, such as finding editions or explications of literary texts they are setting to music. Since the late 1940s, some composers have used electronic equipment and computers to produce or manipulate sound, which can be used to create a composition or a part to be used with live performers. More recently they have also been able to produce, by means of music printing software, many kinds of musical notation meant to be used by composers for composing, music instruction, music publishing, and reading by performers. Of course, music libraries are repositories for musical compositions in notated and recorded form, analyses of compositions, as well as works about the history and practice of composition and music theory; but these are byproducts of the creative act instead of fodder for it. The composer's work is future-oriented, while the library is a repository for work of the past.

Similarly, performing musicians have no unequivocal need to consult libraries in preparing for a performance. They may use libraries to read scores, hear recorded performances, study analyses of compositions, consult background literature to prepare program notes, or seek translations of texts set to music. Performers striving to reconstruct a historically accurate performance may also read treatises on performance practices of the past, consult scholarly editions to find the most accurate version of the music, and read relevant commentaries. As with the composer, the performer's work is an essentially individual artistic undertaking that does not depend primarily on the work of others found in libraries.

Musicologists, on the other hand, depend on the resources of the library as the primary element of their work. Their musical investigation is historical, cumulative, and document-based. They need materials contemporary to the topic under investigation as well as historical and current research related to it. Musicology is always related to the music and writings of others found in a variety of print and nonprint sources in libraries. In this historical discipline neither primary nor secondary source materials "go out-of-date," but are added to by new literature. Depending on the type of research undertaken, different library materials may be the focus of different researchers. For example, while musicologists need primarily print and manuscript sources for their work, ethnomusicologists rely on recordings. In addition to musicologists, teachers, students, independent researchers, and journalistic critics conduct musical research at a variety of levels and for differing purposes.

The serious academic researcher communicates with other scholars and the wider public through publication of journal articles, monographs, and other kinds of professional writing. The meetings and conferences of professional organizations of musicologists, music theorists, ethnomusicologists, and others also provide an important forum for scholarly communication through general discussion and formal presentation of papers. Many organizations also publish their own journals, thereby providing a very important means of scholarly communication. Personal communications among scholars with similar interests allow another kind of national and international interchange to occur. Most music scholars have institutional connections and, thus, have personal contact with other faculty and researchers within music and with members of the broader academic community. In addition to keeping current with professional literature and research activities, music scholars also follow contemporary concert life and trends in composition.

Music Library Materials, Equipment, and Facilities

Music libraries have traditionally had many special features distinguishing them from other humanities libraries, whose collections center around books and book-like materials. In addition to books and periodicals, music libraries also have as central to their collections scores for works of music. Microforms play an important role as a means of making available both manuscript and printed music as well as writings on music. Since the rise of sound recordings in the early twentieth century, libraries have collected music in recorded as well as notated form. Although scores, recordings, and book materials continue to hold the primary place in music library collections, the recent upsurge in other nonprint forms with relevance to music has begun to diversify these collections even further.

Notable new nonprint materials in music libraries include visual recordings of musical performances and master classes that are valuable for performers and scholars alike. The availability of commercially produced, standardized format videorecordings of operas, ballets, and other musical works with a visual component has facilitated collection growth in these materials. However, videorecordings do not play the essential role in most music instruction that sound recordings do. Although not yet a part of many music library collections, computer software and CD-ROM technology will surely have a major impact on all areas of music and music library materials in the coming years. Software for music instruction, notation systems to print music, and reference works on CD-ROM are already available in some libraries. Hypertext technology, which allows a multidimensional approach and can include both sound and visual images along with text, has many potential applications of import for both music instruction and library reference materials and is already seen in some commercial products.

Virtually any form of material collected by general libraries can be found in music libraries. Many music research libraries contain special collections and archival materials. Among these are rare books and scores in manuscript or printed forms, historical sound recordings, visual forms such as photographs and blueprint plans drawn from historical musical instruments, and ephemeral materials of all kinds. Some music libraries have collections of realia, such as musical instruments or materials for music education. Others collect music for performance with individual parts for use by members of large performing groups such as orchestras or opera companies.

Because a significant portion of a typical music library collection comprises materials other than books, special conditions for storage, physical organization, preservation, and use of these materials are required. Since music library materials vary substantially in physical format, size, and requirements for use, different types of materials are ordinarily shelved apart from each other. Separate shelving of physically alike materials affords not only efficient use of library space but better conditions for preservation of the materials. However, different forms must frequently be used together in music study, and library facilities should provide for integrated use of materials. For example, recording playback stations should have table space so the listener can follow a score while hearing the music.

Many works in music libraries have accompanying material in another physical format, or are mixed-media works. Sound recordings often have inserted notes of varying degrees of physical or intellectual substance. Books or even periodical issues may be published with accompanying sound recordings that are housed in a pocket or physically separate. Regardless of how they were issued by the publisher or intended to be used, such materials are often physically separated and shelved with others of their type for conservationally sound and secure storage, especially if their importance or physical intractability suggests it. This treatment is not usually a problem for users already accustomed to a division of materials according to physical form.

The diverse forms of materials collected in music libraries require a variety of specialized shelving as well as means for user access. There must be space for users to examine print material of varying sizes, to play audio and videorecordings individually or in groups without disturbing other users, to examine rare or fragile materials in a secure and safe area, and to use computer-based resources in the library's collection. There should be photocopy machines with paper large enough to copy musical scores (11 by 17 inches) and microform readers with printers, essential for making copies of the music to be played. An electric piano with earphones is useful for playing musical examples or trying out musical editions that do not circulate.

Scores share much in common with books, since both are print materials. However, most classification schemes divide them into different shelving sequences for reasons of content and form. The average score is larger and thinner than the average book and is usually issued unbound. Therefore, shelving for scores needs to be deeper (12 inches), backed, and with more frequent and taller supports. Scores need to be bound in order to be shelved safely and to be preserved during use. Special binding techniques are needed for music, whether bound in-house or commercially. Binding should allow scores to lie flat on a music stand. Parts for individual players must be treated so that they may be stored together but used separately from each other or from a score with which they may have been issued. Although the average score is between 30 and 40 centimeters tall, libraries also collect large numbers of miniature scores, less than 20 centimeters tall, for study purposes. These are often kept in a separate shelving sequence distinguished by a designation of size added to the call numbers. Scores of contemporary music are often issued in many nonstandard oversizes. They are also shelved apart from other scores, standing upright or lying flat, depending on their size. Printed scores with an electronic music part on tape or music existing in computer-read form require only physical separation and storage suitable for each component part.

While the forms in which scores are issued have been quite static, the forms of sound recordings have changed and continue to change vastly with continuing advances in technology. An essential part of music library collections, sound recordings have nonetheless been an expensive proposition because the materials and equipment wear out or are superseded by new forms. Most libraries withdraw outdated forms of sound recordings or remove them to archival collections. Sound recording archives keep all forms of recordings as well as the means to play them back and to record copies for study. Sound recordings of events in the past are valuable historical documents; they can be a primary source for understanding historical performance practices and for studying improvisatory or un-notated music, such as jazz, popular music, and music of non–Western cultures.

Libraries have collected and continue to collect current forms that are available for purchase. The first form collected in a major way by libraries was the 78 rpm disc, 10 or 12 inches in diameter, heavy, and breakable. The long-playing (LP) 33⅓ rpm disc, usually 12 inches in diameter and made of unbreakable vinyl, became the main collected form beginning in the 1950s. The dominant form for nearly forty years, the LP requires oversized (12 inches deep) shelving for the large, thin, heavy discs in cardboard containers. Magnetic recording tape was developed in the 1940s, but commercial prerecorded tapes were not immediately available; later, they usually merely duplicated disc versions. Music libraries often had open-reel tape collections of locally recorded concerts or of anthologies compiled by faculty for required listening assignments. In the 1960s, stereophonic sound became the standard, and cassette tapes began to be a widely distributed commercial form. Digital sound recordings appeared in the 1980s, and by the end of the decade, compact disc (CD) recordings replaced the LP as not only the predominant commercially available form but also the form in which musical repertoire of interest to music libraries is being published and collected. Less than 5 inches in diameter and played with a laser/computer, CDs seem ideal for library collections since repeated playing does not degrade the surface as was the case with 78 and 33⅓ rpm discs. The cueing and ability for direct access to any segment on the CD is of great utility in studying music since listeners often need to repeat a segment of music many times. The CD's small size is at once a space-saving advantage and a potential problem for circulation control. Each of these recording forms requires its own particular type of playback machine, and a change in equipment is needed with each new form introduced. The selection of playback equipment for libraries should be based on durability, ease of use, and availability of repair.

Although rather new in music library collections, videorecordings share with sound recordings the same issues of rapidly changing forms, uncertainty over what will become the standard forms, and the need for diverse durable and repairable playback equipment. At the present time, most videorecordings of music are videocassettes in VHS format. Musical works are also available on videodiscs, which are laser discs like CDs but 12 inches in diameter. Some playback machines can play both sound CDs and videodiscs, but the availability of inexpensive CD-only playback machines and the need for a monitor for videodiscs makes dual use of such machines uneconomical. Videorecording collections in academic music libraries are not as well developed as those in public libraries. In the former, they are not yet seen as essential to most music instruction, while in the latter they are widely used for avocational or recreational purposes.

Computers have played a part in music libraries since the 1970s, but they were not for public use until recently. Bibliographic utilities, such as OCLC and RLIN, have been used by many music libraries for cataloging their collections. This computerized cataloging was first used to produce cards for the card catalog and later for online public access catalogs that replaced or supplemented the card catalog. Computerized indexes of value to music, which needs access to retrospective as well as current literature, have been not as well developed as those for other disciplines, especially those in the sciences. However, online searches of indexes such as *Arts and Humanities Citation Index* (Philadelphia, Pa.: Institute for Scientific Information, 1976–) and recent parts of *RILM Abstracts of Music Literature* (New York: International RILM Center, 1967–) are available for a fee, searched by a librarian instead of the user, through brokers such as BRS and DIALOG. Others, like Expanded Academic Index, which includes several music journals, have been loaded as separate databases in online library catalogs such as the University of California's MELVYL system. The catalog user may use such databases without mediation or charge.

Two new types of computer applications are becoming important in music library collections: one primarily for instructional, creative, or research activities and another for bibliographic needs. A variety of commercially and locally produced music software programs are now available for use with different microcomputers. As yet there is little standardization, and the publication of these materials is aimed at the individual user, rather than libraries. Most music libraries have not yet made strong commitments to buy and make available software for use either inside the library or for circulation. Because of the issues of many incompatible forms, purchase and space requirements of equipment to use the software, and copyright considerations, a sure course of action has not yet been suggested. At present, most music software use is found outside the library in the music department. Software is often developed

or used by faculty members with access to research or instructional funding for equipment and materials not available to the library, and the use
may not typically be thought of as a library activity. For example, use of
software for ear training or notating music takes a long time at a computer
station. Use of such programs in the library could be seen as analogous
to practicing an instrument, which takes place outside the library, even
when using music from the library. Therefore, these sorts of computer
facilities, which are extensions of other instructional activities, traditionally
have been and likely will continue to be housed in the music department.

On the other hand, CD-ROM technology is making available products
that are fully in keeping with the library's traditional function. Quite
a few reference works of some relevance to music have appeared and
many more are planned, including those of fundamental importance to
music research like *RILM Abstracts, MUSE CD-ROM* (Baltimore, Md.:
National Information Services Corp., 1989–) and *The Music Index on
CD-ROM* (Alexandria, Va.: Chadwyck-Healey, 1991–). Computer stations
for these materials may need earphones for sound as well as a monitor
for text and graphic images. Computer stations can be linked to file
servers and CD drives on which various CD-ROM reference works are
stored, providing shared access to single copies of these works. Floppy
disks are fragile, subject to damage from heat, magnetism, and touch; they
require protective storage and careful use. In contrast, CD-ROM laser discs
are the same size and type as audio CDs; thus, they are highly durable
for library use and can be easily and safely stored.

Special Considerations in the Music Library

Most musicians accept a music library's mission to preserve music for
continuing use by many users and buy their own copies of music they
need for study and performance. However, on music borrowed from the
library, circulation staff often find markings that must be erased upon
return, hastening the deterioration of the copy. The fragile nature of music
and recordings relative to their use causes special problems for preservation or replacement. Microfilming is not a viable preservation method
for most music since hard copy is necessary for use. Music published in
individual parts, as well as sound recordings issued in multiple discs,
requires attentive inventory and circulation control. Libraries usually do
not permit interlibrary lending of their sound recordings and special
collections materials because these materials are fragile or unique and
they require strictly controlled use.

Interpreting the music library's collections for the public requires
special approaches to reference service, collection-based exhibits, and

publicity. Reference work in music has particular challenges. It is frequently a lengthy process to identify and locate a particular piece of music because of the many variant and fragmentary title forms known to the user. Patrons of music libraries serving the general public often expect the reference librarian to identify a piece of music from the patron's humming or from a fragment of the text of a song.

In addition to their research value, music library materials frequently have an artifactual value that can be put to good purpose in promoting and publicizing the library. The variety and attractiveness of these materials make them suitable for exhibition as well as useful for concerts or events associated with the material exhibited. Some libraries even sponsor live or recorded concerts of music in their holdings, especially to showcase music that is important or unique but otherwise rarely heard.

Copyright and performance right laws covering music and recordings are evolving, complicated, and different from those for books. Music librarians must keep abreast of these laws and interpretations of them in literature on the music business and their own professional literature. The Music Library Association's Legislation Committee monitors legislation on copyright and performance rights.

Cataloging and Classification

There are several systems for the classification of music materials. The two most commonly used in the United States are the Library of Congress and the Dewey decimal classification systems. Many music libraries, especially research libraries, have adopted the Library of Congress classification system, though Dewey remains in wide use. Some specialized systems for music scores, like the Dickinson classification developed for the Vassar College Library,[1] were devised to organize music in a manner more suitable for study than performance. Such specialized systems and others locally devised to meet the needs of a particular collection are not frequently used. The ability to easily share cataloging through computerized bibliographic databases has given libraries increased economic reason to adopt a nationally recognized classification system and cataloging code. Outside the United States, decimal classifications based on Dewey are most commonly found.

---

1. Carol June Bradley, *The Dickinson Classification: A Cataloguing & Classification Manual for Music; Including a Reprint of the George Sherman Dickinson "Classification of Musical Compositions"* (Carlisle, Pa.: Carlisle Books, 1968).

Both the Library of Congress classification system and recent editions of the Dewey decimal classification system separate music scores from writings on music. The Library of Congress schedule, class M, is divided into three main sections: class M, Music; class ML, Literature of Music; and class MT, Music Instruction and Study. Class M, devoted to music itself, is further divided into miscellaneous collections, instrumental music, and vocal music categories. Class ML is most broadly subdivided into type or form of book (including periodicals, libretti, dictionaries and encyclopedias, bibliography), history and criticism, and philosophy and physics of music. Class MT is divided chiefly into music theory, instrumental and vocal techniques, and pedagogical subdivisions. The Dewey decimal classification 780s were originally designed to intershelve books and music, unlike the Library of Congress system. Later editions of the Dewey decimal system suggested a division between books and music by adding an M to the classification numbers for scores. Dewey also classifies music into categories for miscellaneous collections, instrumental music, and vocal music, but it subarranges these categories differently from the Library of Congress class M. The music schedule of Dewey was substantially revised in the recent twentieth edition. The structure of "Phoenix 780" is now a unified arrangement according to the type of performance medium alone and provides special faceting to organize music more logically and consistently.

In most music libraries, both the book and score collections are classified and available for direct patron access. Often sound recordings and other nonprint materials in large collections are not classified or available in open stacks. These materials are often thought not to be physically amenable to browsing, they usually require special care for storage and use, and their initial novelty makes them subject to theft in unmediated access. Most recordings are thin, so it is difficult to read the title on the spine when they are shelved. Since many individual pieces or compositions of diverse instrumentation can be recorded together on a single sound recording, classification by Library of Congress or Dewey frequently results in a classification number so broad as to be meaningless. In public libraries with smaller collections of more varied content, sound recordings (or their containers) are often placed in bins or racks in broad categories for browsing as in a record store. Some use a classification system devised for public libraries called ANSCR, which organizes recordings primarily by type of music or spoken content instead of by instrumentation.[2] However, none of these systems adequately resolve the problems of shelving and access,

2. Caroline Saheb-Ettaba and Roger B. MacFarland, *ANSCR: The Alpha-Numeric System for Classification of Recordings* (Williamsport, Pa.: Bro-Dart, 1969).

and as a consequence, the most important access to sound recordings is through the library catalog.

Although recordings and other nonprint materials could usually be classified according to the systems noted, many libraries prefer not to use them. In libraries where nonprint materials are paged by library staff instead of being browsable by users, accession numbering can result in a more economical and useful shelf arrangement, allowing new recordings to be added at the end of a compacted shelving sequence. Locally devised prefixes can separate materials of a particular physical format from others.

Some libraries shelve sound recordings by manufacturer's label name and number. Such an arrangement is not always simple to establish and maintain because of changes in names and numbering systems resulting from complex, changing relationships of record companies and their licensees. This is particularly true when the library collection includes both current and retrospective recordings from both United States and foreign companies. However, an arrangement by label name and number not only gives the librarian a visual assessment of the library's holdings from a particular company but also a means of access to uncataloged recordings through trade discographies such as the Schwann catalogs.

Videorecordings, while sharing many properties of sound recordings, are more classifiable in that there is ordinarily not more than one work per item. Nevertheless, as for sound recordings, many libraries do not classify videorecordings and do not shelve them in open stacks. Unless videorecordings are browsable by the patron, classification has little value except, perhaps, to the initiated, who may use it as a browsing point for additional subject access in a library shelf list in manual or online form.

The most commonly used subject heading list for music is *Library of Congress Subject Headings*. Subject headings for books on music parallel those for other disciplines, focusing on topical subject headings. Works of music, on the other hand, are not "about" anything. Instead, works of music are given headings that indicate instrumentation (medium of performance) or form of composition. A feature of the Library of Congress subject heading structure is that form takes precedence over instrumentation. If a composition is written in a specific musical form, the heading will begin with the form name qualified by the instrumentation. If a composition is not in a named form, the heading gives instrumentation only. Thus, the Library of Congress classification scheme provides primary access according to instrumentation, whereas Library of Congress subject headings divide compositions for the same instrumental combination in the catalog. As a consequence, the shelf list provides the only access to what a library holds for a particular combination of instruments. The development of the MARC format for music and sound recordings provides for both specific instrumentation and form of composition in coded form regardless of the type of subject headings applied. Even with the MARC music format providing additional coded access related to subject, form, and instrumentation, Library of Congress subject headings are complicated, inconsistently constructed, and difficult to use. For example, a book about the sonata form is given the heading Sonata, and music written in sonata form, whether for a single sonata or for collected sonatas, is given the heading Sonatas. Whereas a book about Gregorian chant is given the heading Chants (Plain, Gregorian, etc.)—History and Criticism, music for the chants themselves is given the heading Chants (Plain, Gregorian, etc.). Although not ideal for music of the Western art tradition, these subject headings, even with recent additions and changes to the list, are quite inadequate for jazz, popular music, and music of non-Western cultures. Individuals and groups such as the Music Library Association have published special lists for music "other than Western art" and continue to try to improve the MARC format for coded access appropriate to these subjects.[3]

Most music libraries of any size use the *Anglo-American Cataloging Rules* (2d ed., rev., Chicago: American Library Assn., 1988) for description and access in their library catalogs. AACR2 can be used for any level of cataloging, from minimal level to full cataloging as applied by the Library of Congress. Many music libraries follow AACR2 as a national standard, through the Library of Congress published rule interpretations.

Description and access for books on music present no special problems that set them apart from books on other subjects. Music scores, sound recordings, and other nonbook materials require the application of specialized rules in AACR2 to describe them physically and intellectually. Music scores have their own peculiarities of publication, version, and form of musical presentation. Most music remains of enduring interest and may be republished with or without modification by the same or different publishers over many years. Music often has no title page, or a different kind of title page from books. Publication dates are frequently lacking. Publisher's numbers and plate numbers found on many pieces of music are important for determining the publication date and history of an edition.

3. Judith Kaufman, *Recording of Non-Western Music: Subject and Added Entry Access*, MLA Technical Reports, no. 5 (Ann Arbor, Mich.: Music Library Assn., 1977) and *Library of Congress Subject Headings for Recordings of Western Non-Classical Music*, MLA Technical Reports, no. 14 (Philadelphia, Pa.: Music Library Assn., 1983).

Music for more than one performer may be issued in several forms of musical presentation: as a score, or as a score with all parts. (*Score* is often used to describe any notated music. The term is used more precisely as music for more than one performer with all parts written so that they can be read simultaneously. Therefore, music for a single instrument cannot properly be called a score. A *part* is the single line of music followed by an individual when performing as part of a group.) A composition can also be issued in several versions that are needed for different purposes. For example, an opera might be published as a full score, as a vocal score (with instrumental parts reduced for piano), as a voice score (with no indication of instrumental parts), or as a libretto (with no music at all). An orchestral work might be published in more than one full score version: a large size intended for use in performance by a conductor or as a miniature score for study. The same composition may be issued in different editions—from unedited scores, or *Urtext*, to those heavily marked by an editor to show an opinion of the ideal text and how it should be performed. A musical work can be arranged in whole or in part for different instruments or voices, or the work can be used as the basis for a new composition. The different editions, forms of presentation, versions, and arrangements of a work must be noted in cataloging music so the user can find the type desired. Changes in form will, of course, affect the selection of the subject heading.

Sound and videorecordings share the same problems of intellectual access as written music, but their different physical characteristics must be described so that the user can determine the format of the work and what kind of equipment is needed to use it. Additionally, details about the performance and performers are described and given access, the latter by means of added entries. Since sound recordings often contain numerous compositions requiring analytical composer-uniform title added entries, their bibliographic records are typically several times longer than those for scores or books. These bibliographic records are expensive to create not only because of their length but because of the authority work involved. As with scores, publishers' numbers for sound recordings are important access points, since recorded "editions" (performances) are identified more precisely and efficiently by means of the publisher's label name and number than by place of publication, publisher, and publication date.

Music publications have two characteristics that have particular implications for cataloging and access: A composer frequently writes many compositions, some with the same indistinctive form title, e.g., "symphony"; and a single composition is often issued in many editions, versions, or arrangements. Furthermore, a composition is likely to be published under many different versions of its title, with each variation potentially in any language. For example, Beethoven's *Moonlight Sonata* might be published with that title in English or as *Mondscheinsonate* in German. It could be issued with its generic title, instrumentation, key, and numbering in any order or language, with all or some of these elements, or in combination with its distinctive title. Thus, the work could also be published with titles like *Sonata quasi una fantasia per il clavicembalo o pianoforte. Opera 27. No. 2* (its original title), or *Sonata (Moonlight) in C sharp minor. Op. 27, No. 2*. The language of the title page and editorial commentary in a piece of music may bear no relationship to the work itself, even when it has sung text. With such vast possibility for variation in title for a single work, uniform titles are routinely given to works of music in order to bring together in the library catalog all editions, versions, and arrangements of a work. Authority control is essential in music library catalogs for guiding the user to the desired work by providing cross references from title variants to uniform titles.

Under AACR2, the title selected as the uniform title is the composer's original title in the language in which it was presented. If the title consists only of the name of a type of composition, the uniform title is constructed in English in a conventional order: name of type of composition, instrumentation, numeric identifying elements, and key. Publishers do not always provide sufficient information to identify a composition without research. In such instances, a comparison of the music or sound on the recording with a thematic catalog that provides the opening notes of a composition or other editions of music can provide the information necessary to construct a uniform title. The numeric identifying element given in uniform titles for those composers for whom a bibliographer has prepared a thematic catalog is the number assigned to that work by the bibliographer, rather than incomplete or unclear opus numbering assigned by the composer or the publishers to those works; e.g., K. 429 would indicate that the composition is number 429 in Köchel's thematic catalog.[4]

All music librarians need to be informed about music cataloging issues in order to build, interpret, or catalog a music collection. Richard Smiraglia's *Music Cataloging: The Bibliographic Control of Printed and Recorded Music in Libraries* (Englewood, Colo: Libraries Unlimited, 1989) provides a comprehensive overview of descriptive cataloging, subject headings, classification systems, the MARC music format, and authority control for music materials. The *Music Cataloging Bulletin*,

---

4. Ludwig Ritter von Köchel, *Chronologisch-thematisches Verzeichnis sämmtlicher Tonwerke Wolfgang Amade Mozarts* (Leipzig, Ger.: Breitkopf & Härtel, 1862; numerous later eds.).

published monthly since 1970 by the Music Library Association with regular input from the Library of Congress, is essential reading for keeping up with current issues in music cataloging as well as current and proposed rule interpretations and classification and subject heading changes. Numerous other tools are available to aid the music cataloger and other music librarians.

Selection

In large research libraries, music librarians characteristically perform or oversee staff performing all library functions within the microcosm of the music library. Even in a setting with centralized operations for technical services, such activities as the acquisition, cataloging, and physical processing of music materials are usually performed in the music library or by specialist staff reporting to the music librarian. Not only are music materials inherently different, they are acquired from specialized sources and require specialized technical processing by persons who understand the nature and use of these materials.

The selection and acquisition of printed music presents special challenges to the librarian. In addition to different publishing and distributing firms, there is also a lack of systematic bibliography for music. Since there is no equivalent to *Books in Print* for music, librarians must rely on a variety of sources. *Music in Print Series* (6 vols. and annual suppls., Philadelphia, Pa.: Musicdata, 1974–) attempts to provide exhaustive lists of internationally published music, but it is impeded by inconsistency in the ways music publishers describe their offerings and by their imperfect cooperation in reporting new publications to the publisher. Music librarians also rely on lists of music currently received in professional and scholarly journals, the Library of Congress Cataloging Distribution Service (CDS) Alert Service slips, and catalogs and announcements from publishers and dealers. Foreign music dealers like Blackwell's Music Shop (Oxford, England), May and May (Salisbury, England), and Otto Harrassowitz are important sources for the acquisition of music published outside the United States. Harrassowitz's *European Music Catalogue* (Wiesbaden, Ger.: Harrassowitz, 1974–), published nine times a year, serves as a basic trade bibliography for Europe, including Eastern Europe, and is of lasting reference value because of its thoroughness and annual indexing. Similar dealers in the United States, like Theodore Front (Van Nuys, California), Jerona Music (Hackensack, New Jersey), and European American Retail Music (Valley Forge, Pennsylvania), are important sources for music published in North America, although they handle foreign music as well. The European American catalog is available electronically for both searching and ordering online.

In contrast to printed music, recorded music has good discographic control of current recordings. The Schwann catalogs are regularly issued guides to currently available sound recordings in North America. Published since 1949 with title variants to reflect coverage of new sound recordings formats, the Schwann catalogs are now published in three parts by Schwann Publications (Chatsworth, Calif.): *Opus: America's Guide to Classical Music*, monthly; *Artist Issue*, annual; and *Spectrum: Your Guide to Today's Music*, monthly. "Schwann" is the equivalent to *Books in Print* for sound recordings, as well as providing excellent retrospective coverage because of its long, uninterrupted publication run. Publications like the *Gramophone Classical Catalogue* (Harrow, Middlesex, Eng.: General Gramophone Publications, 1953–) in England and the *Bielefelder Katalog* (Bielefeld, Ger.: Bielefelder Verlaganstalt, 1962–) in Germany provide similar in-print discographies for other countries.

An excellent and thorough discussion of issues and sources for the selection and acquisition of all kinds of music materials has been written by Michael A. Keller.[5] In addition to printed music and sound recordings, Keller covers videos, writings on music, periodicals, reference books, and rare and antiquarian material. A useful bibliography of selection sources appears at the end of his essay.

The Music Library Association has complied a bibliography intended to aid the nonspecialist librarian faced with selecting or strengthening a basic music collection. *A Basic Music Library: Essential Scores and Books* by Pauline Shaw Bayne (2d ed., Chicago: American Library Assn., 1983), compiled under the auspices of the Music Library Association Subcommittee on the Basic Music Collection, is a bibliography of books on music and scores deemed essential by professional music librarians. The basic list of scores can also be used as an aid in selecting a basic sound recording collection.

Profile of Music Librarianship

Training and Continuing Education

Music librarianship is a specialty that requires the practitioner to have subject knowledge in order to function at all as a music librarian. Knowledge of music as an academic discipline and as a performing art is necessary to build and interpret a music collection. A music librarian must be able to understand and appreciate the information needs of a

---

5. Michael A. Keller, "Music" in *Selection of Library Materials in the Humanities, Social Sciences, and Sciences*, ed. Patricia A. McClung (Chicago: American Library Assn., 1985), 139–63.

wide-ranging clientele, from the specialist scholar to the casual reader, listener, or player. Although the requisite level of music expertise can be gained without special academic training, the equivalent of under-graduate studies in music history and theory as well as some applied music study are generally accepted as minimum background for work as a music librarian. Foreign language facility is also necessary since music collections usually contain a high percentage of materials in foreign languages, especially German, French, Italian, and Latin. Many research and large academic libraries prefer to have a music librarian with an advanced degree in music. In fact, several distinguished librarians of the past were musicologists who learned the principles and practices of librarianship on the job. Today, however, it is generally recognized that a music librarian needs special training in both librarianship and music.

The development and articulation of professional standards has long been a national and international concern of music librarians. J. Bradford Young has summarized these efforts and the emergence of a music librarianship specialty within library education.[6] During the past twenty years an increasing number of courses in music librarianship and music bibliography have been offered in schools of library science. Some library schools have recently developed masters degree programs with a concentration in music librarianship. The *Directory of Library School Offerings in Music Librarianship* compiled by Lisa M. Redpath (4th ed., s.l.: Education Committee, Music Library Assn., 1992) identifies and describes these courses and programs. Continuing education for music librarians takes place in a variety of ways. Most music librarians partici-pate actively in the Music Library Association and other professional organizations, attending or giving its programs and actively furthering the organization's goals by committee work or other contributions. The as-sociation's Education Committee, established to devise and coordinate activities related to professional and continuing education for music librari-anship, holds a preconference on a topic of current interest before each annual meeting.

Many music librarians keep up with current issues of music librarian-ship through subscription via LISTSERV to the Music Library Associa-tion's electronic mail system, MLA-List, hosted by Indiana University. Heavily used by more than 200 subscribers, it is a forum for informally discussing any topic related to music libraries, including reference quer-ies, cataloging issues, and the like. MLA-List is also useful to report such items as news and publication deadlines, which benefit from rapid and

6. J. Bradford Young, "Education for Music Librarianship," *Notes* 40, no. 3 (Mar. 1984): 510–28.

wide-scale distribution. The recent addition of file serving capability makes it possible to store messages of substance, like reports of meetings or bibliographies, for later retrieval and Music Library Association archival purposes.

Professional Associations

Music librarianship as it is now known is a highly developed professional specialty of distinctly North American origin. Since its inception, it has been a specialty characterized by cooperation among music libraries and strong ties with other library organizations and scholarly music societies.

Recognizing the special problems of administration, organization, and bibliographic control of music collections, a group of interested American Library Association members founded the Music Library Association in 1931. Its mission was to serve the aims of musical research through cooperative effort by promoting the establishment, growth, and use of music libraries. Brought together by a mutual interest in improving bibliographical access to music materials, both librarians and musicologists worked together to found this group. Since many members of the Music Library Association were also musicologists and members of the American Musicological Society, the two groups met jointly for many years to pursue their common goals. Some of the original concerns included the indexing of periodical literature, *Festschriften*, and music in collections; the development of cataloging standards to facilitate shared cataloging; the establishment of educational standards for music librarians; and the publication of a journal, *Notes for the Members of Music Library Association*, published between 1934 and 1942.

Never officially part of the American Library Association, the Music Library Association was incorporated as an independent nonprofit organization in 1945. The national organization, with headquarters now in Philadelphia, currently has about 1,300 individual members and more than 700 institutional members, including more than 100 outside the United States. The Music Library Association has a highly organized administrative and committee structure, with strong organizational connections to many related groups for projects or committee work of mutual interest. Among these related groups are the American Library Association, with representation to many of the Music Library Association's divisions or sections; the American Musicological Society; the International Association of Music Libraries, Archives, and Documentation Centres; the Music Publishers Association; and the National Information Standards Organization (Z39). The Music Library Association's committee structure reveals the topics of concern in music librarianship: Administration (automation, music library facilities, personnel, statistics),

Bibliographic Control (descriptive cataloging, MARC formats, subject access, authorities, electronic music, popular music sources, and uniform titles), Legislation, Preservation, Public Libraries, Reference and Public Service (bibliographic instruction, bibliographic standards for reference works, information sharing, online reference services, reference performance), and Resource Sharing and Collection Development. Although the general concerns of the founders are ongoing topics of interest, music librarianship has since attained sophisticated standards for cataloging, shared networks of electronically transmitted information, cooperative collection development programs, and advances in music bibliography. The organization has also broadened somewhat in scope beyond its academic library focus. Roundtable topics show more specific areas of current interest: American music, archives, band, bibliography, conservatories, film music, jazz and popular music, large research libraries, music cataloging practice, organ music, research in music librarianship, small academic libraries, social responsibilities, subject access to contemporary music, video, women in music, and world music. These groups meet annually at a national meeting held at various locations in the United States.

The Music Library Association also has an active publication program. A new series of its journal, renamed *Music Library Association Notes*, was initiated in 1943. Later named *Notes: Quarterly Journal of the Music Library Association* (Canton, Mass.: Music Library Assn., 1948–), it contains scholarly articles, bibliographical and discographical contributions, reviews of books and music, and notes and communications. It has many special features of great utility to music librarians. Among them are lists of new music, books, periodicals, and music publishers catalogs; indexes to CD and record reviews; reviews of audio and video equipment; obituaries; and a special section devoted to music software. The Music Library Association also publishes the quarterly *MLA Newsletter*, the monthly *Music Cataloging Bulletin*, and two monographic series: *MLA Index Series* and *MLA Technical Reports*. In addition to the national organization, regional chapters have long had their own organizations, programs, projects, and publications.

The International Association of Music Libraries, Archives, and Documentation Centres, known as IAML after its original name, held its first general assembly in Paris in 1951. IAML was founded to promote international cooperation among music libraries in the development of standards for cataloging, personnel training, and levels of service as well as the exchange of information and materials. It has established working commissions for public, conservatory, radio, research, and sound recordings libraries, for music information centers, and for standardization of cataloging and bibliographical research. IAML has individual and institutional members in about thirty-seven countries, and national groups in fifteen. IAML–U.S. has its own administrative structure, and its membership and goals overlap with those of the Music Library Association. Through IAML–U.S., music librarians participate in international inventories of music resources, like RISM, RILM, RIdIM, and RIPM.[7] IAML cooperates with the International Musicological Society in the sponsorship of these projects, paralleling the close links the Music Library Association has enjoyed with the American Musicological Society. IAML and some of its national groups have published other noteworthy publications of interest to music librarians including *Fontes Artis Musicae* (Paris, Fr.: International Assn. of Music Libraries, Archives, and Documentation Centres, 1954–), the quarterly journal, which contains reports of meetings, scholarly articles, and reviews and lists of new publications.

Other organizations of particular interest to music librarians are the Association for Recorded Sound Collections (ARSC) and the International Association of Sound Archives (IASA). ARSC was founded in 1966 to promote the preservation and study of historic recordings in all fields of music and speech. Its membership includes both sound archivists and private collectors. As with the Music Library Association and IAML, ARSC holds annual conferences, has local chapters, sponsors projects like the *Rigler and Deutsch Record Index* (977 microfiche, Washington, D.C.: Assn. for Recorded Sound Collections, 1981–1983) and publishes a journal and newsletter. IASA is IAML's counterpart for sound archives. Both IAML and IASA have ties to the International Federation of Library Associations (IFLA).

The Literature of Music

Unlike most other humanities collections, special types of library materials compose a major portion of music collections. These materials include music scores, libretti, microforms, sound and videorecordings, computer forms, visual materials, and musical instruments. Although writings about music in books and periodicals are an important part of a music collection, the music itself in scores and sound recordings dominates music collections.

Music Scores

Music, in a variety of manuscript and printed versions, is the central nonbook form collected by music libraries. Sketches and full autograph

---

7. Répertoire International des Sources Musicales (International Inventory of Musical Sources), Répertoire International de Littérature Musicale (International Inventory of Music Literature), Répertoire International d'Iconographie Musicale (International Repertory of Musical Iconography), Répertoire International de la Presse Musicale (International Inventory of the Musical Press).

manuscripts show the evolution of a work as well as contain markings that give some clues to how the composer wished the music to be performed. Manuscripts prepared by copyists for performance or publication as well as contemporaneous editions published with or without the composer's supervision may show additional history of a work. From their origins through the present day, manuscript, publishing, and printing traditions for music have differed from those for books and have been performed by different organizations or individuals.

In the broadest sense, music manuscripts and original printed editions of any era can be considered primary source material. However, as with books, music predating the nineteenth century forms a body of literature with special problems of description and location of rare or unique items. The most comprehensive work for music manuscripts and printed editions through 1800 is *Répertoire International des Sources Musicales* (*International Inventory of Musical Sources*) [Series A & C (Kassel, Ger.: Bärenreiter, 1967–); Series B (Munich, Ger.: Henle, 1960–)], commonly known as *RISM*. An ongoing project begun in 1952 under the auspices of the International Association of Music Libraries and the International Musicological Society, RISM describes and locates worldwide works of individual composers, collections of music, and music of a particular type or era in a number of self-contained subseries. RISM in part updates the work of a single scholar, Robert Eitner, whose *Biographisch-bibliographisches Quellen-Lexicon* (10 vols., Leipzig, Ger.: Breitkopf & Härtel, 1898–1904) and *Bibliographie der Musik-Sammelwerke des XVI. und XVII. Jahrhunderts* (Berlin, Ger.: L. Liepmannssohn, 1877), both begun in the late 1870s, provide remarkably exhaustive and detailed coverage of sources known at the time. A variety of additional current and retrospective finding tools supplement RISM by providing further description about a source or additional sources. Among these are published catalogs of music libraries and antiquarian music dealers' catalogs that may provide provenance and sales information.

While some music study requires the examination of the original manuscript or edition, much can be learned through the use of facsimile editions or microform copies. Numerous facsimiles of music have been published separately or as part of printed books or editions of music.[8]

Historical editions of music, definitively prepared from and justified by the sources, are also considered primary source material in music

---

8. See Claude Abravanel, "A Checklist of Music Manuscripts in Facsimile Edition," *Notes* 34, no. 3 (Mar. 1978): 557–80; James Coover, "Music Manuscripts in Facsimile Edition: Supplement," *Notes* 37, no. 3 (Mar. 1981): 533–56; and "Composite Music Manuscripts in Facsimile," *Notes* 38, no. 2 (Dec. 1981): 275–95.

libraries. The aim in all historical editions is to produce as accurate a musical text as possible bringing to bear full current scholarly knowledge. These editions, typically prepared under the editorial direction of a group of specialist scholars, include critical commentary, a description of all the sources used to prepare the edition, and perhaps thematic or other indexes, bibliographies, and facsimiles. Usually issued in multivolume sets, they are of two types: collected, complete works of a composer and collections of music to preserve the repertory of a particular musical heritage. The latter are called monuments (*monumenta*) or *Denkmäler*. The German term *Denkmäler* is in common use by English-speaking musicians since the earliest important sets were of German origin. Similarly, the German term *Gesamtausgabe* is commonly used as a term for the complete editions of a composer's work prepared with a scientific method. The earliest critical set, *Denkmäler der Tonkunst* (Bergedorf, Ger.: Expedition der Denkmäler, 1869–1871), began to be published in 1869 followed by sets for other repertoires in Germany and other countries. The first collected critical edition of an individual composer's works is Johann Sebastian Bach's *Werke* (Leipzig, Ger.: Breitkopf & Härtel, 1851–1926), known as the *Bach Gesellschaft Ausgabe*, issued by the Bach Gesellschaft beginning in 1851. In keeping with the concept that the *Gesamtausgaben* are definitive texts, a new edition of the works of Bach titled *Neue Ausgabe sämtlicher Werke* (Kassel, Ger.: Bärenreiter, 1954–), known as the *Neue Bach-Ausgabe*, incorporates later scholarly findings. A useful index to the contents of historical editions, Anna Harriet Heyer's *Historical Sets, Collected Editions, and Monuments of Music* (3d ed., 2 vols., Chicago: American Library Assn., 1980) provides access to individual compositions in these large sets. A plan to issue the next edition of this essential index in machine-readable form for improved access and update is being undertaken by a team of scholar-bibliographers under the direction of George Hill.

Notated music is published in many ways to serve the needs of performance or study. A composition may appear as composed or as arranged for different instruments, in full or as an excerpt. A piece of music can be issued in many different editions, from one with no editorial content (sometimes called *Urtext* edition) to one with extensive markings and commentary to convey the editor's ideas on how the piece should be played. Since notated music is subject to a variety of possible performance interpretations, many editions of an important piece of music are likely to have been published, and a variety of them collected in a single music library. An edition by a famous performer gives some indication of his or her performance style and the style characteristic of that performer's era. Instructional editions give more explicit guidance to students learning to play a piece. Music for more than one performer can be issued in score form, in individual parts from which each performer plays, or in score with accompanying parts. Most music libraries collect music in parts for small ensembles or chamber music only. Music for use by large performing groups with multiple players on a part bring special problems of inventory control, storage, and marking of parts for use in performance, which are beyond normal music library concerns. Large sets of orchestral parts or copies of choral octavo scores are usually maintained outside the library or rented by the groups who perform them. Study scores, often called miniature scores, are available for much repertoire for study rather than performance. With notation in reduced size, these scores can be studied by themselves or used while listening to recorded or live performance. Anthologies of music, sometimes with accompanying sound recordings, have also been published especially to be used with classroom instruction. Larger vocal works with orchestra, such as operas and oratorios, are often published in piano-vocal score (also called vocal score) form, with the orchestral parts reduced to two staves and playable on a keyboard instrument. Operas and other large vocal works in vocal-score form are heavily collected by music libraries.

The term *sheet music* is used to identify publications of single pieces of music of short duration, usually of a popular or instructional nature. Such ephemeral music is usually acquired by music libraries only as a special collection; for example, American popular music of a particular era or examples of short piano pieces written to teach children. Sheet music presents special problems of storage and access. As unbound music of only a few pages in length, it is usually housed in vertical files or storage boxes. Lack of indexing and the expense of cataloging have precluded standard bibliographic access to sheet music, although some sheet music collections now have been cataloged through OCLC and RLIN using the recently developed minimal level cataloging standard for music. Sheet music of the nineteenth century and earlier gains the status and treatment of rare material, especially in significant collections of the genre. Published catalogs like the *Newberry Library Catalog of Early American Printed Sheet Music* compiled by Bernard E. Wilson (Boston, Mass.: G. K. Hall, 1983) provide a measure of bibliographic control for older sheet music.

Libretti

Libretti are publications of texts of musical works without the music. Opera libretti in the original language and in translation are an important source of music study. In addition to the text itself, they may include the cast of characters, scene descriptions, plot summary, and other background information. Since they were often published for sale to the audience at a performance, those especially from the seventeenth through nineteenth centuries may also include the date, time, and location of the performance as well as the names of singers and other performers associated with it. Several published bibliographies of opera libretti give varying degrees of coverage of the literature. The recently initiated RISM Libretto Project is an attempt to comprehensively identify and catalog through the RLIN computer network the vast number of early opera libretti.[9]

Song texts in the original languages and in translations are also published in collections and are frequently sought by musicians for study or inclusion on concert programs.

Microforms

Published and unpublished microforms of music, treatises on music, periodicals, dissertations, and iconographical sources are frequently found in music libraries. Original materials often can be made available for study off-site by means of microfilm copies made for an individual scholar or those already available in microform for purchase. For example, an extensive project to microfilm early music manuscripts held in British libraries has been undertaken for commercial publication by Harvester, which has also issued printed indexes to the collections. A number of reference works provide access to existing microforms available from the Deutsches Musikgeschichtliches Archiv (DMA) and some national libraries. The DMA's collection is covered in *Katalog der Filmsammlung* (comp. and ed. by Harald Heckman, Kassel, Ger.: Bärenreiter, 1955–).

Music libraries participate in national cooperative projects to microfilm library materials for preservation, such as that undertaken by the Research Libraries Group. Information about titles preserved on microfilm masters is available through RLIN and OCLC.

Recordings

Compared with books and music scores, sound recordings are a very recent phenomenon, dating from the turn of the twentieth century. Yet several already-obsolete forms of sound recordings and machines to play them back document an era of musical performance whose composers and original performers are no longer living. As such, sound recordings are primary sources for performance practice and improvised music of any era.

---

9. Marita P. McClymonds and Diane Parr Walker, "U.S. RISM Libretto Project: With Guidelines for Cataloguing in the MARC Format," *Notes* 43, no. 1 (Sept. 1986): 19–35; John Andrus and Diane Parr Walker, *Searching for U.S.–RISM Libretto Project Records in RLIN: A Guide* (Charlottesville, Va.: University of Virginia, 1990).

Historical sound recordings in their original formats are collected as special collections or by specialized sound archives whose goal is to preserve the history of recorded sound. The *Rigler and Deutsch Record Index* is an extensive union list of pre-LP sound recordings held by five major sound archives in the United States: Library of Congress, Rodgers and Hammerstein Archive of the New York Public Library, and Stanford, Syracuse, and Yale universities. The *World's Encyclopedia of Recorded Music*, by Francis F. Clough and G. J. Cuming (London, Eng.: Sidgwick & Jackson, 1952–1957; reprint, Westport, Conn.: Greenwood Press, 1970) which indexes all commercially issued 78 rpm recordings of classical music through 1955, provides additional coverage. Other discographies and trade catalogs issued by individual record companies also provide access to early sound recordings.

Many libraries collect noncommercial sound recordings, but these collections are usually limited to special groups of materials such as recordings of local concerts. Unpublished recordings, usually open-reel or cassette tapes, are collected primarily by archives or in collections serving ethnomusicological research for which field recordings are the fundamental source of investigation.

Commercially available videorecordings of interest to music libraries began to appear in the 1980s in video tape-cassette and video laser-disc forms. Videotaped opera and other musical performances, master classes, and special sets for music history instruction or ethnomusicological study have also recently appeared.

Sound recordings are primary sources for performance practice, providing more information about musical performance than can be conveyed by verbal descriptions and musical notation, no matter how highly edited. Videorecordings go another step in documenting how music is performed. They are especially valuable in capturing many of the visual components of musical theatre works, in showing how musicians produce their sound, and in revealing some of the extra-musical context in recordings of music events outside the Western art tradition. Although videorecordings produced as instructional materials are not widely used in college level classroom instruction, they add another resource.

Computer Forms

Since the 1970s, many music libraries have been cataloging materials for their collections using a computer network such as OCLC or RLIN. These large databases have not been available for direct use by library patrons, except partially and indirectly when the library's own cataloging becomes the nucleus of an online public access catalog, replacing or supplementing the library's card catalog. Recently, however, both RLIN and OCLC have moved toward the concept of "personal searching." RLIN makes accounts available to faculty and others while OCLC is marketing EPIC, a subject-searchable catalog for librarians, and FirstSearch, for undergraduates. Although online databases of interest to other disciplines, especially the sciences, have been available since the 1970s through commercial bibliographical retrieval services like BRS and DIALOG, virtually no music databases existed until quite recently. For example, RILM Abstracts, an important index for all kinds of music material of academic interest, became available online in the 1980s, but it only covers literature from 1971 onward. Because it has been years behind in abstracting currency and because music research usually depends on retrospective as well as current publications, expensive mediated online searching of a limited body of literature has not been popular with library patrons who can search *RILM Abstracts* in paper form more thoroughly and quickly.

The recent development of music databases in CD-ROM form for use on microcomputers brings machine-readable databases more economically into the music library for direct patron use. Since 1990, music reference works including portions of *RLIM Abstracts* and *Music Index* have begun to be issued in CD-ROM. A number of large bibliographic databases have also appeared, like the music catalog of five large music libraries in the Netherlands[10] and Silver's Platter's OCLC Music Library for musical sound recordings. OCLC's *CAT CD450 Music Cataloging Collection* affords access both to the OCLC database and the means to perform cataloging of music scores and sound recordings offline.

A recent publication on floppy disk that combines a database with a records-management system is OLIS, produced by the American Symphony Orchestra League. It combines an extensive database of information on orchestral works with a planning tool so that an orchestra can select and record information on repertoire and artists and other planning information.[11]

Another technological innovation is the computer multimedia presentation, which combines sound, video, graphics, and text using hypertext technology. For example, Robert Winter has designed a multimedia work on the Ninth Symphony of Beethoven in which the "reader" at a microcomputer with audio and video display can hear the music and choose to see the score with scrolling analysis, to read biographical information or definitions of terms, and to see pictures related to

---

10. Muziek Catalogus Nederland, *Musicrom, CD-ROM* (Hilversum, Neth.: MCN Musicrom, 1990–).

11. OLIS (Orchestral Library Information Service), version 2.01 for the IBM PC, 6 high density floppy disks and manual (Washington, D.C.: American Symphony Orchestra League, 1990).

Beethoven, stopping and starting any feature or combination of features at will.[12] A number of other interactive multimedia presentations have been prepared and may prove an important new means for music instruction.

Visual Materials

Visual materials related to music are sometimes consulted by musicologists, instrument makers, performers, publishers, and others for scholarly and practical use. In 1971 the *Répertoire International d'Iconographie Musicale* (International Repertory of Musical Iconography), or RIdIM, was established under the sponsorship of the International Association of Music Libraries, the International Musicological Society, and the International Council of Museums to establish standards for the classification, cataloging, and inventory of collections of iconographical materials and to establish research centers throughout the world. RIdIM publishes a newsletter, a yearbook containing scholarly papers entitled *Imago Musicae: International Yearbook of Musical Iconography* edited by Tillmann Seebass (Basel, Switz.: Bärenreiter; Durham, N.C.: Duke University Press, 1985–), and a number of occasional publications, including the sponsorship of a microform set of pictures, *European Musical Instruments on Prints and Drawings: Collection Music Department Haags Gemeentemuseum* (Zug, Switz.: Inter Documentation Co., 1973). In 1986 RIdIM also began to publish *RIdIM/RCMI Inventory of Musical Iconography* (New York: Research Center for Musical Iconography, 1986–).

Musical Instruments

Although most musical instrument collections are found in museums or separate collections under specialist curatorship, some music libraries have musical instrument collections. Such collections do not fit comfortably within the scope of a library since requirements for acquisition, description, maintenance, and use of these collections are more like that of a museum than a library. The scientific study of musical instruments, organology, includes in its goals the classification and comparative study of musical instruments across cultures. Musical instruments as artifacts are primary source materials for furnishing historical or ethnological evidence. They also illustrate technological developments, serve as models for construction, and are used in performance of music contemporary to them. Iconographical sources and a variety of secondary material, including encyclopedias such as Stanley Sadie's three-volume *New Grove*

---

12. Robert A. Winter, *Ludwig van Beethoven, Symphony no. 9: CD Companion* (Santa Monica, Calif.: The Voyager Company, 1989).

Dictionary of Musical Instruments (London, Eng.: Macmillan, 1984), catalogs of musical instrument collections, and treatises on instrument building provide the main sources of information on musical instruments in music libraries.

Writings on Music

The term "music literature" is often used to apply specifically to writings on music as opposed to musical scores. Writings on music are chiefly textual material in book form, whether monographs or serials.

Writings on music date back to antiquity. Although only a few fragments of music from ancient Greece survive, there are numerous writings on the power of music and the role it played in many aspects of life. Music was closely allied with poetry and drama, and in most instances the poet was also composer. While little is known about how music actually sounded, the theory of Greek music, transmitted to the West primarily through Boethius's *De Institutione Musica* (ca. A.D. 500), is referred to in numerous music treatises throughout the Middle Ages and early Renaissance.

Theoretical treatises and other early writings on music of the West and Middle East are also covered in *RISM* in several separate volumes including ones for printed writings on music before 1800, musical theoretical treatises in manuscript up to 1400, and volumes devoted to Hebrew and Arabic music. As they do for early music, Robert Eitner's bibliographies, library catalogs, and other bibliographies further describe and locate sources of early music literature.

As in all disciplines, some areas in music, such as world music (national and folk), jazz, popular music, dance music, musical instruments, music criticism (scholarly and journalistic), musical aesthetics, music publishing and printing, music education, and music therapy, have a separate or significant body of literature devoted to them.

Histories of Music

Histories of music are an important part of a music library's collection. The first general histories of music date from the late eighteenth century. Giovanni Battista Martini's *Storia della Musica* (Bologna, It.: Lelio dalla Volpe, 1757–1781; reprint, Graz, Aus.: Akademische Druck- und Verlagsanstalt, 1967), though not completed beyond music of the ancients, served as a valuable source for later historians. Charles Burney's four-volume *A General History of Music* (London, Eng.: Printed for the Author, 1776–1789; numerous reprints) and Sir John Hawkins's five-volume *A General History of the Science and Practice of Music* (London, Eng.: Payne and Son, 1776; numerous reprints) cover music history from

ancient times to Burney's and Hawkins's period. These two English historians are credited with the beginnings of music historiography. Another
important figure for the development of modern musicology, Johann
Nikolaus Forkel, published the first full history in German, *Allgemeine
Geschichte der Musik* (Leipzig, Ger.: im Schwikertschen Verlag, 1788–
1801; numerous reprints), although its coverage extended only through
the early sixteenth century. A number of multivolume histories of music
have since appeared. Recent histories of music range from *The New
Oxford History of Music* (ten vols. to date, with accompanying set of
recordings issued under the title *The History of Music in Sound*, London,
Eng., and New York: Oxford University Press, 1954–), devoted to a
period or genre and written by international contributors, to the frequently
reissued single-volume history *A History of Western Music*, originally
by Donald Grout with later revised editions by Claude Palisca (3d ed.,
New York: Norton, 1980). Histories of music limited to particular national
groups, periods, genres of music or combinations thereof, abound on
music library shelves. Chronologies and histories of music in pictures,
originated by Georg Kinsky in his 1929 publication *Geschichte der
Musik in Bildern* (Leipzig, Ger.: Breitkopf & Härtel, 1929; Eng. trans.,
A History of Music in Pictures, London, Eng.: Dent, 1930; 2d ed., New
York: Dover, 1951), are other historically oriented forms. Several compendia of historical documents, such as records of the royal courts, have
been published as sources for information about the employment and
social status of musicians of a particular place and time.

Biographies and Writings of Musicians

Another large group of writings on music are biographies of composers
as well as performers and others associated with music. Works of individual biography predominate and frequently focus on a composer's works
as well as details of his or her life. Documentary biographies, such as Otto
Erich Deutsch's *Franz Schubert: Die Dokumente seines Lebens und
Schaffens* (Eng. trans., *Schubert: a Documentary Biography*, New York:
DaCapo Press, 1977), consist of a variety of documents related to a composer's life. Autobiographies, diaries, and letters of composers and other
musicians provide insight into their life, work, and times. Scholarly biographies often include authoritative and complete bibliographies or
discographies of the biographee's work. Popular biographies intended for
general readers are not collected by academic research libraries unless
they fill a need in the collection. Collective biographies for musicians related in some way form a smaller group of biographical books.

Although many biographies contain as much about a composer's
works as his or her life, they ordinarily do not contain full analyses of
individual works. Frequently sought by students seeking to understand

the musical structure of a composition, analyses can be found in separately published monographs, periodical literature, and dissertations. Harold J. Diamond's *Music Analyses: An Annotated Guide to the Literature* (New York: Schirmer Books, 1991) provides a comprehensive index to analyses of individual musical compositions of a wide range of composers found in both periodicals and books. Less technical analyses can be found in analytical guides to frequently performed concert or recorded repertoire, a popular genre aimed to enhance the appreciation of music by the general reader.

Theoretical, Technical, and Instructional Works

Books on music theory have to do with such subjects as melody, harmony, counterpoint, rhythm, scales, tuning, form, and analysis. Numerous historical works mark milestones in the development of music theory. They range from the transmission of the ideas of the ancient Greeks in Boethius's *De Institutione Musica* of circa A.D. 500 (Eng. trans. by Calvin M. Bower, New Haven, Conn.: Yale University Press, 1989) to the codification of tonal harmony in Jean-Philippe Rameau's *Traité de l'Harmonie* (Paris, Fr.: Ballard, 1722), and on to the dissolution of tonality described in the theoretical writings and musical compositions of Arnold Schoenberg. The theorist Heinrich Schenker developed an approach to musical analysis that was especially influential in the United States. His theoretical writings culminated in *Der Freie Satz*, published in Vienna in 1935 as the third volume in his *Neue Musikalische Theorien und Phantasien* (Eng. trans. by Ernst Oster, New York: Longman, 1979). Other technical subjects include the processes of composition and orchestration, conducting, improvisation, opera production, and pedagogical techniques. Works for teaching the rudiments of music, such as elementary harmony and ear training, are used for classroom and individual instruction. Music theory is a field with connections to physics and acoustics, cognitive psychology, mathematics, and computer science. Treatises and instruction books on instrumental and vocal techniques have a long history and can provide insight into historical as well as current performance practices.

Programs

Music libraries have long collected concert programs. Local programs may be collected chiefly to document the history of an institutional or local performing group. Programs from distinguished performing groups may also be collected by music libraries for information on repertoire, dates and places of performances by groups and artists, and especially for their detailed and authoritative notes on the works performed. Program notes are focused on the composition and may provide concise information about the piece of music, including works written about it and its history.

Music Periodicals

Both retrospective and current periodical literature is important to the study of music. Depending on their purpose, periodicals may contain research articles; current events; reviews of books, music, and recordings; criticism of performances; lists of new publications and advertisements; and professional opinions in editorials and letters. In addition to journals, yearbooks, congress reports, and conference proceedings are important music serial publications.

Johann Mattheson's *Critica Musica* (1722–1725), the first music periodical, is typical of eighteenth-century periodicals by one author. Modern music periodicals, with a variety of contributors and articles, reviews, and current events, began to be published at the turn of the nineteenth century. The first such periodical was the *Allgemeine Musikalische Zeitung*, which began publication in Leipzig in 1798. The establishment of musicology in the second half of the nineteenth century gave rise to periodicals emphasizing research articles; the first being Friedrich Chrysander's *Jahrbuch für Musikalische Wissenschaft* and Robert Eitner's *Monatshefte für Musikgeschichte*.

About 6,000 music periodicals have been published. Many are issued by music societies and may focus on musicology, music of a particular genre or era, theory, composers, instruments, vocal music, popular music and jazz, ethnomusicology, current events, recordings, bibliography, or education. Some representative English language music periodicals are the *Musical Quarterly, Musical Times, Journal of the American Musicological Society, Early Music, 19th Century Music, Perspectives of New Music, American Music, Latin American Music Review, Ethnomusicology, International Review of the Aesthetics and Sociology of Music, American Record Guide*, and *Notes*. Academic and research music libraries collect numerous music periodicals in foreign languages as well as in English.

Reference Tools

Until the end of World War II, few music reference works existed. Many of the most fundamental tools we depend on today were first published in the 1950s. New reference works, especially those with broad coverage, appeared over the next decades at a steady pace. In part due to the use of computers to produce such works, the 1980s brought a proliferation of new reference tools, many for specialized topics. Reference works in computer-readable forms have begun to appear in the 1990s and may well characterize the decade.

The earliest dictionaries, bibliographies, histories, and editions of music were the work of a single scholar, a characteristic that continued with the first generation of musicologists in the nineteenth century. Single-scholar works of a general nature or broad scope gave way to works with many specialist contributors working under an editorial committee. Music bibliography has benefited by a number of bibliographical projects of international scale, especially those joint projects of the International Musicological Society and International Association of Music Libraries, Archives, and Documentation Centres. Notable among them are RISM, RILM, RIPM, and RIdIM, which aim to provide international bibliographical control for early music and music literature, current music literature, nineteenth-century music periodicals, and musico-iconographic documents.

The first guide to music reference works, Vincent Duckles's *Music Reference and Research Materials*, was originally published in 1952. Now in its fourth edition with Michael A. Keller as second author (New York: Schirmer Books, 1988, rev. 1992), it remains the essential annotated bibliographical guide to music reference works. Other annotated guides, such as Guy Marco's *Information on Music: A Handbook of Reference Sources in European Languages* (3 vols. to date, Littleton, Colo.: Libraries Unlimited, 1975–), complement Duckles's relatively selective work. Keith Mixter's *General Bibliography for Music Research* (Detroit, Mich.: Information Coordinators, 1976) deals with music coverage in general reference works. Specialized guides, such as Bruno Nettl's *Reference Materials in Ethnomusicology* (Detroit, Mich.: Information Coordinators, 1967) describe reference materials of relevance to particular areas of music research. Numerous guides to the literature of a subdiscipline or specific topic within music appeared in the 1980s.

Johann Walther's *Musikalisches Lexicon* (Leipzig, Ger.: Wolffgang Deer, 1732; numerous reprints) was the prototype for music dictionaries and encyclopedias. Two kinds of works evolved from it: large-scale, multivolume encyclopedias with extended articles and concise, single-volume dictionaries for quick reference.

The monumental and up-to-date *New Grove Dictionary of Music and Musicians* (London, Eng.: Macmillan, 1980) is the standard comprehensive music encyclopedia in English. In twenty volumes, edited by Stanley Sadie, it includes long, signed articles on all aspects of music, including terms and biographical entries. The articles include extensive bibliographies, and those for composers include works lists that are frequently the most complete and accurate lists available. The articles on topics such as sources, periodicals, and libraries also provide the most complete and current lists for those subjects. Until the *New Grove* was published, the major comprehensive music encyclopedia was the seventeen-volume German set, *Die Musik in Geschichte und Gegenwart* (Kassel, Ger., and Basel, Switz.: Bärenreiter Verlag, 1949–1967), edited by Friedrich Blume with continuing supplements. A work of international scope and highest scholarship, it remains of great value despite the appearance of the *New Grove*. Other general multivolume encyclopedias in English and German as well as in French, Italian, and other languages may be collected; the latter especially for articles about their own country or language group.

Music reference collections also include single-volume general dictionaries such as Oscar Thompson's *International Cyclopedia of Music and Musicians* (New York: Dodd, Mead, 1985), first published in 1939 with many subsequent editions (the 11th edition is by Bruce Bohle). Many other music dictionaries have a more limited focus, devoted to biography, a type of music, instruments, or terms, and the like. For example, encyclopedias such as the *New Grove Dictionary of American Music* (ed. by H. Wiley Hitchcock and Stanley Sadie, 4 vols., London, Eng.: Macmillan, 1986), the *New Grove Dictionary of Jazz* (ed. by Barry Kernfeld, 2 vols., London, Eng.: Macmillan, 1988), and the *New Grove Dictionary of Musical Instruments* (ed. by Stanley Sadie, 3 vols., London, Eng.: Macmillan, 1984) include many articles and detailed information not in the general *New Grove*. *The New Harvard Dictionary of Music* (ed. by Don Michael Randel, Cambridge, Mass.: Belknap Press of Harvard University Press, 1986) is the standard reference work in English for concise articles on musical terms and other nonbiographical subjects. *Baker's Biographical Dictionary of Musicians* (8th ed., rev. by Nicolas Slonimsky, New York: Schirmer Books, 1992) is the most extensive and authoritative biographical dictionary of music in English.

Music periodical indexing was spotty and fragmentary until the *Music Index* was begun in 1949. The standard index with the widest coverage and longest duration, it currently indexes more than 500 periodicals by subject and author. Several other periodical indexes covering a specialized literature are currently being published, such as *Jazz Index* (comp. by Norbert Ruecker and C. Reggentin-Scheidt, Frankfurt, Ger.: Ruecker, 1977–) and *Music Psychology Index* (Denton, Tex.: Institute for Therapeutics Research, 1978–). Many other publications index a completed run of a single periodical or group of periodicals. Retrospective indexing of important musicological periodicals is partially afforded through publications such as Ernst Krohn's *The History of Music: An Index to the Literature Available in a Selected Group of Musicological Publications* (St. Louis, Mo.: Washington University, 1952). Yet another international venture, *Répertoire International de la Presse Musicale du XIXe Siècle (RIPM)* (Ann Arbor, Mich.: UMI, 1988–) provides access to the extensive music periodical literature published in the nineteenth century.

RILM Abstracts of Music Literature, published under the aegis of the *Répertoire International de Littérature Musicale* (International Inventory of Music Literature), abstracts all current music literature of scholarly import, including books, dissertations, *Festschriften*, and congress reports. It began publication in print form in 1967, became available for online searching beginning with the 1971 volume, and is now available in CD-ROM form for the years 1970–1984 as *MUSE*. Two publications index the articles in *Festschriften* and congress reports prior to *RILM Abstracts*: Walter Gerboth's *An Index to Musical Festschriften* (New York: Norton, 1969) and John Tyrell and Rosemary Wise's *A Guide to International Congress Reports in Musicology, 1900–1975* (New York: Garland, 1979).

In addition to Heyer's *Historical Sets, Collected Editions, and Monuments of Music*, an index to music in collected scholarly editions, there are a number of indexes to individual songs, hymns, and popular music selections in collections. The prototype for this genre was Minnie Sears's *Song Index* (New York: H. W. Wilson, 1926, with suppl., 1934), a work still useful today.

Besides the expected array of bibliographies of music and writings on music, two kinds of bibliographic works have special prominence in music collections: thematic catalogs and discographies. Thematic catalogs, also called thematic indexes, are bibliographies of the works of an individual composer or collection, which include musical incipits for each composition or section of a composition. These incipits are valuable because it is often necessary to see the opening notes of a piece to positively identify it. Thematic catalogs also usually provide the place and date of composition, instrumentation, key, original title, and author and language of a text set to music. The best thematic catalogs provide extensive bibliographical descriptions of the works listed in it. In such thematic catalogs one can expect to find the location to the autograph manuscript and copies, information about the first edition and other editions and arrangements published during the composer's lifetime, and a bibliography of references to the work. They also include indexes to titles, text incipits, names associated with the work, and publishers found in the thematic catalog. The first thematic catalogs date to the eighteenth century and include partial, simple thematic catalogs of both Haydn's and Mozart's works. Thematic catalogs based on a bibliographer's thorough scholarly investigation of a composer's output including full bibliographical information began to flourish in the nineteenth century, often coinciding with the preparation of the composer's collected works. Köchel's thematic catalog of Mozart's works, first published in 1862, was the first monumental scholarly thematic catalog. Thematic catalogs for many, but by no means all, of the important composers have been published. The use of computers to prepare thematic catalogs has greatly facilitated the mechanical part of the thematic cataloger's work today. An annotated bibliography of published and unpublished thematic catalogs, both of composers and collections, can be found in Barry Brook's *Thematic Catalogues in Music* (Hillsdale, N. Y.: Pendragon Press, 1977) published as part of the RILM Retrospectives series.

Discography serves the same function for recorded sound as bibliography does for printed and manuscript materials. The best discographies not only list related recordings, but fully describe their intellectual and technical content. This description includes identification of the music contained on the recording, performing and recording personnel, instrumentation, date and place of recording, and the physical characteristics of the recordings' published form. It also includes the catalog numbers and matrix numbers associated with a recording, which help to identify a "take," or individual recording event. As with bibliographies, discographies can be separately published monographs, articles, or appended to articles. They may focus on the recordings of a particular performer, the recorded works of a composer, the output of a recording company, or a musical genre, topic, or form of recording. The wide variety and scope of available discographies is apparent in the *Bibliography of Discographies* (New York: Bowker, 1977–), the most comprehensive and scholarly work in the field. Three volumes have appeared to date: *Classical Music, 1925–1975*, by Michael H. Gray and Gerald D. Gibson; *Jazz*, by Daniel Allen; and *Popular Music*, by Michael H. Gray. Future volumes will be devoted to ethnic and folk music as well as general discographies of music, speech recordings, and natural sounds.

Professional Readings

Arneson, Arne Jon, and Stuart Milligan. "Index to Reviews of Audio and Video Equipment." Annual feature started in *Notes* 40 (Sept. 1983–).

Barsart, Ann. "Criteria for Weeding Books in a University Music Library." *Notes* 36, no. 4 (June 1980): 819–36.

Bayne, Pauline Shaw. *A Basic Music Library: Essential Scores and Books*. 2d ed. Chicago: American Library Assn., 1983.

Benton, Rita, ed. *Directory of Music Research Libraries*. RISM Ser. C. Kassel, Ger., and New York: Bärenreiter, 1983– .

Bowles, Garrett H. *Directory of Music Library Automation Projects*. MLA Technical Reports, no. 2. Rev. ed. Philadelphia, Pa.: Music Library Assn., 1979.

Bradley, Carol June. *American Music Librarianship: A Biographical and Historical Survey*. New York: Greenwood Press, 1990.

———, comp. *Music Collections in American Libraries: A Chronology*. Detroit Studies in Music Bibliography, 46. Detroit, Mich.: Information Coordinators, 1981.

———, ed. *Manual of Music Librarianship*. Ann Arbor, Mich.: Music Library Assn. Executive Office, 1966.

_____, ed. *Reader in Music Librarianship*. Washington, D.C.: Microcard Editions Books, 1973.

Bratcher, Perry, and Jennifer Smith. *Music Subject Headings: Compiled from "Library of Congress Subject Headings."* Lake Crystal, Minn.: Soldier Creek Press, 1988.

Brockman, William S. *Music: A Guide to the Reference Literature*. Reference Sources in the Humanities. Littleton, Colo.: Libraries Unlimited, 1987.

Burkat, Leonard. "The Challenge of Music Librarianship in the Public Library." *Notes* 38, no. 1 (Sept. 1981): 7–13.

Byrne, Frank P., Jr. *A Practical Guide to the Music Library: Its Function, Organization, and Maintenance*. Cleveland, Ohio: Ludwig Music, 1987.

Cassaro, James P., ed. *Planning and Caring for Library Audio Facilities*. MLA Technical Report, no. 17. Canton, Mass.: Music Library Assn., 1989.

_____. *Space Utilization in Music Libraries*. MLA Technical Report, no. 20. Canton, Mass.: Music Library Assn., 1992.

Coover, James. *Antiquarian Catalogues of Musical Interest*. London, Eng., and New York: Mansell, 1988.

Coral, Lenore, et al. "Automation Requirements for Music Information." *Notes* 43, no.1 (Sept. 1986): 14–18.

Council on Library Resources. *Retrospective Conversion of Music Materials: Report of a Meeting Sponsored by the Council on Library Resources, July 18–19, 1984*. Wayzata, Minn.: Council on Library Resources, 1984.

Druesedow, John E., Jr. *Library Research Guide to Music: Illustrated Search Strategy and Sources*. Library Research Guides, 6. Ann Arbor, Mich.: Pierian Press, 1982.

Duckles, Vincent H., and Michael A. Keller. *Music Reference and Research Materials: An Annotated Bibliography*. 4th ed. New York: Schirmer Books, 1988.

Duggan, Mary Kay. "CD-ROM, Music Libraries, Present and Future." *Fontes Artis Musicae* 36, no. 2 (Apr./June 1989): 84–95.

Fling, Robert Michael. *Shelving Capacity in the Music Library*. MLA Technical Reports, no. 7. Philadelphia, Pa.: Music Library Assn., 1981.

Fontes Artis Musicae: Review of the International Association of Music Libraries, Archives and Documentation Centres. Kassel, Ger.: Bärenreiter, 1954– .

Gaeddert, Barbara Knisely. *The Classification and Cataloging of Sound Recordings: An Annotated Bibliography*. MLA Technical Reports, no. 4. Rev. ed. Philadelphia, Pa.: Music Library Assn., 1981.

Gray, Michael H. "Discography: Its Prospects and Problems." *Notes* 35, no. 3 (Mar. 1979): 578–92.

Green, Richard D., and Kären Nagy. *Foundations of Music Bibliography*. New York: Garland. Forthcoming.

Hathaway, Edward W. "Developing a State Archive of Local Music Materials." *Notes* 45, no. 3 (Mar. 1989): 483–94.

"Improving Access to Music: A Report of the MLA Music Thesaurus Project Working Group." *Notes* 45, no. 4 (June 1989): 714–21.

International Association of Music Libraries. *Guide for Dating Early Published Music: A Manual of Bibliographic Practices.* Compiled by D. W. Krummel. Hackensack, N.J.: Joseph Boonin, Inc.; Kassel, Ger.: Bärenreiter, 1974.

Keller, Michael A. "Music." In *Selection of Library Materials in the Humanities, Social Sciences, and Sciences,* edited by Patricia A. McClung, 139–63. Chicago: American Library Assn., 1985.

Kunselman, Joan D., Peggy Daub, and Marion Taylor. "Toward Describing and Assessing the National Music Collection." *Notes* 43, no. 1 (Sept. 1986): 7–13.

LeSueur, Richard. "Index to CD and Record Reviews." Regular feature started in *Notes* 5 (1948–).

Mann, Alfred, ed. *Modern Music Librarianship: Essays in Honor of Ruth Watanabe.* Festschrift Series, no. 8. Stuyvesant, N.Y.: Pendragon Press, 1989.

Milligan, Stuart. "Music and Other Performing Arts Serials Available in Microforms and Reprint Editions." *Notes* 37, no. 2 (Dec. 1980): 239–307.

Munstedt, Peter A. "Recent Sources in the Preservation of Music Library Materials." *MLA Newsletter* 71 (Nov./Dec.1987): 7–8.

Music Cataloging Bulletin. Canton, Mass.: Music Library Assn., 1970– .

Notes: Quarterly Journal of the Music Library Association. Canton, Mass.: MLA, 1948– .

Redpath, Lisa M. *Directory of Library School Offerings in Music Librarianship.* 4th ed. s.l.: Education Committee, Music Library Assn., 1992.

Shaw, Sarah J., and Lauralee Shiere. *Sheet Music Cataloging and Processing: A Manual.* MLA Technical Reports, no. 15. Canton, Mass.: Music Library Assn., 1984.

Seibert, Donald. *The MARC Music Format from Inception to Publication.* MLA Technical Reports, no. 13. Philadelphia, Pa.: Music Library Assn., 1983.

_____. *SLACC: The Partial Use of the Shelf List as Classed Catalog.* MLA Technical Reports, no. 1. Ypsilanti, Mich.: University Library, Eastern Michigan University, 1973.

Skinner, Robert. "Microcomputers in the Music Library." *Notes* 45, no. 1 (Sept. 1988): 7–14.

Smiraglia, Richard P. *Cataloging Music: A Manual for Use with AACR2.* Lake Crystal, Minn.: Soldier Creek Press, 1986.

_____. *Music Cataloging: The Bibliographic Control of Printed and Recorded Music in Libraries.* Englewood, Colo.: Libraries Unlimited, 1989.

_____. *Shelflisting Music: Guidelines for Use with the Library of Congress Classification, M.* MLA Technical Reports, no. 9. Philadelphia, Pa.: Music Library Assn., 1981.

Tatian, Carol. *Careers in Music Librarianship.* MLA Technical Reports, no. 18. Canton, Mass.: Music Library Assn., 1990.

Thompson, Annie F. "Music Cataloging in Academic Libraries and the Case for Physical Decentralization." *Journal of Academic Librarianship* 12, no. 2 (May 1986): 79–83.

Thorin, Suzanne E., and Carole Franklin Vidali. *The Acquisition and Cataloging of Music and Sound Recordings: A Glossary.* MLA Technical Reports, no. 11. Canton, Mass.: Music Library Assn., 1984.

Tucker, Ruth W., ed. *Authority Control in Music Libraries: Proceedings of the Music Library Association Preconference, March 5, 1985.* MLA Technical Reports, no. 16. Canton, Mass.: Music Library Assn., 1989.

Watanabe, Ruth T. "American Music Libraries and Music Librarianship: An Overview in the Eighties." *Notes* 38, no. 2 (Dec. 1981): 239–56.

Weitz, Jay. *Music Coding and Tagging: MARC Content Designation for Scores and Sound Recordings.* Lake Crystal, Minn.: Soldier Creek Press, 1990.

Wurster, Richard B. *In Celebration of Revised 780: Music in the Dewey Decimal Classification, 20th Edition.* MLA Technical Reports, no. 19. Canton, Mass.: Music Library Assn., 1990.

CHAPTER 5

Performing Arts

Nena Couch and Nancy Allen

Profile of the Performing Arts

The phrase *Performing Arts* has had a variety of meanings over the years and even at this writing does not have a definition that would be universally accepted. In his *A Classification for the Performing Arts*, Simon Trussler considers the coverage of the discipline to be:

> for works relating to the performing arts in general, and anterior and related studies; for all aspects of theatre and dramatic history, study and technique; for musical theatre and opera, dance and ballet; forms of popular entertainment, puppetry and animal showmanship; film and broadcasting; recreative and leisure activities; and sports and games.[1]

The International Association of Libraries and Museums of the Performing Arts/Société Internationale des Bibliothèques et Musées des Arts du Spectacle (SIBMAS), employs a somewhat narrower definition, serving organizations that document theatre, dance, motion picture, radio and television, festival, marionette, circus, and mime performance.

Probably the more generally held, traditional view is expressed in *An International Dictionary of Theatre Language*, which considers the performing arts to be "those arts, such as theatre, dance, and music, that result in a performance."[2] By virtue of this definition, film may easily and logically be included as one of the performing arts. The extension of theatre into the area of film, which some consider the great art form of this century, makes for an interesting combination of disciplines, rang-

---

1. Simon Trussler, *A Classification for the Performing Arts* (London, Eng.: British Theatre Institute, 1974), vi.
2. Joel Trapido, Edward A. Langhans, and James R. Brandon, *An International Dictionary of Theatre Language* (Westport, Conn.: Greenwood Press, 1985), 639.

ing from what is often considered the most ephemeral, dance, to a film performance, which will always play in essentially the same way. Film artists have learned from the traditional theatre, even though at least one informed writer feels that "it has been a calamity that historically cinema has been so closely associated with dramatic art and that this relationship has and is holding back the movies from being finer cinema."[3] Nevertheless, film as an art has developed its own uniquely expressive identity. For the purposes of this chapter, film as a dramatic art will not emphasize education or training films or the use of video technology to record historical events. It should be recognized, however, that all these types of film are based in artistic principles, and they reflect the creativity and talent of many people.

Although each of the performing arts areas could easily be the subject of its own book, in this chapter theatre, dance, and film are considered the performing arts, while music is considered elsewhere. Theatre, dance, and film are related in that they all have a visual aspect as a primary component, often with motion and sound as characteristics (although lack of motion or sound may characterize works in these fields). Because each field will have its own separate collection in a large research library, information unique to each field will be discussed.

Theatre is often viewed as divided into two categories: drama, which is the literary component, and theatrical production, that which is related to performance. However, a strict separation of these two categories is inappropriate since neither is fully realized without the other. Once this broad distinction is made, theatre quickly breaks down into a number of areas that relate to the performance, the dramatic literature, or both. These areas cover forms of theatrical productions that include legitimate stage, burlesque, vaudeville, tent shows, circus, puppet theatre, toy theatre, festival and pageant, mime, performance art, mechanical theatre, commedia dell'arte, musical theatre, opera. Also included are areas of activity of practitioners in the theatre, such as playwrighting, acting, directing, dramaturgy, design, arts administration, and stage management, and of the performance space including theatre architecture and stage technology. Theatres may include those with differing missions and audiences, some of which are children's theatre, educational theatre, street theatre, regional theatre, experimental theatre, and commercial theatre. Subfields of theatrical inquiry that provide structures for the examination and assessment of its effects and significance as an art, in the arts, and as an aspect of human endeavor may include aesthetics, the history of theatre, the study of dramatic literature, and theatre criticism. Theatre

---

3. Robert Steele, *The Cataloging and Classification of Cinema Literature* (Metuchen, N.J.: The Scarecrow Press, Inc., 1967), 9.

scholars may use a variety of theories or methodologies in their work including approaches borrowed from other disciplines.

Dance has a dual aspect in its theatrical and recreational natures that makes it both an almost universally known, if not practiced, activity as well as perhaps being a factor in the slowness with which the discipline has been accorded full status as an art worthy of scholarly inquiry. As with theatre, dance could be seen as divided into performance and primary material components. The primary material aspect of this discipline would be the choreographies of dances. Unlike theatre, for which the primary component has generally been literary, dances have historically been passed from dancer to dancer, in a way that approximates the great oral traditions of literature, and are now being preserved in written, filmed, and videotaped forms. Dance notation, the way in which a dance is written down, has been an area of great concern for those interested in preserving what has been a frustratingly fleeting art form. Dance history, dance aesthetics, and dance criticism are subfields that, while certainly not new in this century, are gaining momentum and strength as legitimate, important areas of investigation. Many of the aspects of production previously mentioned for theatre also relate to those dances that are theatrical in nature.

Motion pictures, with a history of barely a century, are a newer art form than either theatre or dance. The literature of this field covers many topics since there are many kinds of films. Feature films, educational films, animated films, documentary films, films for broadcast, newsfilm, and even advertising films and music videos are some of the vastly varying and widely seen forms of this art. In fact, motion pictures are now viewed by many artists as a conservative art form, whose production values may be restricted by distribution and economic factors, in contrast to video art.

Film is studied for many of its aspects. Some see it as a visual art chiefly influenced by the art director or designer; others see it as a narrative art form where the screenwriter is the dominant creative force. Technical aspects of motion picture production have recently begun to fascinate some viewers and scholars, while others focus on the photographic power of the cinematographer or on the conceptual influence of the editor. The persuasive and educational power of film, the role of the director as *auteur*, and the importance of the actors' performances are studied as central to the medium. Creativity and performance are considered by all as chief elements of the art form. Each approach to the analysis of film, clearly a highly collaborative art form, may require differing kinds of primary resources.

Film-related collections can be reels or tapes of films, published materials about films, or unpublished materials affiliated with the process of creating films. Each type of collection or element of collecting is different, requiring different types of management, preservation, and access.

Nature of Performing Arts Collections

Because performing arts collections exist in a variety of settings that influence the organization and use of those collections, generalizations regarding the nature of such collections would be fruitless. However, it is possible to describe some of the situations in which performing arts materials are collected. As part of a general collection, a defined subject area unit within a library, a major division, or a separate library, performing arts materials may appear in academic libraries, public libraries, or research libraries. It should be noted that these three types of libraries are not mutually exclusive—two of the major performing arts research libraries in the United States are the Billy Rose Theatre Collection and the Dance Collection, both of the New York Public Library's Performing Arts Research Center.

Special Libraries and Collections

Performing arts libraries may also be special libraries developed for use by the staff of a particular business or by the membership of an organization. For example, the Theatre Communications Group (TCG) maintains a library of theatre and arts periodicals, reference books, and files, and the Dance Notation Bureau (DNB) has libraries of dance research, analysis, and notation scores of dance and movement at its primary location in New York and its extension at The Ohio State University in Columbus, Ohio. Film archives of importance are also located in special collections of organizations, such as the American Film Institute (AFI) and the Academy of Motion Picture Arts and Sciences (AMPAS), as well as in academic institutions. Motion picture production studios have their own libraries, which may contain information on the history of the studio or of films produced by the studio, but which are generally reference or picture libraries for those involved in the film production process. These libraries may not be open to the public at all, or they may be open to scholars for an hourly access fee. While many American theatre and dance companies have not preserved their company archives in any organized way, some few maintain their own archives while others have established archives in outside libraries. Public access to these records may vary greatly according to restrictions placed by the companies.

Major research collections for film are found all over the country, but more materials are located on both coasts, chiefly in the Los Angeles and New York areas, with some exceptions such as the University of Texas and the University of Wisconsin. The widely scattered collections of primary research material are described in a number of reference volumes specific to film study[4] as well as in more general catalogs of manuscript collections.

Because of the popular appeal of the performing arts to a wide variety of people, many fine private collections have been and continue to be developed. While these collections are sometimes broken up on the death or loss of interest of the owner, many do make their ways into library collections.

On occasion, collections of performing arts materials may be found in academic departments, where they are administered by the department and are not affiliated with the library system. Performing arts materials may also reside in the special collections divisions of libraries, in libraries of historical societies, in museums, in art collections, in libraries and archives of performing arts groups or organizations, and in private collections.

Academic and Public Libraries

In an academic library, performing arts materials often are housed and administered as part of the library's general collection. The nature and depth of those materials will reflect the overall collection development policy of the library, the subject-area expertise and interests of the bibliographers who have selected materials over the years, and the academic departments with which the performing arts are associated. For example, library materials on dance in an institution in which dance is part of the physical education program will probably be different from those materials that support dance in a performing arts program. Likewise, library materials supporting a graduate history, literature, or criticism theatre program could differ greatly from materials supporting a graduate acting, directing, or design program, thus reflecting the programs' philosophies.

There are not many separate film-study collections in university libraries; film literature and other related materials are generally acquired by those responsible for related areas such as communication, theatre, or literature. Archives of films themselves are almost always administered separately from documentation collections, and public or university libraries containing large collections of nonprint material such as slides,

---

4. Nancy Allen, *Film Study Collections: A Guide to Their Development and Use* (New York: Ungar, 1979), 71–78, 124–68; Kim Fisher, *On the Screen: A Film, Television, and Video Research Guide* (Littleton, Colo.: Libraries Unlimited, Inc., 1986), 152–65; Linda Harris Mehr, ed., *Motion Pictures, Television, and Radio: A Union Catalog of Manuscript and Special Collections in the Western United States* (Boston, Mass.: G. K. Hall, 1977).

still photographs, or posters about films may separate these materials as well.

Even when a performing arts collection is recognized as being self-contained, it may be housed with a related collection. For example, a library often will group together its collections for dance and music, for theatre and dance, for theatre and film, or other combinations.

Special Considerations in the Performing Arts Library

In an issue of *Library Trends*, "Music and Fine Arts in the General Library," the editors identified five aspects of music and fine arts collections that are equally applicable to theatre, dance, and film:

> (1) that there are appreciable differences between these two collections [i.e., music and fine arts] and the rest of the library; (2) that they present different problems with regard to staffing, financing, and acquisition of materials; (3) that their bibliographic control is different and often more difficult; (4) that their use must be regulated differently; and (5) that while physical access should not be hampered, physical protection of the collections must be emphasized at all times.[5]

The performing arts librarian must adequately support the programs offered by the institution by acquiring appropriate materials, ensuring the physical well-being of those materials, and making them available to patrons. Within the mission and mandate of the institution, the librarian should also make efforts to collect in, and support, the performing arts activities of the local and regional areas.

At the same time a joy and a frustration, the great variety of materials that frequently appear in performing arts collections provide wonderful research opportunities, attract public interest, and cause problems for the librarian responsible for the collection's organization, handling, and access. Besides books, musical scores, microforms, recordings, audio- and videotapes in several formats, film, and slides, the performing arts collection often consists of a great many ephemeral materials in a variety of formats that document those arts. For example, these ephemeral, or fugitive, materials may include playbills, programs, posters, press releases, advertisements, program inserts, souvenir booklets, newspaper and journal clippings of all sorts, tickets, scrapbooks, photographs, contracts, financial records, itineraries, correspondence, diaries, notebooks, material used for research, promptbooks, manuscripts of plays and books,

---

5. Guy A. Marco and Wolfgang M. Freitag, eds., "Music and Fine Arts in the General Library," *Library Trends* 23 (Jan. 1975): 322.

original sketches, renderings, maquettes, scenic properties, light plots, ground plans, architectural plans, engravings, illustrations, realia, and memorabilia.

Because film is such a complex and collaborative production process, the major film documentation collections contain some surprising materials. As noted previously, a number of libraries collect slides and photographs, often "outtakes" from the production process, or publicity materials for the production. Publicity materials might also include posters, press releases, and billboards. These can be useful in documenting costume design, lighting, editing, business aspects, or historical aspects of the film's production. Less common artifacts include cels from animated films, set or costume designs, story boards, matte drawings that produced either special effects or the illusion of exterior shots actually filmed on a sound stage, furniture from sets, miniatures, costumes, glass negatives, or even early cameras or other equipment used to make films. There are a great many private collections of correspondence now available in libraries or archives, some of which include versions of the scripts used in production. Several university libraries and many of the major research collections in film now contain large collections of these unpublished scripts, with substitute pages and marginalia. Other kinds of scripts are also useful in research, including release scripts, scripts deposited for copyright purposes, or story scripts. In addition, other kinds of documentation are useful to scholars, such as studio business records, shooting schedules, and personal correspondence.

Even beyond collecting, at least one writer on popular culture dance feels that "libraries can and should schedule and otherwise promote dance experiences as a regular feature of community outreach activities."[6] Obviously, this is not a practical suggestion for many libraries or collections, but it does point up what often seems to be the feeling of patrons and librarians of performing arts collections alike—that the librarian, as the party responsible for the collection, must be in some way actively involved in the art in order to adequately represent that art.

Film librarians, in public and academic libraries as well as those in special libraries, are far more likely to be involved with or to be providers of community access to films than theatre and dance librarians are to be presenters of actual performances. Public libraries of all sizes have film series for the general public; academic libraries with collections of films often sponsor film programs for the general community or the academic community and, even more often, provide copies of films to campus film societies. These activities are crucial to the community's access

---

6. John M. Forbes, "Libraries and the Preservation of American Popular Culture Dance," *Drexel Library Quarterly* 16 (1980): 95.

to high-quality film, since commercial film theatres rarely provide show-ings of foreign films, art films, older films, or even independent films. This means that librarians responsible for collections of films commonly take on the role of film programmers. Audiovisual librarians in public libraries and film archivists in academic libraries need to know how to find distri-butors for films, how to arrange bookings and showings, and other tasks not generally thought of as the responsibility of librarians.[7]

Recently, public and academic libraries have provided collections of videotaped films for the public. This has caused some controversy, since a great many businesses rent films on video, and tax-supported libraries usually provide the films to the public at a very low rental cost. In con-trast to video rental businesses, libraries may have a different kind of col-lection with less emphasis on current films and a greater emphasis on a well-balanced collection of historical, foreign, or "art-film" titles. In many cases, academic libraries have had to make decisions about public access to films on video, since the main purpose behind the purchase of such films is usually to support the teaching and research programs of depart-ments of film study.

Dance is a field with unique problems in terms of building a library collection. At least in theatre, the text of a play generally continues to exist whether or not any permanent record of a particular performance remains. In dance, often nothing exists after the performance other than the memories that the audience may take away with their programs (if they keep them) and, perhaps, a published review. For centuries, choreographers have grappled with the difficulties of preserving their creations in a form that allows the reconstruction of the work. The sad truth has been, however, that once a dance tradition dies, the system of notation created for that tradition ceases to adequately function since the "givens" or assumptions of the system are no longer universally understood and probably not applicable to the movement vocabulary of the succeeding dance tradition. Today, one could see any number of differing but reasonable reconstructions from the Renaissance dance manual *Le Gratie d'Amore*, and it is most likely that none of those reconstructions will be quite the dance that Cesare Negri thought he was publishing at the beginning of the seventeenth century.

Nevertheless, it is possible to use early notational systems to recon-struct dances. Some of the early Western European notational systems that have been investigated by both dance and music scholars and from which dances are now regularly reconstructed and performed include a

---

7. James L. Limbacher, comp. and ed., *Feature Films on 8 mm, 16 mm, and Video-tape: A Directory of Feature Films Available for Rental, Sale, and Lease in the United States and Canada* (New York: Bowker, 1985).

fifteenth-century system of single-letter abbreviations of step names, the discursive descriptions of dance steps and floor patterns of fifteenth- and sixteenth-century Italy, Thoinot Arbeau's placement of step names beside the related musical notes in his *Orchesographie* of 1589, and the Beauchamp/Feuillet system first published in France in 1700 that provides symbols for steps and a track for the floor pattern. Other notation systems have approached the problem of describing movement through a variety of means including the use of stick figures, music notes, or mathematical, anatomical, and kinetic methods.[8] Labanotation, known for its comprehensiveness as well as its great capability for movement description, is widely taught today and is being used to notate and preserve the works of contemporary choreographers as well as works that have been retained only in dancers' memories. While a time-consuming system, Labanotation is benefiting from innovative work in computerized notation being done several places including the Department of Dance at The Ohio State University.

Choreographers and dancers frequently develop their own personal systems of describing their dance work; however, the usefulness of these systems is restricted. Personal systems are intended to allow the choreographer to re-create work but generally are not designed to give outsiders that same opportunity. While these systems may protect the choreographer's work from others, they may also prove to be inadequate even for the developer to reconstruct the original movement.

Many dance companies with ongoing traditions have dealt with the problem of preservation by not letting the tradition die—by passing stylistic characteristics and techniques as well as specific ballets and roles from one performer to another in a master-apprentice style. Of course, this method does not ensure that changes will not occur. After all, memories do grow dim over time and each individual will introduce something personal to a role or delete something instituted by a previous dancer. However, this oral and physical tradition has served many of the great dance companies of the world for decades and probably will continue to be important in the transmission of dances.

In this century, film and video have provided a third method of dance conservation. Prior to that, visual records of dance were provided by paintings, sculptures, and the various visual arts, including still photography, but at the most, these representations can only be considered intriguing and helpful in supplementing a notational system. Movement cannot be accurately re-created from still poses. Many dancers and choreographers

---

8. For a discussion of notation systems, see Ann Hutchinson Guest, *Choreo-Graphics: A Comparison of Dance Notation Systems from the Fifteenth Century to the Present* (New York: Gordon and Breach, 1989).

have hailed the advent of film and videotape as the solution to the problem of saving a dance for posterity. Although there are some questions in the dance and preservation communities as to the adequacy of this solution, it remains a valuable tool that, when used in conjunction with the developing notational techniques and the oral tradition, provides our current choreographers with a greater chance at immortality for their work than earlier choreographers have had.

Recreational and ritual dancing have the same problems of preservation, although perhaps more severe, as does theatrical dancing. Because of the changes in national boundaries this century, the ease of travel, and the widespread availability of television, radio, print media, and film, the societal traditions that had previously been quite stable are changing with great speed. Dance is only one of the aspects affected by these transitions, and it is sad to know that these traditions are being lost even as the ability to preserve them is being made available.

The implications for the librarian in considering the ephemeral aspect of dance are great. In order to provide the environment in which one has the tools to reconstruct a dance as one would have the tools in the music library to reconstruct a particular piece of music, the dance library must offer as much as is available, including a notated dance score, the tools to allow for the interpretation of that notational system, videotapes or films of the dance, critical works on the dance, reminiscences of performers and viewers, anthropological studies of the dance in its culture, aesthetic works viewing the dance as an artwork in relation to other artworks, and recordings of the dance music.

Similarly, a theatre collection may need the literary works, that is, the plays; promptbooks and scripts with annotations by prompters, directors, stage managers, or actors; memoirs of the artists; and critical works of the literature as well as of performances. The collection also may require technical works; the visual artwork such as scene, costume, makeup, and lighting designs; sound recordings; scores; and films or videotapes. Both the theatre and dance collections should acquire the important reference works in the field including bibliographies, indexes, periodicals, dictionaries, catalogs, encyclopedias, guides, and other specialized sources.

A strong film-study collection requires similar documentation of the creative processes involved with making a film. Much of the scholarly output on the topic of films is based on careful historical study of filmmakers in their various roles (editors, writers, directors, actors, etc.). The intent of the filmmaker, like the intent of the novelist, poet, or playwright, is subject to much analysis. Clues about creative intent are often to be found only in scarce research resources such as those of the large special collections of film documentation. But it certainly is possible for an academic library to search for and either locate or obtain research resources for its film scholars. A number of bookshops specializing in cinema materials produce catalogs regularly containing scripts, photographs, drawings, and other primary-research resources for film scholars. Unpublished records, models, artifacts, script marginalia, or even financial records will provide a film historian with insight into the forces at play in the creation of a complex film production—from the narrative to set design to filming to editing to marketing.

It is quite likely that the most severe problem that any performing arts librarian will face is insufficient financial support or lack of funding for the needs of the collection and the demands of patrons. When cutbacks are made, the arts are often the first, and most severely, restricted. Even when the climate is one of economic health, the librarian should avoid being lulled into a false sense of security and should plan accordingly. Many shared and cooperative projects and proposals are an outgrowth of the financial necessity to avoid duplication of effort and to share resources. An example of such cooperation is the Consortium of Popular Culture Collections in the Midwest, whose members are the special collections libraries, all holding performing arts materials, at Bowling Green State University, Kent State University, Michigan State University, and The Ohio State University. Consortium activities include, but are not limited to, the sharing of collection development policies, referral of donors to other consortium members in the case of material inappropriate for the first-contacted institution, consideration of joint preservation projects, and agreement to loan materials from one special collection to another under previously determined conditions for use.

Users of Performing Arts Collections

Depending on the nature of a performing arts collection, the users may range from casual inquirers to dedicated scholars (with others from all points between) and may be from a variety of disciplines, or strictly from one of the performing arts. Louis A. Rachow has identified four major categories of theatre library patrons:

> (1) writers, biographers, historians, dramatic critics, and feature writers supplemented by students of the stage and screen preparing for professional careers; (2) practical workers in the theatre: designers, producers, directors, press agents, and technicians who find theatre material of constant service in the preparation of a production; (3) research workers for film companies in search, chiefly, of historical accuracy; and (4) members of the theatre audience seeking information about a play or players.[9]

9. Louis A. Rachow, "Care and Preservation of Theatre Library Materials," *Special Libraries* 63 (Jan. 1972): 26.

The Dance Collection of the New York Public Library counts among its patrons "the dancer who seeks advancement, the scholar engaged in research, the performing company in its development, faculty and students in their teaching or preparation of coursework and, finally, the amateur searching for a deeper understanding of this lively and profound art."[10]

Patrons of film collections are similar to those of theatre and dance collections, although most librarians specializing in film will say that they spend considerable time answering questions that may seem trivial to some. The fact that films are so widely available to the general public means that people will have many questions about films. Late-night film viewing on television often results in dogged pursuit on the following day of answers to questions on cast, production information, other roles played by performers, and additional so-called trivia. Fortunately, most of this factual information is readily available in reference resources, especially for films produced prior to the current year. There is a well-developed body of reference work that continually grows with the production of new films, and it seems that every few years an up-to-date comprehensive credit listing appears.[11]

The types of patrons a performing arts collection will attract may depend on a variety of factors including the nature and the mission of the parent institution and its departments; the nature of the collection in size, quality, subject areas, forms of materials, and access to those materials; the geographic location; and the way in which the collection is or is not publicized. Researchers from a variety of disciplines, including psychologists, anthropologists, sociologists, health practitioners, athletic trainers, physical therapists, religious practitioners, and educators, may use aspects of the performing arts in their professions. Theatricality exists in life, and life as seen and portrayed by theatre artists exists on the stage and in film. In that sense, theatre, dance, and film truly lend themselves to interdisciplinary research and creative use and may be of primary importance to many disciplines.

The Literature of the Performing Arts

Primary Sources

It is likely that almost any library will have some primary source material for the performing arts even if that material is no more than a dance

10. New York Public Library, *Dictionary Catalog of the Dance Collection: A List of Authors, Titles, and Subjects of Multi-Media Materials in the Dance Collection of the Performing Arts Research Center of the New York Public Library* (New York: The New York Public Library; Astor, Lenox and Tilden Foundations, 1974), viii.

11. Jay Robert Nash and Stanley Ralph Ross, *The Motion Picture Guide* (Chicago: Cinebooks, 1985–); Nash and Ross, *The Motion Picture Guide Index* (Chicago: Cinebooks, 1987).

program in a vertical file, a colorful movie poster on the wall, or a play script in a rare books and manuscripts collection. Many libraries have videotapes or films of theatre and dance performances as well as of feature films. In addition, facsimile and microform editions of historical documents including dance manuals, theatrical treatises, journals, manuscript collections, plays, scene and costume designs, and photograph collections to mention only a few have become increasingly available. This availability enables libraries to provide access to primary materials that otherwise could not be acquired.

In contrast, access to primary sources for film students is a problem. Subjecting films to repeated trips through a standard film projector will quickly result in a collection of damaged films. But film students doing papers on specific aspects of an assigned film usually see the film only once or twice in class and very often request additional viewings. The answer may be found in videotaping a copy of the film, purchasing the film in video format (if available), or in providing students access to an expensive viewing table. Clearly, a library may not be able to invest in any of these solutions, and the film student remains frustrated by limited access to primary source material—the film itself. Secondary resources such as critical writings are fairly widely available for most films taught in colleges and universities, but the number of published scripts remains low. This creates pressure on the library to seek unpublished scripts— one of the several challenges of collection development for film librarians.

Because of the varied natures of the items that constitute primary material in the performing arts, it should not be surprising that many different institutions house that material, and librarians and researchers alike should keep in mind that needed research material may not necessarily reside in the large performing arts libraries. Local and state historical societies and museums have often been the recipients of collections of performing artists or companies from the area. Likewise many performing arts professionals who have developed national and international reputations deposit or leave their collections to their alma maters, schools in their home towns, or institutions that at first glance seem to have no connection with the particular performer or the performing arts. For example, the playwright William Inge left a major portion of his collection to Independence Community College in his hometown of Independence, Kansas. Not only has the library there continued to acquire related materials to supplement the collection, but the school holds an annual William Inge Festival that brings to Independence, and honors, major American playwrights. Francis Robinson, whose career as a theatrical press agent and longtime assistant manager of the Metropolitan Opera brought him into intimate contact with professionals in theatre, music, and dance, deposited his extensive and rich collection at Vanderbilt University, his alma mater.

As works of arts serving one of the performing arts, visual materials such as scene and costume designs and actual stage drops and costumes may be found in art collections and museums as well as in libraries. As the evidence of production, these designs and their realizations can provide invaluable documentation for the historian and inspiration for the designer. These are only a few of the examples that may exist in many different kinds of collections and that prove that many librarians, curators, and archivists may be responsible for performing arts material even though they are not called performing arts librarians.

A particular problem of musical theatre is that a researcher will need access to the book (the text), the musical score, a sound recording, and any videotaped or filmed performances. A student may learn through exposure to others' performances, particularly by the acknowledged greats in the field. To deny access to these performances (which, depending on geographic location and financial status could well be the only professional performance the student may view) may be to force that student to work in a vacuum, or worse, with inferior role models.

Acquisition of ephemeral materials for performing arts collections is often by donation from a variety of sources. Donors may be enthusiasts, researchers, practitioners, or families of practitioners who have collected evidence of their interests and activities, often over a period of years. Frequently these collections focus on one area of interest and, therefore, are simultaneously limited in scope but comprehensive in coverage of that single area.

In addition to acquiring ephemeral materials that have already been assembled into a coherent collection, libraries frequently develop their own collections. For instance, in response to the need to assist theatre students and support programs in black and feminist theatre, the University of Washington Drama Library actively developed a collection of ephemeral materials on theatre companies.[12]

Secondary Sources

In addition to those donated materials that so often enrich a collection and give it a unique character, massive amounts of published materials should be acquired to cover the field. Interests of researchers often are

12. Liz Fugate, "Theatre Companies in the United States: An Ephemeral Collection at the University of Washington Drama Library," in *Arts and Access,* Vol. 15, *Performing Arts Resources* (New York: Theatre Library Assn., 1990), 1.

cyclical, so that judicious coverage in a variety of areas may find many portions unused at any given time and other portions inadequate to serve demand. This is particularly true in institutions that offer theatre productions since local researchers' interests very likely may be directly related to those productions. For instance, the production staff may require a combination of primary and secondary source material in critical writings on the play, reviews of performances, photographs of performances showing costume and scene designs, descriptions and plans, mechanical devices, and lighting plots. Therefore, it behooves a librarian to stay abreast of the season schedules for the school as well as of the performing arts activities in the community to provide adequately for researchers of upcoming performances.

As in every collection, reference services and collection development policies must be based on the patrons and their needs and the types of materials that are generally acquired for the collection. Because of the broad scope of the performing arts, librarians must be able to approach reference questions from multiple access points since questions may come from patrons in a variety of disciplines. The librarian also must keep many types of material in mind, including a heavy emphasis on primary resources that record or document the performance itself. Often a patron has no idea of the availability of such primary resources, and the librarian must be able to refer a serious inquiry to collections located in other states by keeping current contacts with key library and archival staffs elsewhere. No performing arts resource medium is entirely outside the collecting sphere of the large research library.

Film and Television

Because of the currency of film and television, periodicals play an important role in access to information about these fields. *International Film, Radio, and Television Journals* (ed. by Anthony Slide, Westport, Conn.: Greenwood Press, 1985) and *Union List of Film Periodicals* (Westport, Conn.: Greenwood Press, 1984) are examples of sources that provide useful information regarding periodicals. Kim Fisher's *On the Screen: A Film, Television, and Video Research Guide* (Littleton, Colo.: Libraries Unlimited, 1986) is a good overall guide to film-study resources of all kinds including reference books, journals, and bibliographies. Other helpful sources include Frank Manchel's *Film Study: A Resource Guide* (Cranbury, N.J.: Fairleigh Dickinson, 1987) and Bruce Austin's *Current Research in Film* (New York: Ablex, 1985).

Dance

As a field that has only recently begun to be considered in widespread scholarly inquiry, dance has not yet developed the array of secondary literature found for theatre, music, or even film. A 1982 study of the indexing of dance literature revealed that coverage by indexing and abstracting services was woefully inadequate, thus rendering dance information found in periodicals virtually inaccessible.[13] Serious efforts are being made to correct this problem. *Index to Dance Periodicals* (Boston, Mass.: G. K. Hall, 1991–) provides access to periodicals indexed by the Dance Collection of the New York Public Library. *Dance Abstracts and Index* (Los Angeles, Calif.: Dance Database Project, 1991–) includes not only periodicals but also relevant book chapters, dissertations, conference proceedings and reports, and book reviews. Other access to dance periodical literature is found in sources such as the *International Bibliography of Theatre* (New York: Theatre Research Data Center, 1982–), and periodicals themselves may be located through guides such as Doris Robinson's *Music and Dance Periodicals: An International Directory & Guidebook* (Voorheesville, N. Y.: Peri Press, 1989) as well as through reference tools with broad scopes.

Due to the increased demands by both dance performers and scholars, much-needed aesthetic, critical, bibliographical, and biographical works have been recently published, are forthcoming, or are proposed. A major work, international in scope, that should prove to be an extremely valuable resource in the field is *The International Encyclopedia of Dance*, edited by Selma Jeanne Cohen (Berkeley, Calif.: University of California Press, forthcoming). Garland Publishing's series, the Garland Library of Dance, will publish bio-bibliographies of choreographers as well as dance reference books, some of which were previously published in the Garland Reference Library of the Humanities series.

Other works include *Dance History: A Methodology for Study* (ed. by Janet Adshead and June Layson, London, Eng.: Dance Books Ltd., 1983); Fred R. Forbes, Jr.'s *Dance: An Annotated Bibliography 1965–1982* (New York and London, Eng.: Garland Publishing, Inc., 1986); *Researching Theatrical Dance: A Guide to Basic Collections, Bibliographies, Reference Books, Serials Historical Surveys, Manuals, Special Studies, Films, Addresses, and Other Essentials* (Washington, D.C.: ERIC, 1982) by Edward Pease; *French Court Dance and Dance Music: A Guide to Primary Source Writings, 1643–1789* (Stuyvesant, N.Y.: Pendragon Press, 1987) by Judith Schwartz and Christena Schlundt; and Alice Adamczyk's *Black Dance: An Annotated Bibliography* (New York: Garland Publishing, Inc., 1989).

Biographical sources include Barbara Cohen-Stratyner's *Biographical Dictionary of Dance* (New York: Schirmer Books, 1982) as well

13. Daniel Clenoot, "The Need for a Dance Periodical Index," *RQ* 23 (Fall 1983): 87–90.

as sources with broader scopes such as *A Biographical Dictionary of Actors, Actresses, Musicians, Dancers, Managers & Other Stage Personnel in London, 1660–1800* (Carbondale, Ill.: Southern Illinois University Press, 1973–) edited by Philip Highfill, Kalman Burnim, and Edward Langhans; and *Performing Arts Biography Master Index* (2d ed., Detroit, Mich.: Gale Research, 1981) edited by Barbara McNeil and Miranda Herbert. Because of the intimate relationship between dance and music, significant information on dance and dancers may be found in *The New Grove Dictionary of Music and Musicians* (London, Eng.: Macmillan, 1980). *Dance Film and Video Guide* (Princeton, N.J.: Princeton Book Co., 1991) provides information on more than 2,000 films and videos with access by choreographer, composer, dance company, dancer, director, and subject. This publication was compiled by Deirdre Towers for Dance Film Association, which also provides online telephone access to the information database for its members.

Theatre

As a long-established scholarly discipline in the performing arts, theatre has a major body of secondary literature for researchers at all levels, and numerous guides to that literature exist. While in need of updating, Claudia Jean Bailey's *A Guide to Reference and Bibliography for Theatre Research* (Columbus, Ohio: Publication Committee, The Ohio State University Libraries, 1983) remains a useful tool. Similar in concept but limited to post-World War II work is Irene Shaland's *American Theater and Drama Research: An Annotated Guide to Information Sources, 1945–1990* (Jefferson, N.C.: McFarland, 1991).

Two series provide other useful resources in theatre. Bibliographies and Indexes in the Performing Arts is a series published by Greenwood Press. Recent additions to this series include works on scenic, lighting, and costume designers and other biographical works, as well as resources on particular theatre companies, projects, or periods in theatre history. Gale Research Company's American Literature, English Literature, and World Literatures in English series includes guides to drama and theatre.

Charles Carpenter's *Modern Drama Scholarship and Criticism 1966–1980* (Toronto: University of Toronto Press, 1986) is international in scope and is supplemented in the journal *Modern Drama*. A useful examination of theatre theory is Marvin Carlson's *Theories of the Theatre: A Historical and Critical Survey, from the Greeks to the Present* (Ithaca, N.Y.: Cornell University Press, 1984). *Interpreting the Historical Past: Essays in the Historiography of Performance* (Iowa City, Iowa: University of Iowa Press, 1989), edited by Thomas Postlewait and Bruce A. McConachie, provides essays by scholars currently active in theatre historiography and a bibliography of recent works on theatre history as well as art history, literary history, cultural history, and general historiography.

While dated and limited in usefulness for those who do not read Italian, the *Enciclopedia dello Spettacolo* (Rome, It.: Casa Editrice le Maschere, 1954–1962) will continue to be a very important source due to its extensive historic coverage and excellent articles. More recent information may be found in *The Cambridge Guide to World Theatre* (Cambridge, Eng.: Cambridge University Press, 1988) edited by Martin Banham, and Oxford University Press publications including *The Oxford Companion to the Theatre* (Oxford, Eng.: Oxford University Press, 1983) edited by Phyllis Hartnoll, *The Oxford Companion to American Theatre* (New York: Oxford University Press, 1992) edited by Gerald Bordman, and *The Oxford Companion to Canadian Theatre* (Toronto, Can.: Oxford University Press, 1989) edited by Eugene Benson and L. W. Conolly. A major theatre reference work of international proportions, the *World Encyclopedia of Contemporary Theatre* (6 vols., London, Eng.: Routledge) is in progress under the sponsorship of the International Theatre Institute (ITI) and will cover theatre from 1945 to the present.

An ongoing project for theatre is the *International Bibliography of Theatre* sponsored by the American Society for Theatre Research and the International Association of Libraries and Museums of the Performing Arts in cooperation with the International Federation for Theatre Research. This annual publication covers all aspects of theatre publications of research significance for the given year. Theatre literature produced in 1982 was the first covered. After the initial volume, the lag time between year of coverage and year of publication has narrowed, and retrospective bibliography has begun on pre-1982 literature. As this publication develops, the taxonomy, which is a necessary component of the editors' approach, also develops, thereby providing researchers and librarians alike with a tool to use in the knotty question of theatre terminology and the lack of a standardized vocabulary. The *International Bibliography of Theatre* is affordable in print form for libraries and, although not yet publicly available online, has that capacity. As the database increases in size, consideration will be given to nonprint methods of dissemination.

Cataloging and Classification

As the systems in widest use in general collections in the United States, the Dewey decimal and the Library of Congress classifications are frequently used, either in original or modified forms, for performing arts collections since many collections that consist primarily of books follow the practice of their institutions and use one or the other of these systems. For large, comprehensive collections in theatre, dance, or film, neither system of classification is entirely satisfactory for the performing arts librarians or, often, for the patron. Robert Steele cites his frustration as a library patron interested in film literature as his initial motivation in writing *The Cataloging and Classification of Cinema Literature*.[14] Although the problems of cataloging and classifying performing arts materials have been widely discussed, no universally acceptable standards or systems have emerged. Of course, libraries that collect nonprint resources can catalog and classify them using standard cataloging rules and the same classification scheme as used for print materials. However, it is more likely that realia, properties, photographs, costumes, etc., are housed separately from print materials and, therefore, are cataloged in the archival manner by collection and arranged in a manner suited to the preservation of the resources. As with many disciplines, the overall application of classification systems varies so much from library to library that scholars may find themselves unable to apply accustomed search strategies in a strange library even if the classification system is familiar.

Four courses of action have been identified as the most common results of inadequate classification systems for theatre collections:

(1) the collection remains unclassified; (2) an existing classification scheme is endured in its original form, however unsuitable; (3) a scheme is modified to meet the needs of a specialized theatre collection; or (4) an entirely new classification for theatre collections is devised.[15]

Although the specific problems of the Dewey or Library of Congress classifications schemes are beyond the scope of this discussion a few examples of problems from several of the performing arts fields should suffice for illustration. The Dewey system places dance in 793.3, Indoor Games and Amusements, with the exception of ballet, which is located in 792, Theatre (Stage Presentations). Theatre is assigned one number, 792, and the decimal divisions also include ballet, 792.8. The separation of ballet from dance in Dewey may cause difficulties for patrons browsing in a large collection for all dance materials, but even more importantly, the interrelationship of ballet and other forms of theatrical dance is obscured by this separation. Similarly, relevant materials for film are located in several areas in Dewey. For instance, film production is found in 778, while film criticism is in 791.43. A similar problem occurs in

---

14. Steele, *Cataloging*, 13.
15. Lee R. Nemchek, "Problems of Cataloging and Classification in Theatre Librarianship," *Library Resources & Technical Services* 25 (Oct./Dec. 1981): 375.

the treatment of theatre in Dewey classification, which "committed . . . the cardinal sin of rigidly separating theatre as a mere 'recreation' from drama, which was duly sandwiched between each country's poetry and its prose as an aspect of 'literature.'"[16]

In theatre, dance, and film the Dewey system is simply inadequate for such far-reaching and comprehensive art forms. Therefore, librarians who are restricted to that system have often responded by modifying the system and creating their own decimal expansion. Yet even while making modifications, these librarians have acknowledged the inadequacy of their efforts.[17] Both theatre and dance have grown exponentially over this century; arts practitioners particularly, have an increased awareness of the need for publications to serve as forums for communication with others in the field. Of equal importance, there has been a growing commitment to document the ephemeral performance, a continuing extension of dance technique, a continued development and refinement of notation systems for dance, and a phenomenal advance in technical areas of theatre and dance.

The Library of Congress classification schedules for the performing arts, while much larger and more flexible than the Dewey classification, are still considered to be too general and lacking in both room for expansion and subject detail for many performing arts collections. The Library of Congress system places dance in GV—Recreation. This placement highlights the recreational rather than theatrical aspect of dance, thereby downplaying its artistic nature. This problem of placement affects not only theatrical dance but also any dance form, such as dances of the Renaissance and Baroque courts of Europe, that might occur in a social setting but that have broad cultural significance. An examination of the classification schedules shows that over the years, the Library of Congress system has been responsive to changes and advances in the dance field by expanding certain portions of the schedule to accommodate ever-growing amounts of materials. An unfortunate aspect of the schedule changes is in the subsuming of some smaller countries and regions, particularly Eastern European, into the national entry, thereby ignoring the individuality of regional dance traditions whose only link to a country may be official boundaries.

One adaptation of the Library of Congress system that resulted in the collocation of dance and theatre with the visual arts and music was developed for the Juilliard School Library. Dance was shifted from GV

16. Trussler, *Classification*, v.

17. A. M. C. Kahn, ed., *Theatre Collections: A Symposium, Library Resources in the Greater London Area*, no. 4 (London, Eng.: The Library Assn., 1955), 8–9; and A. M. Johnston, *Theatre Librarianship* (Sheffield, Eng.: University of Sheffield, 1979), 34–35.

to NN and NP, and books on the theatre were moved from P to N.[18] It should be noted that this solution of one problem causes another in the separation of theatre and dramatic literature, the same situation that exists with the treatment of theatre in Dewey classification. The standard Library of Congress placement of theatre in P reflects the historical treatment of theatre in terms of its literary component, drama. However, even the placement of both theatre and dramatic literature in P does not result in a close juxtaposition of all related materials since play texts are classified with the literature of each country.

Because of the varied nature of materials related to the performing arts, a number of specialized systems have been developed or proposed. Of these systems, three that were published have evidently never been put into practice in a library but are frequently cited in theatre library literature. Mary Ambler's *Classification for Theatre Libraries* allows for consideration of theatrical materials in four categories: buildings and architecture, plays and drama, personnel, and stagecraft and production. In addition, this system also provides for the classification of ephemeral materials that are so often found in performing arts collections.[19] The system published by Antony Croghan in *A Faceted Classification for and an Essay on the Literature of the Performing Arts* is generally considered too cumbersome and complex to be put into practice. It is also doubtful that a dance librarian would be willing to use a system whose developer considers ballet "a lesser art. . ." that "can never reach the heights of drama."[20] The third system, Simon Trussler's *A Classification for the Performing Arts*, was developed to be

> . . .adaptable, reasonably economical in notation. . ., mnemonic in the use of systematic schedules, and expansive according to need,. . .to exemplify and synthesize all these structural features in applying the principle of collocation. . . .[21]

In this system, which was applied and tested in bibliographies published in *Theatre Quarterly*, Trussler uses twenty-six main classes that move from general to historical to theoretical to practical and three schedules for classification by form, by history of drama and theatre, and by areas and countries.[22] Although the classification itself does not provide for

---

18. Bennet Ludden, "The Dance Classification System of the Juilliard School Library," *Theatre Documentation* 1 (Fall 1968): 22.

19. Nemchek, "Problems of Cataloging," 377.

20. Antony Croghan, *A Faceted Classification for and an Essay on the Literature of the Performing Arts* (London, Eng.: Antony Croghan, 1968), 10.

21. Trussler, *Classification*, viii.

22. Trussler, *Classification*, xxi, 54–57.

ephemera, the problem could be solved by adopting James Ellis's suggested Schedule IV[23] or by adding ephemera to Schedule I, classification
by form.[24]

One published system developed in response to the needs of a particular theatre collection is the Research Classification System at The Ohio
State University's Library of the Jerome Lawrence and Robert E. Lee
Theatre Research Institute. When the system was devised in the 1950s,
the largest part of the Institute's holdings was a microfilm collection of
historical theatrical documents obtained from European and American
libraries and museums. Since much of the microfilm was iconographic
in nature, it was considered important to have frame-level access. The
system developed is a faceted one with six elements that create a unique
identification: historical period, general subject (artist, costume, lighting,
staging, play, scene design, theatre), medium (cinema, circus, commedia,
dance, legitimate theatre, mechanical theatre, pageant, television, non-
theatrical, satirical print), subdivision of the subject, country of origin,
and individual piece number. Although this system has been used as a
model for other theatre collections, it is very specific to the needs of a
particular collection and to the research methods encouraged there during the developmental stages of the system. There are obvious omissions
in coverage, particularly in the areas of modern stage technology and design. The system provides very limited general subject and title access
and is inadequate for the textual materials that make up an increasing
part of the collection's acquisitions. Nevertheless, for the materials that
the system was intended to serve, access can be quick and in-depth.

A number of special collections, including the Library of the Lawrence
and Lee Theatre Research Institute and the Performing Arts Collection
of the Wagner Labor Archives at New York University, have developed
collection databases that run locally on microcomputers, may or may not
be MARC-based, and provide in-depth access to collection materials.[25]
In many special collections, collection-level records in the Archives and
Manuscripts Control format are created and input to OCLC or RLIN. While
providing some limited access on the national level, this two-pronged approach has disadvantages: detailed information is available only at the

---

23. James Ellis, "A Taxonomy of the Theatre: Simon Trussler's *A Classification for
the Performing Arts*," *Theatre Research International* 1 (May 1976): 221–22.

24. Nemchek, "Problems of Cataloging," 378.

25. Nena Couch, "The Theatre Research Institute and Its Collections within a Large
Institution: The Jerome Lawrence and Robert E. Lee Theatre Research Institute of The Ohio
State University," in *Arts and Access*, Vol. 15, *Performing Arts Resources* (New York:
Theatre Library Assn., 1990), 48–49; Martha Schmoyer LoMonaco, "Putting Performance
On-Line," in *Arts and Access*, Vol. 15, *Performing Arts Resources* (New York: Theatre
Library Assn., 1990), 51–57.

local level, and data in individually developed database systems are not easily transferrable.[26]

Librarians have frequently expressed dissatisfaction regarding the inadequacy of lists of subject headings for the performing arts. For comprehensive collections or collections that collect comprehensively in defined areas, the commonly used *Library of Congress Subject Headings* (LCSH) fails to provide in-depth access and is slow to respond to changes and advances in the artistic fields or to cover areas of historical interest. As an example, there is no Library of Congress subject heading for tent shows—a popular form of entertainment for rural areas and small towns in the nineteenth and first third of the twentieth centuries. Vaudeville is a good subject heading and related term, but not all tent shows were vaudeville.

The lack of in-depth subject headings has led major research facilities such as the New York Public Library's Billy Rose Theatre Collection and the Dance Collection to develop their own subject headings. *Theatre Subject Headings* (Boston, Mass.: G. K. Hall, 1966) reflects the development of a detailed subject heading list for theatre since the establishment of the theatre collection in the New York Public Library in 1931. Two subject heading systems are currently in use at the Billy Rose Theatre Collection: for books cataloged since 1971, Library of Congress subjects headings have been used; however, for nonbook material, the richest and most well-known component of the collection, the subject heading list developed there continues to be used.

As a result of their catalog automation project, the Dance Collection staff found that both the Library of Congress and the New York Public Library subject headings were inadequate. A comprehensive list of subject headings and cross-references was devised to provide the detailed subject access necessary for a collection of such magnitude. The catalog automation project was successfully completed resulting in publication of the *Dictionary Catalog of the Dance Collection* (New York: The New York Public Library; Astor, Lenox and Tilden Foundations, 1974), now on CD-ROM as well as in print, and its annual update, the *Bibliographic Guide to Dance* (1975–   ). Performing arts librarians worldwide may reap the benefits of the pioneering work done by Dance Collection and New York Public Library staff not only in the creation of a major subject, name, and title authority but also in the catalog automation project itself.

Subject headings for film are notoriously difficult to use. The policy of superimposing rules for descriptive cataloging has created layers upon

---

26. For one library's efforts to serve both national standards and local needs, see Martha M. Yee, "Cataloging at the UCLA Film and Television Archive," in *Arts and Access*, Vol. 15, *Performing Arts Resources* (New York: Theatre Library Assn., 1990), 59–72.

layers of archaic subject terms connected by a shaky and labor-intensive system of cross-references for most areas of the performing arts. Old headings still in place in most card catalogs for film-related topics are mixed in with some improvements such as direct entry terms (for example, the direct entry "animated films" rather than "moving pictures—cartoons"). But in many libraries a searcher must use such astounding terms as "Cinematography—trick" for special effects. Since most academic libraries use the Library of Congress subject headings list of terms, the cinema librarian invariably must create a guide for doing cinema research in the library that includes instructions on the most useful subject terms. Hundreds of such user guides exist across the country.

Two project proposals that were not implemented but that reflect the concern of theatre librarians and researchers about the general inadequacy of bibliographic control of theatre materials were the Conference on Automation and Documentation in Theatre Research Libraries that the Charles MacArthur Center for American Theatre attempted to organize and the Big Ten Performing Arts Document Inventory Project spearheaded by Alfred S. Golding of The Ohio State University. As part of a program to: "locate, describe, and make accessible all primary and major secondary theatre research materials," five ambitious objectives for theatre research materials and libraries were identified for the Conference on Automation and Documentation:

> [to develop] (1) a standard terminology . . ., (2) [an] initial framework and [a] commitment for the development of a modern classification scheme, (3) [the] compilation of an informal directory of holding locations . . . and the formulation of plans for a national inventory, (4) [the] formulation of plans for a national theatre information system, (5) [and plan] for a "consortium" of theatre research libraries.[27]

The Big Ten Project was intended to inventory theatre holdings in the collections of the participating universities and to form a regional online databank. Although the project was ultimately not funded, "A Thesaurus for the Big Ten Performing Arts Document Inventory Project" (Columbus, Ohio: The Ohio State University, 1978), an outcome of the extensive work done in preparation, provides one approach to a source of performing arts terminology as well as a rationale for the thesaurus. It is unfortunate that lack of funding was instrumental in bringing both these projects to a standstill, leaving the problems addressed but unsolved.

The advent of online catalogs in libraries of all sizes with such features as good authority control systems, automatically produced lists of

27. "Conference on Automation and Documentation in Theatre Research Libraries," (Tallahassee, Fla.: The Charles MacArthur Center for American Theatre, 1974, Photocopy), 1–2.

new headings used, and keyword searching will continue to bring improved access in areas such as performing arts in which the standard thesaurus is awkward or inadequate. As large, old card catalogs become converted to machine-readable format through retroconversion projects, as name and subject headings are "flipped" to headings used by *Anglo-American Cataloging Rules*, Second Edition, and as users of online catalogs become more sophisticated in their search construction, many of the problems posed by card files will disappear.

Retrieval of journal literature in many of the interdisciplinary areas of scholarship related to film, theatre, and dance; performance reviews; film and theatre industry news and other research literature such as dissertations, theses, and conference papers, is being automated as well. Online databases provided by vendors such as BRS and DIALOG are increasingly available in the arts. Several hundred American Library Association conference attendees at a recent Association of College and Research Libraries (ACRL) Arts Section program entitled "Databases in the Arts" heard speakers including James Monaco, who presented information about his new film-industry index called Baseline, discuss the thesaurus, indexing structure, and contents of several online files. Although the arts and humanities literature is not represented by as many databases as the sciences, access is improving, usually through interdisciplinary files such as Arts & Humanities Search (the online version of the *Arts & Humanities Citation Index*) or RILM Abstracts of Music Literature. Moreover, compact discs that will improve access to literature in some areas of the arts are appearing on the marketplace for libraries. One particularly important example is the Film Literature Index databases covering both film and television through the Wilsondisc product line. A German online database that promises to provide past and present production information for European countries is TANDEM, developed at the Deutsches Theatermuseum in Munich. TANDEM will also provide location information for materials. Other theatre databases do exist, but "automation apathy" among researchers in the performing arts must be partially to blame for the slow development of such resources in the arts and humanities.[28]

One exciting result of technological advances is the advent of electronic mail, which allows scholars worldwide quick and easy communication with individuals and groups. As an example, SHAKSPER, an electronic conference operating from the University of Toronto, provides its membership of scholars, students, and interested parties with a variety of online options including a forum for communication and exchange of

28. Helen K. Bolton, "Development and Use of Theatre Databases," *Advances in Library Administration and Organization* Vol. 8 (Greenwich, Conn.: JAI Press, 1989), 142–43.

ideas and access to information and developments in Shakespeare activities as well as to directories, works in progress, and papers submitted by members.

But possibly the greatest change expected in the area of performing arts documentation will be in the area of the use of compact discs and videodiscs to store and retrieve images. The technology is available to store and manipulate images with laser technology, and as libraries continue to invest in equipment that provides access to compact discs and laserdiscs, the market is likely to increase for products that store a digital recording of a performance or selections from a performance. Not only archival but instructional use can be made of such technology. Interactive videodisc productions for teaching films already have been developed in several universities. Computer-assisted instructional programs linked to digitized images are relatively easy to design using commercially available products for IBM-compatible and Macintosh microcomputers. The increasing availability of computers, development of flexible database-management software, and training of librarians and the general public in the use of computers offer great promise for the performing arts collection. At the least, libraries will begin to computerize the great variety of finding aids that traditionally have been prepared for the types of materials that do not lend themselves to standard cataloging procedures. If adequate planning is devoted to the construction of the database and to the desired access points, these finding aids may yield much greater information to researchers than in the past.

Library Facilities for Performing Arts

Because of the specialized nature of much of the material found in performing arts collections, some special needs may exist for equipment and facilities. Of primary importance is a facility that provides for the security and preservation of the collection. Measures must be taken to prevent theft or mutilation of materials and to control the environment to prevent deterioration of materials from light, temperature, humidity, and dirt. Some materials may require nothing more than a table for viewing and perhaps gloves for the researcher to use in handling, while others may require more specialized types of equipment.

A guide to equipment supporting performing arts library research is found in editor George Boston's *Guide to the Basic Technical Equipment Required by Audio, Film and Television Archives* (s.l.: Coordinating Committee for the Technical Commissions of the International Organisations for Audio, Film and Television Archives, 1991) jointly sponsored by the Fédération Internationale des Archives du Film, Fédération

Internationale des Archives de Télévision, International Association of Sound Archives, International Council of Archives, and the United Nations Educational, Scientific, and Cultural Organisation.

Equipment that might be standard for a performing arts collection includes record and tape players with amplifiers, speakers, and headphones, and video and film equipment. Since the collection may well hold a variety of audio, video, and film formats, the librarian may have to acquire and maintain types of equipment that are no longer in common use or have to locate that equipment as the need arises for hearing or viewing an older format. In some cases the material may have to be converted to another format for ease of use and for preservation purposes. Many university media centers, for instance, have converted 16mm films to video. Theatre, dance, and cinema collectors must make decisions about the primary format of their collections of moving images. In addition, the archival copy and the use copy may be in different formats. Certainly, reformatting may not be possible in all cases due to the cost, the condition of the original, and copyright considerations.

A slide projector and screen are often necessary pieces of equipment for the highly visual disciplines of dance and theatre. Many film archives that serve scholars interested in frame-by-frame analysis of motion pictures provide viewing tables, which are not as destructive to the film as are standard projectors. For microforms, a variety of readers and reader-printers may be required for the formats included in the collection. For the care of all materials, and for the long life of the equipment, it is important that all equipment be cleaned and maintained on a regular schedule. As many libraries have found, equipment of this type is often highly desirable and, therefore, susceptible to theft, so it is important to provide a secure area in which to use the materials and, thus, protect both the collection and the equipment.

Archival collections of film, theatre, or dance documentation require standard preservation supplies such as acid-free boxes, window covers to provide protection from daylight, or encapsulation equipment. It is fairly well-known that early films produced on nitrate are now a major preservation problem being addressed by the American Film Institute, the Library of Congress, and other archives of early films. These nitrate films literally dissolve, and there have been recent instances of large-scale destruction of nitrate films from explosions. In California, special local ordinances sometimes prevent viewing of films on nitrate, and those organizations involved in preservation must house the films in special vaults prior to the films' conversion to safer forms of film or tape.

The issue of video preservation is one of great concern to performing arts librarians since it is such a useful medium to capture movement as well as speech. Unfortunately, videotape is not a preservation medium, and information is already being lost from unique videotape documentation of performing arts. Deirdre Boyle's "Video Preservation: Insuring the Future of the Past" in *The Independent* (Oct. 1991: 25–31) summarizes the issues that face video archivists and others and offers some partial solutions to those problems.

Profile of Performing Arts Librarianship

Education of the Performing Arts Librarian

Within the framework of the given library and the nature of the collection, the librarian in the performing arts acquires, cares for, and makes available for use materials that provide information to researchers—easily said, but not so easily accomplished. A number of abilities and skills, some basic for adequate performance by any librarian and some unique to the performing arts, must be learned and developed. Two of the most important qualities a librarian should have for this work are a subject interest in one of the performing arts and the willingness to learn about the others in order to be well-rounded and able to provide adequate assistance to researchers. Most librarians come to this field of librarianship with at least a love of the subject matter, while a significant number come as performer-scholars.

Specialized education for performing arts librarianship has been under discussion sporadically for decades in the United States.[29] In the past, many performing arts librarians have brought a subject-area specialization and interest to the field from their previous positions, often as teachers, performers, or collectors. Frequently these librarians have had no library training but learn about library procedures and develop their skills in those procedures on the job. Although this may continue to be the case for some libraries, recent job listings for performing arts librarians in academic and research libraries seem to indicate a move toward the requirement of a Master of Library Science (MLS) degree. A 1990 survey of theatre librarians showed that 70 percent of respondents held library degrees in contrast to 60 percent in a 1979 survey.[30] It is also interesting to note that there is a crossover of arts librarians from subject-area training in one performing art to work in another. As in any field, subject specialization enables the librarian to communicate with the

29. See Johnston, *Theatre Librarianship;* and Lee R. Nemchek, "Education for Theatre Librarianship," *Journal for Education for Librarianship* 21 (Summer 1980): 49–62.

30. Susan C. Jewell, *Education for Theat* Librar** (Albany, N.Y.: State University of New York at Albany, School of Information Science and Policy, 1990), 19.

patron. Although either subject knowledge or library management skills *can* be learned on the job, it is preferable to seek individuals with previous training and experience in both.

Hopeful performing arts librarians with an MLS degree may come to the profession in several ways: with an interest in one of the performing arts, with an undergraduate or graduate degree in one of the performing arts, with experience in one of the performing arts, or with specialized training in the performing arts made available in the MLS program.

In 1959 George Freedley, curator of the Theatre Collection of the New York Public Library, taught a course on theatre librarianship at the Columbia University School of Library Service, the first course of its kind offered by a school of library science. Columbia continued to be a leader in specialized training for performing arts librarians with its course, Literature of the Performing Arts: A Survey of Reference Tools and Information Sources in the Performing Arts: Music, Recordings, Dance, Theatre, Film, Radio, and Television.[31] Other courses that could be of value in the performing arts include literature of the humanities, field work in special libraries, preservation of library and archival materials, and popular culture.

In 1976 to 1977, Florida State University School of Library Science, with the Charles MacArthur Center for American Theatre, offered a specialization in theatre librarianship. The university was considering for implementation a number of services and projects including an ongoing MLS degree with specialization in performing arts librarianship and "institutes, workshops and seminars on performing arts librarianship to be given regionally... as continuing education opportunities."[32] Unfortunately for the development of professional training programs of performing arts librarians, the course did not continue. In 1980 the Department of Drama at the University of Manchester, Great Britain, announced a one-year diploma course entitled Performing Arts Archives and Collection Studies that included work in the departments of the History of Art and Extra-Mural Studies, the University Library, and practicums in theatre collections. The program covered "theory, practical skills and techniques... including selection and classification, cataloguing and information retrieval, conservation and restoration, exhibition work, publicity, and relevant administration."[33] The Manchester program fared no better than the MacArthur program and was also discontinued.

Courses are available to students in several graduate programs of library science, but they are often taught by auxiliary faculty on an infre-

31. *Columbia University Bulletin, 1986–1987*, School of Library Service, 20 (Jan. 1986).

32. "Conference on Automation and Documentation," 1–2.

33. "Performing Arts Archives and Collection Studies," *Broadside* n.s., 8 (Fall 1980): 4.

quent basis. Only a few programs have regularly available course work on performing arts or film literature in the curriculum. One of these is the Division of Library and Information Science at San Jose State University that offers Resources in the Performing and Visual Arts on a regular basis at San Jose and occasionally at the Division's Fullerton campus.

For book collections of theatre and dance, special courses other than standard literature or bibliography courses in humanities or arts, which tend to cover some of the major materials in the field, do not seem commonly to exist. The UCLA Graduate School of Library and Information Science has placed interns at the Academy of Motion Picture Arts and Sciences (AMPAS), the American Film Institute (AFI), the Huntington Library, and the J. Paul Getty Museum Library. In addition, students may petition to have prior course work that clearly shows a relationship applied to the chosen specialization in the library science program, so that it is possible to tailor programs to meet career objectives.[34] The Graduate School of Library and Information Science at the State University of New York–Albany offers a course on film librarianship, and the recent combination of several library science programs with communication programs may allow students even greater flexibility when seeking course work in the performance media.

It is obvious that for most library science degree programs, it will be necessary for those with an interest in specialization as performing arts librarians to devote some careful planning to their studies in order to incorporate a subject area specialization into a library degree program. It is possible to choose schools with good library science departments as well as performing arts departments, especially ones that offer graduate degrees in the history of the discipline. The library science program would need to be one that allows outside electives, or the student should plan to stay longer to take specialized courses that might include any research methods or bibliography courses offered through theatre, film, and dance departments. Particularly desirable are programs that are located conveniently to performing arts collections and that not only provide opportunities for practicums, internships, and field work but also actively assist the student in securing those opportunities. In this way, an interested student would be able to construct an individualized program that combines the necessary training in librarianship with focused study in the subject area and with on-the-job work experience.

With the increasing awareness in recent years of the special handling needs of the nonprint materials, such as those frequently found in performing arts collections, and an awareness of the general conservation

34. *UCLA Graduate School of Library and Information Science, 1987–88* (Los Angeles, Calif.: UCLA Public Affairs Department, Academic Publications, 1986).

needs of all materials, more library science courses on preservation and conservation will be available to performing arts librarians.

Professional Associations and Continuing Education

In the United States, the performing arts librarian has been served since 1937 by the Theatre Library Association (TLA). This organization represents not only librarians and curators of collections but also performing arts practitioners and scholars. Established "to bring together librarians and individuals interested in the collection and preservation of material relating to the theatre, and to stimulate general interest in the making and use of theatre collections,"[35] the statement of purpose was broadened in 1975 to read as follows:

> the advancement of public knowledge of the theatre and theatre arts by (a) furthering the interest of collecting, preserving and using theatre material in libraries, museums and private collections; (b) assisting in the preparation of programs for library schools about the preservation of theatre materials; (c) encouraging discussion about the particular problems of librarianship in theatre and other performing arts collections; (d) answering questions about theatre library problems; (e) sponsoring courses and seminars in librarianship in the theatre and theatre arts; and (f) publishing occasional newsletters and other publications on the subject.[36]

From the early years of TLA to the present time, the association has supported dance and film in addition to theatre as shown in its coverage of those arts in the TLA-sponsored publications *Broadside, Theatre Annual, Theatre Documentation*, and *Performing Arts Resources*. As a result of this service to dance and film as well as theatre, a motion was entertained in 1978 to change the name of the organization to the Performing Arts Library Association. Although the name was not changed, TLA continues to provide a forum for the greater community of performing arts librarians and scholars.

TLA produces two regular publications that provide readers with helpful information in many aspects of the performing arts: *Broadside* and *Performing Art Resources*. *Broadside*, the association's newsletter, highlights new collections, those collections that have acquired new materials or undergone changes that would be of interest to members, and previously unknown collections. The newsletter also provides book reviews, reports on meetings and notices of related conferences, lists of

35. Sarah Chokla Gross, "The Theatre Library Association and *Broadside*," *Wilson Library Bulletin* 38 (Apr. 1964): 664.
36. Louis A. Rachow, "The Theatre Library Association," *Encyclopedia of Library and Information Science* 30 (1980): 415.

books received, and works in progress. *Performing Arts Resources*, an annual TLA publication, has covered various aspects of a particular theatre topic, has made available the texts of historical theatrical documents that are not easily accessible, and has described collections of interest and the ways in which those collections are processed and made available for use. A particularly helpful volume of *Performing Arts Resources* (vol. 15), *Arts and Access: Management Issues for Performing Arts Collections*, deals with a variety of issues facing performing arts librarians, including the establishment of a collection; collection management topics such as preservation, fundraising, cataloging, and bibliographic access; and service issues.

A TLA publication, *Preserving America's Performing Arts Resources: Papers from the Conference on Preservation Management for Performing Arts Collections* (1985), includes essays by experts in the fields of performing arts and conservation. The bibliography and technical information provided are of great value for librarians faced with the preservation needs of materials that were often designed to be discarded. In line with its commitment to make available theatrical materials, TLA sponsored the publication of *Three Centuries of English and American Plays* (New York: Readex Microprint, 1942–), a massive project to provide microform access to all extant plays, whether in print or in manuscript, from the sixteenth through the eighteenth centuries. This project has made available plays that are obscure, difficult to obtain, or available only in manuscript; it is a major contribution to the field of theatre scholarship.

The American Society for Theatre Research (ASTR), an organization with which the TLA has overlapping membership and often holds joint meetings, is dedicated to promoting knowledge of the history of theatre and to serving American theatre historians. ASTR has provided a forum for scholarly work in its various publications, which include occasional monographs on aspects of theatre history, conference papers, and the semiannual journal *Theatre Survey*. Established in 1956 as a result of the 1955 International Congress on the History of the Theatre in Venice, ASTR has had a close and continuous affiliation with the International Federation for Theatre Research (IFTR), an international umbrella for public and private organizations as well as individuals active in theatre research.[37]

Another international organization that serves institutions, collections, and individuals is the Société Internationale des Bibliothèques et Musées des Arts du Spectacle/International Association of Libraries and

---

37. Thomas F. Marshall, "The First Quarter Century of ASTR," *Theatre Survey* 22 (Nov. 1981): 117–24.

Museums of the Performing Arts (SIBMAS). The purpose of SIBMAS is to promote practical and theoretical research in the documentation of the performing arts; to establish permanent international contacts among specialized libraries, museums, and documentation centers; to coordinate the work of members; and to facilitate international exchanges.[38] SIBMAS publishes *Bibliothèques et Musées des Arts du Spectacle dans le Monde/Performing Arts Libraries and Museums of the World* (4th ed., Paris, Fr.: Éditions du Centre National de la Recherche Scientifique, 1992), which attempts to supply worldwide coverage of performing arts collections. Information supplied to SIBMAS by individual libraries, museums, and collections includes general characteristics, policies on access and reader assistance, the history and nature of the holdings, and other activities of the organization. Each new edition of this major reference work has been greatly expanded from the previous edition, reflecting the establishment of new collections, inclusion of previously unidentified collections, and additions to known collections.

Dance librarians do not have a distinct professional society although they have had representation in TLA from the inception of that organization, and through the international organizations SIBMAS and IFTR. Very recently, a group of dance librarians also approached the American Library Association's Association of College and Research Libraries (ACRL) Arts Section, and formed a discussion group to consider relevant dance issues as well as to publish a regular column in the Arts Section newsletter. There are two related organizations serving scholars in the field of dance to which many performing arts librarians belong: The Congress on Research in Dance (CORD) and the Society of Dance History Scholars (SDHS). CORD promotes research in dance as well as interdisciplinary research related to dance. Its publication *Dance Research Journal* contains book reviews, provides a bibliography of new works in the fields of dance and related disciplines, discusses collections, and publishes articles on aspects of dance including technique, scholarship, notation, education, and aesthetics. CORD's *The Dance Research Annual* has consisted of conference proceedings and papers and collected essays on aspects of a particular topic or has been a monograph. SDHS is concerned with research in dance history. Operating in the early stages under the umbrella of CORD, it is now an independent organization that sponsors an annual conference. *Proceedings* of the Society's conferences are published and provide information of great use to the dance librarian and scholar alike.

---

38. Application for membership, Société Internationale des Bibliothèques et Musées des Arts du Spectacle/International Association of Libraries and Museums of the Performing Arts.

The indexing of dance periodicals and other problems were addressed at the Bibliography of Dance Studies Research Conference held in 1985 at the Library of Congress. The dance scholars and librarians attending had three goals:

> (1) to develop a working taxonomy for the dance field; (2) to develop a network of bibliographers and scholars committed to the ongoing task of indexing and abstracting research materials; and (3) to begin discussions on practical aspects essential for the realization of the project.[39]

Since the conference, the taxonomy has been developed and ongoing work has resulted in the publication of *Dance Abstracts and Index*.

A group whose membership is not currently open but whose work will ultimately benefit dance librarians has been funded by the Andrew W. Mellon Foundation. The planning group, consisting of representatives from the Dance Collection of the New York Public Library, the Harvard Theatre Collection, the Library of Congress, and the San Francisco Performing Arts Library and Museum, will propose a coalition to deal with a variety of issues on dance documentation. This project is an outgrowth of a study jointly funded by the National Endowment for the Arts and the Andrew W. Mellon Foundation. The report of that study is *Images of American Dance: Documenting and Preserving a Cultural Heritage* (Washington, D.C., and New York: National Endowment for the Arts and the Andrew W. Mellon Foundation, 1991).

Perhaps because the scholarly community of film is so new, there is not a well-developed professional community for film librarians. Librarians are not particularly active in the scholarly organizations for film faculty, and there is not a separate film librarians' organization. From 1977 to 1985, there was a forum for film library information and discussion within the American Library Association's ACRL called the Cinema Librarians' Discussion Group. This group often cosponsored meetings with TLA. Recently, programs and membership of the former Cinema Librarians' Discussion Group have been picked up by the ACRL Arts Section. This move, as does the recent involvement of dance librarians in the ACRL Arts Section, supports the trend toward interdisciplinary professional discussion among the visual and performing arts. For the last several years, librarians interested in film as well as dance information have attended programs sponsored by the Arts Section and, as members of the Arts Section, received *Arts Newsletter*.

39. "Conference on Dance Bibliography Establishes New Data Base Project," *Library of Congress Bulletin* 44, no. 16 (22 Apr. 1985): 85–86.

Relevant organizations on an international level include the International Federation of Film Archives (FIAF) and International Federation of Television Archives (FIAT), which produce *International Index to Film Periodicals* (New York: Bowker, 1972–), *International Index to Television Periodicals* (London, Eng.: FIAF, 1979–), *Subject Headings: International Index to Television Periodicals* (London, Eng.: FIAF, 1992), and *Subject Headings: International Index to Film Periodicals* (London, Eng.: FIAF, 1990). In addition to producing these indexes through shared indexing by members, regular meetings of FIAF are held in Europe in which the few U.S. members of FIAF (including the Library of Congress and the American Film Institute Library) participate. Another international association related to film study is the International Association of Mass Communication Research (IAMCR). Meetings of the IAMCR include sessions for bibliographers at which literature on film as a mass communication medium is discussed.

As evidenced by the joint meetings of TLA, ASTR, and occasionally SDHS, the performing arts and scholarly endeavor regarding those arts are also interdisciplinary in nature. Scholars in the performing arts have tended to communicate through professional societies and conferences and organizations' newsletters and journals. The results of scholarly endeavors are disseminated in association publications, conference proceedings, other periodicals, and monographs. Therefore, the value of these professional societies, whether officially dedicated to a performing arts library specialization or not, is of significance to librarians, scholars, and practitioners in these arts.

In addition to the previously discussed organizations (which are related by subject matter), continuing education needs of performing arts librarians have been reflected over the years in the development of related programs in other societies and institutions. In 1968 the Graduate School of Library Science at the Drexel Institute of Technology sponsored a workshop on "Librarianship in the Performing Arts."[40] In the Society of American Archivists (SAA), a Performing Arts Roundtable has been established whose mission is "to promote the exchange of information on historical and contemporary documentation of the specialized categories of music, dance, theatre, motion pictures and other performance media."[41] Recognizing a growing need, SAA held a meeting in Chicago entitled "Performing Arts Collections: Issues and Challenges." As is the case with the ACRL Arts Section, SAA's Performing Arts Round-

---

40. "TLA's Year in Review," *Broadside* o.s., 28 (Oct. 1969): 3.
41. "About SAA . . ." [promotional literature] (Feb. 1987), 3.

table provides what seems to be an expanding forum for interested librarians and archivists.

There are also frequent workshops on preservation and conservation that are offered by the Society of American Archivists and other organizations. PRESERVE: The Coalition for Performing Arts Archives is a not-for-profit organization that conducted workshops on archival organization and preservation methods in 1989 and 1990 for more than 450 representatives of performing arts organizations across the United States and that continues to provide instruction and assistance in the area of preservation of performing arts documentation.[42]

The AFI's Meyer Library annually offers a one-week intensive workshop in film and television documentation that introduces librarians and scholars to the full array of documentation, to issues in preservation, and to topics in collection development, access, reference, and cataloging that are unique to these disciplines. Site visits to Los Angeles–area collections are especially interesting and, in the past, have stressed film preservation programs for nitrate film stock. Of particular interest was a 1981 AFI session attended by more than 80 librarians, including several representatives from the United Kingdom, on uses of computers in film and performing arts libraries. This conference, held in Washington, D. C., was called the Film and Television Archival Cataloging and Documentation Conference.

Conclusion

The performing arts library offers patrons the opportunity to look into the past, investigate the present, create, and preserve for the future in disciplines that are vital aspects of human existence. Although the nature of performing arts collections, difficulty of access to materials, lack of adequate funding, and as-yet undefined standards for librarianship complicate progress in the field, the problems are not insurmountable. Work is being done on many fronts and by many supporters to provide assistance in the solution of these problems. The increasing awareness of the performing arts as a rich aspect of our heritage by all involved— the library profession, administrators, conservators, researchers, donors, and the general public—will lead to the recognition and support of performing arts librarianship and libraries.

---

42. Leslie Hansen Kopp, "PRESERVE: Assuring Dance a Life Beyond Performance," in *Arts and Access*, Vol. 15, *Performing Arts Resources* (New York: Theatre Library Assn., 1990), 13.

Professional Readings

Blazek, Ron, and Elizabeth Aversa. "Accessing Information in the Performing Arts" and "Principal Information Sources in the Performing Arts." In *The Humanities: a Selective Guide to Information Sources*, 166–261. 3d ed. Englewood, Colo.: Libraries Unlimited, Inc., 1988.

Boston, George, ed. *Guide to the Basic Technical Equipment Required by Audio, Film and Television Archives*. s.l.: Coordinating Committee for the Technical Commissions of the International Organisations for Audio, Film and Television Archives, 1991.

Clenott, Daniel. "The Need for a Dance Periodical Index." *RQ* 23 (Fall 1983): 87–90.

Cohen, Selma Jeanne. *The International Encyclopedia of Dance*. Berkeley, Calif.: University of California Press, forthcoming.

Cohen-Stratyner, Barbara Naomi, ed. *Arts and Access: Management Issues for Performing Arts Collections*. Vol. 15, *Performing Arts Resources*. New York: Theatre Library Assn., 1990.

———, and Brigitte Kueppers, eds. *Preserving America's Performing Arts: Papers from the Conference on Preservation Management for Performing Arts Collection, April 28–May 1, 1982, Washington, D.C.* New York: Theatre Library Assn., 1985.

"Columbia Pioneers for Theatre Librarians." *Broadside*, o.s., 20 (Winter 1959): 1–2.

"Conference on Automation and Documentation in Theatre Research Libraries." Tallahassee, Fla.: The Charles MacArthur Center for American Theatre, 1974. Photocopy.

Couch, Nena. "The Theatre Research Institute and Its Collections within a Large Institution: The Jerome Lawrence and Robert E. Lee Theatre Research Institute of The Ohio State University." In *Arts and Access*, 45–50. Vol. 15, *Performing Arts Resources*. New York: Theatre Library Assn., 1990.

Croghan, Antony. *A Faceted Classification for and an Essay on the Literature of the Performing Arts*. London, Eng.: Antony Croghan, 1968.

Ellis, James. "A Taxonomy of the Theatre: Simon Trussler's *A Classification for the Performing Arts*." *Theatre Research International* 1 (May 1976): 216–22.

Forbes, John M. "Libraries and the Preservation of American Popular Culture Dance." *Drexel Library Quarterly* 16 (1980): 89–99.

Freedley, George. "The Need for the Training of Theatre Librarians." *Educational Theatre Journal* 8 (Mar. 1956): 25–28.

———. "Teaching Theatre Librarianship." *Journal of Education for Librarianship* 2 (Summer 1961): 20–27.

———. "Theatre Librarianship." *Bulletin of the New York Public Library* 66 (Jan. 1962): 53–57.

———. "Theatre Librarianship" in "Education for Special Librarianship." *The Library Quarterly* 24 (Jan. 1954): 18–19.

Fugate, Liz. "Theatre Companies in the United States: An Ephemeral Collection at the University of Washington Drama Library." In *Arts and Access*, 1–6. Vol. 15, *Performing Arts Resources*. New York: Theatre Library Assn., 1990.

Golding, Alfred S. "A Thesaurus for the Big Ten Performing Arts Document Inventory Project." Columbus, Ohio: The Ohio State University, 1978. Photocopy.

Gross, Sarah Chokla. "The Theatre Library Association and *Broadside.*" *Wilson Library Bulletin* 38 (Apr. 1964): 664.

Jewell, Susan C. *Education for Theat* Librar**. Albany, N.Y.: State University of New York at Albany, School of Information Science and Policy, 1990.

Johnston, A. M. *Theatre Librarianship*. Sheffield, Eng.: University of Sheffield, 1979.

Kopp, Leslie Hansen. "PRESERVE: Assuring Dance a Life Beyond Performance." In *Arts and Access*, 7–18. Vol. 15, *Performing Arts Resources*. New York: Theatre Library Assn., 1990.

LoMonaco, Martha Schmoyer. "Putting Performance On-Line." In *Arts and Access*, 51–57. Vol. 15, *Performing Arts Resources*. New York: Theatre Library Assn., 1990.

Ludden, Bennet. "The Dance Classification System of the Juilliard School Library." *Theatre Documentation* 1 (Fall 1968): 21–29.

Marco, Guy A., and Wolfgang M. Freitag, eds. "Introduction, Music and Fine Arts in the General Library." *Library Trends* 23 (Jan. 1975): 321–27.

Marshall, Thomas F. "The First Quarter Century of ASTR." *Theatre Survey* 22 (Nov. 1981): 117–24.

Nemchek, Lee R. "Education for Theatre Librarianship." *Journal of Education for Librarianship* 21 (Summer 1980): 49–62.

———. "Problems of Cataloging and Classification in Theatre Librarianship." *Library Resources & Technical Services* 25 (Oct./Dec. 1981): 374–85.

New York Public Library. *Catalog of the Theatre and Drama Collections*. Boston, Mass.: G. K. Hall, 1967. Supplements: *Catalog of the Theatre and Drama Collections*; *Dictionary Catalog of the Theatre and Drama Collections*; *Bibliographic Guide to Theatre Arts*, 1973– .

———. *Dictionary Catalog of the Dance Collection: A List of Authors, Titles, and Subject of Multi-media Materials in the Dance Collection of the Performing Arts Research Center of the New York Public Library*. New York: The New York Public Library; Astor, Lenox and Tilden Foundations, 1974. Annual supplement: *Bibliographic Guide to Dance*. 1975– .

———. *Theatre Subject Headings: Authorized for Use in the Catalog of the Theatre Collection*. Boston, Mass.: G. K. Hall, 1966.

Oswald, Genevieve. "Creating Tangible Records for an Intangible Art." *Special Libraries* 59 (Mar. 1968): 146–50.

"Performing Arts Archives and Collection Studies." *Broadside*, n.s., 8 (Fall 1980): 4.

Performing Arts Resources. New York: Theatre Library Assn., 1974– .

Rachow, Louis A. "Care and Preservation of Theatre Library Materials." *Special Libraries* 63 (Jan. 1972): 25–30.

———, ed. "Theatre and Performing Arts Collections." *Special Collections* 1 (Fall 1981): 1–166.

———. "The Theatre Library Association." *Encyclopedia of Library and Information Science* 30 (1980): 413–15.

Sheehy, Carolyn A. "Chicago Dance Collection: A Case in *Pointe*." *American Archivist* 53 (Summer 1990): 432–40.

Steele, Robert. *The Cataloging and Classification of Cinema Literature*. Metuchen, N.J.: The Scarecrow Press, Inc., 1967.

"Theatre Librarians Take the Stage." *Broadside*, o.s., 14 (June 1953): 1.

Trussler, Simon. *A Classification for the Performing Arts*. London, Eng.: British Theatre Institute, 1974.

Veinstein, André, and Alfred S. Golding. *Bibliothèques et Musées des Arts du Spectacle dans le Monde/Performing Arts Libraries and Museums of the World*. 4th ed. Paris, Fr.: Éditions du Centre National de la Recherche Scientifique, 1992.

Yee, Martha M. "Cataloging at the UCLA Film and Television Archive." In *Arts and Access*, 59–72. Vol. 15, *Performing Arts Resources*. New York: Theatre Library Assn., 1990.

CHAPTER 6

Philosophy

Richard H. Lineback

What is philosophy? Over the last twenty-five centuries the word philosophy has had a variety of meanings. For the Greeks, philosophy meant literally "love of wisdom." Jacques Maritain in his *Introduction to Philosophy* asserts that "philosophy is concerned with everything, is a 'universal science.'"[1] In contrast, William James, in *Some Problems of Philosophy*, maintains: "philosophy in the full sense is only man thinking...."[2] Although each of these definitions is helpful, none of them is totally satisfactory. Certainly philosophy does not have a corner on thinking, science, or the love of wisdom. What these three definitions do show is that one's definition of philosophy reflects a philosophical position. Hence, there may be as many definitions of philosophy as there are philosophical positions.

Profile of Philosophy

The traditional concept of philosophy describes more or less accurately what philosophers have called philosophy over the last twenty-five hundred years. This traditional concept of philosophy is clarified by giving due attention to the problems addressed, the attitudes encouraged, and the methods employed by philosophers. Studying these features enables us to distinguish philosophy from other disciplines.

---

1. Jacques Maritain, *Introduction to Philosophy*, trans. E. I. Watkin (New York: Sheed and Ward, 1962), 65.
2. William James, *Some Problems of Philosophy* (Cambridge, Mass.: Harvard University Press, 1979), 14.

Philosophers consider numerous and varied problems. They include the perennial questions that virtually all human beings have pondered from time to time. What exists? Does God exist? Is the universe real? Do I exist? If so, how do I know? What is knowledge? What is truth? What is beautiful? What is good? What ethical principles should I live by? The answers to these and related questions make up philosophies to be discussed and disputed. The answers to these questions are frequently labeled as one *-ism* or another, such as realism, idealism, empiricism, or rationalism.

In addition to the problems addressed by philosophers, philosophy is characterized by a particular attitude. Most philosophical activity begins when an individual is perplexed or begins to wonder. Perhaps perplexed by the untimely death of a loved one, one begins to wonder if God really exists. Given that philosophers disagree on almost everything, a philosopher must be open-minded concerning the views of others and tolerant of those who disagree. Dogmatism is the antithesis of philosophy. A philosopher is willing to be guided by reason and experience and to change views as reason and experience require. A philosopher stresses reason and seeks to avoid the emotional.

The method of philosophy is basically one of rational reflection. Since everyone uses rational reflection to address problems and to seek solutions, what differentiates the philosopher from anyone else? The philosopher uses logic, including inductive and deductive reasoning, and carefully considers the meanings of the words used, the truth of the assertion put forth, and the relationship between the assertion being made and other related ideas. For example, consider the question "Does God exist?" Before attempting to answer the question, one must be very clear about the meaning of the word *God*. Similarly, one would need to be clear about the meaning of the word *exists*. When we use the word *exists*, do we mean "exists in the minds of human beings" or "exists independently and outside human minds"? After clarifying the meaning of the key terms, philosophers seek to support or prove the truth of their assertion. Again using the example of God's existence, philosophers throughout the history of philosophy have sought to give proofs that God does truly exist. After establishing the truth of their claim to their satisfaction, philosophers also regularly explore the relationship of their assertion to other related claims. For example, given that the existence of God is proven, how is it compatible with the concept of evil in the world?

Implicit in the foregoing is an important fact: philosophy deals with problems that by their very nature are not empirical. The physical sciences usually deal with empirical questions, such as what is the melting point of gold. The social sciences deal with empirical questions concerning the conduct of individuals and groups of individuals. In contrast, the philosophical problems mentioned previously do not lend themselves to straightforward empirical solutions. There is no critical experiment that can be done to determine if capital punishment is right or wrong. Although philosophical problems cannot be solved by appeals to empirical facts, empirical facts do play an important role in philosophical arguments. The premises that philosophers present to support the truth of their assertions are typically both empirical claims and nonempirical claims. For example, consider the following argument:

1. Murder is morally wrong.
2. John murdered his wife.
3. Therefore, it was morally wrong for John to murder his wife.

In the argument, the first premise is a nonempirical claim and the second is an empirical claim. Both the empirical claim and the nonempirical claim are required to support the conclusion.

Also implicit in the argument is the fact that philosophy differs from mere opinion and from "popular philosophy," which is characterized by less rigor and less rational arguments. However, legitimate philosophic thought may be found in good literature. Even though philosophers may disagree on the answers to many of the perennial questions, their views are more than mere unsupported opinions. The essence of philosophy is the support of assertions by rational arguments. The work of a philosopher can be critically evaluated by considering the accuracy with which the key terms of the treatise have been defined, the logical soundness of the arguments, and the consistency of the assertions with other assertions that have been made.

Given that philosophers do disagree, one may well ask why philosophers bother philosophizing. Does philosophy make a difference? In terms of one's conclusions, the answer is probably that philosophy does not make much difference. Most philosophers and students of philosophy end up holding the same views with which they start. However, this does not mean that philosophy is useless. Taking time to carefully ponder some of the perennial questions is beneficial in a number of ways. First, by carefully considering the meanings of the words we use, like the word *God,* we come away with a much clearer concept of what we are talking about. Second, after careful consideration of the alternatives, we see our view in a truer perspective. Even though we still disagree with other philosophers, we have a clearer understanding of their reasons. This leads us to be more open-minded and less dogmatic about our beliefs. We become more tolerant of the different views of others. To conclude, the value of philosophy may not be its ability to transport us from one position to another, but rather the value of philosophy resides in what we learn along the way.

Fields of Philosophy

A consideration of the fields of philosophy helps one become familiar with the breadth of the discipline. In this section twelve areas of philosophy are discussed, although there is not complete agreement concerning how philosophy should be divided.

Metaphysics (the study of being) is a synonym of ontology. Some of the basic questions of metaphysics include: What does it mean for something to have being? What is being? What kinds of things exist? The topics most often discussed in metaphysical treatises include the existence of God, the nature of man, and the nature of the universe.

Philosophy of religion, although related to metaphysics, is usually thought of as a separate field. Philosophy of religion is the systematic study of the elements of religious consciousness. It differs from theology in that it assigns priority to reason over faith. More specifically, philosophy of religion deals with arguments both for and against the existence of God, the nature of the human soul, the immortality of the human soul, the nature of evil, and the nature of religion itself.

Epistemology is the study of knowledge and, hence, is referred to as "the theory of knowledge." Epistemology includes a consideration of what knowledge is and how humans obtain it. Empiricists stress the role of experience in obtaining knowledge, while rationalists stress the importance of reason. Epistemology is closely tied to metaphysics in that it is important to establish that one's metaphysical beliefs or assertions are true.

Logic deals with the analysis of arguments and is usually divided into informal and formal logic. Informal logic usually deals with everyday reasoning and particularly with fallacies, which are to be avoided. Formal logic deals with axiomatic systems in which the form of arguments is separated from their content. Formal logic includes the traditional syllogistic logic of Aristotle, along with propositional logic and predicate logic. Propositional logic deals with propositions as a whole, whereas predicate logic breaks propositions down into subject and predicate terms.

The philosophy of science is the systematic study of the nature of science, including its concepts, assumptions, and methods. Philosophers of science are concerned with how scientific theories can be confirmed, how theories explain the data, and how theories may be used to predict the future. The study of the philosophy of science is often associated with and combined with the history of science, which belongs within the field of history rather than within philosophy.

Ethics, or moral philosophy, studies judgments concerning what is good or bad, right or wrong, concerning our actions, goals, and dispositions. Today, ethics is usually divided into normative ethics and metaethics. Normative ethics seeks to answer the question of what ought to be done, while metaethics concerns itself with the meaning and justifications of ethical statements. The two most common schools of normative ethics are utilitarianism, which was proposed by John Stuart Mill, and deontology, which was defended by Kant.

Social and political philosophy are both related to ethics. Whereas ethics usually concerns itself with the individual, social philosophy deals with groups, such as families and organizations, while political philosophy deals with the role of the state. Political philosophy is particularly concerned about the powers of the state vis-à-vis the individual and the relative merits of the different forms of government, such as democracy and communism. In contrast, social philosophy is particularly concerned with the consideration of appropriate public policy for a society and for the various groups and institutions that compose it. Social philosophy considers such questions as whether we ought to raise federal taxes or reduce federal spending. Should we increase expenditures for social programs and decrease defense expenditures or vice versa?

Aesthetics, or the philosophy of art, studies the nature of beauty and examines how we make judgments that certain things are beautiful. Aesthetics includes not only analyses of the concept of beauty but also a consideration of the nature of art, the nature of our aesthetic experiences, and a consideration of the alternative theories of aesthetics.

Philosophy of language examines the nature of language and studies how languages are used. Of particular importance is the problem of meaning, and many significant works have been written in an attempt to resolve this problem.

Philosophy of education studies the role of education in our society. John Dewey is the most famous philosopher of education. In the broad sense, philosophy of education includes all that contributes to the development of human knowledge. In the narrower sense, philosophy of education deals more particularly with the place and the function of schools in our society. Common discussions in this field center around the goals and objectives of education, the most appropriate curriculum, and the most appropriate teaching methods.

Philosophy of history studies both the understanding of history and the metaphysics of history. The latter provides a metaphysical basis of interpreting historical events. For example, the Christian view is that history is the endless struggle between an individual's will and God's will. Historical explanation addresses the question of how the events of history are to be explained. To answer this question, some philosophers of history have used models of scientific explanation. Indeed, some view philosophy of history as a subdivision of philosophy of the social sciences and, hence, of philosophy of science itself.

In addition to these areas of study, others are sometimes added in the broad discipline of philosophy. Axiology, the study of values, complements ethics and aesthetics. Philosophy of mathematics can be considered a separate field or combined with logic. While the philosophy of psychology is sometimes considered a separate field, it also may be viewed as a subdivision of the philosophy of science. Philosophy of mind and philosophy of law, although associated with one of the twelve larger areas of philosophy mentioned previously, are becoming important fields of philosophy in themselves.

History of the Major Movements

The study of the history of philosophy is important for several reasons. First, it helps us to better understand the nature and function of philosophy. By studying the most important works of the world's greatest philosophers one can come to a better understanding of the problems that philosophers consider, of the attitudes they manifest, and of the methods they use. Second, a study of the philosophers of the past helps us to understand the sources of our own presuppositions and views. And third, studying the history of philosophy helps us to understand what constitutes a genuine advance in philosophy. A very brief outline of the history of Western philosophy is included here to provide librarians with an overview and to call attention to important primary works. Non-Western philosophy is omitted for two reasons. First, few philosophers in the Western world pursue Eastern philosophy as their area of specialization. Second, it is difficult to separate Eastern philosophies from Eastern religions.

Western philosophy began in Greece in the sixth century B.C. The first Greek philosophers are referred to as pre-Socratics because they preceded the famous philosopher Socrates. These philosophers used reason to question popular religious beliefs and practices and to examine and explain the nature of the universe. The pre-Socratic period includes Thales, the first Greek philosopher; Pythagoras, the mathematician; and Democritus, the first to suggest the theory of atomism. The pre-Socratics laid the foundation for the four most important philosophers of ancient philosophy: Socrates, Plato, Aristotle, and Plotinus.

Socrates (470–399 B.C.), who saw distinguished military service in his early life, turned in his maturity to philosophic inquiry and social criticism. The method of Socrates was dialogue; he questioned and probed his opponents with persistence. In this way he allowed those with whom he spoke to discover that they really knew little and that their preconceived notions of the good life were flawed. He taught that the good life was the virtuous life, a life characterized by justice, understanding, courage, and temperance. Late in his life he was charged with not believing in the Athenian gods and with corrupting the youth of Athens. He was convicted and sentenced to death, and died after drinking hemlock. Although Socrates taught many students, he wrote nothing. Hence, our best picture of Socrates comes from the early works of Plato.

Plato (427–347 B.C.) established his own school of philosophy, called the Academy, in Athens. Plato described reality as twofold: the physical world, which is constantly changing, and the world of Forms, which is eternal and unchanging. According to Plato, the goal of philosophy is to obtain a knowledge of the Forms or Ideas in the real world. Plato, like Socrates, also emphasized the importance of right living and the importance of the basic social principles that made life in the Greek city-state possible. Plato's concept of the ideal city-state is portrayed in *The Republic*, which is perhaps Plato's most famous work.

Aristotle (384–322 B.C.) was Plato's most famous student. He, too, founded his own school of philosophy, the Lyceum. Aristotle was a great encyclopedist and, as such, sought to collect and summarize all knowledge. He collected the works of other philosophers and established the first major Greek library. Aristotle's logic, which is sometimes referred to as "traditional logic," is still taught in many universities today. In his *Metaphysics*, Aristotle rejected the dualism of Plato's theory of Forms and provided important analyses of such concepts as form, matter, potentiality, actuality, substance, causality, time, and the prime mover. In *Nicomachean Ethics* Aristotle argued for the doctrine of the golden mean, in which the virtuous action is the mean between two extremes. For example, courage is the virtue between cowardice and rashness.

As the Greek city-states declined, Greek philosophy turned from complete philosophical systems to practical philosophies that would help citizens cope with everyday life. The two most important philosophies of this period were epicureanism and stoicism. Epicureanism, named after its founder Epicurus (341–270 B.C.), suggested that citizens maximize their pleasure and minimize their pain by looking for happiness in this life, by limiting their desires for the unnecessary, by cultivating friendship, and by fearing neither the gods nor death. In contrast, stoicism suggested that citizens should carry out their duties and not worry about such things as pleasure, happiness, health, or material possessions.

Early medieval philosophy was a period of transition from Greek philosophy to the Christian religion. It was characterized by attempts to synthesize the philosophical concepts of Platonism and Christianity. The result was known as neoplatonism, which was set forth by such philosophers as Plotinus and Augustine.

Plotinus (205–270) is perhaps the greatest of the neoplatonists. He believed that reality was based upon and arose from a single source, which he called the One. The One manifests itself as Mind, as a world soul from which all individual human souls are derived, and as Matter, which makes up the physical world. Salvation is liberation of the soul from the bondage of the material body and the reunion of one's soul with the One. These ideas are set forth in Plotinus's principal work, *The Enneads*.

Augustine (354–430) is usually considered to be the first great Christian philosopher. He established faith, hope, and charity as the three theological virtues to complement the four cardinal moral virtues of Greek philosophy, which were justice, temperance, courage, and understanding. His theme was faith seeking understanding. In his *Confessions* Augustine shares his experience of redemption and of faith seeking understanding. He viewed God as the creator of the universe, which was good, and evil as the absence of good and as something not created by God. According to Augustine, persons are free agents who can only be saved from sin by God's grace. The influence of Augustine is significant for the remainder of the Middle Ages and is seen in the Reformation theologies of Luther and Calvin.

Anselm (1033–1109) is mainly known for his ontological argument presented in his *Proslogion*, in which he sought to establish the existence of God by arguing that his idea of God, as that of which nothing greater can be conceived, exists in reality. This argument, which was based on the neoplatonic and Augustinian tradition, influenced many modern philosophers such as Descartes, Leibniz, and Kant. Anselm also marks the beginning of scholasticism, which is the view that the truths of religion, although they may be beyond reason, are not contrary to reason. Thus, although God may be beyond reason, it is fitting to use reason to confirm by rational arguments that God exists.

Thomas Aquinas (1226–1274) is the scholastic philosopher whose influence has been most enduring. He has not only influenced the philosophers who followed him but his views are still promulgated by the Roman Catholic church today. Aquinas sought to synthesize Aristotle's philosophy and Christianity. Aquinas is perhaps most famous for his five proofs of the existence of God, which are contained in his *Summa Theologica*. Here, again, rational arguments support the revelation that God exists.

William of Ockham (1285–1349), author of *Summa Logicae*, is perhaps best known for his work in the area of logic and for separating logic from metaphysics and theology. In particular, he is known for his principle, Ockham's Razor, which asserts that what can be explained by fewer principles should not be explained by more. In reference to the problem of universals, Ockham defended nominalism, which holds that universals such as goodness do not reside in the essence of things, but are merely names for the characteristics of things.

As suggested previously, medieval philosophy was dominated by three major problems: the existence of God, the problem of universals, and the problem of evil. During the fifteenth and sixteenth centuries, Renaissance philosophy was characterized by a reaction against scholastics and a movement in the direction of humanism. An emphasis on the individual and liberation from authority characterized a new approach in philosophy. The rise of science led philosophers like Francis Bacon to shape a new philosophy. The Renaissance served to prepare the way for modern philosophy.

René Descartes (1596–1650) is usually considered the father of modern philosophy. Descartes, as a rationalist, found in reason a basis for certain knowledge. After doubting everything, his "clear and distinct" perception of his own consciousness convinced him that his own existence was beyond doubt. He said, "I think, therefore I am." Also using reason, Descartes concluded that God must exist and that there is a real distinction between the mind and the body. These ideas are contained in his *Discourse on the Method* and *Meditations*. Following in the footsteps of Descartes, Spinoza (1632–1677) sought certain knowledge by the use of his "geometric methods." In his chief work, *Ethics*, Spinoza concluded that reality is one and that God is the totality of that which exists. According to Spinoza, God is manifested through two attributes, mind and nature. Leibniz (1646–1716) is the third rationalist of modern philosophy. He argued that reality is composed of an infinite number of monads, which, while not affecting one another, are organized in a divinely created preestablished harmony.

One philosophical reaction to rationalism is empiricism. In empiricism, experience and not reason is the basis of all knowledge. Thomas Hobbes (1588–1679), John Locke (1632–1704), George Berkeley (1685–1753), and David Hume (1711–1776) are the four most famous empiricists. Hobbes, both an empiricist and a materialist, argued that only material bodies exist; thoughts are motions in bodies. Hobbes also believed that all human beings are naturally selfish and, as a result, that life will be unpleasant unless and until people enter into a social contract and form a civil society. Locke argued in *An Essay on Human Understanding* that a person is born with a blank mind. According to Locke, all of one's ideas come from experience of the material world or from reflection on experiences of the material world. Locke was also a strong supporter of democracy, and the essentials of his political theory are reflected in the United States Constitution and in the Declaration of Independence. Berkeley concluded in his *Treatise on the Principles of Human Knowledge* that nothing exists except minds or spirits and their contents, ideas. That is, to be is to be perceived. Following in the empiricist tradition, Hume argued in his *Enquiry Concerning the Human*

Understanding that all ideas originate from immediate perceptions. Hume's empiricism led him to skepticism and, hence, to doubt the existence of both God and himself.

Immanuel Kant (1724–1804) sought to produce a synthesis of rationalism and empiricism. As a compromise, Kant argued in his *Critique of Pure Reason* that knowledge comes from sensation like the empiricists proposed, but that it is organized by the mind as the rationalists believed. In the area of ethics, Kant argued for a deontological position that human beings have a duty to act only on the principles that a person would be willing to have made a universal law for all persons.

After Kant, philosophy moved in several different directions. Many of these movements—including idealism, positivism, Marxism, existentialism and phenomenology, pragmatism, process philosophy, and logical positivism—began in the nineteenth century and continued into the twentieth century. Georg Wilhelm Friedrich Hegel (1770–1831), the first important philosopher of the nineteenth century, defended absolute idealism, which is the view that all reality is a single ultimate all-encompassing Spirit. All change is a reflection of the Absolute Spirit as it evolves from the thesis through the antithesis to a new and higher synthesis. Using this view, Hegel was able to give a dialectic account of the entire history of philosophy. Hegel developed these views in several works, *The Phenomenology of Mind, Science of Logic*, and *Encyclopedia of the Philosophical Sciences*. Hegel's idealism continued to influence other idealists for more than a century.

John Stuart Mill (1806–1873) endorsed positivism, with its emphasis on observable facts and the use of the scientific method. Mill is known for his work in economics, logic, and particularly, ethical theory. In *Utilitarianism*, Mill agreed with other utilitarians that an action should be judged by its consequences, but he went beyond them by distinguishing between higher and lower pleasures. In addition, Mill argued strongly in favor of individual liberty. Mill's utilitarianism and emphasis on liberty continue to influence philosophy today.

Karl Marx (1818–1883), with the help of Frederick Engels, developed the economic, political, and social principles known as Marxism. Marx, although influenced by Hegel, emphasized the material side of life. He sympathized with the oppressed and argued that only through a revolution would the working class attain political freedom. In *Das Kapital* Marx wrote of the ideal society, which would be a classless society in which private property would be replaced with common ownership. The work of Marx continues to influence contemporary Marxism, Leninism, and Maoism.

Existentialism began with Sören Kierkegaard (1813–1855), who frequently has been referred to as the father of existentialism. Existentialism stresses that a person's existence precedes the determination of one's essence and that each individual is free to determine that essence. Kierkegaard, reacting against Hegel, argued that an individual is free to make a "leap of faith," i.e., to endorse Christianity, that is absurd to the human reason. Frederick Nietzsche (1844–1900) followed in the steps of Kierkegaard and argued in favor of individual responsibility and against entanglement in philosophical systems. Nietzsche contrasted the slave morality of the weak with the master morality of the strong in *Beyond Good and Evil*. His "over man" rises above the traditional constraints of human culture and, being beyond good and evil, creates his own values. Jean-Paul Sartre (1905–1980), an important literary figure, popularized existentialism in his plays, novels, and short stories. Sartre explains in *Being and Nothingness* how some human beings are reflective and recognize that their existence is prior to their essence. These people live in "good faith." In contrast, those who deny their freedom and responsibility live in "bad faith."

Phenomenology, although sometimes confused with existentialism, is another important philosophical movement. Phenomenologists maintain that philosophers should seek to describe the universal characteristics of objects to gain an insight into the essential structures of the phenomena. Edmund Husserl (1859–1938) is usually thought of as the founder of the phenomenological movement. In his numerous writings, he carefully described whatever presented itself to his consciousness and was not concerned about the reality of the objects. In other words, Husserl suspended his previous beliefs and bracketed all his presuppositions about reality to concentrate on the pure phenomena as he perceived them. Martin Heidegger (1889–1976), both a phenomenologist and an existentialist, used the methods of phenomenology to describe human life in existential terms. His ideas are presented in his most influential work, *Being and Time*. Both phenomenology and existentialism have been influential not only in philosophy but also in other areas such as psychology and art.

Pragmatism is perhaps the most American of the philosophic movements of the nineteenth and twentieth centuries. Charles Peirce (1839–1914), usually thought of as the father of pragmatism, argued that all differences of meaning are reflected in practice. Consistent with his training in logic and science, Peirce reminds us that all our beliefs are fallible and that they might have to be revised in the light of additional information. William James (1842–1910) applied pragmatism particularly to the area of religious beliefs. He argued in *Varieties of Religious Experience* that religious beliefs should be considered good because of their favorable consequences, even though they might not be provable by science. John Dewey (1859–1952), America's most famous twentieth century philosopher, concentrated on ethics and norms of groups. He viewed education and democracy as the continuous reconstruction of experience. For Dewey, pragmatism provided a means for correcting erroneous beliefs and for solving the problems that confront us. Dewey's views are clearly stated in his most popular book, *Reconstruction in Philosophy*.

Process philosophy, along with process theology, is another movement that has its roots in Hegel. Alfred North Whitehead (1861–1947) is probably the most famous proponent of process philosophy. During his early years, Whitehead was primarily a mathematician; he wrote *Principia Mathematica* with Bertrand Russell. However, most interpreters of Whitehead emphasize his metaphysics. In his latter works, including *Adventures of Ideas* and *Modes of Thought*, Whitehead argued that process is the creative advance in which all events emerge, evolve, and die through absorption in their offspring.

The final movement of the twentieth century is logical analysis. In their early days, both George Edward Moore (1873–1958) and Bertrand Russell (1872–1970) were idealists in the tradition of Hegel. Moore, with the publication of his *Principia Ethica* in 1903, changed the direction of British philosophy. He rejected idealism and replaced it with a philosophy of common sense. Moore's emphasis on the analysis of the meanings of propositions made him one of the early proponents of linguistic analysis. In 1914 Russell published *Our Knowledge of the External World*, which set forth his metaphysics of logical atomism and his method of philosophical analysis. Russell's epistemology was empirical and stressed that physical objects are logical constructs from sense data. Ludwig Wittgenstein (1889–1951) carried the work of Moore and Russell forward. Wittgenstein's early works developed a picture theory of language. Later he rejected many of his early ideas and stressed that meaning is use within the language-game. As a result, Wittgenstein asserted that philosophy should concentrate on describing the ordinary uses of words and upon removing conceptual confusion. Karl Popper (1902–) chose falsifiability rather than verifiability as the criterion used to distinguish science from metaphysics. His emphasis on falsifiability set him apart from the earlier logical positivists. Further developments of the philosophies of Wittgenstein and Popper continued to flourish in Britain.

While a knowledge of these major movements in philosophy is necessary, it is important to recognize that many other philosophers have contributed to a vast body of thought representing other movements. In addition, the current work of philosophers may develop into the movements for tomorrow as well as provide reconsideration and new thought on traditionally held views as shown, for example, by recent feminist perspectives in philosophy.

Philosophers' Methods of Communication

Philosophers regularly define their terms, usually early in their works. The two most common types of definitions are those that report on how a word is generally used in the language and those that stipulate the way the author will use the word within the context of a given document. After analyzing definitions, philosophers generally analyze arguments. The analysis of an argument involves a working knowledge of logic; philosophers frequently classify arguments as inductive or deductive. If the argument is inductive, the strength of the argument is evaluated; if the argument is deductive, the validity of the argument is determined. After considering the argument and its soundness, philosophers regularly turn to several related considerations, such as whether the premises are true or whether all the assumptions are contained in the premises. Also, philosophers examine the conclusion and consider whether the author's claim is empirical or normative. An empirical claim reports on a state of affairs, while normative claims reflect value judgments. Philosophers frequently reject conclusions because they imply undesirable consequences or because they do not adequately consider and incorporate all of the facts presented.

To share their ideas with an audience, philosophers generally employ one of five types of essays: criticism of a particular view, defense of a particular view, considerations of a particular dispute between two or more philosophers, consideration of a general problem, or defense of an original position. In contrast to those writing philosophical essays, those writing textbooks generally would not use any of these five approaches. To assist philosophers with the publication of their works, there are more than 300 professional philosophy journals and almost as many publishers of philosophy books.

Over the past twenty years there has been a shift in the topics that philosophers have chosen to discuss. This trend is revealed by a study of the number of articles and books assigned to seven major subject headings in *The Philosopher's Index* (Bowling Green, Ohio: Philosophy Documentation Center, 1967– ; also available on CD–ROM from DIALOG). During the 1960s 16 percent of the documents concerned metaphysics, whereas in the 1980s, only 15 percent concerned metaphysics. Similarly, documents in philosophy of religion are down from 11 percent to 8 percent. Turning to logic and the philosophy of science, publications concerning logic decreased from 12 percent to 11 percent and publications about philosophy of science went from 13 percent to 9 percent. In contrast, interest in ethics, social philosophy, and political philosophy is increasing. Writings about ethics rose from 11 percent to

14 percent, social philosophy increased from 4 percent to 12 percent, and publications in political philosophy are up from 2 percent to 6 percent. In other words, in the literature of philosophy there has been a major shift away from metaphysics, religion, logic, and the philosophy of science. There has also been a trend toward applied philosophy, as illustrated by the field of medical ethics. In the entire decade of the 1960s, only four articles and books cited in *The Philosopher's Index* dealt with medical ethics. In sharp contrast, in the period of the 1980s, 675 documents dealt with medical ethics. The same trend is confirmed by the number of graduate degree programs that concentrate in the area of applied philosophy and also by the number of centers that have developed in recent years that are devoted to various aspects of applied philosophy, such as The Hastings Center (Briarcliff Manor, N.Y.) and the Kennedy Institute of Ethics (Georgetown University, Washington, D.C.).

Philosophy and Libraries

The history of Western philosophy clearly reveals the interdisciplinary nature of philosophy. The pre-Socratics were interested in both philosophy and physics. Plato was interested in both philosophy and mathematics, while Aristotle was interested in philosophy, physics, biology, politics, and poetry. Turning from ancient to modern philosophy, Descartes was both the father of modern philosophy and a great mathematician. Locke and Malebranche made significant contributions in the area of politics. Leibniz is remembered for his windowless monads and for his development of calculus. Moving to the nineteenth century, Mill is known for his work in economics as well as in logic, philosophy of science, and ethics. William James is recognized as both a philosopher and a psychologist. Whitehead and Russell, two twentieth-century philosophers, are well known for their work in the foundations of mathematics.

A consideration of the twelve major fields of philosophy also reflects the interdisciplinary nature of the discipline. The names given to six of the twelve fields of philosophy clearly reflect their connection with another discipline: aesthetics or philosophy of art, philosophy of education, philosophy of history, philosophy of language, philosophy of science, and philosophy of religion. In addition, the fields of social philosophy and political philosophy likewise suggest the close affiliation of these fields with other disciplines. Even the four remaining fields bear important relationships with other disciplines. Metaphysics certainly considers physics, logic regularly deals with the foundations of mathematics, ethics concerns sociology, and epistemology is related to the psychology and sociology of knowledge. Hence, philosophy contributes to each of these interdisciplinary areas and, hence, to research in the sciences, the social sciences, and the other humanities.

It is the interdisciplinary nature of philosophy that makes philosophy more difficult to define in terms of its unique subject matter. A cohesive body of literature exists that is of major interest to philosophers and that may be classified as "philosophy." However, philosophy attached to the subject areas may be spread throughout the library, thereby complicating access since all works will not be together physically.

Users and Their Needs

Users of philosophy collections may be university faculty members, scholars, graduate students, undergraduate students, or general readers. The needs of the general reader can usually be satisfied by the use of standard reference works, such as *The Encyclopedia of Philosophy* (reprint ed., New York: Macmillan, 1972); by popularized accounts of the history of philosophy, such as Will Durant's *The Story of Philosophy*; and by a small collection of original works by philosophers from Plato through Sartre. As in many other academic disciplines, there are very few philosophy books intended for general readers; the vast majority of books and other sources are intended for undergraduate and graduate students and the professional scholar. Perhaps this results from the fact that philosophy, unlike many other fields in the humanities, is rarely taught in the secondary schools; however, some attempts to do so are currently being made. Consequently, many of the books published for the general reader do not concern philosophy, as defined earlier, but rather deal with psychic phenomena, the occult, or serve as recipe books on how to find happiness or how to solve other perennial problems.

Students as a group have their needs much better addressed than are those of the general reader. Of particular importance to undergraduates are quality histories of philosophy, original works by philosophers from the history of philosophy and of today, and some of the better anthologies covering historical periods or fields of philosophy. Graduate students, particularly those working on papers, theses, and dissertations, have many needs that are not easily satisfied. The graduate student expects extensive reference collections, complete original works by philosophers in both the original language and in translation, a wide variety of professional journals including back issues, and a collection of books that includes the older "classics" and up-to-date materials. The graduate student in philosophy is expected to be familiar with existing philosophy resources and then to go beyond them with original thought.

Philosophy graduate students and faculty alike generally work with the five types of essays previously identified, all of which require library resources.

The needs of faculty members and others doing professional research in philosophy are similar to those of the graduate students; however, faculty members have more opportunity to visit with their fellow professionals who have similar interests at conferences and conventions. According to an American Philosophical Association survey in the late 1970s, the two research tools that professional philosophers use most are *The Philosopher's Index* and the *Encyclopedia of Philosophy*. Current investigation into the research patterns of philosophers indicates that *The Philosopher's Index* is still heavily used but that *The Encyclopedia of Philosophy* is increasingly dated.

A marketing survey conducted in 1980 by the Philosophy Documentation Center (Bowling Green, Ohio) showed that philosophers were not interested in a selective dissemination of information service to help keep them current. Rather, the most common ways scholars keep abreast of their fields of philosophy are reading mail advertisements and catalogs, scanning journals received by their university libraries, scanning acquisition lists of their university libraries, discussing ideas with their fellow scholars, visiting book displays at conferences and meetings, and scanning journals that they purchase. Conversations with philosophers done by the Research Libraries Group indicate that inclusion of philosophy research in the database Research in Progress would be helpful, although the same study indicates that few philosophers use the online version of *The Philosopher's Index* due to cost.[3] Comparatively few philosophers scan indexes, abstracts, or bibliographies in an effort to keep up; in general, philosophers are the most traditional of all the humanities scholars in their approach to information gathering.[4]

This is further demonstrated by Cynthia Corkill and Margaret Mann in their *Information Needs in the Humanities: Two Postal Surveys*, where they show that the needs of those doing research in philosophy differ from the needs of those doing research in the other areas of humanities. Their research revealed that philosophers are generally more satisfied with their libraries' own collections than are scholars in English, French, history, and music. They discovered that philosophers make less use of interlibrary loan than researchers in the other four fields. Also, researchers in philosophy are the least likely group among the humanities to ask librarians for help with bibliographical problems or for help in locating items. In keeping with the above, a greater percentage of

3. Constance C. Gould, "Philosophy," in *Information Needs in the Humanities: An Assessment* (Stanford, Calif.: Research Libraries Group, 1988), 30.

4. Gould, "Philosophy," 33.

philosophers use their own books and journals, as opposed to library materials, than do scholars in the other fields. As one might expect, almost 60 percent of the philosophy scholars surveyed said that non-local materials were not important. Philosophers also scored lowest by a wide margin on the use of unique materials, such as letters or manuscripts.[5] To conclude, philosophers as original thinkers depend more heavily upon their local collections and are more satisfied with their local collections than are researchers in the other areas of the humanities.

The Literature of Philosophy

Primary Sources

Given the nature of philosophy, the heart of any philosophy collection must be primary sources, or the major works of the world's most important philosophers. As noted previously, philosophers are not in agreement on a single list of the most important philosophers. However, *The Philosopher's Index*, which during the period 1940 to 1985 cited well over 100,000 documents, listed only 13 philosophers who were discussed in more than 1,000 documents. They are Kant, Aristotle, Plato, Hegel, Aquinas, Marx, Wittgenstein, Heidegger, Hume, Descartes, Husserl, Russell, and Dewey. An additional 19 philosophers were discussed in more than 500 documents: Quine, Sartre, Locke, Whitehead, Nietzsche, Augustine, Leibniz, Popper, Kierkegaard, Mill, Peirce, Freud, Spinoza, Berkeley, Hobbes, Moore, Frege, Carnap, and James. In addition to major works of the most important philosophers, the collected works of important philosophers are essential primary sources. For example, Kant's *Gesammelte Schriften* in twenty-three volumes is the standard critical edition of Kant's works.

Translations of the principal works of important philosophers are also very important. Only two of the ten philosophers who are most often cited in *The Philosopher's Index* wrote in English. Certainly the vast majority of students and scholars are not going to read Aristotle in Greek. Hence, translations like the *Works of Aristotle*, translated by J. A. Smith and W. D. Ross in 12 volumes, are of central importance.

Autobiographies do not play a major role in philosophy. Research indicates that autobiographies are comparatively scarce and are seldom used; however, the few autobiographies that do exist, such as the *Philosophy of Martin Buber*, are usually valuable. Among a number of series of primary sources, perhaps the most important is editor Paul A.

---

5. Cynthia Corkill and Margaret Mann, *Information Needs in the Humanities: Two Postal Surveys* (Sheffield, Eng.: British Library, 1978), 93–103.

Schilpp's The Library of Living Philosophers series (La Salle, Ill.: Open Court, 1939–), which has published many volumes on individual philosophers.

While essential primary sources include the major philosophers, do not forget that philosophy is a vibrant field, and philosophers continue to offer new philosophical perspectives. These works are also primary sources and should be represented in the library collection.

Philosophy journals, of equal importance with books, provide both primary and secondary sources. Since the history of journal publication in philosophy is long established, this medium has provided, and continues to provide, major access to thought in the field. In 1952 the Library of Congress published *Philosophical Periodicals: An Annotated World List*, which contained more than 450 scholarly journals devoted to philosophy in whole or in part. Ulrich's *International Periodicals Directory 1986–1987* listed 600 titles under the heading of philosophy. The *Bulletin Signalétique: Philosophie, Sciences Humaines* (Paris, Fr.: Centre de documentation du C.N.R.S., 1956–) draws from some 400 journals described as predominantly philosophical, while *The Philosopher's Index* regularly indexes and abstracts more than 360 journals devoted exclusively or primarily to philosophy. The vast majority of philosophy periodicals are professional journals intended for scholars and advanced students; however, there are a few semipopular magazines published in the area of philosophy, such as the *Humanist*, which has a circulation of approximately 12,000. Librarians seeking a shorter list of philosophy journals to subscribe to should consider the interests of their philosophy faculty and students and, secondarily, the circulation and date of founding of each journal.

Secondary Sources

The secondary sources most important to the study of philosophy are histories, biographies, and textbooks, all of which provide information related to the field but are not works developing original philosophical thought. Histories of philosophy are particularly important because they provide readers with information on particular philosophers' lives, works, and thoughts, as well as information on how the particular philosophies fit into the broader movements of history. Although there are many excellent histories of philosophy, four deserve particular consideration: Émile Bréhier's *The History of Philosophy* (Chicago: University of Chicago Press, 1963–1969), A. Robert Caponigri and Ralph McInerny's *A History of Western Philosophy* (Notre Dame, Ind.: University of Notre Dame Press, 1964–1971), Frederick Charles Copleston's *A History of Philosophy* (New York: Image Books, 1985), and W. T. Jones's *A History of Western*

Philosophy (New York: Harcourt Brace Jovanovich, 1969–1975). While most histories of philosophy are scholarly in nature, there are a few, such as Durant's *Story of Philosophy*, written for a general audience.

Although histories of philosophy usually supply some biographical information, biographies of philosophers are essential complementary secondary sources. Biographies exist for virtually every major philosopher, including those of the nineteen and twentieth centuries. Perhaps the best listing of available biographies is contained in *The Philosopher's Guide* by Richard T. De George. Although most histories of philosophy and biographies are scholarly in nature, at least a few were written for more general audiences, such as Louis Browne's *Blessed Spinoza*.

Textbooks form the largest class of secondary sources. Textbooks traditionally consider the definition of philosophy and its methodology, the various fields of philosophy, the major philosophical movements, and the philosophies developed in various nations or regions of the world. Textbooks as a class seek to present information about particular philosophers or philosophical positions.

Reference Tools

Reference sources in philosophy include dictionaries, encyclopedias, bibliographies, indexes and abstracts, and catalogs of major libraries. Dictionaries of philosophy are important because they provide not only definitions but also explanations of philosophical terms and information about how these terms are used by important philosophers throughout the history of philosophy. The classic dictionary of philosophy is editor James M. Baldwin's *Dictionary of Philosophy and Psychology* (reprint ed., Gloucester, Mass.: P. Smith, 1960), which was originally published between 1901 and 1905. Although a classic, this dictionary does not include information on persons and topics of the twentieth century. Hence, many today turn to more up-to-date sources. Among the dictionaries frequently used are the following: *The Dictionary of Philosophy* (rev. ed., New York: Philosophical Library, 1983), edited by Dagobert D. Runes, which first appeared in 1942; the *Dictionary of the History of Ideas* (5 vols., New York: Scribner, 1973–1974), by Philip P. Wiener; *A Dictionary of Philosophy* (2d ed., London, Eng.: Routledge & Kegan Paul, 1986), by A. R. Lacey; and *The Concise Encyclopedia of Western Philosophy and Philosophers* (rev. ed., London, Eng., and Boston, Mass.: Unwin Hyman, 1989), by James O. Urmson and Jonathan Rée.

The Encyclopedia of Philosophy is the encyclopedia most often used by philosophers. Although this encyclopedia is a valuable research tool, it is now out-of-date and some philosophers believe that it is too sympathetic to analytic philosophy. Two other encyclopedias are useful: editor Hermann Krings's three-volume *Handbuch philosophischer Grund-begriffe* (Munich, Ger.: Kösel, 1973) and the six-volume Italian *Enciclope-dia Filosofica* (2d ed., Florence, It.: Sansoni, 1968–1969). *The Handbook of Western Philosophy* edited by G. H. R. Parkinson (New York: Macmillan, 1988) deals with contemporary, primarily British, philosophy in six areas: meaning and truth; theory of knowledge; metaphysics; philosophy of mind; moral philosophy; and society, art, and religion.

In addition to dictionaries and encyclopedias, several bibliographies provide important information to those doing research in philosophy. Richard T. De George's *The Philosopher's Guide to Sources, Research Tools, Professional Life, and Related Fields* (Lawrence, Kans.: Regents Press of Kansas, 1980) includes information on reference tools; the history and branches of philosophy; schools and movements of philosophy; national and regional movements; philosophical serials; philosophical organizations; and related fields, such as religion, the fine arts, the social sciences, the physical sciences; and related professions. *Research Guide to Philosophy* (Sources of Information in the Humanities no. 3, Chicago: American Library Assn., 1983), by Terrence N. Tice and Thomas P. Slavens, is also very useful. Taking the approach of seeking issues for investigation by students, *Research Guide* includes chapters on historical periods, major movements, and sixteen fields of philosophy. More than 3,000 books are cited in this bibliography. Hans E. Bynagle's *Philosophy: A Guide to the Reference Literature* (Reference Sources in the Humanities series, Littleton, Colo.: Libraries Unlimited, 1986) is more up-to-date than *Research Guide* and contains thorough annotations for each title. Bynagle devotes four chapters to bibliographies subdivided by schools, periods, geography, and individual names. In Ron Blazek and Elizabeth Aversa's *The Humanities: A Selective Guide to Information Sources* (Littleton, Colo.: Libraries Unlimited, 1988), one chapter deals with access to information in philosophy and another provides an annotated list of primary information sources.

The three major indexes that provide ongoing information on the books and journal articles published in philosophy are the *Bibliographie de la Philosophie*, the *Bulletin Signalétique*, and *The Philosopher's Index*. Since 1954 the *Bibliographie de la Philosophie* (Paris, Fr.: Institute International de Philosophie, Librairie Philosophique, 1937–) has been devoted to publishing abstracts of scholarly philosophy books. Original scholarly books are abstracted; translations and new editions are merely listed. While approximately 1,000 books are listed each year, coverage is primarily of European and North American publications. Abstracts are in the original language for English, French, Spanish, Italian, or German texts. Texts written in other languages are abstracted either in English or in French. The *Bibliographie* is considered by many to be the best source to consult on non-English–language books. The back of the fourth quarterly issue of each volume contains several indexes: a combined author and title index, an index of names of the philosophers, and an index of publishers. Instead of a subject index, the broad classification scheme, comprising 10 broad categories, arranges material topically. The *Bibliographie* is not available online.

The *Bulletin Signalétique*, published regularly since 1956, is the successor of the *Bulletin Analytique: Philosophie* (Paris, Fr.: Centre de documentation du C.N.R.S.), published from 1947 to 1955. The *Bulletin* cites about 4,000 documents each year and is published in French. Many consider the *Bulletin* to be the single best source to consult for non-English–language journal articles in the field of philosophy. According to its own statistics, 98 percent of the documents are journal articles, while 2 percent are works, reports, theses, and congresses; about 60 percent of the documents are accompanied by an abstract; 15 percent of the documents indexed are in French, 50 percent are in English, and 35 percent are in other languages. The abstracts are all in French and average 50 to 100 words. The documents are listed according to a classification scheme, and each quarterly issue of the *Bulletin* includes an index of the journal covered, a subject index, and an author index. The *Bulletin* is available online through FRANCIS, the French retrieval automated network for current information in the social and human sciences.

The *Philosopher's Index*, founded in 1967, provides the most comprehensive coverage of English-language articles and books. Complete coverage of English-language philosophy journals and books goes back to 1940. Coverage of journals in other languages began in 1967, and books in languages other than English have been included since 1980. The *Index* includes scholarly works, textbooks, and translations, as well as original contributions from anthologies and other multiauthored works. Of the approximately 8,000 new documents cited in the *Index* each year, about 50 percent are in English and 50 percent are in other languages. Journal articles account for 70 percent of the documents, while books account for 15 percent, and contributions from multiauthored works account for the other 15 percent. Approximately 60 percent of the documents have abstracts, often written by the author of the document and published in the language chosen by the author. The *Index* contains a subject index, an author index, and a book review index. In addition to the print product, the information contained in the *Index* is also available online through DIALOG and on CD-ROM.

Although not an index unique to philosophy, the *Arts & Humanities Citation Index* (Philadelphia, Pa.: Institute for Scientific Information, 1976–), available in print and online, also should be noted as it is useful to those tracing citation locations of particular works of philosophers.

Because of the interdisciplinary nature of philosophy, reference works such as this in related fields and works devoted to the humanities in general are often helpful.

Concordances play a limited role in philosophical research, i.e., they are generally used only in the study of the history of philosophy. Major concordances exist for the works of Plato, Aristotle, Descartes, Malebranche, Leibniz, Kierkegaard, Nietzsche, Heidegger, and Wittgenstein. In addition, two very large projects center on the works of Aquinas and Kant. The *Index Thomisticus* is the product of Roberto Busa, S.J., in cooperation with IBM. This voluminous work includes a 10-volume index, a 31-volume concordance to 118 of Aquinas's works, an 8-volume index to 61 related works, and a 7-volume set of the works of Aquinas in Latin. The *Allgemeiner Kantindex zu Kants gesammelten Schriften* was started by Gottfried Martin, who died in 1972. To date only two volumes have been published; it remains for his colleagues to complete the project. Because of the increasing availability of computers, more concordances of major works no doubt will be produced in the future.

There are only two directories of philosophy that have been regularly updated. The first, edited by Archie J. Bahm, is the *Directory of American Philosophers* (Bowling Green, Ohio: Philosophy Documentation Center, 1962/1963–), which is published every two years and which covers the United States and Canada. It lists information on individual philosophers, philosophy departments, societies, institutes, journals, and publishers, as well as graduate assistantships. The other is the *International Directory of Philosophy and Philosophers* (7th ed., Bowling Green, Ohio: Philosophy Documentation Center, 1990), edited by R. Cormier et al. This directory is published every four years and covers all countries, except the United States and Canada, in which philosophy is taught. It, too, provides information on philosophers, departments, societies, institutes, journals, and publishers.

Reference collections in philosophy contain two major library catalogs. The first, the *Catalog of the Hoose Library of Philosophy, University of Southern California* (Boston, Mass.: G. K. Hall, 1968), is published in six volumes and lists 37,000 books. The *Dictionary Catalogue of the Library of the Pontifical Institute of Medieval Studies, Toronto, Canada* (Boston, Mass.: G. K. Hall, 1972; supp., 1979–) lists 83,000 titles. These two catalogs are important because they are the two largest published catalogs of philosophical collections.

Using collections located through catalogs and bibliographies sometimes involves travel. There are only a few major philosophy special collections in North America, including those at University of Southern California, University of California–San Diego, University of Michigan, the Weston College Library in Cambridge, Massachusetts, the University of

Pennsylvania Library, Columbia University Library, and McMaster University Library in Hamilton, Ontario. They are briefly described, along with a number of international information centers for philosophy, in Blazek and Aversa's *The Humanities*.[6] In addition to these special collections, some large research libraries have considerable philosophy collections with separate service points, such as the University of Illinois at Urbana's History and Philosophy Library.

Selection

If access to published works is not a major problem for philosophers, there are some problems for librarians doing materials selection.[7] In libraries using approval plans, philosophy selectors will note that a subject-based approval plan brings in many books that are popular in nature; books on the philosophy of life for the general reader usually are not selected for a scholarly audience. It is difficult to prevent these items from arriving through approval plans; therefore, the rejection rate for philosophy books can be quite high. A publisher-based approval plan can work much better, especially one that involves university presses because in this country, it is the university presses that support scholarly works on philosophy; therefore, the university press approval plan is most helpful to selectors in narrowing the search for appropriate material. In addition to an approval plan that "automatically" brings university press books to be reviewed by the selector, approval plans with European vendors, especially those covering German and Dutch publishers, can be very helpful, even for those materials published in English.

Selectors working from reviews will find that the time frames for review literature are problematic. Reviews in the journals are published very late, and the books reviewed are often out of print by the time the reviews are published. It is generally a difficult field for current-materials selection, especially for materials not published by major publishers.

Cataloging and Classification

Access to the primary and secondary works does not seem to be a major problem in philosophy despite the existence of problems in classifica-

---

6. Ron Blazek and Elizabeth Aversa, "Accessing Information in Philosophy," in *The Humanities: A Selective Guide to Information Sources*, 3d ed. (Littleton, Colo.: Libraries Unlimited, 1988), 33–36.

7. For a helpful and concise discussion on selection in philosophy, see Andrew D. Scrimgeour, "Philosophy and Religion," in *Selection of Library Materials in the Humanities, Social Sciences, and Sciences*, ed. Patricia A. McClung (Chicago: American Library Assn., 1985), 98–121.

tion schemes as applied to philosophy. Most scholars and students of philosophy engaged in significant research usually begin building their bibliographies by using the reference tools mentioned. Having found the basic bibliographic information in these and related sources, philosophers then use the author/title catalog to get the call numbers for the books they seek. Subject cataloging, with its wide variety of subject headings relating to different areas and problems of philosophy, provides adequate access for those who prefer this approach. As the traditional card catalog is replaced in more and more libraries by online catalogs with more powerful search software, and as it becomes easier and easier for "traditional" scholars such as philosophers to tap into distant online catalogs through telecommunication links invisible to the searcher, philosophers will enjoy extended access to library materials.

Philosophers throughout the centuries have been concerned with the classification of knowledge in general and of philosophy in particular. Aristotle thought that philosophy was made up of logic, metaphysics, ethics, physics, politics, and aesthetics. This division of philosophy significantly influenced Dewey when he sought to classify philosophy. Francis Bacon, an early modern philosopher, divided philosophy into three major areas: the divine, the natural, and human. Human philosophy was further subdivided into the philosophy of humanity, the body, the soul, and civil philosophy. Bacon's conceptual divisions influenced the classification schemes of both Dewey and the Library of Congress.

In the Dewey decimal system philosophy occupies the 100 classification. This section is further subdivided into philosophical works classified by form (100, e.g., 105 is for philosophy periodicals); metaphysics, including ontology, cosmology, epistemology, teleology, etc. (110 and 120); metapsychology (130); philosophical systems and doctrines (140); general psychology (150); logic (160); and ethics (170). Ancient and Oriental philosophers are in the 180 section and modern philosophers, subdivided by nationality, then chronologically, and then by individual philosopher, are in the 190s.

The Dewey decimal system has been criticized for its inherent weaknesses, such as the requirement to divide all subjects into ten divisions, although questions concerning Dewey's classification of philosophy are more relevant here. Why did he put philosophical systems and doctrines (140) between metapsychology (130) and general psychology (150)? Why did he separate philosophical systems and doctrines (140) from the philosophers who espoused the views (180s and 190s)? Why did he not include aesthetics in the 100 classification, instead of the 700s?

The Library of Congress classification system for philosophy constitutes the B-BJ classification, which is subdivided into numerous sections. Theory and method, including general discussions of the relation of philosophy to other disciplines, and history and systems, subdivided chronologically and geographically, are located in B. Individual philosophers are placed in their appropriate national and chronological sequence. Logic is assigned the BC class, while general philosophical treatises are in BD. In BF, psychology is followed by metapsychology and the occult sciences. Aesthetics occupies the BH class, while ethics is assigned to the BJ class, which includes manners, social customs, and etiquette.

The Library of Congress classification improves on the Dewey decimal system by placing psychology adjacent to metapsychology and by including aesthetics in the section with the other major divisions of philosophy. However, one wonders why the occult sciences were classified as philosophy, as opposed to religion, and why manners, social customs, and etiquette are included in philosophy, as opposed to sociology. Although neither of these classification systems is totally satisfactory, both have proven to be useful over a significant period of time.

Three other classification schemes more recently have been devised by philosophers themselves. They are the systems employed by the *Bibliographie de la Philosophie*, *Bulletin Signalétique*, and *The Philosopher's Index*. The classification scheme of the *Bibliographie de la Philosophie* has the advantage of dividing philosophy into nine major fields, using the tenth for form publications. The nine fields are more precise than the broader divisions of the Dewey and Library of Congress systems; psychology, the occult sciences, and manners have been omitted from the scheme. Although the *Bibliographie de la Philosophie* is not concerned with classifying books to be placed on shelves, the system is a genuine classification system in that the bibliographical information and abstract concerning a book must be placed in one of the ten sections. As in all classification systems, problems arise when a publication does not fall clearly into one of the ten divisions; hence, multiple entries and cross-references are employed.

The *Bulletin Signalétique*, like the *Bibliographie*, uses its classification scheme to group citations and abstracts under appropriate categories, which have evolved over time. While in 1972 there were only six broad categories in the *Bulletin*, the current scheme has expanded to take advantage of twenty-four more-specific headings. In general, the *Bulletin* is more specific than the *Bibliographie*. The *Bulletin* recognizes epistemology, or theory of knowledge, as a field by itself. In addition, the *Bulletin* has a subject index in the back, which refers users to the appropriate citation and abstract. While the citation to a book dealing with Kant's ethics and aesthetics, for example, will be located in only one of the main sections, multiple entries in the subject index under Kant, ethics, aesthetics, or other appropriate headings will lead the reader to the citation.

The Philosopher's Index employs yet another classification scheme to categorize the philosophy journal articles and books that it indexes. The goal in establishing this classification scheme was to accurately reflect the classes actually used by philosophers and to allow for efficient online retrieval. A comparison of systems devised by *The Philosopher's Index*, *Bibliographie*, and the *Bulletin* reveals that *The Philosopher's Index* employs a narrower classification scheme.

To many in the field of philosophy, the classification systems of the *Bibliographie de la Philosophie*, the *Bulletin Signalétique*, and *The Philosopher's Index* are preferable to the Dewey decimal system and the Library of Congress system because they provide more specific and more up-to-date access to information. However, as philosophy continues to develop in new and sometimes unexpected ways, these classification systems will need to respond to change or they also will become outdated.

Profile of Philosophy Librarianship

The small field of philosophy librarianship expands when general-humanities librarians whose subject area responsibilities include philosophy and librarians who handle philosophy and religion are counted. In addition, public and technical services librarians for specific language areas may be responsible for philosophical works published in those languages. The educational requirements for philosophy librarians vary depending upon the general quality of the library and the extent of its commitment to the philosophy collection. Ideally, philosophy librarians should have at least a master's degree in library science and in philosophy. Because some Ph.D.s in philosophy have had difficulty finding jobs teaching philosophy at the university level, some have taken a degree in library science. For this reason some philosophy librarians have doctorates in philosophy. However, it is impossible for any philosophy librarian to be as well-read in a narrow area of philosophy as a philosopher who specializes in that narrow area. Nevertheless, a librarian with a good knowledge of the history of philosophy and its major movements will be able to assist the vast majority of persons with their research. In addition to a degree in philosophy, a reading knowledge of foreign languages is helpful. The two most useful languages for philosophy librarianship are German and French. Others that are desirable include ancient Greek, Latin, Spanish, and Italian.

Philosophy librarians find little support from professional philosophy societies. The American Philosophical Association, the largest and most influential society, has no special-interest group for librarians. In like manner, no other philosophy association or society in the United States or

Canada has such a group. The American Library Association's Association of College and Research Libraries does have a Philosophical, Religious, and Theological Studies discussion group. However, the only society specifically for philosophy librarians is the Association of British Theological and Philosophical Libraries. And the only publication for philosophy librarians is the *Bulletin of the Association of British Theological and Philosophical Libraries* (London, Eng.: The Association, 1956–). Philosophy librarians who have a particular interest in some area of philosophy could seek membership in one of the many associations that are devoted to special areas of philosophy. Examples of such societies include The American Society for Aesthetics, the American Society for Political and Legal Philosophy, the American Society for Value Inquiry, and The Metaphysical Society of America. However, none of the many specialized societies offers philosophy librarians programs or publications dealing with philosophy librarianship. Research and study in the librarianship of philosophy is very limited.

Perhaps the best hope for philosophy librarians lies in related fields and the humanities in general. Many philosophy librarians find that they have been asked to assume responsibility for one or more related fields. Responsibility for philosophy and religion is one such common assignment. Librarians holding such joint appointments can find professional opportunities from such organizations as the American Theological Library Association. And all philosophy librarians can find some opportunities in groups and publications devoted to librarianship in the humanities, some of which are described in other chapters.

Professional Readings

Arnold, Charles Harvey. "Philosophy and Religion." *Library Trends* 15 (Jan. 1967): 459–77.

Asheim, Lester. "Philosophy." In *The Humanities and the Library: Problems in the Interpretation, Evaluation and Use of Library Materials*, 61–99. Chicago: American Library Assn., 1957.

Blazek, Ron, and Elizabeth Aversa. "Accessing Information in Philosophy." In *The Humanities: A Selective Guide to Information Sources*, 17–36. 3d ed. Littleton, Colo.: Libraries Unlimited, 1988.

———. "Principal Information Sources in Philosophy." In *The Humanities: A Selective Guide to Information Sources*, 37–53. 3d ed. Littleton, Colo.: Libraries Unlimited, 1988.

Carr, Reg. "Religion and Philosophy in Cambridge University Library: A General Introduction." *Bulletin of the Association of British Theological and Philosophical Libraries* 26 (Mar. 1983): 3–6.

Cornish, G. P. "Provision for Philosophy and Theology at the British Library Lending Division." *Bulletin of the Association of British Theological and Philosophical Libraries* 5 (Mar. 1976): 12–16.

De George, Richard T. *The Philosopher's Guide to Sources, Research Tools, Professional Life, and Related Fields.* Lawrence, Kans.: Regents Press of Kansas, 1980.

Diemer, A. "Die Idee Einer Enzyklopadischen Systematischen Philosophie und die Moderne Dokumentation." *Nachrichten für Dokumentation* 19 (Feb./Mar. 1968): 1–4.

Duckett, R. J. "Philosophy and Religion in Dewey 19." *Bulletin of the Association of British Theological and Philosophical Libraries* 18 (June 1980): 12–16.

_____. "Philosophy on the Public Library Shelves." *New Library World* 87 (June 1986): 104–7.

_____. "Theological and Philosophical Libraries and Librarianship." In *British Librarianship and Information Science 1971–1975*, edited by H. A. Whatley, 252–59. London, Eng.: Library Assn., 1977.

Gould, Constance. "Philosophy." In *Information Needs in the Humanities: An Assessment*, 29–33. Stanford, Calif.: Research Libraries Group, 1988.

Henrichs, Norbert. "Philosophische Dokumentation: Literature-Dokumentation Ohne Strukturierten Thesaurus." *Nachrichten für Dokumentation* 21 (Feb. 1970): 20–25.

Lamble, W. H. "The Role of the Library of Social Sciences, Philosophy and Religion." *Australia's Special Libraries News* 10 (Dec. 1977): 155–58.

Preuss, Werner. "Gemeinschaftsarbeit in der Philosophischen Information." *Ziid Zeitschrift* 15 (Apr. 1968): 71–73.

Reister, Gernot. "Entwurf Einer Annotierten Grundbestandsliste Philosophie." *Buch und Bibliothek* 36 (Feb. 1984): 138–53.

Scrimgeour, Andrew D. "Philosophy and Religion." In *Selection of Library Materials in the Humanities, Social Sciences, and Sciences*, edited by Patricia A. McClung, 98–121. Chicago: American Library Assn., 1985.

Tice, Terrence N., and Thomas P. Slavens. *Research Guide to Philosophy.* Chicago: American Library Assn., 1983.

Walsh, Michael J. "Religion and Philosophy." In *Reviews and Reviewing: A Guide*, edited by A. J. Walford, 37–52. London, Eng.: Mansell, 1986.

CHAPTER 7

Religion

Gary Ebersole and Martha S. Alt

Religion is one of the central fields of knowledge in the humanities. Indeed, over the centuries and millennia of human history, religion has been the soil out of which many other fields were created. Scholars have clearly demonstrated that much of the impetus in early developments in art, music, dance, architecture, philosophy, astronomy, the other sciences, and so on, came from the religious concerns and world views of different human cultures. To look at a few types of architecture as examples, one discovers that the designs of the Hindu temple, the Egyptian pyramids, the Gothic cathedral, the Iroquois longhouse, and the Plains Indian tepee were all informed by the world view of the respective culture in which they had their genesis. The design, form, and uses of all these buildings were an expression of the desire to have the house—be it a domicile (the longhouse and tepee), a house of worship (the temple and cathedral), or a mortuary house (the pyramids)—be a miniature model or microcosm of the universe as each culture understood it. For religious men and women living in a house modeled on the cosmos, life in the world, including many aspects one may now consider "secular" (e.g., eating, bathing, sexual activity), has had a religious value. One of the signs of modernity and secularization is that one no longer thinks in terms of a building as a microcosm of the universe. Architecture is only one example of the way religion has influenced many fields that are no longer always immediately associated with the sacred. Yet there are few elements of cultural history that can be properly understood without taking the influence of religion into consideration.

Profile of Religion

Religion as a historical phenomenon is both difficult to define and impossible to categorize neatly. Naming only a few of the subfields—the philosophy of religion, the sociology of religion, the history of religions, the psychology of religion, religion and literature, religion and the arts, the geography of religions, the anthropology of religion—suggests something of the breadth involved. In the twentieth century the academic study of religion has been characterized more by a focus on subject matter than by a methodology applied to this study. Indeed, some influential scholars have even argued that the concept of "religion" is a Western hegemonic historical construct that is no longer of use and, thus, should be abandoned.[1] While such arguments may be of interest to scholars of religion as they strive to be conscious of both the ideological implications of their framing (and thus creation) of their subject matter and of their methodologies, it is equally true that the term *religion* has a currency in our culture that must be acknowledged as libraries consider their holdings and plan future acquisitions. The library's role is to serve as a repository of documents and information pertinent to the study of religion.

A Definition of Religion

As a general working definition of religion, one might begin with that offered by the anthropologist Clifford Geertz, since it has proven to be serviceable for scholars in a wide variety of fields. Geertz's definition, found in his essay "Religion as a Cultural System," reads:

> A religion is a system of symbols which acts to establish powerful, pervasive and long-lasting moods and motivations in men by formulating conceptions of a general order of existence and clothing these conceptions with such an aura of factuality that the moods and motivations seem uniquely realistic.[2]

This general definition of religion has several important implications that should be duly noted. First, religion is not an individual or private affair but is understood more properly as a corporate or collective cultural phenomenon. One may have a private philosophy, but religion involves a community of believers who share "a system of symbols which acts to establish powerful, pervasive, and long-lasting moods and motivations." The respective set of symbols that orients human beings in the universe and that is value-producing constitutes what historians of religions and anthropologists have come to call a "world view." Culturally meaningful acts are those participating in a shared world view permitting these acts to be understood and interpreted in a commonly and largely uncon-

---

1. See Wilfred Cantwell Smith, *The Meaning and End of Religion* (New York: Macmillan, 1963).
2. Clifford Geertz, "Religion as a Cultural System," in *Anthropological Approaches to the Study of Religion*, ed. M. Banton (London, Eng.: Tavistock Publications, 1966), 4.

sciously held consensual manner. Such a cultural and religious world view, however, is not simply a given passed on unchanged to the next generation nor is it a passive reflection of the existing society and social structures. Rather, as scholars in all fields of knowledge have come to recognize, culture (including religion) is not a thing or an abstraction but rather is a socially constituted web of meaning and structure that is created and re-created continually through every level of social interaction and communication.

Communities and the individuals within any given culture are involved continually in an ongoing process of constructing, apprehending, utilizing, and challenging the operative symbol systems. This process is inevitably social and anonymous insofar as it is never under the complete control of any single individual or group. This fact gives the individuals who find themselves born into or enmeshed in a social web of interrelationships, beliefs, and practices based on systems of symbols a sense that these systems are in some sense autonomous. Émile Durkheim, the "father of modern sociology," was one of the first to suggest that much of the power of symbolic systems and associated systems of morality comes from this sense of their autonomy. Cultural patterns or symbolic complexes are external sources of information through which traditional understandings of reality are transmitted from one generation to the next and from one social group to another.

The second point to note is that the symbol system that constitutes a religion is not an intellectual abstraction nor is it simply a speculative philosophy. It structures or informs both social and psychological reality *and* seeks to channel human responses to this reality. That is to say, a religion seeks to provide people with the truth concerning the way the universe *really* is beyond the superficial or phenomenal world one can know through the senses as well as the truth concerning the human condition. In providing these truths, though, religion also creates values (*this* is a higher truth than *that*; this is illusion or delusion; this is proper action, that is not). In this sense, religion provides both *a model of the universe and humanity's place in it* and *a model for meaningful activity* within it. One of the primary goals of library acquisitions in religion should be to maintain a collection allowing future generations to retrieve the rich variety and multitude of other expressions of human religiosity from the past as well as from the contemporary world.

Humanity's ability to create and use symbols (i.e., to represent the world and to think through symbols) is a central—if not *the* central—point that differentiates human beings from animals. As Geertz notes, for example, a beaver inherits a genetically transmitted model of a dam in his physiology and, thus, instinctively is able to build a hydraulic control device/home that serves to create an environment conducive to beaver life. Unlike humans, however, the beaver cannot give the structure of the dam a higher meaning or value through symbolic thought. Nor, for that matter, is a beaver able to consciously alter the design of the structure to better represent a conception (old or new) of the structure of the universe or of anything else for that matter. With humans, though, the matter is quite different. Traditional architecture, as hinted at earlier, was designed in order to represent conceptual images of the universe *and* to stimulate certain cognitive and emotive responses in people upon entering the architectural structure, in viewing it, in inhabiting space ordered precisely along symbolic and cosmological lines, etc. This latter element is what Geertz means by saying religions seek "to establish powerful, pervasive, and long-lasting moods and motivations in men." One need only consider the Gothic cathedral[3] to see how various concepts, ideals, and psychological elements could be translated into a plastic[4] form, which in turn evoked shared responses. For example, when medieval Christians entered the cathedral at Chartres, they saw at once the vault of heaven, sculptural and pictorial images of central biblical narratives and the life of Jesus, had their eyes turned heavenward, and experienced the awe and grandeur of the Christian deity and the relative insignificance of humankind.

This example may serve as an introduction to the next important point found in Geertz's definition of religion. Religion provides conceptions of a general order of existence that take on "an aura of factuality." The rhetorical claim and, if accepted as true, the sense that religious conceptions provide access to ultimate reality or eternal truth in turn lead individuals to hold firm and specific convictions about reality (a cosmology), the human condition (an anthropology), and questions about morality (ethics). Moreover, religion provides a general conception not only of how the world really is structured, ordered, and so on, but also of what it ideally should be like. In other words, religion is not only descriptive, it is also prescriptive. Religion seeks to provide guidelines for meaningful action in the world and often to change the human condition in some fundamental way, to prepare for or to achieve a higher spiritual state, a desired afterlife, and so on.

Religions, then, make far-reaching claims on persons. Participating in or joining a religion always involves some kind of acceptance of authority that transforms the individual's experience and understanding of the world. For "religions of the book," authority will tend to be located in a sacred scripture or canon (the Torah, the Bible, the Qur'an, the sutras,

---

3. See Otto von Simson, *The Gothic Cathedral*, 2d ed. (New York: Harper & Row, 1964).
4. "Plastic" in this sense refers to tangible materials, physical objects; for example, paintings, sculptures, pottery, etchings.

for example). Thus, it is important that all library collections include translations of the most important sacred texts of the religions of the world and, in collections supporting the relevant languages, in the original language. In addition, major commentaries and exegetical texts are important. However, texts are not the only loci of authority in religious traditions.

In many religions the origin of their claims to authority may be located in the transformative experience of an individual, as in the cases of the Gotama Buddha, Jesus, St. Paul, and Muhammed. Such individuals become paradigmic figures for their respective religious traditions or role models for living a holy life. The Buddha, for instance, claimed to have achieved the highest state of spiritual insight possible, enlightenment, while meditating under the boddhi tree. In the enlightenment experience he discovered the Four Noble Truths and the Eight-Fold Path, which thereafter became basic guides for the Buddhist faithful, providing not only a universal anthropology and cosmology but also a way of overcoming the suffering that characterizes existence. In yet other religious traditions, the source of spiritual authority may be located in the vision of a shaman (a specialist of the sacred who has mastered the techniques of ecstasy), a prophet, or the extraordinary experience or teaching of some other religious functionary. Whatever the case may be, however, every religion includes a claim of privileged access to ultimate authority, truth, and reality. For the religious individual, the first step toward really understanding the world and living a meaningful life is to accept the authority of someone or something (a text, a revelation, a traditional teaching). This acceptance, when deeply felt and internalized, reorganizes the individual's experience of the world. It involves more than just a rational or cognitive acceptance of a given set of propositions, for it involves the whole person, including unconscious, nonrational, and emotional aspects.

The teachings and essential conceptions of a religion are transmitted not only through word of mouth or written texts but also through the performing arts, myths, iconography, the plastic arts, and so forth. Thus, it is not enough that the library holdings consist only of doctrinal, theological, philosophical, and other texts. The full richness and complexity of religion or of the cultural expressions of human religiosity can be conveyed through a balanced collection in the major dimensions of religion. Every area of the humanities encompasses concerns related to religion.

The general definition of religion presented previously suggests that religion is a cultural phenomenon that impinges upon many dimensions of human life and society. Religion and/or religious expressions are not easily divisible into discrete parts that may be viewed in isolation. Yet the richness and complexity of the subject matter of religion make it useful to group certain dimensions of religion for study (a list that undoubtedly could be expanded or trimmed), but with the understanding that these must ultimately be reintegrated: the doctrinal, the mythic, the ritual, the social, the ethical, the expressive or artistic, and the experiential.

The Doctrinal Dimension

Every religion has a belief system, a doctrinal dimension. When most people think of religion, they think first of the beliefs of various religious traditions rather than the other dimensions previously mentioned. Religious doctrines are attempts to give a systematic order and clarity to the beliefs and tenets of a community of the faithful. The doctrinal dimension of religion includes *theology* in theistic religions, but it is not limited to this as this term is generally understood in the Western monotheisms (Judaism, Christianity, and Islam). It also includes elements of the mythic dimension (discussed later). Moreover, not all religions are theistic (i.e., subscribe to a belief in the existence of a god or goddess [monotheism], multiple divinities [polytheism], or multiple manifestations of a single divinity [henotheism]). Theravada Buddhism, for example, is a nontheistic religion, for in this tradition Gotama the Buddha (literally "the enlightened one") is not considered a god but rather as the first human being to have achieved enlightenment, a spiritual state now potentially open to all sentient beings.

Religious doctrine includes the basic and essential beliefs that are shared by a given religious community. These beliefs have an inclusive function as they help to define the community and membership therein, but they also have an exclusive function in that these same doctrines may define others as outside the community. Doctrines are frequently not uniformly held by all persons within a religious tradition at any given time, and even less so over greater expanses of time and space. This lack of doctrinal uniformity is a result of the general historical process that might be termed "internal differentiation," through which smaller communities under the umbrella of a larger tradition (e.g., Christianity) come to hold differing doctrinal beliefs, often leading to splits, schisms, and sectarianism. In the history of Christianity one need only think of the differences between the Eastern Orthodox and Roman Catholic traditions, the Reformation, the Counter-Reformation, and the subsequent proliferation of Protestant denominations to recognize that this process is found in religious traditions great and small.

Doctrines in any religion are subject to change over time as well as to variation at any given time within different communities of the same faith. All religions have their genesis and development in history, and as such they are subject to change over time and space. As a rule of thumb, then, librarians should be wary of purchasing only general introductions to religions that present a "flat" list of the doctrines of given religious traditions. We will return to the question of basic holdings in the area of religious doctrine later; however, a good library collection will include: (1) the basic sacred texts of the major religions of the world, including those of nonorthodox, minority, or peripheral groups; (2) the major influential interpretations of these texts from within the respective religious traditions; and (3) doctrinal histories by modern academic scholars. In considering the doctrinal dimension, or any other dimension of religion for that matter, librarians need not (and should not) make any judgments about the truth claims of the religious traditions of the world. Normative claims by significant religious figures and religious communities, both orthodox and heterodox, are important pieces of historical "data" for students of religion and, as such, have a place in library collections, though these claims need to be complemented by academic and critical studies that will locate them in their socio-cultural contexts. Insofar as possible, libraries should strive to provide their patrons with a clear sense of the richness, diversity, and complexity of the religions of the world, including internal diversity over time and space.

The Mythic Dimension

The mythic dimension of religion consists of the paradigmatic sacred narratives or myths that hold special meaning for a religious tradition. In common parlance the term *myth* has been devalued and is often used in a derogatory sense in the modern and largely secular world. Consequently, when one prefaces a remark with "It's a myth that . . .," the implication is usually that "such-and-such is false." However, in religious studies and in religious traditions themselves, *myth* means just the opposite—i.e., a "true story." Myths tell how something or some condition in the world, be it human mortality, sexual and gender distinctions, or a given ritual, came to be the way it is through the actions of the gods, supernatural beings, the ancestors, or in some other manner.

Myths are a basic repository of the truths religions claim to possess. In this general sense the New Testament narratives or the Qur'an are myths in the same way the Navaho sacred stories or the Vedas are. Living myths are not empty stories or fantastic tales but are deeply connected to the lives of the faithful. Used in this nonderogatory fashion, then, religious scholars consider the sacred narratives of the world's religions, from the Bible to the Vedas, as myths. Myths are studied in order to better appreciate the symbol systems that have given meaning to the world for the adherents of the religions of the world. Myths are also often interesting narratives for readers to begin with in learning about religions, although they must be supplemented and contextualized along with the other dimensions of religion mentioned. Although by their very nature myths rhetorically present themselves as timeless or eternal, like every other dimension of religion they, too, have a history of their own that also may be the object of study. All libraries will want to have representative holdings in the mythic traditions of the world's religions.

The Ritual Dimension

Ritual is one of the basic forms of expression found in religion. It includes such things as worship, prayer, fasting, the practice of meditative techniques, pilgrimage, sacrifice, and offerings. Ritual can be both private and public, though even private ritual practices, such as prayer, are performed according to standard forms and procedures. Indeed, ritual activity of every kind is characterized by being a patterned activity. Every ritual is always based upon a prior paradigmatic action, often from the mythic past. Ritual activity usually seeks to overcome ordinary and mundane (profane) time and space and to (re)create a sacred time and space. Ritual is intimately related to the mythic dimension of religion, expressing and enacting elements of myth, even as the myths inform the actions and intentions in the ritual performance. When Christians, for example, participate in the Eucharist, it is held by some that they thereby become contemporaneous with the apostles who shared the original Last Supper with Jesus. In this single example one can glimpse an important general fact—the doctrinal and mythic elements of religion are also involved in the tradition's interpretation of the meaning of a given ritual. A "living" ritual is one in which the participants and observers are aware of the religiously and traditionally ascribed meaning of what is being performed, while an "empty" ritual is one that has become separated from the mythic and/or doctrinal dimensions with the result that when it is performed the actors are simply "going through the motions." In seeking to learn about any given religion, one needs to study not only what a member of the religion believes, but also what she or he does, i.e., how the symbolic belief system finds expression in collective rites, in individual ritual actions, and in motivating an individual to act in value-directed ways.

Studies of the ritual dimension of religion will be of various sorts. There are descriptive and interpretive ethnographical monographs that present in detail the unfolding of a ritual or ritual complex, as well as the symbolic associations or valences that come into play both consciously and unconsciously within a culture or community. Then, there are phenomenological studies that attempt to distill the "deep meaning" of different types of religious rituals. Mircea Eliade's study *Rites and Symbols of Initiation* (New York: Harper and Row, 1958) is an excellent example of the latter sort. This type of synthetic, comparative, and interpretive study is especially important in assisting the general reader in gaining an appreciation of the general religious meanings shared in the otherwise overwhelming volume of factual detail and descriptive minutiae of specific examples collected and recorded by the scholarly community over the centuries. In general, libraries will want to maintain a balance between culture, religious tradition, group or tribe-specific studies, and well-researched and balanced integrative studies. Just as Freud wryly noted that a cigar in a dream is sometimes just a cigar (rather than a phallic symbol), so too librarians must beware of reductionistic studies that would identify all religions or elements therein as essentially the same.

It is also important to note that rituals have their own histories. Although a ritual is essentially a patterned repetitious performance of specific ordered actions, rituals enjoy widespread currency at some points in time and space and varying currency at others. Thus, one can also find historical studies of certain rituals (e.g., baptism in Christianity or the Feast of the Dead among the Algonquian-speaking Amerindians) tracing the vicissitudes of these. Such studies are important because we often tend to assume that a ritual we know (or have read about) is somehow normative or standard, that it has always been performed as it is now, or when it was recorded, by all persons of that religion. In addition, such historical studies serve as a corrective to one of the weaknesses of the ethnographic monograph genre: the descriptive sections are usually cast in the present tense, thus creating what has come to be known as the "ethnographic present." This style of writing suggests to the uncritical reader that the ritual and the ritual participants are somehow "frozen" in time.

The Social Dimension

What is here referred to as the social dimension of religion is one of the more wide-flung categories employed. It embraces all communal and corporative aspects of religious traditions, including among other things ecclesiastical structures and organization, gender roles, familial and kinship organization, the variety of sacred roles found within a religious tradition, the socioeconomic and political dimensions of religion, religious schooling, and so on. As mentioned earlier, religion is always a communal affair, not the preserve of isolated individuals. Thus, almost every aspect of religion may be said to have a social dimension. Even such seemingly private or individual elements as prayer, having a vision or mystical experience, etc., have a social dimension insofar as these experiences and practices are learned, communicated to others, and are either authenticated and validated or challenged and/or invalidated by the religious community as possessing spiritual value or worth. Meaning and value are social constructs.[5] Thus, no aspect of religion can be properly understood if the

---

5. For a useful introduction to this topic see Peter Berger and Thomas Luckmann, *The Social Construction of Reality* (New York: Doubleday & Co., 1966).

social dimensions of religious phenomena are ignored. In many ways, a myth, a rite, a scriptural passage means what the religious community says it means. This is the exoteric aspect, but there may also be a hidden or esoteric meaning known only to the elders, the initiated, or the specialists of some sort. Finally, in the wake of Freud and the discovery of the unconscious, one will find many studies that speak of the unconscious meaning of certain symbols or acts.

The Ethical Dimension

In seeking to give meaning to human existence through ordering and structuring the cosmos, religion also addresses the issue of humankind's place in the universe. In presenting a coherent view of the order of the universe or a cosmology and an understanding of the human condition or an anthropology, most religions assert that in some important ways the world and the present human ontological state are less than perfect, that some rupture (or "Fall") has occurred, resulting in the present situation as we know it. The well-known nursery rhyme of Humpty Dumpty may be thought of as a shorthand expression of the basic position of many religious traditions in this regard. If we take Humpty Dumpty when whole, almost always represented pictorially as an egg, to symbolize the paradisal state of the beginning (and many myths of this cosmic egg as well as pictorial and iconographical expressions from around the world and over the entire length of human history would suggest this reading), then the Humpty Dumpty who "had a great fall" would, in his shattered state at the foot of the wall, symbolize the present. The nursery rhyme goes on, of course, to suggest that "all the King's horses and all the King's men couldn't put Humpty Dumpty together again." This we may understand to be saying that neither secular authority nor secular power alone are sufficient to repair the damage.

While the nursery rhyme ends there, religions inevitably go on to suggest that the situation is not hopeless. Rather, religions often claim to have the way or path to "put Humpty Dumpty together again," i.e., to restore the original, primal state. The described path differs, of course, from religion to religion and even within religious traditions over time and space or among different groups. What is important to note, however, is that the path often includes not only the proper performance of prescribed rituals according to the mythic paradigms or models but also the ordering of human actions in everyday life according to a higher or cosmic perspective. This latter aspect usually translates into a series of prescriptive and proscriptive commands that constitute the ethical dimension of religion.

Religious ethics differ from secular ethics in that they involve the spiritual well-being of humans, either in this world or a posited other world

or state. The legal prohibition in a state against the consumption of alco-
holic beverages before a certain age may be largely unrelated to any religious concerns, while a similar prohibition in certain ritual situations,
specific existential situations, or whatever may involve religious concerns.
Religious ethics are found not only in the doctrines of any given religious
tradition but also in the commentaries on scripture, in sermons and
preachings, in school textbooks, and in monastic and lay guides.

Of course, religious ethics could be considered under the social dimension of religion, but it is such an important element in most religions that
it perhaps deserves mention and attention in its own right. Like many
dimensions of religion, religious ethics is not an airtight compartment,
but one that overlaps with or is integrated with several others as well.
Religious ethics are not eternal and unchanging; they also have a history
that needs to be reflected in the holdings of any library.

The Expressive or Artistic Dimension

Religious expressions of various sorts have long been recognized as the
wellsprings of many of the arts. Ritual performances of various sorts no
doubt helped to stimulate song, dance, the theatre, ventriloquism, mime,
poetry, and pictorial representation. Moreover, the arts have always been
primary vehicles for communicating information about religion through
all of the senses. Thus, no study of religion can ignore the artistic expressions of the variety, complexity, and richness of human religiosity. Human beings create and express meaning not only through language, oral
and written, but also through gestures and the plastic arts. Indeed, in terms
of human history—and for many persons even today—religious teachings
and meanings are communicated through other nonwritten means, including the visual and aural arts. The study of religion that is restricted
to texts or perhaps doctrines will be impoverished. Thus, libraries must
strive to make available the full range of human cultural creations, including the artistic expressions of human religiosity. On the other hand,
religious arts or artworks cannot be appreciated fully in isolation from
the other dimensions of religion, so that even art libraries must include
in their collections basic holdings in these as well.

The Experiential Dimension

The experiential dimension of religion encompasses the individual's experience of religious phenomena as well as communal experience. It involves elements that might be thought of as psychological in nature.
Religious individuals are not only intellectually convinced of the correct-
ness of certain beliefs and doctrines but are immediately engaged as persons both emotionally and spiritually. In Geertz's definition of religion
cited earlier, he maintains that religion is "a system of symbols which

acts to establish powerful, pervasive, and long-lasting moods and motivations" in people. The symbol system does not merely present an image of reality; in important and pervasive ways it structures the human experience of the world and our responses to it.

In order to appreciate the experiential dimension of religion, one must turn first to the testimony of individuals and communities. The experiential dimension may be found, among other places, in mysticism and mystical texts, in meditative practices, in prayer, in the accounts of pilgrims and others, in confessions (e.g., those of St. Augustine). This testimony itself becomes one type of data for the student of religion. Individual or communal experience, then, is never "raw," however, but is always readily structured and mediated by culturally available interpretive frames. The study of religion is not limited to a simple cataloging of reports of experiences but also includes the ways in which different cultures validate or give meaning to disparate experiences. Studies in the psychology of religion and psychobiographies of major figures are important interpretive works for libraries to hold, but religious individuals and communities should also be allowed to speak for themselves in confessional statements, autobiographies, diaries, etc. First-person accounts, testimonials, and so forth, are in many ways the primary sources in religious studies. We will return to this point in the section on "The Literature of Religion."

Even with this brief survey of a few of the major dimensions of religion, it should be obvious that religion is a complex and multidimensional human cultural phenomenon. Consequently, library holdings in this field must be both multidisciplinary and cross-cultural. Librarians have a special social responsibility in this regard. We can no longer afford to be comfortable in an unexamined Eurocentricism or in any other parochialism. To be sure, it is important to have extensive holdings in the major Western religious traditions, but bibliographers must also make concerted efforts to provide patrons with a global perspective on religion. Only by locating Western traditions in the total history of humankind can one truly appreciate the commonalities these share with other religions as well as the uniqueness and integrity of each religious tradition.

Terminology of the Discipline

The discipline that has as its primary goal the description and interpretation of religious phenomena is most commonly known as religious studies, although other terms such as simply "religion," "comparative religion," "the history of religion(s)," "*Religionswissenschaft*," "science of religion," and so on, are also used. Religious studies is in some ways an awkward term since the student of the subject need not be religious any more than one must be musical in order to appreciate and study music. Nor is the academic study of religion in itself a religious act or enterprise. Nevertheless, this term, religious studies, has come to be the most commonly used in North American colleges and universities for designated departments and programs engaged in the academic study of religion. Theology, on the other hand, is more commonly used to suggest a confessionally based study.

In considering their collections, public libraries and most college and university libraries will want to think of the subject of religion in terms of the general history of religions, for this more properly locates religion in the humanities as a historical phenomenon. "History of religions," however, does not restrict the subject to history as it is generally taught in history departments. History in that sense is not the whole of what constitutes the subject matter of religious studies. "The history of religions" is the English phrase that has been adopted by the major international professional organization of scholars of religion, the International Association for the History of Religions, to designate "*Allgemeine Religionswissenschaft.*" Thus, this designation might be adopted for the sake of consistency and convenience if nothing else.

History of the Academic Study of Religion

As a field of academic inquiry the study of religions is a relatively recent one, having its inception in any significant form only in the nineteenth century. A number of factors and historical developments—the founding of universities in Europe and England, the Renaissance and Enlightenment, European exploration and colonization, the rapid increase in world trade, Christian missionary activity—had by that time combined to bring other cultures and other cognitive and symbolic worlds of meaning into the consciousness of the West. The appropriation of other cultures and people through knowledge gained through contact with and the study of these other cultures (whether this knowledge was accurate or not) had important ideological dimensions and cultural/historical consequences. It also set the stage for the emergence of a general history of religions wherein the Western monotheisms could be located for the first time in the larger, and non-Eurocentric, history of humankind. Such a history of religions is now establishing itself within the various types of academic institutions of North America.

In order to understand the place of the history of religions in the humanities today, a brief sketch of the history of the academic study of religion may be useful.[6] Within this context it is impossible to do more than mention a few of the significant intellectual movements and theories found in the study of religions from the nineteenth and twentieth centuries. Many of these theories of religion are thoroughly discredited or outmoded. Chief among these are what may be termed evolutionary theories of religion, which argue in some form or another that all religions passed through a set series of developmental stages. One of the most common developmental schemas had culture passing from animism to magic to religion to science. Whatever the specific evolutionary scheme offered, however, the West and the authors themselves inevitably were found to be at the highest developmental stage. Such condescending evolutionary (and a few devolutionary) schemas had, of course, no historical validity whatsoever. Moreover, they usually confused industrial and technological development with spiritual and intellectual development.

An example of a devolutionary theory of sorts was expounded in the writings of the nature-myth school. Friedrich Max Müller (1823–1900) was one of the main representatives of this school of thought that claimed that the deities of antiquity were at base the personification of natural phenomena such as the sun, stars, thunder, and dawn. Müller suggested that the various phenomena discovered in the foggy past by humankind in nature had evoked a sense of the infinite and the divine, but that these feelings or intuitions could only be thought of through metaphor and symbol. Müller argued that religion, at least in its theistic form, was the result of a regrettable "disease of language" that led humans to take their own metaphors and symbols as real rather than as what they were. The only way to recover the original intuitive insights of humankind was through philological and etymological research, restoring the pristine meaning of the names of gods and goddesses. Müller's works, while classics in the field, are now of largely historical interest. Müller's most enduring legacy, perhaps, is having edited the famous series of translations of sacred scriptures, *The Sacred Books of the East* (Oxford, Eng.: Oxford University Press, 1879–1910; reprint ed., Delhi, India: Motilal Banarsidass, 1965). The works of Müller may serve to remind us of an important point, however. All critical academic studies are superseded sooner or later and

6. For fuller discussions, the reader may consult E. E. Evans-Pritchard, *Theories of Primitive Religion* (London, Eng.: Oxford University Press, 1965); J. Waardenburg, *Classical Approaches to the Study of Religion*, 2 vols. (The Hague, Neth.: E. J. Brill, 1978); Eric J. Sharpe, *Comparative Religion: A History* (London, Eng.: Duckworth, 1975); Mircea Eliade, "The History of Religions in Retrospect: 1912 and After," in *The Quest: History and Meaning in Religion* (Chicago: The University of Chicago Press, 1969); and Joseph M. Kitigawa, "The History of Religions (*Religionswissenschaft*) Then and Now," in Kitigawa, ed., *The History of Religions: Retrospect and Prospect* (New York: Macmillan Publishing Co., 1985).

become obsolete. Nevertheless, their value in academic collections does not end, it changes. Even when studies of various aspects of religion are no longer on the cutting edge of the field, they may still be very important documents of intellectual history, cultural history, and other such fields.

Edward Tylor is another nineteenth-century scholar who tried to explain religion through a theory of its origins. Tylor coined the term "animism," which has a long history of ambiguity contributing to the imprecision that long characterized the study of religion. Tylor suggested that primitive people had posited the existence of a soul or animating spirit in order to make sense of death, dreams, visions, trance states, and other altered states of consciousness. There was, alas, no real historical evidence for this thesis. Tylor's work is representative of what might be called an intellectualist interpretation of religion in that he, like many others, assumed that people arrived at religious conceptions through rational and deductive thought, even if these were sometimes faulty and immature.

Sir James Frazer is famous for his *The Golden Bough*, an immensely popular compilation of bits of information and misinformation gathered from around the world on religious beliefs and practices. First appearing in 1900 as *The Golden Bough: A Study in Comparative Religion*, this work went through multiple editions, revisions, and enlargements over the next thirty years and grew into the famous multivolume set under the general title *The Golden Bough: A Study in Magic and Religion* (London, Eng.: Macmillan, 1911–1915). It is still available in a thirteen-volume reprint edition and an abridged one-volume version edited by Theodore H. Gaster, *The New Golden Bough* (New York: Criterion Books, 1959). Like many of his contemporaries, Frazer erroneously assumed that all human cultures pass through the same evolutionary stages from magic to religion to science. Similarly, he took the modern West as the pinnacle of human cultural advancement toward which all other cultures would necessarily evolve. Insofar as other cultures differed from the West or did not share Western aesthetic values, they were judged to be inferior. Frazer also took bits of information out of context, thus distorting their meaning. Moreover, he failed to take note of the difference in human behavior in religious ritual situations (i.e., in sacred time and space) and outside these in secular time and space.

Other major theories of religion came from such individuals as Herbert Spencer, Lucien Lévy-Bruhl, Rudolf Otto, William James, Sigmund Freud, Karl Marx (who defined religion as "the opiate of the masses"), Émile Durkheim, and so on. Most theories can be categorized as either psychological theories or sociological theories. While librarians will want to have all the "classics" of the history of religions in their collections, they will also want to acquire the major modern secondary studies of these works and authors as well as intellectual histories, both as correctives and to locate the texts and scholars within their generative cultural contexts.

The Literature of Religion

We have already seen that the field of religious studies is both interdisciplinary and multidisciplinary in nature. This fact alone would suggest that the number of publications concerning religion will be large, but because religion plays such a central role in ordering and giving meaning to people's lives, it also generates a tremendous amount of material published by and for specific religious communities as well as academic studies.[7] No library collection can hope to be able to cover the entire field of religious studies.

The literature of religion can be thought of in a number of different ways. Stephen Peterson has divided it into the categories of source literature, critical literature, and historical literature.[8] *Source literature*, as used by Peterson, indicates materials published by and for specific religious communities. *Critical literature* refers to scholarly and academic works about religion and religious phenomena. Finally, *historical literature* indicates now-obsolete critical works (i.e., scholarship that has been superseded in the field of religious studies). This division has much to recommend it, and many librarians may want to think in these terms in considering not only acquisitions but also disposal policies.

Religious literature—whether considered primary or secondary; source, critical, or historical—is available in both print and nonprint formats. Print formats include monographs, journals, guides to the literature, reference works, and special materials such as pamphlets and manuscripts. Microforms, audiovisual materials, and computerized data are examples of nonprint formats. Religious materials are produced by well-known houses such as HarperSanFrancisco, Zondervan, and Oxford University Press, and by specialized publishers such as Tri-Star Publishing, producer of the CD-ROM *Master Search Bible* (*MSB*).

Source Literature

Source literature is produced by and for specific religious communities. It includes the sacred texts of the religious traditions of the world, works that are confessionally based (i.e., that come out of the religious life and

---

7. See publishing statistics in William J. Hook, "Approval Plans for Religious and Theological Libraries," *Library Acquisitions: Practice and Theory* 15 (1991): 215–27.

8. Stephen Lee Peterson, "Documenting Christianity: Towards a Cooperative Library Collection Development Program," *Summary of Proceedings* (American Theological Library Assn.) 32 (1978): 83–103.

convictions of the author or community), works that aim to provide guidance in everyday life according to the religious community's precepts (e.g., sermons, devotional literature, inspirational works), and the official documents and statements of a religious body. Such works are of use to others outside the religious community insofar as they provide the most immediate access, other than fieldwork studies, to the beliefs, practices, and ethics of that group.

The term *primary sources* is used to refer to the basic or central religious texts of each religious community. These may be either in the original language or in translation. They are not studies of the sacred texts or of their history, though in modern editions these will often be appended or included in an introduction, but rather the sacred texts themselves. It is the respective religious communities themselves, not the academic scholars of religion, that determine which texts are sacred. At first it might seem to be a fairly easy task to assemble the sacred texts of the religious traditions of the world. There are any number of one or multivolume sets claiming to be collections of the sacred texts of the world, either in full or condensed form. Max Müller's series of translations mentioned earlier is a classic example of a collection of primary texts. However, librarians must be aware that such collections, while useful in many ways, may also seriously distort the historical reality if they are not complemented by other more detailed studies because any such collection is selective of necessity in the number and size of texts included. As a result, most compilers and editors tend to base their inclusion decisions on criteria such as a determination of which texts have been most influential, been recognized by the largest sect(s), etc. While quite rational in some ways, such editorial decisions result in the exclusion of many smaller sects, minority groups, and so on, that are given little representation or voice. What most people think of as "classical Hinduism," for example, is as much a function of Müller's editorial decisions and of other early Orientalists as of anything else. Fortunately, a number of annotated bibliographies on non-Western religions have appeared, and continue to appear, so that the bibliographer need not be a Buddhologist, a Japanologist, and so forth, to do justice to the various religious traditions.

A careful consideration of the matter will reveal that history once again has complicated the bibliographer's job, for the canon of a religious tradition is often fluid. That is, the determination of which texts are sacred and which are not, or which are more sacred than others, is not a constant either diachronically over time and space or synchronically over space. Just as the Christian canon has a history, so do other sacred texts, be they oral or written. Different communities within a broad religious community such as Hinduism, for example, may hold different texts sacred or assign different relative values to certain texts than other

Hindu communities do. To give a more familiar example, one cannot assume that the King James Bible represented the sacred text of Christianity as a whole over its entire history, for this translation had its genesis at a specific point in time and circulation or currency in a circumscribed area of Christendom. It is also a Protestant Bible, not a Roman Catholic or Eastern Orthodox one. This example may serve as an exemplar of the fact that different groups or sects within a religious tradition may hold differing beliefs concerning the content of the sacred canon and the relative valuations placed upon those within it. Thus, if one wanted to accurately represent the Bible as the central sacred text of Christianity in a library collection, at a minimum one would want to have various versions and include, for example, the Douay-Rheims Version, the New American Bible, the King James Version, the New International Version, and the Apocrypha. Research libraries, seminaries, and schools of theology will, of course, include many other translations and versions.

Sacred texts, then, have a history. To provide patrons with access to this type of history, when considering the purchase of a translation of any given sacred text librarians should give preference to scholarly annotated versions, preferably with an appended introductory essay on the text's history, its impact, etc. Examples would include the Bell and the Pickthall translations of the Qur'an and *The New Jerusalem Bible*.

Sometimes the situation is even more complicated, however. In Buddhism, for example, scholars do not talk about a single canon but of multiple canons—the Pali canon, the Sanskrit, Tibetan, Chinese, Japanese canons, and so forth. Each of these in turn has a complex history of its own, which in some cases is only now beginning to be reconstructed by scholars. Research libraries will want to have much larger holdings in these areas than will other libraries, although every library should aim to build a collection that will help locate the texts in their generative contexts and detail their reception and interpretation over the centuries.

Primary sources also include examples of source literature that have become especially important for a religious community in either its practice or its doctrinal history. For example, the theological works of St. Augustine, St. Thomas Aquinas, Martin Luther, John Calvin, and so on, are today primary sources in the study of the history of Christianity, although at the time of their genesis these writings were secondary literature.

Sacred Literature

Another type of source literature may be thought of as primary literature as described earlier. In its most general terms, this sacred literature includes not only the sacred texts of the religious traditions of the world but also the major commentaries, critical editions, theological or exegetical treatises that have proven influential within the traditions, etc. In

Christianity, for example, it is a foregone conclusion that the writings of the Church Fathers, Aquinas, Luther, Calvin, and so on, will be a part of every collection. While it is less obvious, perhaps, it is no less important to have equivalent works by influential thinkers in other religious traditions. Here again the various bibliographical guides to the specific religious traditions will be of assistance to those unfamiliar with a given religious tradition.[9]

Some libraries may want to build and maintain collections of primary materials in specific areas such as church, diocesan or synagogue records, the formal deliberations of ecclesiastical bodies, the papers and other writings of significant religious figures (theologians, writers, social activists, religious leaders, etc.). Librarians, in conjunction with faculty and others, will want to identify areas in which unique or especially strong collections should be built.

Popular or Confessionally Based Literature

Popular and confessionally based literature need not be scholarly in tone or format, although in some cases it may be of high intellectual caliber. This type of literature represents the largest percentage of works published in religion each year. It includes, but is not limited to, religious diaries and autobiographies, works of pastoral counseling, study guides to the sacred texts, guides to living a religious or sanctified life, published sermons, and religiously colored works of fiction. Some of the literature may be polemical in tone or politically biased. Much of it will be focused on topics and issues of contemporary interest and concern. Examples of contemporary sources include works by C. S. Lewis, Billy Graham, Charles Swindoll, Kahlil Gibran, and Shirley MacLaine. In general, literature of this type deals with contemporary issues that impinge upon the lives of the members of the religious community and discuss these in terms of the author's understanding of the religion. Every academic library collection in religion must make a place for such literature, although it will necessarily be a fairly limited one. Not only the various dimensions of religion in the past or in other cultures but also those in the contemporary world constitute the subject of study in religious studies.

Acquisition of contemporary, confessionally based literature poses special problems. Understandably some librarians have shied away from acquiring these materials because of their "popular" and nonacademic nature. Certainly, any library with a limited acquisitions budget will want to carefully consider and monitor purchases of popular literature in religion. At the same time, however, librarians should not ignore the fact

---

9. See, for example, Jean Holn, *Keyguide to Information Sources on World Religions* (London, Eng.: Mansell, 1991).

that it is such literature that provides an important source of data on "grass-roots" religion, both for researchers today and in future generations. Thus, while no budget should be expended primarily on such sources neither should such sources be completely slighted.

The spring and fall religious books issues, the "Religious Publishing" features, and the "Religious Bestsellers" columns of *Publishers Weekly* (Bowker, 1872–); the occasional articles on religion in *Library Journal* (Bowker, 1876–); and the monthly issues of *Bookstore Journal* (Christian Booksellers Association, 1968–) provide reviews, information on publishers and publishing trends, and suggestions for the selection and handling of popular publications in religion.

Some libraries will want to have representative holdings in the popular literature of non-Western religious traditions as well. It may be very important, for example, to have works published by the Baha'i or the Japanese "new religion" Tenri-kyo, to name only two communities outside the "mainstream" of North American culture but which, nevertheless, represent an active minority presence. These two groups, like hundreds of others, also publish their own magazines to which research libraries may want to subscribe. Once again, the sheer number of publications is overwhelming, and many librarians despair of ever being able to do justice to all of the religions of the world. This difficulty, always with us, is ameliorated by several factors. First, simply recognizing that no one library could ever hope to be comprehensive in its holdings opens the way for individual institutions to evaluate their needs and those of the surrounding and cooperative libraries in order to determine where each might be able to make the greatest contribution for a realistic budgetary expenditure. Second, out of necessity, all but the major research libraries will limit their holdings primarily to Western-language materials.

Critical and Historical Literature

Critical and historical works in religion include all of the materials that are of academic interest but that do not fall in the category of source literature. In many cases a library's holdings of secondary works in religious studies will outnumber the primary sources. Given the complexity of the field and the number of dimensions of religion, this is to be expected. All of the different dimensions and the different disciplinary approaches and methodologies applied to the study of religious phenomena should be represented in a research-level collection so that these dimensions may be studied individually, collectively, and comparatively.

Monographs

Monographs make up the bulk of most religion collections and include general studies, textual interpretations, text-critical studies, textual histories, histories of religious traditions, and theological works, including apologetics (those works that deal with the reasons for faith, the proofs of the veracity and efficaciousness of the application of the faith to daily life, and works written for those within the faith who need encouragement to reaffirm their commitment). Commercial publishers, university presses, association presses, denominational houses, and presses of particular religious communities and viewpoints all share in producing the monographs included in library collections in religion.[10]

Publishing titles in monograph series is a technique used by publishers in religion in an attempt to capture the heart and standing-order budget of librarians. Many excellent series are available in the field, and titles in the series can usually be trusted in their quality since they are overseen by editorial boards composed of eminent scholars. Such series include Semeia and Semeia Studies (Decatur, Ga.: Scholars Press); Studies in Oriental Religions (Wiesbaden, Ger.: O. Harrassowitz); Contributions to the Study of Religion (New York: Greenwood Press); ATLA Monograph Series (Evanston, Ill.: American Theological Library Association); those published by university presses, such as the Religion in North America series (Bloomington, Ind.: Indiana University Press); and those published by university-affiliated institutes, such as the Institute of Buddhist Studies series (Berkely, Calif.: Pacific World).

Journals

The number of serial publications in the area of religion seems infinite at times, with several new titles being produced every year. All of them are not of academic significance, of course, and titles must be reviewed in light of curricular and patron needs, available funds, and value as compared with titles already in the collection. At times, funds may be better spent in filling gaps in the journal collection to provide greater depth of collection for researchers rather than in adding new titles. Donations from organizations or interested individuals of subscriptions and back issues are good ways to boost a library's holdings.

Titles basic to collections supporting a department or program of religion include the *Journal of the American Academy of Religion* (*JAAR*) (Atlanta, Ga.: Scholars Press, 1933–), *Journal for the Scientific Study of Religion* (*JSSR*) (West Lafayette, Ind.: Society for the Scientific Study of Religion, 1961–), *Journal of Religion* (Chicago: University

10. See issues of *Publishers Weekly* for discussions of religious publishing and publishers, as well as Rev. Jovian P. Lang, "Religious Publishers and Their Specialties," *Catholic World* (Nov.-Dec. 1989): 111–18; Phyllis Tickle, "Religious Publishing: the Cult of Mission," *Small Press* 8 (Oct. 1990): 34–38, 26, 8 (Dec. 1990): 30–39; and Barbara Hoffert, "Spiritual Guidance," *Library Journal* (1 Nov. 1990): 58–63.

of Chicago Divinity School, 1921–), *Religion* (London, Eng.: Academic Press, 1971–), and *Religious Studies Review* (Macon, Ga.: Council of Societies for the Study of Religion, 1975–). Some journals emphasize a particular aspect of religious studies. *Church History* (Indialantic, Fla.: American Society of Church History, 1932–), *History of Religions* (Chicago: University of Chicago, 1961–), and *Numen* (Leiden, Neth.: Brill, 1954–) contain frequently cited articles on historical topics. *Missiology: An International Review* (Wilmore, Ky.: American Society of Missiology, 1973–) is a key resource on missions; the *Journal of Biblical Literature* (Atlanta, Ga.: Scholars Press, 1881–) is a key resource on biblical studies.

Libraries connected to or supported by particular religious organizations will have as a high priority in their serials and processing budgets those titles that represent official organs or voices of their organizations, such as the *American Baptist Quarterly* (McMinnville, Oreg.: American Baptist Historical Society, 1982–), and the *Catholic Biblical Quarterly* (Washington, D.C.: Catholic Biblical Assn., 1939–). A list of periodicals by organization or religion may be found in Charles Lippy's *Religious Periodicals of the United States: Academic and Scholarly Journals* (Westport, Conn.: Greenwood Press, 1986).

Reference Tools and Guides to the Literature

A librarian new to the field of religious studies would profit from looking at guides to the literature to become familiar with the standard reference works. These include James Kennedy's *Library Research Guide to Religion and Theology* (Ann Arbor, Mich.: Pierian Press, 1984) and John Trotti's introductory chapter in *Theological and Religious Reference Materials: General Resources and Biblical Studies* (New York: Greenwood, 1984). The chapters "Accessing Information in Religion" and "Principal Information Sources in Religion" in Ron Blazek and Elizabeth Aversa's *Humanities: A Selective Guide to Information Sources* (Littleton, Colo.: Libraries Unlimited, 1987) provide information on 130 religious reference sources. John F. Wilson and Thomas P. Slavens's *Research Guide to Religious Studies* (Chicago: American Library Assn., 1982) provides a detailed introduction to the field of religious studies and to the various religious traditions as well as listing basic reference works categorized by general resources and resources pertaining to particular persuasions. James Patrick McCabe's *Critical Guide to Catholic Reference Books* (3d ed., Research Studies in Library Science, 20, Englewood, Colo.: Libraries Unlimited, Inc., 1989) supplies information on more than 1,500 important reference books related to Catholicism. The "Religion" section of *Topical Reference Books: Authoritative Evaluations of Recommended Resources in Specialized Subject Areas* (New Providence, N.J.: Bowker, 1991) includes a small number of titles. Charles Adams's *A Reader's*

Guide to the Great Religions (New York: Free Press, 1977) and John R. Hinnells's *Handbook of Living Religions* (Harmondsworth, Middlesex, Eng.: Viking, 1984) both provide an overview of the major religious traditions and suggestions for further reading. Lists of new reference titles appear annually in the *Catholic Library World* (Haverford, Pa.: Catholic Library Association, 1929–) and in the *American Theological Library Association* (ATLA) *Newsletter* (Evanston, Ill.: American Theological Library Assn., 1953–). Annotated bibliographies of reference materials for particular religions include Ed Starkey's *Judaism and Christianity: A Guide to the Reference Literature* (Englewood, Colo.: Libraries Unlimited, 1991), *Asian Religious Studies Information* (Carmel, N.Y.: The Institute for Advanced Studies of World Religions, 1987–). Other guides to non-Western religions include titles in the G. K. Hall (Boston, Mass.) series, The Asian Philosophies and Religion: David Dell's *Guide to Hindu Religion* (1981), Frank Reynolds's *Guide to Buddhist Religion* (1981), and David Yu's *Guide to Chinese Religion* (1985). C. L. Geddes's *Guide to Reference Books for Islamic Studies* (Denver, Colo.: American Institute of Islamic Studies, 1985) and H. Byron Earhart's *Japanese Religion, Unity and Diversity* (Belmont, Calif.: Wadsworth, 1982) are additional non-Western religion guides. Several guides to religious periodicals are available, including James Dawsey's *A Scholar's Guide to Academic Journals in Religion* (Metuchen, N.J.: Scarecrow, 1988), Eugene Fieg's *Religion Journals and Serials: An Analytical Guide* (New York: Greenwood, 1988), John J. Regazzi and Theodore C. Hines's *A Guide to Indexed Periodicals in Religion* (Metuchen, N.J.: Scarecrow, 1975), and *Religious Periodicals Directory* (Santa Barbara, Calif.: ABC-Clio, 1986) edited by Graham Cornish.

Encyclopedias

The most ambitious recent endeavor of the religious studies world was published in 1987 by Macmillan Publishing Company (New York). This sixteen-volume work, *The Encyclopedia of Religion*, attempts to present the fruits of the labors in the field in this century. Edited by Mircea Eliade, the renowned historian of religions from the Divinity School of The University of Chicago, the project took only six years to complete, a phenomenal accomplishment of coordination of 1,400 contributors from more than 50 countries. This work complements and often supersedes James Hastings's *Encyclopedia of Religion and Ethics* (New York: Scribner, 1908–1927) and the *New Schaff-Herzog Encyclopedia of Religious Knowledge* (New York: Funk and Wagnalls, 1908–1912). For the next several years the bibliographies at the ends of the articles will serve as good sources of titles for retrospective purchasing.

Numerous less comprehensive encyclopedic works that cover specific periods of time, geographic areas, and religious traditions are available.

These include the *Encyclopedia of Judaism* (New York: Macmillan, 1989), J. Gordon Melton's *Encyclopedia of American Religions* (Detroit, Mich.: Gale, 1989), and his *Encyclopedic Handbook of Cults in America* (New York: Garland, 1986).

Indexes and Abstracting Sources

Religious studies publications are well-served by index and abstracting services, both in print and electronic versions. The general periodical sources, *Readers' Guide, Humanities Index,* and *Social Sciences Index,* all provide access to religious topics in both general and religious journals.

The most in-depth indexes specifically for religion, however, are produced by the American Theological Library Association (Evanston, Ill.). *Religion Index One: Periodicals (RIO)* (1977–) indexes articles in more than 450 periodicals. *RIO* included book reviews and author abstracts until 1986. *Religion Index Two: Multi-Author Works (RIT)* "indexes essays from collected works, *Festschriften,* conference proceedings and congresses, and reprints of articles not previously included in the ATLA indexes."[11] *Index to Book Reviews in Religion (IBRR),* begun as a separate publication in 1986, indexes approximately 14,000 reviews of more than 9,000 titles.

Other less-comprehensive indexes and indexes with a particular religious focus include *Guide to Social Science and Religious Periodical Literature* (Flint, Mich.: National Periodical Library, 1965–), *Christian Periodicals Index* (Cedarville, Ohio: Christian Librarians Assn., 1956–), *Catholic Periodicals and Literature Index* (Haverford, Pa.: Catholic Library Assn., 1967–), *The Quarterly Index Islamicus* (London, Eng.: Mansell, 1977–), and *Index to Jewish Periodicals* (Cleveland Heights, Ohio: Index to Jewish Periodicals, 1963–).[12]

Abstracting resources include *Old Testament Abstracts* (Washington, D.C.: Catholic Biblical Assn., 1978–), *New Testament Abstracts* (Cambridge, Mass.: Catholic Biblical Assn. of America and the Weston School of Theology, 1956–), and *Religious and Theological Abstracts* (Myerstown, Pa.: Religious and Theological Abstracts, Inc., 1958–). *RIO* discontinued author abstracts in 1986.

Bibliographies

Bibliographies abound in the field of religion. Perhaps the most comprehensive and current sources are those compiled by G. E. Gorman and Lyn Gorman, *Theological and Religious Reference Materials* (New York:

---

11. "Preface," *Religion Index Two: Multi-Author Works* (Chicago: ATLA, 1960/1969–), page number varies according to date.
12. For descriptions of some of these indexes, see Seth Kasten, "Religious Periodical Indexes: A Basic List," *Reference Services Review (RSR)* (Jan./Mar. 1981): 53–55.

Greenwood, 1984–), with one volume each on the topics of general
resources and biblical studies, systematic theology and history, practical
theology, and a projected fourth volume on comparative and non-Christian
religions. Robert J. Kepple's *Reference Works for Theological Research:
An Annotated Selective Bibliographic Guide* (3d ed., Washington, D.C.:
University Press of America, 1992) and Ernest Robert Sandeen and
Frederick Hale's *American Religion and Philosophy: A Guide to Information Sources* (Detroit, Mich.: Gale, 1978) provide bibliographic access
to general resources. As with other types of reference materials, listings
of bibliographies for specific religious groups are best found in special-
ized works as listed in Gorman and Gorman, in Wilson and Slavens's
Research Guide to Religious Studies, and in Blazek and Aversa's
Humanities.

Yearbooks and Directories

Statistical sources are used primarily by researchers for sociological and
historical studies. Census data and other general statistical sources frequently provide information on religion; the *Yearbook of American and
Canadian Churches* (Nashville, Tenn.: Abingdon, 1916–) and the yearbooks and almanacs of specific religious groups provide specialized data.
The Gallup Organization conducts a "Religion in America" poll approximately every two years; results of the survey are issued as part of its *Gallup Report* (Princeton, N.J.: The Gallup Poll, 1981–) and as separate
publications. On occasion the Gallup Organization is contracted by other
organizations to conduct specialized surveys on religion, and it includes
questions on religion in "virtually every survey that goes into the field."[13]
These sources are frequently cited by both the popular and scholarly
presses.

   Directories are used as in other fields to provide the user with information on specific groups or individuals. The *Encyclopedia of Associations* (Detroit, Mich.: Gale, 1956–) and the *Directory of Religious
Organizations in the United States* (3d ed., Detroit, Mich.: Gale, forthcoming) are examples of sources that provide addresses and general information for associations and general headquarters of religious groups.
Denominational yearbooks and almanacs often include names and addresses for the various departments, programs, and individual congrega-
tions of that group. The Council of Societies for the Study of Religion
issues directories of the schools and departments of religion in North
America and the names and brief biographical information of the faculty
of those programs. *Who's Who in Religion* (Chicago: Marquis, 1992) not

---

13. George Gallup, *The People's Religion* (New York: Macmillan, 1989), xvi.

only gives biographical data but a brief statement of the personal philosophies of the biographees.

Special Materials

Special materials for the field of religion include pamphlets and manuscripts containing sermons or essays; archives of correspondence, photographs, proceedings and notes of historical conferences, and diaries; and rare editions of religious writings, such as holdings of early religious periodicals. Information on the more noted library and archive collections is available through compiler Lee Ash's *Subject Collections* (6th ed. rev. and enl., New York: Bowker, 1985). Guides with a special focus include, for example, *Religion in Indiana* (Bloomington, Ind.: Indiana University Press, 1986), an annotated listing of sources about religion in Indiana, and *Christianity in China* (Armonk, N.Y.: Sharpe, 1989), a directory of U.S. library holdings of the papers of missionaries.

Microforms

Special-format resources are produced and used in religion as in other fields. Historical documents, rare and brittle books, personal papers, church records, and journals and periodicals that are no longer readily available are being preserved through the microfilming process. The InterDocumentation Company (IDC) has made available to libraries throughout the world many collections of church and religious history records, and University Microfilms has made accessible religious serials in microformat. Since 1955 the American Theological Library Association (Evanston, Ill.) has filmed approximately 1,200 serial titles; in 1985 it began a systematic program of filming approximately 4,500 monographs a year. Phase 1 (1986–1987) covered biblical studies; Phase 2 (1987–1988), biographies of missionaries, Near Eastern studies, religious education, and Catholic theology; Phase 3 (1988–1989), biblical studies; Phase 4 (1989–1990), church history from the patristic period to the early twentieth century; Phase 5 (1990–1991), systematic theology; Phase 6 and continuing (1991–), biblical studies and works in the Denominational Filming Project, in which it hopes "to document not only the American religion of the time, but also the migration of religious ideas, thought, and culture from Europe, Africa, and beyond."[14] To accomplish this, librarians and scholars contribute recommendations for titles to be included in the bibliographies that will be used for soliciting books for filming.

---

14. Karl Frantz, "Monograph Preservation Program Update," *ATLA Program Notes* 2 (July 1990): 2.

Many projects have been initiated to preserve special collections, such as the Hilandar Project at The Ohio State University Libraries[15] and the filming program at the American Jewish Archives in Cincinnati, Ohio.[16] The Hilandar Project began in the 1970s with the filming of the holdings of the Hilandar Monastery, Mt. Athos, Greece, and now includes film from many other monasteries and libraries in Europe to make it the largest collection of medieval Slavic manuscripts in microformat in the Western Hemisphere.

Audiovisual Materials

Audiovisual materials have received greater recognition and use in public libraries than in academic libraries, but the increased accessibility of equipment for use of audio- and videotapes has increased their acceptance in the religions collections of various types of libraries or in the teaching resource center of the institution. Sources of these materials can be found in *Media Review Digest* (Ann Arbor, Mich.: Pierian, 1973/1974–) and in *Audio Video Market Place* (New York: Bowker, 1984–). In 1981 Anima Books (Chambersburg, Pa.) published two guides to audiovisual resources to accompany the respective bibliographic guides published in the G. K. Hall Asian Philosophies and Religions Resource Guides series: *Focus on Hinduism: A Guide to Audio-Visual Resources for Teaching Religion* and *Focus on Buddhism: A Guide to Audio-Visual Resources for Teaching Religion* include reviews of the audiovisual materials and lists of distributors and filmmakers. Peter P. Schillace's "The 'Reformation' in Religious Video" (*Sightlines* 21 [Fall 1988]: 8–11) includes descriptions of the major religious video distributors.

Computerized Data

Bibliographic databases and CD-ROM products in the field of religion have greatly enhanced access to religious topics. Current and some retrospective entries from *Humanities Index* are online and on CD-ROM as are the ATLA indexes—*RIO, RIT, IBRR,* and *RIM* (*Research in Ministry,* an index of doctoral and ministry theses and reports). Religious news services and bulletin boards are also available through computer utilities.

---

15. See introductory information by Predrag Matejic and Hannah Thomas in *Catalog: Manuscripts on Microform of the Hilandar Research Library (The Ohio State University)* (Columbus, Ohio: The Resource Center of the Hilandar Research Library, in cooperation with the Ivan Dujchev Research Centre for Slavo-Byzantine Studies, Sofia, Bulgaria, 1992).

16. Kevin Profitt, "The Micrographics Program of the American Jewish Archives," *Microform Review* 15 (Spring 1986): 87–90.

Computer technology has opened wide the fields of textual studies and translation through input of religious manuscripts and documents into machine-readable format. "Every word, every phrase, every idea can be automatically indexed and cross-indexed."[17] Several versions of the Bible are available both online and on CD-ROM, as are concordances, theological and biblical dictionaries, and commentaries.[18]

With increased access to information through automated systems, libraries are receiving pressure to obtain the automated products or services that will make the research process easier, faster, and more efficient and to make available either through purchase or interlibrary loan the sources cited in the bibliographic databases the researchers are using. Since financial resources of libraries are limited, it is becoming increasingly difficult to make the choices necessary among the various formats available for the study of religion.

Religious Materials in Libraries

Religious materials have been found in libraries since the beginning of library history—from the early libraries in Egypt and the Near East when writing and books were restricted primarily to religious and political topics and on into the Middle Ages when monastery libraries became the depositories and producers of religious literature of the time. Today, religious materials are found in many types of libraries.[19] The most obvious, of course, is the theological library, usually connected to a school of theology that may be an independent institution, such as Union Theological Seminary in New York, or connected to another institution, such as the Divinity School at The University of Chicago. Prominent collections are also found in the archives and libraries of denominational and diocesan headquarters. Many special institutes have research-level collections for their areas of specialization, such as the Institute for Buddhist Studies in Berkeley, California, and the Institute for Advanced Studies of World Religions in Carmel, New York.

---

17. Parker Rossman, "Computers and Religious Research: *Fish Imagining Fish*," *Summary of Proceedings* (ATLA) 40 (1986): 311–19.

18. See "Offline: Computer Assisted Research for Religious Studies," ed. Robert Kraft, in issues of the *CSSR Bulletin* (Macon, Ga.: Council of Societies for the Study of Religion); relevant sections of *The Humanities Computing Yearbook* (Oxford, Eng.: Clarendon, 1988–); Mark Stover, "Optical Bibles: A Review of Three Bible Concordances and Full-Text Theological Reference Sources on CD-ROM," *Laserdisk Professional* (Jan. 1990): 56–60; and William Griffin, "The Bible in Bytes," *Publishers Weekly* 237 (2 Mar. 1990): 26–30.

19. John F. Harvey, "Scholarly and Popular Religious Libraries," *International Library Review* 19 (Oct. 1987): 359–86.

Large public libraries usually have quite respectable collections of religious materials, frequently emphasizing a particular collection, such as the White Collection for Oriental Studies in the Cleveland Public Library, Cleveland, Ohio.

Colleges and universities affiliated with religious organizations often are repositories of materials about that particular religious persuasion. They usually also maintain a collection of at least a comprehensive level of materials on religion to support their institution's department or program of religion. Libraries of state colleges and universities are becoming more active in collecting religious materials, particularly as religious studies courses become more integrated into the general curriculum of the institution and as the institutions strengthen and expand their religious studies programs.

Due to the diversity of interest in religious materials within institutions, a religion collection may be dispersed among numerous library locations such as the fine arts library, the music library, libraries of the social sciences, area studies units, and humanities collections. It follows then that many library staff will be involved in the development and maintenance of the religious collection as a whole and that coordination and communication concerning the collections is essential.

As mentioned in the introductory section, the study of religions touches many other disciplines, establishing subgroups that influence the collections of the library. Thus, faculty and students in the anthropology, sociology, history, psychology, literature, geography, and education departments may also be active users of the collection of religious studies materials for instructional or research purposes and for personal development purposes. Public library users range from the serious researcher and the local minister, rabbi, or Bible study teacher using biblical text materials to the individual seeking information to establish or enhance personal faith or for general self-education.

Selection and Collection Development

Religious studies, or the history of religions, is an inherently inter- and multidisciplinary and cross-cultural field. This fact has a number of implications for selection and collection development as well as for presenting a few problems. In most cases the goal of an acquisitions policy should be to build and maintain a fairly comprehensive sample of major works in the various dimensions of religion, the religious traditions of the world, and the current state of the field of the history of religions. Holdings should be appropriate to the particular institutional and user needs and usually will be in both the humanities and the social sciences. Moreover, because of the cross-cultural nature of the field, acquisitions will not be confined to any one geographical area of the world. However, how best to accomplish the goal of having a balanced collection will depend, among other factors, upon the size of the library, the internal administrative structure and budget lines, and the profile of the patrons and patron interests. The proliferation of area studies programs in North America since the end of World War II, frequently accompanied in larger libraries by comparable area divisions in library collections, acquisitions staff, budget lines, and so forth, dictates that in some cases librarians must coordinate acquisitions and planning for purchases in religion with other library staff.

Second, librarians need to recognize that religion can be a sensitive subject and is an area in which some patrons may occasionally show an unusual degree of interest in the library's acquisitions policy. Moreover, the nature of religion is such that it can engender strong convictions and emotional responses not only in patrons but in librarians themselves. There is a need to separate personal faith from one's professional responsibilities as a bibliographer. It is the bibliographer's responsibility to represent in the collection the rich diversity of the various expressions of religion found in human history. By viewing religion as a historical phenomenon, the library will be able to better perform its duty to provide its patrons with as much accurate information on this field of study as is possible. To this end, most bibliographers need to "bracket" their own commitments of faith in performing their professional responsibilities. While all religions make truth claims concerning ultimate reality, such as the structure of the universe, the human condition, and the path to salvation, many religions use different forms of the rhetoric of "eternal truth" in proclaiming their doctrines and spiritual paths. Such claims are themselves made (circulated, culturally consumed, affirmed, disputed) in time and space and, thus, are historically grounded. It is these things that are the object of study in the history of religions, where the goal is not to make normative judgments concerning the truth claims.

Religious studies as an academic field differs from theology in that it is not a normative discipline. Works of theology, however, have an important place in library holdings since they provide "insider" views of their respective religious traditions. Theological school libraries, as well as the libraries of religiously affiliated institutions, of necessity will include more works of theology in their holdings than most publicly supported libraries. Even in publicly supported libraries, however, it is important that a representative selection of works of theology be available. Of course, the depth of any collection in religion will depend on the patrons' needs and interests.

With the quantities of materials available, selection for a large budget is just as difficult as for a small one. The first priority for any type of collection is to have a collection development policy that defines the subjects to be included and the depth of the collection. The value of a collection policy is seen when difficult selection choices must be made or when questions of censorship arise. In addition, the process of developing the policy is invaluable in promoting dialogue between the library staff and its clientele, whether they are faculty, students, or other users of the collection. A collection policy for an academic library should address the curricular concerns and trends of the institution.

Assessment of a collection to determine areas of strength and areas needing additional resources can be done by employing both collection-centered and client-centered measures. Collection-centered methods include a comparison of the holdings of libraries with similar programs, shelflist measurement, and a check of the library's holdings against standard bibliographies in the areas of the collection as delineated in the collection development policy; client-centered measures include user surveys and interviews.[20]

Retrospective collection development is conducted by consulting guides and bibliographies such as those already cited in this chapter. Current selection uses the appropriate sections of *Publishers Weekly, Library Journal, Choice* (with occasional bibliographic articles on religious topics), *Reference Services Review*, and *Serials Review*. In addition, current selection includes consulting specialized religion sources such as *Religious Studies Review, ADRIS Newsletter* (St. Louis, Mo.: Assn. for the Development of Religious Information Services, 1971–), and the annual *Critical Review of Books in Religion* (Atlanta, Ga.: produced jointly by The Journal of the American Academy of Religion and The Journal of Biblical Literature, 1988–). Regular perusal of publishers' and book dealers' catalogs and flyers, the book review sections of journals in the field, and listings in the newsletters, journals, and conference programs of religious associations and related organizations is certainly recommended, but since the religion bibliographer usually has many other responsibilities, this may not be possible at all times. For the most part, approval plans ease the pressure of time constraints on the religious bibliographer, but it cannot be assumed that an approval program will cull all materials wanted in the collection; careful monitoring is still essential.[21] A more complete description of the methodology and sources for selecting religious materials may be found in the chapter "Philosophy and Religion," by Andrew D. Scrimgeour in *Selection of Library Materials in the Humanities,*

---

20. See Richard D. Shiels and Martha S. Alt, "Library Materials on the History of Christianity at The Ohio State University: An Assessment," *Collection Management* 7 (Summer 1985): 69–81.

21. Hook, "Approval Plans," 215–27.

Social Sciences, and Sciences, edited by Patricia McClung (Chicago: American Library Assn., 1985).

Cataloging and Classification

As with other subject areas, two major systems are the most widely used in academic and large public libraries for classifying religious materials—the Dewey decimal system and the Library of Congress system. In the Dewey system, the 200 class is the basic division for religion, with subdivisions as follows: Religion (200), Natural religion (210), Bible (220), Christian theology (230), Christian moral and devotional theology (240), Local church and religious orders (250), Social and ecclesiastical theology (260), History and geography of the church (270), Christian denominations and sects (280), and Other and comparative religions (290). It is generally recognized that the Dewey system has a Christian—specifically, Protestant—bias and that fitting in other religious groups is difficult.[22]

The Library of Congress system also has a Christian bias, but recent revisions have attempted to ameliorate this. Most religious materials are classed in subsections of the B class, which covers philosophy and religion. Originally published in 1927 and revised in 1962, Class B, Part II BL-BX, Religion, is now issued in three volumes: Religions, Hinduism, Judaism, Buddhism (BL-BQ); Christianity, Bible (BR-BV); and Christian denominations (BX). Other classes that contain religious subjects are BJ (Ethics), E and F (Native American Religions), and parts of Z (religious bibliography). Religious aspects of many subjects may be classed with those subjects, e.g., abortion in H (social science), anthropology in G, etc.

Since neither system is well-suited to specialized needs of many religious libraries, some libraries have expanded or altered the systems to suit their specific needs.[23] Others have devised alternative systems. In 1954 Jeannette M. Lynn developed a system to be used in conjunction with either the Dewey or the Library of Congress system to meet the needs of Catholic institutions. Revised by Gilbert C. Peterson in 1965 and commonly known as the Lynn-Peterson system, it is still used by some Catholic schools to provide greater specificity for their unique materials. Several alternate systems for Jewish collections have been developed,

---

22. G. E. Gorman, "The Classification of Theological Literature: A Commentary and Annotated Bibliography," *International Library Review* 17 (Apr. 1985): 203–31.

23. See William P. Collins, "Classification of Materials on the Baha'i Religion: Expansion of Library of Congress BP300–395," *Cataloging and Classification Quarterly* 8 (1988): 99–133.

but most Jewish collections in academic institutions use the Dewey or the Library of Congress system.[24]

Another classification system used in predominantly theological collections is the Union, or Pettee, classification system, devised by Julia E. Pettee in the early 1900s for the Union Theological Seminary Library in New York. Although this library no longer uses the system, the Union Theological Seminary Library in Richmond, Virginia, has become the library responsible for revising and updating the system. A few United States and several overseas church and religious institute libraries still use the Pettee system. However, with the advent of automated cooperative cataloging systems such as OCLC and RLIN, many libraries have discontinued use of these systems as well as the Dewey system to take advantage of using online information.[25]

Although two major subject access systems—Sears and Library of Congress—exist, most large public libraries and academic collections use the Library of Congress Subject Headings (LCSH) system. Its large number of subjects appropriate for religious materials and the ability to subdivide nonreligious topics with religious subdivisions (e.g., Marriage—Religious aspects) makes it adaptable to most collections.[26] As with the Library of Congress classification system, LCSH has a Protestant bias. For example, "Lord's Supper" is used rather than "Eucharist," the term Catholic libraries would prefer; "Bible. O.T." is used even though Jewish libraries find the term inappropriate for their sacred texts. Some Catholic institutions use additional terms and subheadings as listed in *Catholic Subject Headings* (Catholic Library Association, 1942–). However, the need for supplemental lists has decreased as the Library of Congress subject headings have been adjusted to reduce their ethnocentrism and as the ease and greater efficiency of using the headings listed in the cataloging utilities is recognized.[27]

Special directories of religious terms used in LCSH exist to aid the cataloger and researcher. *Current Subject Headings in the Field of Religion*, issued quarterly by ATLA, informs its seminary, public, and

24. Bella Hass Weinberg, "Hebraica Cataloging and Classification," in *Cataloging and Classification of Non-Western Material: Concerns, Issues and Practices* (Phoenix, Ariz.: Oryx, 1980) 321–57; and Weinberg, "Defining the Scope of Judaica: Complementary Problems in Bibliographic Control and Bibliographic Organization," *Library Acquisitions: Practice and Theory* 15 (1991): 155–63.

25. Thomas F. Gilbert, "Classification Systems: Where We've Been, Where We Are, Where We're Going," *Summary of Proceedings* (ATLA) 40 (1986): 289–98.

26. Lois Mai Chen, *Library of Congress Subject Headings: Principles and Application*, 2d ed. (Littleton, Colo.: Libraries Unlimited, 1986), 296–305.

27. W. Thomas Nichol, "Theological Subject Headings Reconsidered," *Library Resources and Technical Services* 29 (Apr./June 1985): 180–88; Rabbi Theodore Wiener, "Developments in Library of Congress Cataloging of Judaica," *AJL Proceedings* 11 (1976): 37–42.

university subscribers of terms added or changed since the last edition of LCSH and is less costly than a subscription to the *LC Weekly Lists* issued to the library community on a monthly basis by the Library of Congress. *Library of Congress Subject Headings in Jewish Studies*, 3d ed. (New York: Association of Jewish Libraries, 1992), compiled by Yosef Galron, is based on Library of Congress subject headings and is updated quarterly in *Judaica Librarianship*.

Profile of Religion Librarianship

Librarians and archivists who work with religious collections frequently "fall into" the field through their training in the general humanities. Some have masters in theological studies or divinity degrees, a few have academic degrees in religious studies. However, the majority have developed their expertise in the area through self-education and occasional course work. In the past, theological librarians were frequently teaching faculty with subject expertise rather than knowledge of, or interest in, the administration of the library.[28] Specialists in such areas as Jewish studies, Islamic studies, and East Asian studies usually have advanced academic degrees in their areas. As mentioned previously, many staff members may be involved in the development and maintenance of religious materials— administrators, bibliographers of various collections, catalogers, and audiovisual staff.

Specialized professional development opportunities come to religious studies librarians through the professional literature and professional associations. Journal articles on religious librarianship may be found in many journals as evidenced by the numerous journals cited throughout this chapter; however, Haworth Press has announced a new journal, *Journal of Religious & Theological Information*, that should bring focus to the concerns and informational needs of professionals of all types who deal with religious materials.

Professional Associations

The organization that relates most directly to religious studies librarians is the American Theological Library Association. Although the name implies a membership having special interest in theological materials, approximately 15 percent of its individual members are from nontheological institutions. Recent publications from the group indicate that it is giving increasing attention to non-Christian religions. The papers published in

---

28. Ron Jordahl, "The Interdisciplinary Nature of Theological Librarianship in the United States," *Libraries and Culture* 25 (Spring 1990): 153–70.

its annual *Proceedings* deal with such concerns as classification, subject headings, practices of the Library of Congress, the availability of resource materials, religious publishing sources and trends, and research. The *ATLA Newsletter* reports on ongoing projects of the Association, such as its indexing and preservation programs. Local and regional groups of theological librarians provide forums for sharing ideas and developing cooperative projects.

The American Library Association at one time had a Religious Book Committee that produced an annual list of leading religious books, but it was disbanded in the early 1950s since it was felt that other groups, such as the American Theological Library Association, could better serve that function. In 1990 a Discussion Group on Philosophy, Religion, and Theology was formed within the Association of College and Research Libraries, which will provide a much-needed forum for sharing information.

Several specialized library groups may also provide professional development for librarians of general religious collections. The Association of Jewish Librarians is very active in dealing with problems in cataloging, classification, preservation, acquisitions, bibliographic access, etc.; its publications, the *AJL Newsletter* and *Judaica Librarianship*, contain articles dealing with these issues as well as reviews of books, music, periodicals, and nonbook media. The publications of the International Association of Orientalist Librarians, the Middle East Librarians Association, and the Committee on East Asian Libraries, a subgroup of the Association of Asian Studies, also contain occasional articles relevant to religious studies concerns.

The Academic Section of the Catholic Library Association provides enrichment for its nearly 300 members through its newsletter and conference programming. The Society of American Archivists has a Religious Archives Section that librarians who also work with archival materials may join. Although established to meet the needs of congregational libraries, the Church and Synagogue Library Association, the Lutheran Library Association, the Evangelical Library Association, as well as other denominational library groups can also provide professional development opportunities for the religious studies librarian, particularly on a local level.

Religious organizations that can and do provide information and educational opportunities to librarians abound. At the top of the list again is the American Academy of Religion (and its regional affiliates) and the Society of Biblical Literature. Members of the Council of Societies for the Study of Religion, an organization that facilitates communication and planning among the member groups and issues *CSSR Bulletin*, include the American Society of Missiology, the Catholic Biblical Association, the College Theology Society, the Institute on Religion in an Age of Science, the North American Association for the Study of Religion, plus several other professional religious groups.

The librarianship of religion is at the same time an ancient field and a new, developing one. Theological libraries have existed for centuries. In nineteenth-century America the place of religious materials in a library was not questioned, and yet today, with the concern of separation of church and state, we are seeing and hearing more and more discussion of what role publicly funded libraries should have in providing religious materials to patrons. With the increase of academic programs in religious studies in academic institutions, greater public interest in religion as evidenced by the Gallup polls, and the rise in publication of religious materials, more and more attention will need to be given to the selection and handling of religious materials.

Professional Readings

Alt, Martha S. "Issues in Developing a Religious Studies Collection." *Library Acquisitions: Practice and Theory* 15 (1991): 207–14.

Asheim, Lester. "Religion." In *The Humanities and the Library: Problems in the Interpretation, Evaluation and Use of Library Materials*, 1–60. Chicago: American Library Assn., 1957.

Avalone, Susan. "Receptivity to Religion." *Library Journal* 109 (15 Oct. 1984): 1891–93.

Broadus, Robert N. "Religion." In *Selecting Materials for Libraries*, 320–31. 2d ed. New York: H. W. Wilson, 1981.

Choquette, Diane. "The New Religious Movements Research Collection: A History and Description of Alternative Subject Cataloging." *Technical Services Quarterly* 2 (Fall/Winter 1984): 19–34.

Cunningham, Lawrence S. "Catholic Publishing: A Reflection." *Catholic Library World* 59 (Mar.–Apr. 1988): 212–14, 228.

Dowd, Alice. "The 'New Age' for Libraries." *Library Journal* 114 (July 1989): 44–50.

Ede, David, ed. *Guide to Islam*. Boston: G. K. Hall, 1983.

Geddes, C. L. *Guide to Reference Books for Islamic Studies*. Bibliographic Series, no. 9. Denver, Colo.: American Institute of Islamic Studies, 1985.

Gould, Constance. "Religion." In *Information Needs in the Humanities: An Assessment*, 34–39. Stanford, Calif.: Research Libraries Group, 1989.

Grover, Mark L. "Liberation Theology in Latin America: An Introduction to Library Acquisitions." *Library Acquisitions: Practice and Theory* 15 (1991): 185–93.

Homan, Roger, comp. *The Sociology of Religion: A Bibliographical Survey*. Bibliographies and Indexes in Religious Studies, no. 9. New York: Greenwood, 1986.

Kepple, Robert J. *Reference Works for Theological Research: An Annotated Selective Bibliographical Guide*. 3d ed. Washington, D. C.: University Press of America, 1992.

Lauer, Jonathan D. "Urgency and Overlap in the Dissemination of Information: Five Religion Journals and the Book Reviews They Published in 1986." *Collection Management* 11, no. 3/4 (1989): 113–26.

McCabe, James P. "The New Code of Canon Law: Reference and Research Material for Libraries." *Library Acquisitions: Practice and Theory* 15 (1991): 195–205.

Miller, Karen Gray. "Do Libraries Get Religion?" *Library Journal* 107 (15 Oct. 1982): 1941–43.

———. "Religion Revisited." *Library Journal* 108 (15 Oct. 1983): 1921–23.

Partington, David H. "Islamic Literature: Problems in Collection Development." *Library Acquisitions: Practice and Theory* 15 (1991): 147–54.

Peterson, Stephen L. "From Third World to One World: Problems and Opportunities in Documenting New Christianity." *Library Acquisitions: Practice and Theory* 15 (1991): 177–84.

Sayre, John L., and Roberta Hamburger, comps. and eds. *Tools for Theological Research.* 7th ed. Enid, Okla.: Seminary Press, 1985.

Singerman, Robert, comp. *Jewish Serials of the World: A Research Bibliography of Secondary Sources.* Westport, Conn.: Greenwood, 1986.

Stover, Mark. "Optical Bibles: A Review of Three Bible Concordances and Full-Text Theological Reference Sources on CD-ROM." *Laserdisk Professional* 3 (Jan. 1990): 56–60.

Walsh, Michael J. "Religion and Philosophy." In *Reviews and Reviewing: A Guide,* edited by A. J. Walford, 37–52. London, Eng.: Mansell, 1986.

———. *Religious Bibliographies in Serial Literature: A Guide.* Westport, Conn.: Greenwood, 1981.

Yang, Lena Lee. "Acquiring and Preserving Buddhist Materials in the Library of the Institute for Advanced Studies of World Religions." *Library Acquisitions: Practice and Theory* 15 (1991): 165–76.

Editors and Contributors

Nancy Allen is currently dean of the library, University of Denver Penrose Library, and was previously assistant director for public services, Colorado State University Libraries. She has served as chair of the Association of College and Research Libraries Arts Section and has authored books and articles on a variety of topics including information sources for film studies and communications and media information.

Martha S. Alt is general humanities bibliographer at The Ohio State University Libraries, which includes responsibility for the collection development of the Asian studies, comparative studies, history of Christianity, and religious studies collections. She has published articles on religious librarianship in *Collection Management* and *Library Acquisitions: Practice and Theory.*

James K. Bracken is head of second floor information services; bibliographer for English, communication, and speech; and associate professor, The Ohio State University Libraries. He is the author of *Reference Works in British and American Literature: Volume I: English and American Literature* and *Volume II: English and Authors.* He is coauthor, with Eleanor S. Block, of *Communication and the Mass Media: A Guide to the Reference Literature.* His articles on literature and librarianship have appeared in such journals as *The Library, Studies in Bibliography, College and Research Libraries,* and *Library Resources and Technical Services.*

Nena Couch is curator of the Library of the Jerome Lawrence and Robert E. Lee Theatre Research Institute, The Ohio State University, and was previously project archivist for the Francis Robinson Collection at Vanderbilt University for which she compiled and edited *The Francis*

Robinson Collection of Theatre, Music, and Dance: A Manuscripts Catalog. She serves on the Theatre Library Association board, is a dancer and dance historian, and writes on performing arts librarianship and dance.

Nancy C. Cridland is the history specialist at the Indiana University Libraries, Bloomington, and is currently acting associate dean for collection development. She is president of the Association for the Bibliography of History. Among her publications are *Books in American History* and the chapter "History" in *Selection of Library Materials in the Social Sciences, Humanities and Sciences.*

Gary Ebersole is associate professor of history of religions in the Divinity School, The University of Chicago. He was previously associate professor in comparative studies and East Asian languages and literature at The Ohio State University where he served as director of the religious studies program and was assistant professor of religious studies and East Asian studies at Grinnell College. His recent publications include *Ritual Poetry and the Politics of Death in Early Japan.*

Richard Lineback has served since 1967 as director of the Philosophy Documentation Center at Bowling Green State University where he is editor of *Philosopher's Index* and professor of philosophy. He is assistant editor of *Directory of American Philosophers* and editor of the series Bibliographies of Famous Philosophers.

Elisabeth Rebman is reference librarian in the Music Library and lecturer in cataloging in the School of Library and Information Studies at the University of California, Berkeley, and was previously head of both the music and special collections cataloging sections and was acting head of the Music Library and Archive of Recorded Sound in the Stanford University Libraries. She has taught courses including music bibliography for graduate students and historical dance for music students. She has published articles in *Library Trends* and the *Encyclopedia of Library and Information Science.*

Susan Wyngaard is currently head of the Fine Arts Library in the Wexner Center for the Arts at The Ohio State University. Previously she held positions as art librarian at the University of California at Santa Barbara, and as director of archives at the International Museum of Photography at the George Eastman House. Ms. Wyngaard has served as a review panelist for the National Endowment for the Humanities, as an executive board member of the Art Libraries Society of North America, and as a consultant for art library building projects.